Child of War, Woman of Peace

ALSO BY LE LY HAYSLIP

When Heaven and Earth Changed Places
(With Jay Wurts)

Child of War,

LE LY HAYSLIP

With James Hayslip

Woman of Peace

ANCHOR BOOKS
DOUBLEDAY
New York   London   Toronto   Sydney   Auckland

An Anchor Book

Published by Doubleday

a division of Bantam Doubleday Dell Publishing Group, Inc.
1540 Broadway, New York, New York 10036

Anchor Books, Doubleday, and the portrayal of an anchor
are trademarks of Doubleday, a division of Bantam Doubleday Dell
Publishing Group, Inc.

Child of War, Woman of Peace was originally published in hardcover by Doubleday
in 1993. The Anchor Books edition is published
by arrangement with Doubleday,
a division of Bantam Doubleday Dell
Publishing Group, Inc.

Library of Congress Cataloging-in-Publication Data

Hayslip, Le Ly.
Child of war, woman of peace / Le Ly Hayslip, with James Hayslip.
—1st Anchor Books ed.
     p.   cm.
1. Hayslip, Le Ly.   2. Vietnamese Americans—Biography.
3. Refugees—United States—Biography.   4. Vietnamese Conflict,
1961–1975—Personal narratives, Vietnamese.   I. Hayslip, James.
II. Title.
[E184.V53H38   1994]
973′.049592—dc20   93-21027
CIP

ISBN 0-385-47147-5
Copyright © 1993 by Le Ly Haslip and Charles Jay Wurts
All Rights Reserved
Printed in the United States of America
First Anchor Books Edition: January 1994

13 12 11 10 9 8 7 6 5 4

To our ancestors

CONTENTS

PROLOGUE

Song of the Sau Dau Tree

A LONG TIME AGO, before the world knew better, a young man went to war. Like his brothers, he traveled to all points of the compass, fought many battles, and saw many wondrous and terrifying things—but none so terrible as when, twenty-five years later, he returned to find his village abandoned.

The wind-swept streets were full of weeds and the once fruitful fields were bare and scabbed. The sky was red with dust and the river —once filled with fish—was reduced to a murky trickle. Coconut palms stood like broken flagpoles, their fronds scattered by the summer monsoon; the farmers' houses were collapsed or empty. Only a lone sau dau tree, ancient branches still green with peppers, stood on the riverbank to remind him of the world he used to know.

And remember it he did.

The soldier stretched out under the tree and turned his face to the empty streets. The spiders in their webs became old people gossiping in the shade; the scurrying lizards became children chasing after ducks; the swooping birds, lithe maidens carrying water—casting languorous glances at village boys chopping wood and mending carts.

A dust devil spinning up from a bone-dry garden became dinner smoke rising from his mother's kitchen. As if part of the dream, an elderly woman dressed in black and thin as death hobbled up from a nearby shack.

The soldier jumped to his feet: first in fear that the figure was a spirit-guardian of the village graveyard, then to help the old woman gather peppers when he saw that she was real.

"I used to live in this village," the soldier said, pleased to be helping now, instead of killing. "My family lived there, where the ferry crossed the river. I used to drink coconut milk on hot days and listen to the ferry girl sing."

The old woman did not care for his stories and sullenly went about her labors. "Your old house is ruined now," she told him bluntly, "and the ferryboat ran aground and rotted when the armies dammed the river. The girl was raped and, with her fatherless child, fled to the city where she sings no more. And no coconuts grow since the trees were shot to pieces. Now everything's dried up and shriveled like me. If you're wise, you'll run away before the sun goes down. The village isn't safe at night: too many ghosts. *Too many ghosts!*"

With infinite sadness, the soldier watched the old woman hobble back toward her house. The sun sank lower and the shadow of the sau dau tree crept down the empty street to the place where his own house had stood in happier times. Suddenly, in a voice full of confidence and compassion, born of a soldier's triumphs but tempered with a soldier's regrets, he sang:

> The sau dau tree stands in the sunset
> Leaves flowing around you like river sand.
> Wind and rain have followed my footsteps,
> I have been too long *la nuoc la cai*—
> Lost and lonely in a foreign land.
> *Tu* has been my shadow;
> *Dao* has been my sun.
> What fear can a darkened house hold
> When it used to be your own?

The old lady turned and saw the man bathed in radiant light, twisted limbs of the sau dau tree hanging above him like a crown, glittering with life. Heat rose from the peppers in her basket and the scars of the years melted from her body and the birds *became* maidens and the lizards *became* children and the water flowed again and the ferry girl returned and the song she sang was the Song of the Sau Dau Tree.

Today, when exiles have been away from home too long and their eyes are cried dry and their mouths are full of dust, they need only look into the sunset and sing the Song of the Sau Dau Tree, and the ghosts that haunt them flee and the scars of the years melt away and the soil underfoot, wherever it is, becomes the soil of home. That which was halved becomes whole and they no longer fear the darkened house that used to be their home.

In May 1970, I stepped from the Pan Am airliner that had taken me from the hell my country had become to the heaven I hoped America would be. I was twenty years old with two sons, both by different fathers. I didn't speak much English, and my manners were better suited to peasant villages and Saigon street corners than a suburb of San Diego, which was to be my new home—a place stranger to a Vietnamese farm girl than the dark side of the moon.

My background was not like that of my American neighbors. By age twelve I had lost two brothers and countless uncles, aunts, and cousins to the war. By age fifteen I had been in battle, captured, tortured by the South Vietnamese Republicans, and had been condemned to death and raped by the Viet Cong. By sixteen I was an unwed mother supporting my family on Danang's black market. By the time I was nineteen my father had committed suicide rather than involve me again with the Viet Cong, and I was married to *de quoc My,* "the enemy"—a middle-aged American civilian construction engineer, Ed Munro—in the desperate hope that he would save me and my children from the war.

When he finally brought me to the United States, I learned quickly that the skills I needed to survive in the jungles and corrupt back alleys of my native land didn't count in U.S. supermarkets, department stores, and employment offices. The "traffic signs" I obeyed weren't posted on crosswalks and freeways but were chiseled in my heart as *Dao lam nguoi:* natural law, universal law, the law of karma and life and death. I suddenly faced a world without ancestors—without cause and effect—where I had no yesterday and no tomorrow. I was in *dat khach que nguoi*—lost and lonely in a strange and hostile land. The propaganda of the Viet Cong's midnight meetings in the swamps outside my village was still fresh in my memory. *De quoc thuc dan,* they would tell us: liberate Vietnam from the "capitalist colonial empire." Now the soil of that "evil empire" had become my home. I had condemned myself to live *song tren dat dich*—in the land of the enemy.

This book is the story of my life in the land of "the enemy"—a Vietnamese woman struggling to survive among the "cat-eyed" Westerners whom I had been taught since birth to fear and hate. But it is also something more. It is the story of discovering treasure where you least expect it; of searching for two halves that make a perfect whole. It is about *say me khoai lac:* seeing similarities in different things, and taking delight—finding what is unique and precious—in what is ordinary and overlooked. It is about finding and losing love, letting go of hurt, and getting on with life. Most of all, it is about coming to terms with the past while reaching out for a better future. I have been told it is America's story, written with a bamboo pen. It is the story of anyone—Oriental, European, African, Pacific Island, Middle Eastern, American—who ever found herself dispossessed, abandoned, and swallowed up by the world only to be spat out: a stranger in a strange new place.

I invite you to share in these pages a journey that took me twenty years to complete. Although we'll experience many terrible and wondrous things, none may be more terrible than the fears my story may awake inside you, nor more wondrous than the peace you'll find at its end: for I have seen the sau dau tree and sung its song.

PART ONE

*Living with the Enemy
(1970–82)*

ONE

Yearning to Breathe Free

HONOLULU'S WARM BREEZE caressed me like a mother's hands. A pretty hula girl put a flowered lei—a victor's garland— around my neck. For the first time in my life, I gulped the heady air of a world at peace.

May 27, 1970, the day I stepped onto the ramp at Honolulu International Airport after fleeing the war in Vietnam, marked the beginning of my new life as an apprentice American. It may have been my imagination, but the attendants on the big American jetliner from Saigon seemed exceptionally kind to me and my two boys—three-year-old Jimmy (whose father, a wealthy Saigon industrialist, he never knew) and Tommy, the three-month-old son of my new American husband, Ed Munro, whom we were on our way to join. Liberty and goodwill, like corruption and cruelty, seem to hold each other's hand.

Still, Hawaii was too much like Vietnam to really count as the United States. For one, it was a tropical island—covered with palms and sand—and Honolulu, despite its modern hotels and shops and restaurants, was too much like Saigon: filled with Asians and GIs, tawdry bars and taxis, and people in transit, *khong hieu qua khu*—without a past or future, like me. The thrill of great America would have to wait for our next landing.

As it turned out, San Diego was another Honolulu, if written on a larger page. Our plane arrived after midnight, not a good time for sightseeing, especially by timid immigrants. In Vietnam, the Viet Cong feared the light, so "friendly" areas—cities, towns, air bases, and outposts—were lit up like American Christmas trees. Perhaps to show it was safe for GIs coming back from the war, San Diego, too, left its lights burning all night.

Ed met us at the arrival gate, just as he'd promised. He had been staying with his mother, Erma, in the suburb of El Cajon. Although he looked tanned and healthy and was a welcome familiar face after thousands of miles of strangers, my heart sagged when I saw him. Born in 1915 (seven years after my mother's birth) in Mount Vernon, Washington, he was old enough to be my father—no twenty-year-old's dream husband. Yet, with two brothers and three sisters, he was no stranger to small towns and big families—one reason, in addition to his own maturity, that he understood me so well. His mother had been a waitress at something called a "drive-in" and his father, like mine, had died. Both had been honest, family-loving men who tackled life barehanded. My father had been a farmer who seldom went farther than a day's walk from our home village of Ky La. Ed's dad had been a carpenter and hunter who ventured to Alaska: a wondrous place where, Ed said, ice fell stinging from the sky. In all, Ed's relatives were solid working-class people. Like my peasant family, they loved one another, loved their country, and lived their values every day.

Ed had been married twice before. He knew, as I did, how it felt to lose the game of love. His first wife gave him two sons, Ron and Ed Jr. (navy boys whom we visited in Vietnam), then divorced him and moved to Nevada. His second wife was unfaithful and when Ed found out about it, he did not beat her as a Vietnamese husband would, but sent her a dozen roses and wished her good luck with her new man. In a way, that was what Ed was all about. He put the wishes of those he loved above his own right to be happy. This constant sacrifice, I think, whittled him down and eventually cost him what he treasured most. In this, I would discover, he was not alone among Americans.

The long drive from San Diego's Lindbergh Field to El Cajon was not much different from a drive to Saigon's suburbs, except for more cars and fewer motorbikes on the highway's six broad lanes. Off the freeway, we drove through blocks of tidy homes, all dark except for streetlamps standing like GI basketball hoops in the gloom. We parked in the driveway of a pale yellow house—"ranch style," Ed said, although I couldn't smell any animals—and we went up the narrow walk to a front door bright with light. Before Ed could reach the bell, a shadow hobbled up behind the curtain. The door opened onto a large American woman in curlers, backlit in a nightgown as big as a sheet.

Startled, I bowed low—to be polite and to put the big creature out of sight while I collected my sleep-starved wits.

"Ohhh!" Erma, Ed's sister, screamed, slapping her cheeks, and pulling me to her with beefy arms. "She's so cute—like a little china doll! I want to hug her to pieces!"

She very nearly did—a big, sloppy American bearhug, a show of emotion no proper Vietnamese would dare display on first meeting. It amazed me how quick Americans were to show affection to strangers, even those their menfolk had gone so far from home to destroy.

"And the children—?" Erma peeked around my helmet of ratted hair. Ed had shown her pictures of my two sons.

"In the car!" He poked a dad's boastful thumb over his shoulder.

"Ooo—I can't wait to see them!" Erma scuttled down the walk. "I'll just eat them up!"

Eat them up—my god! Of course, it was just another American figure of speech. I was beginning to discover that English was as full of booby traps as the jungle outside Ky La.

Anyway, Ed's new family impressed her, for better *and* for worse. Jimmy was cranky from crossing time zones, and since he spoke mostly Vietnamese, he cried when this giant brown-haired bear-lady tried to crush him with her paws. Tommy, however, who had slept fourteen hours on the plane and was ready for fun, screeched with delight. Erma knew right away which boy had the bright, upstanding, red-white-and-blue American father and which child was the pitiful third-world refugee. First impressions are lasting. I think that midnight meeting forever biased her in Tommy's favor, although I never dreamed of saying it.

We unloaded the luggage and put the boys to bed, where I stayed with them until they fell asleep. From the depths of this strange-smelling, thick-walled American house, I listened to Ed and Erma chat in too fast English over coffee. I still didn't know what to make of my new environment: American kitchens smelled like sickly hospitals, reeking of disinfectant, not *Ong Tao,* "Mr. Stove's," healthy food. The darkness outside the house was as terrifying as a midnight cadre meeting. I wanted to join them and gossip and laugh like real family, but I understood only a fraction of what they said and part of that was whispered, which to me meant danger, not good manners. Fortunately, the deep, even breathing of the kids won me over and I fell asleep, reminding myself to pay special attention to any spirits who might visit me in my first American dream.

My first full day as an American housewife didn't go so well. I slept poorly in Erma's tight-sealed house and my body still awoke and made water and got hungry on Saigon time. Nobody explained jet lag to me and I thought my strange waves of sleepiness in the middle of the day and spunkiness at four in the morning were just signs of how out of place Orientals were in round-eyed America. I hoped it would pass, like the flu, without my having to consult the neighborhood psychic or witch doctor.

My alarm clock on that first day was a playful slap on the rump.

"Get up, sleepyhead!" Ed yelled with a grin as wide as the band of sunlight streaming in through the window. He looked so happy to have his wife and family with him again that I thought he was going to burst. Like a slug in my mother's garden, I slithered around the sunburst to the shower where I took another ten minutes to wake up.

I dressed and made up with great care, partly because of my new surroundings (unlike Vietnamese peasant houses, American homes have their owner's fingerprints all over them: no two housewives ever put wastebaskets and tissues in the same place!) and partly because I could take no chances with my appearance. Daylight and in-laws are terrible critics.

"Hurry up and dress the kids," Ed commanded. "After breakfast, I want you to meet my mother!"

In Vietnam, meeting in-laws is always a tricky business. This is true especially when the marriage has not been arranged through matchmakers and the couple are of vastly different ages, let alone races—*quen nha ma, la nha chong,* I am at home in my mother's house, but a stranger to my in-laws! I would sooner have met an American battle tank on Erma's lawn than to walk next door unes-

corted and introduce myself to Ed's mother—which, for some unknown reason, was my husband's harebrained plan.

When Jimmy was dressed and fed (Tommy was still asleep and
nobody had the courage to wake him) Ed booted us out and pointed
to the shingled green house next door.

"Oh, go on!" he laughed. "You girls get acquainted. Mom won't
bite your head off!"

Well, I certainly hoped not, but Ed hadn't met a real Vietnamese
mother-in-law. Back in Danang, my mother had never accepted our
marriage, and so never treated Ed like a new family-member-in-
training, with all the horror the position inspires. I dragged my son
across the sunny lawn like a goat on the way to the slaughterhouse.

I squeezed Jimmy's spit-slick fingers and knocked on the door.
Dogbarks from hell—we jumped back! The shadow of a big, Erma-
like figure waddled toward us behind lacy curtains. A grandmother's
high-pitched voice scolded the yappy dogs.

Had this been a Vietnamese house, I would have known instantly
what to do. I would have bowed low, recited the ritual greeting of an
unworthy daughter-in-law to the witch-queen who would transform
me over the next few years into a deserving wife for her son, then
gone into the kitchen and made us both some tea, humbly serving it
with two hands, the old-fashioned way. Then I would have sat silently and waited to be instructed.

But this was an American house: a great sand-castle trap for a
Vietnamese fish out of water. In Vietnam, a matchmaker would have
prepared the way—sold my mother-in-law on my maidenly virtues,
few as those might be. Now I would have to do my own selling,
encumbered with my fatherless child, remembering how I had lost
my virginity not once, but *three* times: bodily to the Viet Cong who
raped me after my kangaroo court-martial; spiritually to Anh,
Jimmy's father, with whom I fell into girlish love; and morally to the
sad little GI in Danang who kept my family off the street by paying
me four hundred U.S. dollars *green money* for a last happy memory of
my country. By any measure, I was unworthy to stand on this fine
woman's stoop, let alone pretend to the honors and duties of a daughter-in-law. It was only because of my continuing bad karma that the
earth did not swallow me up.

Despite my fears, the door opened onto the most angelic old face I
had ever seen.

Leatha (whom I would always call "Mom Munro" and *never* impolitely by her first name) was seventy-five and had silver-blond hair that circled her cherub face the way white smoke twists around a storybook cottage. In Vietnam, such women aged like plucked berries: from the blush of virgin freshness to old age it was quick and downhill. Although a woman's post-birth *buon de* ritual, like our daily regimen of outdoor labor, kept our bodies lean and hard, we had no time or money for beauty treatments. Indeed, in a culture where reaching old age was a real accomplishment, we revered our elderly for being one step closer to the ancestors we worshiped. Old women and old men were sometimes mistaken for one another, and that was no cause for shame. In a way, this blending of sexes with its release from the trials of youth—concern for appearance and catching a mate—was one of aging's big rewards.

But not for Leatha.

Although Ed and Erma later assured me that she was "just an average grandma," I thought her angelic hair, well-fed happy face, plump saggy arms, solid girth, and movie star makeup made her even more spectacular than the painted Buddhas in the shrine beneath Marble Mountain near my village. Her appearance was even more astonishing, since in Vietnam I had seen no American women over fifty. (Most outsiders were men—soldiers or civilian contractors like Ed—or young female nurses.) Although her big hug made me feel better, I continued to stare at her. I tried to imagine my mother's face beneath the silver wreath and felt strangely envious and sad. Until I later found out how most Americans treat their elderly parents, the thought of growing old, fat, and pretty in America seemed to be another dividend of peace.

Of course, Leatha knew who I was at once and invited us inside. We talked only a minute before our polite smiles hurt and our rootless conversation slowed to head nods and empty laughter. I volunteered to make tea but she insisted that was the hostess's duty. Unfortunately, such was my mood that even this unexpected kindness seemed like a slap in the face—a reminder of my foreignness and incapacity. How bad must a daughter-in-law be, I thought, not even to merit a stern lecture on family rules?

Eventually, Ed and Erma came over with Tommy and I felt more at ease. To be strictly proper, I should have sung the "new bride" song in the presence of both my husband and his mother—a kind of ceremonial acceptance of the collar of obedience:

A risen moon is supposed to shine
Except through clouds, when it is dim and weak,
I come young and innocent to be your wife
Please speak of me kindly in your mother's ear.
People plant trees to grow big and strong,
People have children to prosper and protect them.
I cross my arms and bow my head
To please my husband and his mother.
If I do something wrong, please teach me right.
Don't beat me or scold me in public
For some will laugh and others will say
The fist is my husband,
The tongue is she from whence he came.

Instead, Ed put his arm around his mother and told her all about Vietnam, leaving out everything of importance in my black and bloody past—most of which he didn't know himself. Instead, he bragged about his mother's blue-ribbon pies at the Skagit Valley Fair, and I nodded enthusiastically even though I hadn't the slightest idea what pies, blue ribbons, or county fairs really were. After Ed's father died, I learned, Leatha had moved south to California where she took up residence next door to Erma, who shared a house with her husband, Larry, and adult son, Larry Jr., who was seldom around.

I saw much more of her pixie-faced daughter, Kathy, a young woman about my age, who lived with her husband in the neighboring town of Santee. Why Leatha didn't move in with her daughter, who had more than enough room and could share housekeeping and cooking chores Vietnamese style, was beyond my understanding. I guessed that Americans loved their possessions so much that even a lonely old woman valued her own TV set, kitchen, bathroom, spare bedrooms, and garage for a car she couldn't drive more than living with a daughter in her sunset years.

Anyway, the longing in Leatha's eyes told me that she probably would have traded all her possessions for a little room among her family. Her "children" these days were six little dogs that jumped around like kids and yapped at the TV and pestered you for snacks and attention whenever you sat down. She even bought canned food for them at the store, which I thought was the height of decadence.

In Vietnam, a dog was a guardian first, then a pet, and sometimes dinner. It fed itself by foraging, not at the family's expense. I chalked up Leatha's behavior to American ignorance, and it helped me feel less like a bumpkin in their magnificent homes. After all, if they knew that the soul of the dog was really a transient spirit (usually a greedy person who had to earn a new human body by suffering a dog's life—most of it spent guarding someone else's wealth), they wouldn't be so quick to put them up on pedestals and deny them penance. I shuddered to think how Leatha's six "children" must have laughed among themselves in dogbark about their naive American mistress.

Ed and Leatha gossiped away the morning until Erma's son, Larry, joined us. I soon felt like the decorative china doll Erma had dubbed me when I arrived—just unwrapped and put on a shelf, worthy of an occasional glance but no conversation. Jet lag (as Ed now explained it) soon caught up with me again and, depressed and exhausted, I bowed and apologized in Vietnamese, which I knew would sound more sincere, and went for a nap, leaving Ed to contend with the kids. I fell asleep wondering how quickly Ed's womenfolk would begin to complain about the "lazy new wife" he had brought to California.

When I awoke, most of our things had been moved from Erma's house to Leatha's. Ed preferred the company of his aged mom to imposing on his sister, and I agreed enthusiastically. Whereas Leatha seemed to look down on me as one of her puppies, Erma just seemed to look down. I was not prepared for this reversal of roles, for the sister-in-law was supposed to be the young bride's ally—someone who would comfort her when the rigors of wife-training got too bad. In America, it seems, who you are is more important than the role society gives you. Even as Ed's wife, though, I did not seem to be worth too much.

That evening, Erma and Larry came over and I tried to help the women fix dinner. Unfortunately, between my ignorance of American kitchens and a strong desire to avoid looking dumber than I had already, I didn't contribute much.

The first thing that astounded me was the refrigerator—a two-door monster that dwarfed our knee-high Vietnamese models—every nook and cranny of which was packed with food! It occurred to me that this was why Americans got so big: the bigger the refrigerators, the bigger the people. I thanked fate or luck or god that Jimmy would now grow up to be twice the size of Anh, his wealthy Vietnamese father. For a second I held a fantasy reunion: me, more rich and beautiful than Lien (Anh's wife who had thrown me out of their mansion when I got pregnant); my mother—plump and queenly as Leatha; and Jimmy—called Phung Quoc Hung in Vietnamese—tall and powerful as an American Green Beret, stooping to shake his father's little hand. It was a scene that could never come true, although, as everybody said, all things are possible in America.

Erma took out a frosty box with the picture of a glowering green giant (no doubt a character from American fables who devoured children who didn't eat their vegetables), then a slab of meat, frozen solid in a little Styrofoam boat covered with plastic.

"How we eat this?" I asked as the clumpy peas, hard as marbles, rattled into a pan. I was not ready to live in a country where vegetables and meat were sucked like ice cubes.

"Oh, the peas will cook in no time," Erma said, adding water and flipping on her stove's magic, matchless flame. "The round steak we'll have tomorrow. I'll just defrost it in the fridge."

Why not just go to the market and get what you want before you eat it? Maybe that was why Americans had to invent frozen food, so they would have something to put in their expensive freezers. Little by little, I was beginning to understand capitalism.

We sat down for my first American dinner and I shyly waited to see what everyone else did first. I knew some Americans said prayers for their food, perhaps to honor the dead animal they were about to eat, but this seemed like a silly custom. There was a time for praying and a time for eating. Did those same people say prayers when they did other ordinary things—when they made love or went shopping or relieved themselves? I just didn't understand their reasoning, particularly since Americans didn't seem like a particularly spiritual people. Their houses lacked shrines for their ancestors where prayers were said. Anyway, I was happy to see the Munros reach for the food all at once—"digging in," as Leatha called it—like an Oriental family, as soon as we sat down.

My next hurdle was faking the use of their cumbersome eating utensils. In Vietnam, all food was taken with chopsticks or slurped from a bowl. Here, Americans employed as many utensils as the cook had used to prepare the meal. I was sure I'd never master them all, particularly the fork, which everyone held like a pencil, then juggled like acrobats between hands to cut their meat. Why didn't the cook just slice the food into bite-size strips the way we did in the Orient? I went along with the game as far as I could, grasping my fork like a club and politely smacking my lips very loudly so that Erma and Leatha would know I enjoyed the meal—despite the rich sauces that filled me up after two bites. Fortunately, after a few seconds of this, nobody looked at me anymore and Jimmy and I finished our meal winking and poking each other at the kids' end of the table.

After dinner, I wanted to show my new mother-in-law that I could be a good housewife, so I volunteered to do dishes. At first, I was shocked by all the uneaten food. In Vietnam, we believed that the more food you waste in this life, the hungrier you'll be in the next. Then I remembered the full refrigerator and guessed that if people rationed their food as we did in Vietnam, all the freezers and freezer makers would be out of business and go hungry; so, in America, waste was really thrift. I began scraping the plates into the garbage can and, predictably, Ed came up behind me and laughed his amused-daddy laugh.

"No, no," he said. "Dump the garbage into the sink."

"What?" I knew he must be kidding. "You want to clog drain?" I might be new to America, but I wasn't born yesterday.

"It won't get stopped up. Go ahead. Just dump it down the drain. I'll show you some magic."

I peevishly did as he instructed. *Okay, Mister Smart Man, if you want to play plumber after your supper, that's okay with me!*

When a heap of leavings blocked the drain, I turned on the tap and stood back. Sure enough, the water started to rise. Without blinking an eye, Ed threw a switch over the stove and the pile of sludge became a shaking, squirting volcano, and miraculously, the pile collapsed and disappeared. The grinding earthquake became a hum and Ed turned off the switch. Tap water ran merrily down the drain.

Pale and humiliated—again—I could only look at the floor. Tears came to my eyes.

"Here now," Ed put his arm around me. "I didn't mean to scare you. That's just a garbage disposal. A motor under the sink grinds everything up."

I took the wrapper the peas came in and started to shove it down the monster's rubbery throat.

"No, no," Ed corrected me again.

I stopped and blew a wisp of hair from my face.

"No paper," Ed warned, "or bones or plastic or anything like that."

"But you say put trash in sink!" This American miracle now seemed a little fickle to be real magic.

"No trash. Just soft food."

Again, I did as I was told, feeling Erma's critical eyes on my back. With the sink now empty, I could at last get on with washing the dishes—something even an ignorant Vietnamese farm girl knew quite well how to do.

"No, no," Ed said when he saw me stacking the dishes in the sink. "Just load them in the dishwasher." He had the same irritating little smile and I had absolutely no idea if he was making fun of me or trying to be helpful.

"What you talk about?" I slammed the silverware into the sink. I was getting tired again and my tone was not properly humble and subservient. I looked over my shoulder into the dining room. Erma and Leatha politely pretended to be absorbed in their coffee and conversation.

"Here—" Ed flipped down the big metal door beside the sink. Inside was a queer wire basket. "Just put the dishes here." He demonstrated with a plate.

"Okay, but how we wash them when they inside?" It seemed a logical question, but it only made Ed laugh. Under his close supervision, I loaded all the dishes in the stupid machine, wondering how even these mechanically inclined Americans got greasy plates and the tines of their silly, useless forks clean without rags and fingers. When I was finished, he poured some powder into a little box on the door and shut it tight. He punched a few buttons and turned a big dial and the growling noise began again. I thought for a minute that the dishes would be ground up, but the whirring was friendlier this time and I could hear the water splashing.

"See?" Ed smiled proudly. "Nothing to it!"

"Okay," I replied, "so how long we wait to dry them?" I fished for a dishtowel.

Ed laughed again. "You don't have to wait. You wipe the counter and go watch TV!"

Okay—I can do that! My first long day in America was coming to an end and I was ready to accept anything he said at face value. I decided I wouldn't even ask about the machine that put the dishes away.

At the end of the week, Ed went looking for a new construction job so that we could move out on our own. We showed our gratitude to Leatha by doing chores around the house, and Ed even poured a new concrete patio for her backyard. He also paid Leatha rent, although I never knew how much. This last arrangement struck me as odd because, in Vietnam, adult children often lived with their parents to care for them as they got older. Charging even modest rent to your own family seemed like free enterprise gone haywire—a ridiculous contradiction. After all, if the purpose of American freedom was to pursue happiness, what could make a mother happier than to surround herself with her kids? Charging money for something most mothers enjoy seemed silly at best, and in the long run, self-defeating. After all, if you can't be charitable to your own flesh and blood, why would you be charitable to strangers?

That was not the last contradiction I discovered while living with Leatha. For the first time in our married life, Ed and I had our own room and Tommy and Jimmy shared another. In Vietnam, children sleep with their parents until they are married—who else will protect them from evil spirits that stalk the night? When children sleep alone in Vietnam, we give them a knife or sharp stick with which to defend themselves, or put the skull or teeth of a watchdog by their beds. Some Americans think toy animals—little bears and kittens—have the same power; but, having seen bad war ghosts as a kid, I always put my faith in the stick.

For the year we lived in Vietnam, Ed and I slept with only a curtain between ourselves and the boys. I wore my black pajamas; peasants everywhere in Vietnam slept in their clothes, ready to jump for shelter instantly when explosions or gunfire rocked the night. Even when Ed demanded his husband's rights, I tried to keep something on because this impulse to stay covered was so strong. The first lesson I learned growing up in a war zone was to be ready to flee at a moment's notice and never look back. Even in the suburban silence, I couldn't shake the impulse to stay dressed and keep my money handy. When part of your mind is waiting for shells to fall, it's hard to concentrate fully on the task at hand, even when that task is making love.

And making love to Ed—or rather, allowing him to make love to me—was always a task. This problem stemmed not only from our age difference but the entire basis for our marriage, which for me was one of survival, not mutual attraction. (One can honor and serve a savior, but passion takes something more.) Another source of my discomfort was the way I had been raised, as well as everything that had happened to me to that point in my life.

For us, the claustrophobic life of the village—where everything was done in groups and nobody had any privacy—caused us to suppress those urges Americans express so freely. In the paddies, when a young man and woman catch each other's fancy, one will sing a song that requires the other to answer. Leaning on one's hoe and flirting openly just isn't the way it's done. If the girl wants to impress the boy, she does so by working extra hard—gaining a reputation for her serious attitude and dedication to her family. When the boy wants to court the girl, he labors beside her in a village work group, sits nearby during village entertainments (where the young people tell ghost stories or sing songs for the adults), or simply waits to walk with her like a loyal puppy to and from the paddies.

In no case, however, would either reveal their feelings, for that would lead to catastrophe. Sex was a taboo subject, discussed only by distraught mothers and dirty old men. Village girls were brought up to submit to it only for the purpose of creating a family, a duty we took very seriously. When a wife proved barren, in fact, it was her duty to recruit a second or third wife in which her husband could plant his seed. As the old saying went, "A man can have three wives and seven lovers; a woman has but one husband."

We also had practical reasons for disliking the sexual act. As peasants, we slept in the same clothes we wore in the fields. Coming home at the end of the day, we washed our feet and hands so as not so soil our home and food, and braved the dangers of river bathing as infrequently as we could. Women had no underwear or tampons or sanitary napkins, so our "unclean" period messed up more than our happy mood. Besides, after a long day in the fields (which in summertime could last until two or three in the morning, since the daytime was too hot for work), nobody felt like sex—for recreational, procreational, or any other reason.

Even our clothing contributed to our puritanical habits. Our lightweight pants were held up with a single drawstring which, when tightly knotted, posed a formidable obstacle to sex or even urinating in the fields. (We would simply pull up a loose pant leg rather than wrestle with the knot.) In fact, my introduction to this symbolic difference between East and West came when my American boyfriends—and later Ed—gave me Western-style underwear with an elastic waistband. In America clothes implied "no waiting;" in Vietnam, they declared "no way."

So Ed inherited everything I had learned to mistrust and dislike about sex. As a child, I never saw any form of sexual contact until my own double rape at the hands of the Viet Cong. Not even teenage hugging and kissing were permitted. When my female relatives learned of my impending marriage to an older American, they balanced their disapproval with relief that I would at least receive dispensation from sex. *"Chong gia vo tre,"* they would say with a wink, "Old husband, young wife," recalling the title of a cautionary folktale on that subject. Older men were thought to care less about physical pleasure; and every girl carried within her chaste distinctions about fatherly—as opposed to husbandly—love.

In reality, Ed's sex drive was stronger than anyone imagined—fully equal to that of the young Americans I'd known in Danang. In bed, I would let Ed jump on and jump off (frequently twice a day), trying to hurry the process as much as possible. I'd had younger lovers before, of course, and had learned what to pull and where to push to give a man what he needed—but it was all very mechanical, like a machine in a factory. Although I knew the secret attraction every woman feels for forbidden fruit—the delicious inner tingle one gets from a flirtatious glance or the accidental brush of a young man's hand—I neither felt nor expected pleasure during the act of sex. I had been instructed only too well that such was not the woman's privilege. Romance for me remained in the heart and mind, not the body. What you don't know exists, you do not think to ask for, even in the language of love.

Anyway, my string-tied pants and stern moral upbringing were barriers to more than sex. The only dress I had on arrival in America was an *ao dai,* the traditional long-paneled tunic worn by Vietnamese ladies since ancient times. On my first Saturday (shopping day in America), I would find out that dressing up in a way that was right in my old country was very wrong in my new one.

In Vietnam, we had two kinds of shopping: *dao pho mua sam,* which is "dress up and go to town"; and *di cho,* which is to buy food in the local market. So when Ed said, "Get dressed, we're going to get groceries," I assumed he meant we were going to the neighborhood fish market.

"I am dressed," I answered, pointing to my black pajamas—the kind I had worn to the village market all my life.

"Not that!" Ed almost choked. "People will think you're lazy or sick. Put on pants or a dress. You know, something you'd wear outside."

Ed's huffy tone left me confused and a little insulted. Although I was young, I wasn't stupid or without experience. I knew my *ao dai* would leave me overdressed for haggling with fish peddlers, but with my lousy record of mistakes, I figured it was better to be safe than sorry.

Although I was dressed and perfumed for a night on the town, everyone else was dressed for the beach—or bedroom.

"Look at that girl!" I whispered to Ed as we approached the local Safeway. Her big breasts bounced around inside a spongy tube top. Ed had already noticed. Behind her came another woman in high, creased shorts that showed things her doctor would be ashamed to see. I was scandalized and grateful I had left my innocent kids at home with Leatha and Erma. These housewives and schoolgirls were more provocative than anything I had seen outside the sleaziest nightclubs in Danang. In my country, a polite woman hid her body out of consideration for society (what man could work with such distractions?) as well as self-respect. If we felt free to dress like tramps, the men around us would feel free to behave like bums. In a war zone, temptation was the same as provocation.

"So, you don't like my pajamas, eh?" I poked Ed in the ribs. "Maybe next time I shop in my underwear!" The spirits guarding Safeway, obviously pleased at my proper attire, opened the door with unseen hands.

That's when I noticed: American markets don't smell like markets at all. Everything is canned, packaged, wrapped in cellophane, and hidden in boxes where, instead of seeing and smelling the fruit or vegetable or meat or whatever, you get a pretty picture of what the seller wants you to think the product looks like. You pay so much money for a pretty picture! Everything in the supermarket reeked of freon or cleanser or corrugated cardboard boxes. How was I to tell if my husband's steak and potatoes—hidden behind plastic and frost in a refrigerator too cold to touch—was fit to eat? And the produce counters weren't much better. Everything was air conditioned or on crushed ice. I felt as if I were visiting a "fruit hotel" rather than picking out tomorrow's dinner. It was all so strange that my stomach began to hurt. Ed mistook my pained expression for amazement.

"So—what do you think of our big American supermarkets?" he asked proudly, steering our huge metal cart down the aisle. "Pretty impressive, huh?"

"Oh, there are too many choices!" I replied, trying to find something nice to say. "And the wagon they give you is very nice," which was true enough. I was used to shopping day by day, not for a week of groceries at a time.

Ed stopped in the middle of a rainbow of packages.

"Here now," he said, adjusting his glasses like a professor, "you always say we don't eat enough rice—what do you think of this?"

He waved his hand along the shelf. From the pictures on the labels, all the boxes contained rice, although I had no idea what distinguished one kind from another. Of course, I *had* complained (in the nicest way possible) that I sorely missed my daily bowl of rice. The Munros were a steak and potatoes family and liked thick sandwiches of bread and meat for lunch instead of the greens and rice and noodle soup even wealthy Orientals preferred.

In the village, we had a dozen names for rice depending on its stage of preparation. Generally, we had three kinds of finished rice: *tam* rice, or bran rice, which was fit only for animals and beggars; brown (or "autumn"—*gao mua)* rice, which most of us ate every day; and sweet rice, called *xoi*—the white kind served at ceremonies, on holidays, or sacrificed to our ancestors. Here, Americans ate Spanish rice, fried rice, converted rice, steamed rice, wild rice, paella rice, rice pilaf, risotto rice, and dozens more I couldn't pronounce. Ed must've thought I had been a poor rice farmer, because I couldn't tell the difference. Finally, I grabbed a nice-looking box.

"Great," Ed said. "What kind did you get?"

Timidly, I showed him.

"Uncle Ben's?" he said. "Why Uncle Ben's?"

"The label," I tapped it like a smart American shopper. "I want number-one rice for family, right? So, this brand called 'Uncle Ben.' Vietnamese call trusted friend 'Uncle,' right? Like 'Uncle Ho' for Ho Chi Minh? So, Uncle Ben must be very good rice—trusted very much by all Americans, right?"

Ed laughed again and shook his head. I began filling the cart with Uncle Ben's but Ed stopped me after a few boxes.

"Whoa—hold on!" he said. "We aren't feeding the whole neighborhood!"

I was still battling old reflexes—to clean out American goods for resale on the black market. Our credo had been: Stash, hoard, and survive. It was also customary in the Orient to buy rice in hundred-kilo bags, not tiny boxes printed like colorful storybooks. As things turned out, it wasn't the kind of rice I thought it was after all, and Leatha let me spoil a batch before stepping in to show me how converted rice was cooked. She, too, must've thought I was a terrible farmer as well as an incompetent wife. Imagine—an Asian woman who can't cook rice!

When we went to the checkout counter, the male clerk, seeing my *ao dai,* gave me a nasty stare. It was an expression I had seen before—mostly from Vietnamese in Danang who disapproved of my American boyfriends—but here it was something more. The clerk was too young to have been in the service, but he had the warrior's look: hate and fear and sorrow all mixed. Maybe he had a brother or father killed in my country. Maybe he was just one of the many Americans I would meet who were so fed up with the war that they hated anyone who reminded them of it.

Still, this was his country, not mine, so I lowered my eyes. I tried to make myself look humble and even smaller, which was easy next to my big American husband.

Like many in my village, I never really hated American soldiers. We resented them for invading our country, of course, but we didn't take it personally. As a rule, they weren't mean to us for meanness' sake—like the Moroccans or Koreans, or the Japanese in World War II. Americans' funny racial differences—big noses and round eyes on long faces—were objects of amusement and sometimes fear, but seldom hate. As a result, I was surprised to see those embers glowing in the eyes of this angry young clerk.

Even worse, *I* began to take it personally. I thought I must look funny or was standing or gesturing in some way that gave offense. I tried to summon up the guilt I often felt for planting jungle booby traps as a twelve-year-old conscript for the Viet Cong. What had once seemed right and necessary now seemed cruel and useless. Had I actually helped to wound or maim this young man's brother? Had I led his hapless father into a Viet Cong ambush? Today, the breezy, bustling Americans around me seemed no more threatening than a load of tourists. War and "real life" were now as opposite as night and day. War guilt, I had learned, was partly the chagrin you feel for outliving a crisis that once consumed you. One does not strike a match where there is no darkness, although one may still be afraid of the dark.

So I tried to play the role this young man gave me, but I could not. What alarmed me most was the racial anger that popped up inside me like the flame on a GI's lighter. People can reason about anything they have the power to change, like their attitude or their clothes, but when condemned for their race they react like cornered rats. I longed for my father's spirit to cool me, as it had so often those last years in Vietnam. *"Con o dau—ong ba theo do,"* he used to say, assuring me that wherever his children wandered, our ancestors would surely go to comfort and protect us. But how could they find me so far from home? More than a stranger in a strange new land, I was becoming a stranger to myself. I didn't like that feeling one bit.

The clerk rang everything up and Ed didn't haggle about price or freshness, and when the boy told us how much we owed, I almost fell over. Ed, however, wasn't fazed. Instead of handing out cash, he simply wrote the amount on a slip of paper, which he signed and tore out of a book.

"What's that?" I asked.

"A check. I'm paying for our groceries. Surely you've seen somebody write a check!"

"Of course!" I sniffed. I didn't want to appear ignorant in front of the surly cashier.

"Well, maybe our American checks are different," Ed said softly as the clerk copied down more numbers from some cards Ed showed him. "You see, the store gives the check to our bank, which gives them money for us."

No money for food! I was astonished, *Just a paper check! No wonder Americans eat so much!* And no wonder wealthy Vietnamese were the only people in my country to use banks. That's how the rich got rich —because the banks paid all their bills! It also explained why Ed guarded his checkbook the way I guarded my kids. Checks were better than money!

Over the next few weeks, I met many more of Ed's friends and relatives. Usually, I served them tea Vietnamese style, offering the cup with both hands and bowing slightly when they took it. Word must have gotten around, because sometimes they would clap after my "performance." Each visitor would congratulate Ed on his beautiful young wife—as if I were a new TV set or lawn mower—ask me how I liked America, then begin talking to Ed as if I weren't there. True, my English wasn't the best, but I understood a lot and was willing to learn more. For some reason they always asked me questions through Ed—although he spoke no Vietnamese—and I was assumed to be incapable of anything except pouring tea, looking pretty, and caring for my children, who were greeted with a mix of amusement and distaste. "Cute kids," I would hear them say, "but such urchins—especially the one that isn't Ed's." Did they think I didn't have ears?

During these long conversations, I often wondered what these "wise" Americans really knew about life and living, let alone death and survival. How many of them had their world split in two—saw brother fight brother with bullets, bombs, and bayonets? How many had their homes invaded by strange-looking, strange-smelling giants? Had to hide in leech-filled swamps or were tortured with snakes and electricity for information they didn't have? How many sent wives and husbands and brothers and sisters out to work in the morning only to have their pieces come back in a basket? What had their cozy houses and bulging refrigerators and big, fast cars and noisy TV sets really taught them about the world: about back-breaking labor, bone-grinding poverty, and death's edge starvation? Could they imagine their sons and husbands, so peaceful and happy in civilian life, coming into my village and making old men and women beg for their lives? *"Xin ong dung giet toi!"*—"Please, sir, don't kill me!"—was our standard greeting for the American boys in uniform who came our way.

We once watched a TV war correspondent interview a young GI in front of a burning village.

"Do you think your operation was successful?" the journalist asked.

"Yeah, we burned down a lot of Charlie's homes and destroyed the village—really killed a lot of gooks!" the soot-faced young man said with a big grin.

I could only imagine the wailing villagers, unseen by the camera and Ed's relatives. How successful had the "operation" been for them? Did anyone realize how many lifetimes we villagers crammed into our first twenty years on earth? *Tre chua qua, gia da den*—Before youth has left, old age has come! Did Ed's relatives realize what an old lady looked back at them through the tear-moistened eyes of Ed's "lovely young bride"?

When I started crying like this—"for no reason at all," Ed would say after the visitors had gone—I felt more foolish than ever. "The poor dear is homesick," Leatha would say, just out of hearing. "She misses her mother," and that was true enough. "She's just a spoiled crybaby," young Kathy would add, going off to her own lovely house and young husband. Erma would sniff into her coffee mug after glancing around to see if I was near, and say things like, Not that she lifts a finger to help out. She leaves long black hairs around the house and those poor children would *starve* if I didn't fix them a proper meal. Nothing but rice and noodles—how can they live on that? And she never socializes with our guests, have you noticed? Just bows and bats her eyes, then goes into her dream world. Lord knows what she thinks about—probably all the things Ed's going to buy her. He's going through his second childhood, all right, and he's found the perfect playmate!

To tell the truth, I didn't feel like much of a playmate, or even much of a wife or mother. Because Ed enjoyed telling the story of how we met—on a Danang street corner through a girlfriend of mine who used to be a hooker—his family concluded I had been a streetwalker. Even in their more charitable moods, they seemed sure I'd married Ed for his money and a life of ease in America. They couldn't conceive of mere survival as a motive, with gratitude, not greed, the consequence.

I tried to solve their problem with my hair, which now flowed like a waterfall down to my waist, by lopping it off with kitchen scissors —short, like a Chinese rice-bowl haircut. I redoubled my efforts to impress both Leatha and Erma in the only way I knew—by working harder and longer than anyone, but even this tactic only widened the gap between us. When I tried to wash clothes by hand, Erma chided me for not using the automatic washer and dryer. When I scrubbed the floor on my knees, Leatha chuckled at my stupidity and told me to use the mop. When I cooked good fish and rice, they turned up their noses and wondered why I was starving "my boys" of old-fashioned meat and potatoes. When I picked up my kids and carried them around, even when they weren't crying—handling them the way all kids need to be handled if they are to learn love and affection —Leatha pointed to the playpen and said, "Leave them alone, or they'll never become independent!" In a land of instant gratification and miracle conveniences, apparently, there was no room for a spontaneous show of love through the labor of one's heart and hands.

On top of it all, whenever the women took me shopping, the only sizes I could wear were in the children's department, so the kids and I bought our clothes together. I felt more like a foster child than an honorable daughter-in-law with a family of my own.

After a few weeks of this, I began to hate myself as the useless teenager everyone supposed me to be. I hated my hair for being Oriental black, not European brown or blond or silver. I hated my body for being Vietnamese puny and not Polish plump or German hardy or big-boobed and long-legged like the glossy American girls Ed ogled on the sidewalk.

For that matter, being married to "my father" made me feel even more like a child, which was how I responded as a wife, and I hated myself for that. Unable to communicate with anyone in any of the ways I knew, I felt alone, like a stone at the bottom of the sea.

As much as I hated the war, I began to miss Vietnam very much— not for the dangerous and depressing life I used to live, but for the home and family I remembered as a child. The more I tried to make such a family here, the more I ached for the one I had left behind. I waited like a puppy for the American mail carrier, hoping for a letter or postcard from my family. At sunset, I would sit in Leatha's yard and sing to the blood-red sun—in the direction of my absent mother —but the palms of Southern California were not magical sau dau trees, and my soul did not flower in the dirt beneath my feet.

Worst of all was when we gathered after dinner for an evening of TV, which in those days always began with war news from Vietnam —the U.S. invasion of Cambodia and the Kent State massacre that had followed.

"Look at those awful people!" Erma would say when stories about "Viet Cong atrocities" filled the screen. To her and Larry, the enemy had one face. Ed and Leatha, like me, just sat in silence, speaking only when Jimmy's playing got too loud or little Tommy began to cry. I understood the newscasters, and the pictures spoke for themselves. But where the Munros saw faceless Orientals fleeing burning villages, tied up as prisoners, or as rag dolls in a roadside trench (even innocent villagers were "VC" or "Charlie"), I saw my brother Bon Nghe, who fought twenty-five years for the North; my mother's nephew, who was a lieutenant for the South; my sister Lan, who hustled drinks to Americans in Danang; and my sister Hai, who shared sleepless nights with my mother in our family bunker at Ky La. I saw floating on the smoke of battle the soul of my dead brother, Sau Ban, victim of an American land mine, and the spirit of my father, who drank acid to avoid involving me again with Viet Cong terrorists. I saw in those tiny electronic lines, as I saw in my dreams, the ghosts of a hundred relatives, family friends, and playmates who died fighting for this side or that, or merely trying to survive.

When the news changed to a story about a little girl who fell into a well, however, the whole room filled with compassion. In the Vietnam newsreel, children and women and old people had been blown to bits and everyone just yawned, because they were *the enemy*—bad guys on a real-life "cops and robbers" show. Now that one little girl-in-the-well made my in-laws weep bitter tears: because she was *one of them*. I wanted to tell these kind, well-meaning, but ignorant people the truth about my war, their war—*our* war—that my brothers and sisters and that poor trapped little girl were really all one family.

But I didn't know the words, even in Vietnamese.

After striking out in his local job search, Ed finally decided to accept a contract with his old employer in a place called Utah. Ed decided we would visit Yellowstone Park before he reported to work. Erma said it would be a great chance for me to see the country, but I think she and Kathy were secretly pleased to see me leave. When it came time to plan our trip, I was not surprised when they volunteered to keep Tommy in order to make our travels easier. I didn't like the idea of leaving one of my boys with near-strangers, but their affection for Tommy seemed genuine and they were his blood relations. With a strained smile, I agreed.

On the appointed day, we packed the car and pulled out of the driveway. The last thing I saw was Kathy grinning on the curb, holding my little boy like a prize and waving his tiny arm as we drove away.

"Oh, turn off the waterworks!" Ed said gruffly, trying to cheer me up. "Tommy will have a wonderful time. The girls will treat him like he was their own."

I cried even harder.

Within hours of leaving San Diego, though, I had other things to think about: big, desolate America had swallowed us up. The horizon jumped back and I felt smaller and more insignificant than ever. If Vietnam were a delicate teacup, America—with its craggy peaks and endless, dusty plains—was a gigantic banquet platter, inviting hungry immigrants from all over the world to come and sup, to indulge their appetite for a better life. Still, immigrants like me don't arrive with our dreams full-blown. Rather, it seems, we expand our hopes to fit this country's vast horizons.

When our car radio went fuzzy, I sang all the songs I knew (in Vietnamese, of course—Ed couldn't understand a word) and realized that for the first time in five years I could shout anything I wanted—about the damned Viet Cong or greedy Republicans or backbreaking paddy work, or ridicule American soldiers—and not get into trouble. In America, I was as big as my voice and I liked that feeling a lot.

When we were still driving at sunset, however, I began to get nervous. In Vietnam, driving after dark in the middle of nowhere was a quick ticket to your next life. Even if you escaped the land mines and enemy patrols, you could easily be ambushed by what we Vietnamese called "cowboys": renegade Republican soldiers or big-city gangsters who robbed and killed anyone who traveled unescorted—crimes usually blamed on the Viet Cong. Although my head reassured me that the war was thousands of miles away, my heart told me to play it safe.

"You drive down middle," I said, nudging Ed's arm. I knew mines were usually seeded on the shoulder of the road and that cowboys often rolled boulders down from narrow passes to stop a car. I supposed that was why smart Americans painted yellow guide lines in the middle of their highways.

"Don't be silly," Ed replied. "You want us to get killed?"

We chased our headlights into the deepening night and I only felt worse and worse. Finally, a car pulled up to pass.

"Good," I blurted out as the vehicle—our convoy—roared by on the left. "Keep up with him! Don't let him get away!" The sight of those big taillights ahead of us in the vast American wilderness was immensely comforting and I didn't want to lose it.

"What?" Ed laughed. "You're crazy! He must be going ninety!"

I clamped my lips over gritted teeth and didn't say another word. Fortunately, our next stop was at a place that was famous for its lights.

Ed's sons, Ron and Ed Jr., had just left the navy and lived in Las Vegas. I assumed a family reunion would be the main reason for our visit—what else could you do in the middle of a desert?

I soon found out.

We arrived about midnight, but the streets were as bright as day. All I could think of was Saigon, which had the same effect on me when I arrived there as a teenager a half-dozen years before. We were inside a giant jukebox, with the tunes of a thousand upside-down lives spinning all around us: sailors five hundred miles from the sea; husbands looking for girlfriends and wives looking for lovers; poor people dreaming of riches and rich people terrified of losing whatever they had.

Ed told me a joke about a man who "struck it rich" in Las Vegas, arriving in a ten-thousand-dollar Cadillac and leaving in a forty-thousand-dollar bus! I knew we were not among the people arriving rich, despite our comfortable (and by Vietnamese standards, lavish) lifestyle, when Ed told me to look for a motel. I pointed to the first building I saw, a towering high-rise with uniformed doormen, and he said, "No, a *mo*tel, not a hotel."

More American word tricks. "Okay," I asked, "what is difference between hotel and motel?"

"About fifty bucks a night," Ed replied, and laughed his big-daddy laugh.

Finally, he spotted a place he liked and we checked in. It was too late to call Ed's sons, so I suggested we go to bed. Ed would hear nothing of it.

"You don't come to Las Vegas to sleep!" he exclaimed, astonished at my latest stupid idea. "I'll call a baby-sitter so we can go gamble."

Gambling I understood; but calling for someone to sit on my baby was something else. My worry showed on my face.

"You know," Ed explained, "a person to look after Jimmy."

"You mean Ron and Kim?"

"No, a *baby-sitter.*"

"You mean a friend you know in Las Vegas?"

"Nope. You just call the front desk and they send someone up, like room service. Watch."

He picked up the phone and a few minutes later a teenager in high-spun hair, miniskirt, and bracelets appeared at our door. My mouth dropped open. No way was I going to leave my child with a stranger, let alone a girl young enough to need a nanny herself. Besides, when it came to strangers, I'd heard rumors about Asian children being kidnapped for sale on the black market—and my beautiful little Jimmy had all the best features of his race. *No way, Charlie!* We had escaped cowboys on the highway and I wasn't about to press my luck. Ed could go gamble if he wanted to; I would stay with my baby.

Five minutes later, on our way to the casino, Ed explained how he hadn't brought a pretty wife to Las Vegas just to wander around like a bachelor. Frowning, sleepy, and miserable, I followed him into a giant room that looked like a *cho,* a frenzied Vietnamese meat and vegetable market.

"Here's ten bucks," Ed said, slipping a bill into my hand. "Turn it into a million."

I stared at the money as Ed disappeared into a canyon of one-armed bandits. As well-off as we were, Ed rarely gave me cash for anything; he either bought it at my suggestion, gave me a check, or used one of several plastic cards. The first thing I thought of was how much ten dollars in "green" money would buy in Danang: a week's worth of food for me, my mother, and Jimmy; or enough PX goods to breed five times that amount on the suburban black market.

I also recalled how many Vietnamese men had a special weakness for gambling, so it was not something daughters and wives approved of. In the village, whenever we kids passed a man whose habit had harmed his family, we softly sang, *"Co bac bac thang ban; cua nha ban het ra than an may"*—"Gambling is the uncle of the poor and miserable; bet your house and lose your belongings, win a new job as a beggar!" We didn't sing it to be mean, but to show the man we cared about his family. Anyway, despairing of my husband's order, I changed the whole thing into nickels, which had a comforting heft, and began depositing them into the slots like a child feeding goats at the zoo.

Fortunately, Ed wasn't much of a gambler either. I felt a little better when I returned a few dollars a couple of hours later. The Chinese say "where there is no gain, the loss is obvious," and we Vietnamese know the opposite is true as well.

To my great relief, Jimmy survived being sat on by his rock-and-roll nanny, and the next day's visit with Ed's sons went well. Being Vietnam veterans, they understood not only some of what I had gone through, but what both veterans and Vietnamese were still going through in America: the "baby killer" sneers for them and the smoldering "VC Commie" looks for me. We all had regained the ability to see each other as people instead of shooting-gallery targets, and I felt a little sad for ever having accepted war as a way of life. I would later find out that this strange, out-of-body feeling of disconnectedness from life and helpless shame over the past was what many U.S. vets called guilt. I could hear it crackle in the voices of Ed's sons and see its shadow in their eyes. In this respect, encountering a Vietnam vet (soldier or civilian, it didn't matter), whether he hated, respected, or just tolerated me, was like finding a long-lost cousin. A distant cousin may dislike you, but you are united by a bond of blood. For many Vietnamese and Americans alike, the blood bond of battle was stronger than the blood tie of birth. We were all orphans of the same shattered dream.

In Utah, the job Ed had been promised fell through, so after another night in a motel we drove straight on to Yellowstone. I was secretly pleased we didn't stay in Utah. The Indian name must've meant "rocks and dirt"! I felt more at home once we had climbed into the mountains. The superhighway narrowed to more Vietnamese proportions and the view beyond the windows turned cool and green. Eventually, we passed patches of funny white dust—like China Beach!—by the road, then more and more of it, piled even on the rocks.

"What on earth is that?" I asked Ed, rolling up my window. The air had turned frosty like a draft from Erma's freezer.

Ed laughed his famous laugh and I knew I was about to get another lesson on America. "Don't you know what that is? That's *snow!* You know—frozen water!"

I knew Ed was kidding, because frozen water was ice cubes. Nobody would go to the trouble of freezing water then grinding it up and dumping it all over the ground for miles and miles, especially where nobody lived.

Ed saw my doubtful expression and pulled the car off the road. He grabbed Jimmy like a sack of potatoes and plunked him down in the nearest patch of white. Jimmy started to laugh, then cry, then laugh again. I knelt and put my hand in the snow. It crunched like cotton candy and was very, *very* cold.

"Ow!" I pulled my hand back. "It burn! Where does it come from?"

"The sky," Ed said cryptically.

More American magic. I glanced upward, half expecting a freezerload of ice cubes to tumble down on my head. It was strange to feel cold in a green forest—another American contradiction: a freezing jungle.

Farther down the road, we parked with other tourists and Ed led us from the car. I walked, bundled up like an Eskimo, to the edge of a boiling pond. I cried out and jumped back.

Ed, in shirtsleeves, holding Jimmy's hand, asked, "What's wrong?"

"My god! It's *hell!* I see pictures!"

Buddhists, like Christians, believe in the heaven and hell vividly explained to them as children. One difference is that Vietnamese think virtually nobody makes it to heaven whereas Western saints admit almost everyone if they repent before they die. Unlike Christians, though, we Buddhists must atone for the sins of many former lives, not just our current incarnation, so a simple deathbed confession won't do the job.

For example, if I spent my life accumulating wealth and never helped the poor, I might return in my next life as a beggar until I learned the rule of charity. Even good souls have to spend ninety days in limbo before they're assigned a future. It's not that the cosmic god is cruel; just practical. Consequently, his holy men on earth talk mostly about hell because that's where their congregation is likely to wind up. As a Buddhist, I knew from what I had already been through in my short life that I must be atoning for a lot of bad karma.

That day, I remembered especially one book a monk gave me when I was young. It showed ordinary people with the heads of beasts. One man had the head of a water buffalo and another looked like a terrible devil. The buffalo-man, they said, had been cruel to animals, and the witch-headed fellow had had evil thoughts when he was alive, so these were their punishments in hell. The idea that these pictures were really clever symbols meaning something else—that "bull-headed" and "malicious" thinking could create a hellish life— never occurred to us. The notion that a bad act in life would lead to retribution in kind after death, though, made us little kids really sit up and take notice.

The worst picture, I thought, was one of a beautiful woman hanging upside down over a boiling pond, tormented by demons. The devils were sawing off parts of her body and throwing them into molten lava—the punishment for someone who cheats on her husband. The idea of body parts writhing like skewered worms made me sick with horror. A village elder, of course, might have seen in the picture a symbol of how broken vows can "dismember" a family, but such thinking was for monks and wise men, not little kids. Because I was ashamed of many things I had done in Vietnam and was now questioning my new marriage in America, I teetered on the edge of that boiling pond like a woman poked by demons.

"Be careful"—Ed steadied me with a hand—"people have fallen in there and died."

"I don't want to see this," I blurted out, shivering and confused, and ran back to the car.

I heard Ed tell Jimmy in a fatherly voice, "That's okay. Mama's just tired. We'll go see something more fun."

We drove farther into the mountains with the heat on full blast for my benefit—past wedges of snow plowed against the curvy highway. After a while we came to another smoking lake that Ed thought would cheer me up. But when we pulled up to this smoking lake, surrounded by mist and shadows and looking very much like the home of the Buddhist's *Mang Xa* snake—a fire-breathing monster—I refused to get out. "You go ahead," I told Ed. "Show Jimmy the sights. I'm too cold to walk around."

"Okay," Ed said. "We're just going to climb the bridge. We'll be back in a jiffy."

I didn't know how long a jiffy was, but it was long enough to do a lot of worrying. As they were about to disappear from the foggy windshield, I saw something that confirmed everything I had suspected about the United States.

From the edge of the forest, a lone stag approached the lake, antlers bobbing above its shoulders. In the face of such terror—before the very gates of hell—the deer was proud, calm, and strong. I knew then that America really *was* as magical as I had heard—that the mystical things I had been taught as a child were true. To Buddhists, the deer is a symbol of goodness, purity, and peace. When their antlers are prepared *nai to*—cut as buds and ground into a potion— they are said to cure illness and extend life, like the unicorn horns of Western myth. Even more startling, in one of our stories of a great smoking lake, the Buddha himself crossed a bridge and was confronted by the serpent. Instead of crying and trying to run away like other people, the Buddha reached out and quenched the flames with his compassion. Now, in the middle of this hell on earth, I had seen with my own eyes the symbol of purity come down to quench his thirst at the lake of evil. This was no coincidence—and was possibly an omen for me. In a land where ponds boil and ice falls from the sky, my son had walked the *Mang Xa* lake and been kissed by the

Buddha deer. Good and evil lie down together and peace blooms like the buds of enchanted antlers. *This* was why Americans revered this holy place. This was what America is all about!

When Ed and Jimmy came back with rosy cheeks and smoky breath, I gave them each a big hug and asked Ed when we were going to eat. I was starving now and ready for anything from the great American banquet.

We returned to San Diego and four months passed before Ed's Utah boss recalled him. Our life didn't improve much in the interim because we were "short-timers" in San Diego and Ed's faith in his old company kept him from seeking employment elsewhere and allowing us to move away from my in-laws and into a house we could call our own.

Not knowing what his future held, Ed began to smoke too much. Like a dutiful wife, I told him to cut down, pouting like a child when he barked back. When we argued I called him an old man, which to a Vietnamese is a compliment, not a curse. With the best of intentions, I would say, "Old men shouldn't smoke so much!" Ed always took it like a bullet through the heart. Leatha pulled me aside after one of these exchanges and told me *never* to shout at my husband— her perfect son—again. I found myself responding more like an American wife than a Vietnamese daughter-in-law: with frowns and grunts instead of chastened silence. I began to realize why so many American relatives—fractured by hectic, materialistic lives—preferred to live apart. Like leaky pots hastily mended, broken hearts can't hold much love.

Our bedroom life, for me at least, went from bad to miserable. After Tommy was born, Ed had had a vasectomy. This tinkering with god's plumbing seemed to change other things as well. "The blocked ditch always overflows," my father had said, and he was right. Tormented by backed-up seed (or freed, perhaps, from worry about another child), Ed became insatiable. To make matters worse, the false teeth Ed wore (which he never removed in Vietnam) came out with the stars, contributing nothing to the appeal of this wheezing old giant who loomed over me like a rain squall twice a day.

Fortunately, Ed's return to work gave us both relief from our frustrations: me from sex, Ed from his fear of aging. Everyone had told him (sometimes joking, sometimes not) that he was too old for construction work. He'd only laugh and give his almost-a-teenage wife a squeeze or bounce his feisty son on his knee to prove them wrong. Now his old boss had confirmed the myth he had been trying to prove in bed, so he gave up trying so hard with me. Our drive north, with both the boys this time, was much happier than the first.

We arrived in Orem, Utah, on a hot August night and the next day went looking for a place to live. Neither of us wanted to settle down in Utah and Ed knew his project wouldn't last forever. Because, as a construction man, he was used to living in mobile homes and I had seldom lived in a place with more than two rooms, we agreed that buying a house trailer made good sense. We wound up with a fully furnished three-bedroom, two-bath palace with living room and kitchen—just like Leatha's house!—with hot and cold running water and flames that popped out of the stove and a flushing toilet that let you relieve yourself without running into the bushes. The best two things about it, though, were that the carpet and furnishings were red —a lucky color in the Orient. And it was *mine*—no in-laws to ambush me from the cover of language or past relationships. Unfortunately, Ed hated red, though he bought the trailer to please me—a pattern that was becoming all too familiar in our Asian-American marriage.

I showed him my appreciation the only way I knew: with my body, hands, and hard work. In bed, I didn't make him climax so soon but touched him softly. Although we still never kissed or hugged, I made him feel more welcome. Around the house, I treated him like one of my babies: massaging his back and neck, cleansing his skin and pores, trimming hairs from his ears and nose. Now that I had my own territory—my first real home—I would let nothing prevent me from being the good wife my mother had trained.

While Ed puttered with the trailer's connections, I scouted out the local markets and stocked the cupboard with good American brands. As in Ky La, everything I needed was footsteps from my house: food, a place for the kids to play, and friendly, if curious, neighbors— including a retired couple next door whom I wound up calling Mom and Pop. Like any small village, Orem had its festivals and feuds, good gossip and bad feelings, saintly spirits and wounded souls. For a brief time at least, I was back in a world I understood.

Being there, in fact, gave me the peace of mind to do something I had not even contemplated since I arrived in the United States: to write to my mother, whom I had left in Danang without a word of explanation for my "defection" to America. It was not an easy letter to write, especially when it came time to tell—honestly and com-pletely—about my rape by the two Viet Cong guards who had been sent to kill me. Until that letter, my mother never knew the truth. This was important not just to clear my conscience, but to prepare better karma for Jimmy. I knew that if fate or luck or god threw my mother and Anh, Jimmy's father, together again, she must know that he did not take my virginity: that it was sacrificed to the war.

I also wrote to my sister Lan, who, a lifetime ago, first counseled me to find an American husband. I knew she was anxious to marry one herself, so I offered a little sisterly advice.

"Don't be in a hurry to sacrifice your freedom," I wrote in big letters. "Life in America is two parts sour for each part sweet, even if your man is a prince!" I exaggerated a little. After all, how terrible can life be when you have a nice house, good food, and no bombs falling on your head? Still, I wanted to make a point. "Don't marry a GI. Your own war wounds will be hard enough to heal without trusting your soul to an injured doctor. Don't marry an old man, either. You can only have one father, and he doesn't belong in your bed."

To celebrate Ed's first day at work, I decided to make his favorite American dish, pork and beans. I bought some dry beans at the store and soaked them overnight as I had seen Leatha do in San Diego. After Ed left, I put the soaked beans on the stove to boil, gave the kids breakfast, and started their morning: Jimmy in front of the TV, and Tommy chewing on toys in his playpen. I wanted nothing to interrupt the preparation of the perfect meal I owed my husband.

After a couple of hours' boiling, I took the beans off the stove and drained them. I cut into one and realized it was still hard—not soft like Leatha's—so I figured the skins prevented them from cooking. *No problem.* I had the whole day, so I emptied the beans into a big bowl and began peeling each bean with a paring knife in front of the TV, the way, I discovered, most of my American neighbors did their housework.

After all the beans were peeled, I put them back in the pan, added the pork and some water, and put the whole thing back on to cook. It was now lunchtime and two little neighbor girls, Sara and Mary, came over to see if Jimmy could play. *So young and already the girls are after him!* Jimmy picked up English very quickly (he knew a lot already from my American boyfriends in Danang) and remembered every TV jingle and cartoon noise he ever heard. He also remembered his Vietnamese, though less and less of it over time, and it brought tears to my eyes to hear his little voice chirp *"Chao ma"* to me every morning before demanding his Cheerios and Flintstone vitamins.

I made them some sandwiches and they went out to play with Kool-Aid mustaches. Sara was blond, fond of sucking her fingers, and always dressed in blue. Actually, she wore the same blue dress all the time—you could count the days of the week by the spots that bloomed across her skirt. Mary was dark-haired and had sad eyes. I knew they lived in the trailer park, but didn't know where, so I sometimes tried to match them up to residents as they walked down the road in the evenings, but never with any luck.

The remaining daytime shows were spent cleaning and dusting and getting everything ready for Ed's supper when he returned from his ten-hour shift. I set the table with our best dishes and even made myself up a little so that he would know it was a special occasion.

When Ed finally walked through the door, though, I was shocked. He looked like a bum: covered with mud from head to toe. Fortunately, he was already well schooled in Vietnamese manners and left his shoes outside, but his appearance amazed me. In Vietnam, as a supervisor, he wore a tie and told everyone else what to do. Here, as low man on the totem pole, he did roughneck work like everyone else. I could see he was a little dismayed by things himself—not just his loss of status, but his own exhaustion and realization that despite his young wife and towheaded son, he was no longer a youngster. I really felt sorry for him and gave him a kiss, telling him to wash quickly because I had a big surprise. He could smell the beans, of course, so my treat wasn't such a surprise, except that it was me, his little wife, who had cooked them and not his mother—my first victory in the battle between generations. I toted the pot over to Ed and removed the lid, reaching in to serve a big helping of savory beans—but the spoon stuck fast in the bottom.

My smile slid down my face. I withdrew a spoonful of mush and watched it fall back like clay into a swamp. My eyes teared up and I told Ed what had happened.

He laughed his hearty "aren't-you-stupid-but-don't-feel-too-bad-about-it" laugh and went to the refrigerator and fixed himself a sandwich.

"It's the thought that counts," Ed said wearily, then took a shower and went to bed.

The next morning I got up before the sun, determined to make pancakes better than Leatha's or die in the attempt—a Vietnamese suicide attack against a kitchen full of lethal American utensils. Although I couldn't make much sense of the instructions on the box of Bisquick, I tried to remember the ingredients Leatha used; but pancakes were treacherous opponents and I would not underestimate them. Unfortunately, between too few eggs, too much milk, and a lukewarm skillet, Ed had the choice of drinking his pancake milkshake or throwing it out with the beans. This time, though, I was able to laugh with him, but cried as soon as he left. Orem had no Oriental market, so the ingredients I knew from home were unavailable, and every American meal I tried was a flop. I was beginning to believe my karma was to fail as an American wife. How long could my husband persist, let alone survive doing heavy work, on a diet of cold cereal and toast?

About this time, too, I started feeling uneasy about going out alone. Ed never seemed anxious to teach me to drive, so I became the American equivalent of a Vietnamese man without legs. My concern was not so much getting around, although that was a problem, but the good opinion of those around me. The town was friendly enough, and our Mom-and-Pop neighbors often invited me in for coffee—yet my village inhibitions and crushing sense of duty to Ed made me worry about provoking gossip: a young woman should not run around by herself, even with two babies. Thus I always turned down Pop's offer of hospitality when Mom was running errands—not because I was afraid of Ed's jealousy, but from fear of what wagging tongues might say. In Vietnam, my family and I had learned just how dangerous neighbors could be.

Two things saved me from getting depressed.

One was neighbor Mom herself, who saw my growing distress and began to counsel me on the facts of life about "May-December" marriages. As I gradually revealed the details of my relationship with Ed, she would laugh and slap her knee (and sometimes mine) and explain the difference between an "American wife" and a "Vietnamese slave"—a distinction that was only now becoming clear. If nothing else, Mom taught me the many ways in which an American wife says no.

My second savior was Mary and Sara's mother.

The two girls had become such steady lunch customers that their mother got curious about who was caring for her children all afternoon. Of course, I didn't mind. I liked having kids around and they kept Jimmy occupied.

One afternoon their mother appeared at the door and inquired after her daughters. Judy was about ten years older than me, short and round, with frizzy red hair that topped her once pretty face like a TV clown's ratty wig. Her worn-out clothes reeked of cigarettes (one always dangled from her mouth), which at least masked the smell of whiskey when she belched—which was often enough to delight the kids. Nonetheless, she was the first American neighbor-friend I'd met who was remotely close to my age, and I greeted her with full ceremonial honors.

"My name is Le Ly," I said, bowing politely. "Won't you please come into my house?"

"Well, I can only stay a minute." Judy huffed up the steps and flopped down into Ed's favorite chair. I moved to turn off "I Love Lucy," but she said, "Don't touch that dial! I love this one! Lookit that damn Ricky! Ain't he a piece of work?"

I offered her some tea and found out she liked any kind of beer. She asked me where I came from and I told her.

"Well," she said, looking down into the can, "I guess we can't pick our parents."

We talked a long time about our favorite TV shows and how "the damn coin changer in the laundry room rips off the tenants," then the kids started fighting and she decided it was time to go. She thanked me again for watching and feeding her girls and invited me over for lunch the next day at her trailer, two rows behind us. I accepted with gratitude.

That evening, Ed came home to a perfect dinner of Top Ramen— a packaged noodle dish Judy assured me "even a shithead can't screw up." I liked it because it actually resembled Vietnamese noodles, cooked quickly, and went with a number of American foods Ed liked.

The next day I got made up and went to my luncheon date in my lucky red *ao dai*. Judy's mobile home was rusted through like an old tin can and had cardboard instead of glass in one of the windows. The area under her tattered awning was littered with junk and the inside was even worse because it didn't show to neighbors.

"I meant to clean the place up for company," Judy said, sliding a stack of dirty laundry down the kitchen counter to make way for eight slices of stale bread. She was still in curlers and a nightgown, stained chenille bathrobe open to the waist, with smoke from her ever-present cigarette curling around her red head like the fuse on a stick of dynamite. "But, you know how it goes: the damn kids start squawkin' and one thing leads to another. Grab a seat anywhere. TV's busted again, so it don't matter. I got some old tuna salad in the icebox—or do you want peanut butter?"

"Oh, peanut butter sound very delicious," I answered, realizing now it must have been the aging tuna that gave the trailer its distinctive aroma. I could see no space anywhere, including the floor, that was completely free of toys or clothes or half-filled drinking cups or dirty ashtrays, so I carved a place on the cushionless couch. She produced my sandwich on a paper plate and offered me a sudsy beer like hers, which I declined.

"Sorry," I said meekly, "I have ulcer," and pressed my long, painted nails into my slim, firm tummy. She looked at me the way a bullfrog contemplates a mayfly, then shrugged.

"Suit yourself." She chugged the rest of her beer then took a swallow from mine. "Waste not, want not." She belched noisily, crushed the empty can, and tossed it into the sink. "How 'bout some moo juice?"

We ate our sandwiches with Judy swilling her beer and me watching my sour milk curdle in a sunny window. She knew a lot about eating, though, and gave me valuable information on which potato chips to buy and how to make gravy nice and lumpy. Because I came from a big family, I paid her back with tips on how to help her two girls get along. I already sensed that this funny, dumpy lady had a heart as big as her belly, and knew from what she said that she held no illusions about herself or her situation.

"I sure do appreciate you watching the girls like you do," she said for the third or fourth time. "Some folks just have a knack for that shit—like sewing clothes and baking pies. Not me. Hell, most nights I'm lucky just to get the rascals in bed!"

She laughed a not-so-funny laugh and stared out the dirty window. When she wasn't making fun of herself, she spent a lot of time staring out of the window. During one such lull, I glanced at the framed pictures of her relatives—photos of Sara and Mary as babies and a white-haired grandma who looked like Leatha. She also had a photo of a tough-looking, jug-eared, knob-throated man in a military uniform, which she saw me notice.

"You ready for an afternoon eye-opener?" she asked, getting up. "No—that's right, you got a ulcer. I forgot."

She went to the kitchen, poured some bourbon in a coffee mug and came out. She sat down, lit another cigarette, then blew out the match: a blast from a potbellied locomotive gathering steam for an uphill climb.

"Men are assholes," she said finally, as if commenting on the weather.

"Well—some, I guess," I responded in a tiny voice and looked down at the curled linoleum.

"You're probably wondering why you don't see a man around my place, right?"

It was true I'd never seen a man with Judy's children, but, seeing now how she lived, it wasn't such a wonder.

"That man in the picture," she continued, taking a pull from her cup. "That there's my husband. Handsome S.O.B., wasn't he?"

"He's very nice—very nice-looking." I cleared my throat. I knew the beers and the bourbon hadn't been Judy's first, and I had learned long ago from GI boyfriends that the best way to handle moody drunks was to let them do the talking.

"Course, that's an old picture. *Vietnam,*" she said solemnly, tamping out her cigarette as if that said everything.

"I'm sorry," I assumed he'd been killed in action or was a POW.

"*You're* sorry!" Judy laughed a gravelly laugh like Ed's—the laugh of too many cigarettes. "Son of a bitch wrote me a letter six months ago saying how he met this Vietnamese twat. Says he wants to marry the little bitch, can you believe it? Says he wants a goddamn fucking divorce!"

One of the children screamed outside, then all of them laughed.

"I better check the kids," I suggested. I couldn't see the conversation going anywhere good from here.

"Oh, hell, they're fine, Le Ly," Judy said in a pleasant voice, and lit another cigarette. She may have been mad at the Vietnamese girl in the letter, but she didn't seem mad at me. In fact, I got the feeling she wanted very much to tell me the whole story.

"Course, he still sends money stateside for the girls," she added, shaking out the match. "The bastard *has* to send money. The army makes sure of that. And Mom and Dad help out, too, but you can see how far that gets us." She gestured hopelessly around the room. After another long glance out the window, she looked at me directly and said, "You know, I don't really blame that Vietnamese gal. Hell, she's just trying to get by. And I fell in love with the bastard too, didn't I, so who am I to point fingers?" She folded her bathrobe across her lap. "Course, I let myself go a little—out here in the boonies, who the hell you gonna dress up for? No, I blame the fuckin' army. The goddamn war fucked up my family, not that little Vietnamese gal."

Listening to Judy in her sad little trailer made my inside eyes get wider. She didn't blame me. She thought I was the "good" kind of Vietnamese who were just like Americans. But I *could've* been the girl who stole her husband. I had tried to make Red, the navy med tech, fall in love with me then Jim, the civilian mechanic, then Paul, the air force lieutenant—to make me feel more alive and save my little boy and me from the war. By the time I left Vietnam, I had been through the mill and was tired of the killing and cheating and cruelty that passed for normal life in a war zone. It was up to our GI boyfriends to worry about their stateside wives and girlfriends, not us local girls. We treated our men like kings because that's the way we were raised, the way we were taught to treat any man who helped us. We were just trying to discharge our obligations honorably and survive. With luck, a few of us were even able to get the hell out of the bloody sewer our country had become.

More often than not, though, our GI lover just got on a plane at the end of his tour and that was that. Even if we bore his kids, we got no promise of marriage, no "dependent support," not even a goodbye kiss. The best we could hope for was a wink from another GI, and begin it all again—until we got too old, too strung out from whiskey or dope, or dead. These things which I had forgotten in the land of supermarkets and shiny cars and TV now flooded back into my heart as Judy puffed blue rings and bad memories like a mortar spewing shells. I couldn't say what I felt to her face, but I knew she saw what I was thinking.

"Well, we all got our cross to bear, don't we, sweetie pie?" With brave, moist eyes, she gave me the best smile she had—her last treasure, the one she spent most sparingly. "I bet *you* could tell some stories, couldn't you? About the war and all?"

"You are very kind to ask," I said, wiping a tear before it streaked my cheek. "Oh dear, it getting late. I'm such a bad cook, I have to start Ed's supper early so I can throw it out before he come home.

Maybe some time he come over, eh?—looking for lady to make good mashed potatoes. Then American woman can steal Vietnamese girl's husband. Wouldn't that—oh, how you say it? Wouldn't that be a pisser?"

We laughed together and Judy hugged me like a sister.

"Okay, boys," I clapped my hands on her doorstep like a farmer herding ducks. "It time to go. Say goodbye to Sara and Mary. Say goodbye to Judy. Bye-bye. Bye-bye." I turned to wave.

"What the hell." Judy raised her mug of whiskey as we shuffled away. "If the ol' man can fix a TV set, send the bastard over!"

TWO

Jaws of the Tiger

ED NEVER GOT A CHANCE to repair Judy's troubled TV set, or the troubles in our marriage. Just before his fifty-fifth birthday, as the weather turned cold in Utah, he was laid off. Because of the hard outdoor work, his many disappointments, and too many cigarettes, he returned to California looking ten years older. Of course, Ed's women attributed this to my poor care and I was inclined to believe them. I had been anything but a success as an American wife in the kitchen or the bedroom.

At least Ed was appreciated by his Utah boss who quickly steered him into a new job in San Diego. With the promise of a paycheck and the balance of his unused VA loan from World War II—plus "one dollar down"—we purchased a modest five-bedroom house that to me was as big as a hotel.

At first, I couldn't believe how generous America was with its veterans. I wondered how the draft-age protesters who rioted on TV every night could complain about serving in an army that made them rich. In Vietnam, old Viet Minh and Viet Cong fighters were compensated only with gratitude. Even Northern regulars were pensioned with only a few pennies per month. The opportunity to turn Ed's ancient war record into tangible wealth seemed too good to be true. It also rekindled instincts from my bad old days as a black-market hustler in the streets, fire bases, and air strips around Danang.

"A house for one dollar!" I kept repeating, amazed, after Ed explained the deal. "Why don't we buy a thousand houses and rent them out?"

"It doesn't work that way," Ed said with a smile. "You still have to make the monthly payments and I'll be lucky enough to pay for the one we've got."

Somebody was missing the point, but I didn't press the issue. We moved in at the beginning of a ninety-day escrow and filled our little mansion with new furniture, also purchased for no money down. For people who loved cash so much, Americans sure went out of their way to avoid handling it. People who needed money least seemed to borrow most; and those without much cash always had to pay up front. Like so many Western institutions, the system of debt and credit seemed upside down. But who was I to complain? I settled down to try once again to become the best housewife I could be.

Every day I got dressed up like the women in TV commercials and cleaned my house and cooked our meals, using every kitchen gadget I had. Jimmy now had a room of his own and, being almost four, asked when he could go to school with his friends. I stared at him often while he played with his toys or sat leafing through picture books, swinging his legs under the chair at his too-big student's desk, and thanked fate or luck or god that he wasn't dodging shells or smuggling contraband. In my evening prayers at the makeshift Buddhist altar I constructed in our house, I began to thank the Christian God (half in English, half in Vietnamese—who knew what language the Western deity understood?) that my two boys had been spared the soul curse of their race. In the eyes of a strict Buddhist monk, of course, these well-intended prayers were a bit impious; but I knew that my ancestors, and especially my father, would understand and approve.

A few weeks later, though, I began to wonder if my intrusion into the American spirit world hadn't provoked a nest of demons.

When Mom Munro and Erma visited, they always brought sweets and praised my cooking, which gave them both an excuse to leave me alone in the kitchen (a guest bearing food is excused from chores, and good cooks don't need any help), which was fine with me. One October evening, though, they brought a bucket of candy.

"Oh," I cried, "the boys can't eat all this candy! They get sick!"

"It's not for the boys," Erma said, "it's for Halloween."

"Ohhh, Halloween." I nodded knowingly, determined not to reveal my ignorance of *every* American custom.

I put the candy up out of Jimmy's reach and went on with preparing dinner. For the rest of the evening not another word was said about Halloween, and I assumed it would be another jolly holiday like the Fourth of July with whizzing fireworks and so much loud music and feasting that even a displaced Oriental could understand well enough what to do.

I soon found out how wrong I was.

The next day, Ed and I returned from shopping only to find glowing devils scowling at us from neighborhood porches—as if the local spirits had taken advantage of our absence during the day to put the hex on us at night. I grabbed Ed's arm as he spun the steering wheel into our driveway and demanded to know what was going on.

Ed chuckled, then got very serious. After parking the car, he looked at me with a strange expression.

"Spooks," he said solemnly. "And goblins." I had not encountered these words before, and the way he said them made me run to look them up in my dogeared English-Vietnamese dictionary. I was right: *ghosts, ghouls, spirits of the dead.*

After a poor night's sleep and a morning made worse by screaming boys and Ed's puzzling instructions to "get rid of that damned candy early," I was startled by a mysterious pounding in our neighbor's yard. I stepped outside to see Tony, a friendly teenager who often did odd jobs on our block, hammering nails in a coffin.

"Hi Tony." I tried to keep my voice from breaking. "What you doing?"

"Oh, hi Mrs. Munro." He wiped a shock of hair from his sweaty forehead. "How do you like my casket?"

Icy chills ran down my spine. "My god—who die?"

Tony grinned. "Aw, nobody—yet!" He winked conspiratorially as Erma had done when she gave me the candy. "It's for my brother, Joey." He stabbed the air with his hammer like a sword skewering guts and laughed maniacally.

I ran inside and slammed the door, heart pounding. I spent the rest of the day peeping out from drawn curtains while trying to amuse my restless boys with indoor play. Near dusk, while glancing nervously into the carport to see if Ed was home, I saw Tony drag the coffin down his steps. As he tilted it against the porch, I saw inside a ghastly white face, splattered with blood, both eyes torn mercilessly from their sockets. I had seen enough of war and torture in Ky La and at My Thi prison to recognize an atrocity when I saw one, so I ran to the kitchen and began a batch of *chao*—rice soup—and *banh keo*—the sugar rice cookies we use in Vietnam to placate vengeful spirits on Vu Lan, the day when Hell coughs up its tortured souls. I now knew what the big bucket of candy was for and why Ed and Erma were afraid to speak of such things openly. I fished the sweets out of the cupboard with trembling hands.

"Quick, Jimmy!" I barked, spilling candy over the floor. "If anybody—any *thing*—come to the door, give them this! And turn off that TV!" A giant lizard was devouring Tokyo and the last thing I wanted was more monsters in my house.

Just as I placed the first offering of *banh keo* cookies on the family altar, the doorbell rang and my heart jumped out of my mouth. Jimmy, cheeks bulging with expiatory candy, opened the door. On the other side were a dozen half-human monsters—people killed in past centuries: ghosts in burial shrouds, pirates with patch-eyes, beggars in rags, bloody ghouls with oversized heads.

"Trick or treat!" they shouted in singsongy ghost talk.

I jumped between my sons and the devils and threw a handful of candy in their faces.

"Here!" I shouted. "Take all you want! Take everything! Just leave us alone!"

The demons got very quiet, then scooped up the candy from the porch and darted into the darkness. The last to leave peeled up the skin on her face—the death mask of some long-dead princess—and said, "Thank you, Mrs. Munro." The spirit was an ancestor of the six-year-old girl across the street who played with the boys on weekdays after school—the resemblance was amazing. "Maybe next year Jimmy can come with us."

Oh my god—no! I slammed the door and locked it. Fortunately, Ed came home minutes later to handle the roaming spirits. I spent the rest of the night in bed.

A few weeks later we all dressed up and went to Mom Munro's for a "Thanksgiving" feast—an ancestral festival without the ghosts.

Ed gave me a full explanation of the holiday: "You give thanks you've got a turkey, then you eat it." I felt better about this festival because we wore our nicest clothes and all of Ed's relatives would be there (his brothers and sisters and nephews from Washington State and cousins and nephews from the Midwest) just like a Vietnamese family. Despite all the talk I heard later about Pilgrims and Indians, the Munros were thankful mostly because Ed had returned from Vietnam in one piece, a sentiment I understood well. However, many things made Thanksgiving different from the Ta On feasts I remembered as a girl.

In Vietnam, for example, we began thanksgiving feasts on our hands and knees, praying to our ancestors. We thank Ong Troi— "Mr. Sky," the god of all—and *Me dat* (mother earth) for the food in our bellies and the water in our wells and fields. We offer thanks-in-kind (food and rice wine) as well as miniature paper clothes, money, and incense, which we burn to help lost spirits find their way into the light. Only after the burnt offerings have ascended to heaven—*nhan tan khoi lanh*—do we sit down to enjoy our meal. Such niceties, though, are not the American way.

"Okay, everybody," Erma shouted from the kitchen, "come and get it!" From the moment we arrived, the men had either lounged around the living room or were out in the yard with the bigger kids tossing footballs and curious plastic plates that soared like airplanes. Of the women, only a couple helped Erma and Leatha prepare the meal, which seemed the height of rudeness. In Vietnam, on a big holiday like this, the men would tend the altar while all the women and younger children busied themselves in the kitchen. The bigger kids would find firewood and do whatever chores were needed so that the adults could tend to the food and rituals. Leatha's festival was more like a birthday party at a restaurant, with a pretty but spiritless table, servants and guests, but no *thu tu*—order and piety— and overt respect for our ancestors or the elderly who would soon join them.

When everyone was seated willy-nilly—young next to old and men next to women in violation of all propriety—Erma asked everyone to bow their heads. This to me was a position of shame, not prayer. I crossed my arms over my chest, the way we show reverence, and immediately drew rude stares. I think Erma's guests thought I was acting angry and aloof, not pious, but what else was I to do?

After a few rhyming words, which no one repeated except "Amen," her husband Larry began to carve the big American chicken.

"Hope you like turkey, Le Ly," big Larry said in a friendly voice, heaping pile upon pile on my plate. "You're so skinny, you have to eat twice as much!"

"Just give her a wing, Larry," Ed said quietly. "I'll take the rest."

Everybody laughed but I didn't know why. Ed wasn't joking. In Vietnam, letting youngsters pick over the carcass while elders ate their fill was not just good manners, it was survival. In a land where one's teeth seldom lasted past forty, the older generation often depended on the younger to give them the softest food. As long as I had known Ed, I had used my strong teeth to strip and chew bones that had already yielded most of their meat. That night, the turkey proved too tough and dry even for me to eat and, given my nervous stomach, even the wing wound up *co duyen*—decorating my plate.

"Come on, Ly," Erma coaxed, seeing most of my food untouched, "think of all those starving children in Vietnam!" She smiled and half the guests laughed with her.

Leatha interrupted them. "Oh, Erma—leave the poor girl alone. She always eats like a sparrow."

I would've been glad to tell them what I knew of starving children, which was way too much, but my English wasn't up to it. Anyway, a happy feast day just wasn't the time. The void left by my silence was replaced by conversation about the price of turkey and how happy everyone was that Larry could still get things so cheap at the navy commissary. *American* talk.

While they chatted, Erma heaped more mashed potatoes on my plate. The narrow smile on her plump face reminded me of the jack-o'-lanterns that had scared me so much on Halloween.

"Give her a break, Erma," Ed said testily. "She can't eat for her whole damn country!"

"Well, I just want to show her we're being generous. I just want her to be thankful for what she has."

"Thankful?" Ed threw his napkin on the table. "I'll tell you about thankful! In Danang, we lived next door to the regional hospital. Every day I'd come home for lunch past a crowd of peasants from the countryside—people wounded and sleepless from nonstop shelling and stinking with dysentery and God-knows-what other diseases. Half of them couldn't stand up—"

"Well, it's a good thing they had a hospital," Larry offered with a weak smile.

"Hell, half the people didn't have legs!" Ed's face was redder than his wine. "I'm talking about people blown to pieces and sick and starving and you know what? That wasn't the worst of it. What really got to me was when I'd drive by in my fancy American pickup truck, these people would smile and wave to me like I was some kind of goddamn tourist on his way to the beach! That's right! They were *happy* to be there, happy to see me, and thankful as hell they were still alive! So don't lecture Ly about thanksgiving. Don't expect her to do handsprings over your turkey. She knows exactly what she's got, and what she left behind."

After the awkward silence that followed, one of Ed's young nephews asked, "Did you actually see any VC while you were there?"

"Yeah, Uncle Ed," another said, "I hear things have gotten pretty bad over there. A lot of our guys are getting killed."

Ed shrugged. "A lot of people get killed every day over there, not just our Grunts and Charlie. For every American casualty there must be a dozen—two dozen—villagers, farmers, babies, grandmothers—" He looked at Leatha and shook his head. "Hell, half the kids in Quang Nam have been wounded or beaten or walk around in bandages—" He broke off and took a swallow of wine. "I don't know what we can do about it. It was a poor country to begin with and the war sure isn't making things better. Let's just hope the Paris peace talks succeed. Maybe the whole damn nightmare will end."

"Are you saying we shouldn't be there?" the same nephew asked.

"Hey, I just go where they tell me. As far as I can see, we're doing what we think is right. If it *is* right. I mean, who knows for sure?"

The nephew, a young man of military age who seemed to know war only from TV, movies, and comic books, made a face and didn't seem to appreciate Ed's views. As for me, I gave Ed's leg a secret squeeze under the table and was as proud of him as I could be.

Winter in California is the season of the wet monsoon. The days of cold rain, intermixed with patches of summer sky, made me miss Vietnam's Central Coast. My Asian bones told me that Tet—the chief holiday in Vietnam—was coming up.

In America, holidays arrive first in merchants' windows. Since to me all vivid American packaging looked the same, I'd failed to notice the leering pumpkins and goggle-eyed turkeys. Now, the stores were filled with displays of a jolly man in a red suit—like a fat, bearded Uncle Ho—pulled in a sleigh by Buddha deer with big red noses. Because the fat man was in every store and on every package, I knew something big was coming up.

For Tet, we villagers got excited about how many pigs, chickens, and ducks we would slaughter. How much we could eat and how many people would come to help us eat it was a measure of how successful our year had been. Small debts were forgiven and big ones were paid off whenever possible so that everyone could begin the new year with a clear conscience. We swept the graveyards, polished our family headstones, and burnt offerings to our loved ones. Still, the two big celebrations, Christmas and Tet, seemed to have little in common save the winter solstice.

"What is Christmas?" I finally got up the nerve to ask our next-door neighbor, Rose, Tony and Joey's mother.

"Only the best holiday of the year!" she gushed like a little girl. Indeed, I had begun to realize that all of America's holidays were geared in some way to children and spending money in stores. This latter tradition, of course, seemed perfectly natural, since our own custom of burning money to honor our ancestors had been accepted in Vietnam for centuries. In America, though, as nowhere else in the world, money is life; so making and spending it quickly takes on the colors of a religion.

As we sipped our green tea, Rose explained how the orgy of toy-buying formed the very core of this glorious Christian holiday—how the amount of money you spent was a sign of God's favor and a signal to your family of how much you loved them.

"But Jimmy and Tommy have lots of toys," I protested. "And they already know Mom and Dad love them. Anyway, Ed get mad at me if I spend too much!"

"No, he won't," she assured me. "It's Christmas. That's the whole point. In fact, he'll get mad if you *don't* spend money. He'll be pleased you've become so American. Come on. I'll show you how to do it. Shopping is my middle name."

While Tony baby-sat my two boys, we spent the rest of the day on a pilgrimage from one toy temple to another. Since I had to arrange in advance with Ed to get cash or a check for anything, Rose helped by lending me the money for everything I bought. Still, the few things I felt brave enough to take to the register seemed miserly compared to the cartloads of rubber, plastic, and cardboard she purchased for her own two kids. Compared to me, she must have been a fabulous mother and very devout worshiper. When we got home, we wrapped the presents like conspirators.

Ed was not the problem I had feared, showing how infectious the "Christmas spirit" could be. Ordinarily, money fell from his hands like raindrops in a drought. A week before the big day, though, he brought home a small tree like the ones we had seen at Yellowstone.

"Oh, how pretty!" I exclaimed, thinking he had bought a houseplant. "But it won't live long without roots!"

"It's not supposed to," he answered, looking now like a department store Santa—all white hair and red cheeks. "We'll throw it out after Christmas."

This news disturbed me. Trees were sacred. For Tet, we cut only a small branch of the *bong mai* plant and waited for it to blossom. If it did, it meant we'd have good luck the next year. Of course, the reason this plant was selected was because its cut branches tended to flower —a symbol of how our own lives bloom from our ancestors'. Only later did I realize that evergreens held a similar message for Christians and, in some ways, it fit the Christian message even better—that life persists after death.

The "big day" itself came and went like most other Munro holidays, although I lost a little sleep on Christmas Eve waiting for a fat, red-suited burglar to break into our house. It did not seem unnatural to build a holiday around such a shadowy figure, since most Vietnamese holidays were based on ancestral ghosts. What really seemed strange, though, was adults admitting that Santa Claus was a hoax. It seemed cynical, if not hypocritical, to tell your children one thing when you really believed another. Consequently, when I told people I had no problem believing that the spirit of Saint Nicholas visited every house in the world on Christmas Eve, I drew only blank stares. "Poor Ly," I imagine they thought, "the simple child *really* believes in Santa!" Why not? It was the most spiritual thing I had yet seen in America.

In any event, the family got through its Christmas "ceremonies" as quickly as possible. They made no effort to savor the ritual as long as possible—our impulse in Vietnam. Kids and adults ripped open the presents we had so painstakingly wrapped. Each seemed locked in his own little world, forgoing that priceless piece of eternity we had supposedly gathered to share. In the midst of all this "official" happiness, I could feel nothing but sadness.

That night, we drove to Leatha's for a family supper and my stomach knotted up in fear of another Thanksgiving dinner. Instead, everyone talked about who spent how much for what presents and forgave me condescendingly for not knowing I was supposed to buy gifts for all the adults as well as just the children. In the midst of Ed's big family, I missed my own more than ever. On the one day of the year when Americans gather to celebrate eternal life, I felt myself beginning to die. Even an evergreen can't live when its roots have been cut off.

At home after Christmas dinner, after the exhausted and hysterical boys had fallen asleep amid piles of Styrofoam and vinyl and colored paper and flameproof stuffed animals, I told Ed that I had to go back to Vietnam.

The days after Christmas passed in slow motion. To his great credit, and as had become the pattern in our marriage, Ed seemed to know my heart even before I did. For a month he had been quietly looking for new contract opportunities in the war zone—partly because he had gone through his savings faster than he'd hoped (one last high-paying Vietnam assignment would set him up for years), but mostly because he had seen how difficult it was for his relatives to accept his alien young bride as their own. Also, in Vietnam he would live cheaply and supervise others, whereas in America he must toil like a workhorse and pay dearly for the honor of living in the world's richest country.

By New Year's Eve, the idea of returning to Vietnam had blossomed from wishful thinking into a plan. Appropriately, we celebrated this out-with-the-old, in-with-the-new holiday with a young navy couple about to be transferred to Danang. It was the first time I had really felt like celebrating since I had arrived.

Just before twelve o'clock, we put on funny hats and made a ruckus with whistles and kazoos. Although it fit my mood very well, making noise at the stroke of midnight was an odd tradition. In the Vietnamese countryside, we tried to be absolutely still at midnight in order to hear the next year's omens. If you heard a dog bark, for example, it meant you would be troubled by thieves and intruders. If you heard a hooting owl, you knew the gates of hell would open to receive your neighbors. If you heard a rooster crow, which is very unusual for that time of night, you knew the harvest would be good. (Consequently, we were usually prepared for bad seasons.) With so many things to go wrong and so few things that could go right, it's no wonder we peasants strained to listen to nature's voice.

Although I couldn't take the New Year's auspices because of our racket, they must have been propitious. A week or two later, in mid-January 1971, Ed got a two-year contract for a construction project near the town of An Khe: a strategic location in the An Tuc District, a mountain fortress that dominated Highway 19 all the way to the Laotian border. I celebrated this good news privately by cooking up sweet rice as a sacrifice to the Phung spirits, which, just as my father promised, had followed me to this strange new land and seen me through many unexpected trials and torments.

Because the house was still in escrow, we were able to back out of the deal without losing too much money. We put all our nice new furniture into storage, which for me was no sacrifice although Ed's women seemed pretty upset. Ed flew off at the end of the month and I was to follow with the boys a week later after the complex paperwork of a returning Vietnamese national was complete. When I recalled how expensive and exhausting it had been to leave my native country—a tedious, venal process filled with back-door payoffs and administrative booby traps—I was not surprised to see Uncle Sam put a few roadblocks of his own into the path of returning Vietnamese. But I could already smell Danang's salty air. No counselor, fee, or mountain of paperwork was going to change my course.

The week I spent at Leatha's getting ready to go was one of the longest of my life. Ed's relatives were naturally very distressed to see him going back into harm's way just to make more money for "his little Vietnamese gold digger." I avoided them whenever I could, doing extra chores for Mom Munro—sometimes over and over again just to stay occupied and out of the way—but inevitably I would get caught and have to listen to their lectures.

"You know I love my brother very much," Erma said, tears welling. "It hurts me to see him risk his life needlessly just for you."

"Ed want to go back himself!" I answered cheerily. "He want to make more money."

"Is that all you think of, Le Ly?" She shook her head in disgust. "Well, little lady, there's more to life than money. Do you want to see him killed by the Viet Cong?"

Now we were onto a subject I knew something about. "He be okay. I take care of him. Ed number one!"

Erma grunted, "You'll take care of him as long as the money holds out!"

As for Leatha, her happy American grandma's eyes turned Vietnamese old overnight. "I won't be around forever, Ly," she said, rubbing her eyes beneath her glasses. "I want my son to be near me. I know how you feel about your own mother. Surely you can understand my feelings."

I wanted to say, "Yes, I do know how that feels, which is exactly why I have to go home!" but didn't. Instead, I listened to Erma's and Leatha's complaints and laments all the way to the airport.

My heart was airborne well ahead of the big jetliner. The Paris peace talks were going well and I was sure the endless, stupid war—which had wracked my country for so long, pursuing a course and will of its own that defied both sides—would finally be dragged to a halt.

After we settled into our seats, I began writing a letter to Mom Munro and Erma "bequeathing" my fine new furniture, the boy's American toys, and everything else we had left behind to their family. I thanked them for their kindness and attempts to understand me and wished them a happy life. I swore on the bones of my ancestors that they would see Ed—whole and happy—after two years, but after that our future would be found in Vietnam, where builders like Ed would be needed to reconstruct our country. If he chose to stay, I said, he would spend his final years surrounded by the children he loved, a faithful and attentive wife, and a grateful people. Could they offer him anything better than that in El Cajon?

I sealed the letter and tucked it away for mailing in Honolulu. Looking past the boys sleeping peacefully in their seats, I scanned the sparkling blue water and let my thoughts race toward the wonderful life I knew awaited me: the best of both worlds, East and West.

When we finally landed in Saigon, Jimmy pressed his nose against the window and gazed in wonderment at the jungle and paddies from which he came. I had first seen the variegated Mekong River from the air five years before when the overloaded DC-3 from Danang arrived to deposit my mother and me on the sunbaked tarmac at the beginning of our exile from Ky La. It would end a year later with my shameful return to Danang, the birth of little Jimmy out of wedlock, and the start of my new career as a black marketeer. Now, with the prospects of peace at hand, the velvety green landscape seemed as inviting as a tourist poster; the meandering river, a bride's silver necklace instead of a slave's iron chain. My softened, citified feet now itched for the loamy soil of China Beach and the last few paces of their age-long journey: from the pavement of cat-eyed America to the hard-packed dirt floor of the house where I'd been born.

As soon as I stepped from the airliner, though, reality—and the oppressive tropical heat—smacked me in the face.

I had forgotten, even after one brief year, the searing Saigon temperature. My thick American makeup immediately began to melt. Jimmy, who was carrying my bag while I carried Tommy, pulled against my hand and cried hysterically when he saw the first Vietnamese uniform.

"I hate this place, Mama Du!" he shouted, startling me with the first Vietnamese word I'd heard from his lips in months. "I hate these people!" He hid behind my legs until the Republican soldier passed. I bent to comfort him as a flight of four camouflaged American jet fighters screamed low over the runway. We scampered into the terminal like mice in a thunderstorm.

Now Tommy was in tears and it was all I could do to keep from crying myself. We snaked through the crowd to the customs tables, trying to collect ourselves. Bits and pieces of the Vietnamese language, music to my ears, floated by as I wiped my sons' faces and fumbled through my purse for our paperwork. I now became painfully aware of the deadly conflict that lurks in the heart of every wife and mother. As Phung Thi Le Ly, I had put my right to independence above my duty to serve my husband, no matter what. I knew in my heart that if Ed decided to go back to the states and the peace talks eventually broke down, I would still want to stay in this country. As Le Ly Munro, however, I treasured above all else the well-being of my sons. By bringing them back to the only place on earth I felt I could be happy, I had put them in mortal danger. I could feel my father's unhappy spirit grumbling in the jet-blast. Yet hadn't my mother told me, on our exile to Saigon, that "Good seeds grow in any soil"? Why should the shell-pocked land of home be less nourishing to my two good boys than the hard-paved streets of America? It all seemed so clear, yet at the same time murkier than the turbid swamps around Ky La.

We cleared customs easily (getting into Vietnam during the war was always faster than getting out!) and found a cab to take us on the ten-minute drive to the hotel where I would contact Ed and plan the next leg of our trip. The only thing the ragged cabby would talk about was America—what it was like, how he longed to travel to the "land of gold," and how such travel would be easier when the much anticipated treaty between the North and the South was signed. Although I was still upset, with upside-down thoughts about right and wrong and duty and love buzzing around my head, I was happy to hear a lilting country accent and to watch our driver's crafty peasant eyes regard me in the rearview mirror. After one very long year, here were feelings I understood, situations I could handle. I felt my power grow with every dusty, bouncy mile.

Our hotel was a seven-story concrete blockhouse which, although relatively new and the largest on the street, already had a typically run-down, seedy Saigon look to it—especially after San Diego's steel and glass skyscrapers. What had impressed me only a few years before as Saigon's sophistication now looked merely third-world shabby. Inside, the walls and floor were well scrubbed (as they should have been; manual labor was plentiful and cheap and uniformed hotel workers were notably silent and efficient) with rooms that were blessedly air conditioned.

After I took care of Tommy and changed my clothes, I watched my first sunset back on my native soil: a red football slowly sinking behind purple palms, with neon signs flickering over the storefront windows. Through the tightly sealed glass, I studied the bustling street—cars and buses and motorbikes and military vehicles and *siclo* pedicabs and bicycles and pedestrians passing noiselessly as in a dream: a silent movie about my past.

After a blissful night's sleep—the kind of "open palm" sleep you enjoy only on home turf—we got up and went out to buy our airline ticket to Danang. "We're going to see Ba Ngoai—your real grandma," I told Jimmy, preparing his ear for the Vietnamese words he would gradually have to remember.

I sent a wire to Ed, giving him our flight information, then spent the rest of the day padding around the city—at least the parts we could easily reach—stuffing our senses with all the sights, sounds, and smells I'd hungered for in America: the earthy stench of the local fish market; the ranks of vegetables drying like brightly uniformed soldiers in the midday sun; the street children, clothed in little more than smiles and love, darting around our legs. Slowly we acclimated to the searing heat. We returned exhausted and the boys went down for their naps without the usual protest. I brushed my hair out long, went barefoot, and put on my lucky red *ao dai*. Ceremonially, I packed away my American clothes and put them out of my mind. Instead, I thought about tomorrow.

When I had left Vietnam to join Ed a year earlier, I was too ashamed—of marrying an American, a much older man, and of going off to live with the enemy—to tell my mother. Now I felt like *meo mat mua*—a prideful cat coming in from the rain. And what about my sister Lan, who did not suffer me kindly as a little sister even when times were good? How would she receive me now? And Hai, my oldest sister, our mother's only caretaker in our bombed-out, almost-abandoned village? Would she welcome me as she had done on our exile to Saigon, forgiving me all my sins, or would she shelter our poor mother from more heartache by keeping "black sheep sister Ly" at arm's length? I didn't and couldn't know. Nobody but Lan had written to me in America. I could only follow my conscience, my higher self, and right now that little voice inside me had lots of apologies to make.

The next morning we left Saigon, but not my doubts, far behind. In my unsettled state of mind, the flight to Danang seemed longer than our trip across the ocean.

Danang and its big air base, although cooler than Saigon, was as frantic as I'd remembered. With the constant roar of jets and grinding trucks and clanking tanks and the distant *whump* of artillery, my homesick eyes were more anxious to spot a bunker than pagodas or colorful peasants. Getting through the jammed-up streets to our hotel, in fact, was an hour-long nightmare: I'd made the same trek in twenty minutes on my old motorbike. The French-style hotel was open to the air, although a few rooms had evaporative coolers. Our antique bed was festooned with mosquito nets like sails on a wooden ship. It was noisy and uncomfortable, but it was *home*.

Without delay, I readied the boys and took a *siclo* to Lan's house, which had changed little since I'd last seen it a year ago. The only exception was her live-in boyfriend, an American contractor named Peter Bailey. If he turned out to be like Lan's other boyfriends, it would be wise to give him a wide berth. With no telephone to call and no particular reason to send a telegram (which, in wartime, only scared the recipient), I arrived unannounced, if not unexpected. Lan's eyes lit up when she saw me.

"Bay Ly!" She used my family number-name, the title of the

"number six" child. *"Ong cha oi*—Oh my god—come in! You made it after all!" She seemed happy to see me—a good start. She also seemed very pregnant; perhaps a gift from her American boyfriend. The child would be similar to the other Amerasian she had borne with a different GI lover. In this respect, too—creating life from the seed of death-dealers—Lan and I were sisters.

"Where is Ed?" Lan looked past me and the boys to the empty street.

"He's in An Khe. We'll go there after I see everybody."

We followed Lan into the shabby little house. Except for the furnishings deemed indispensable to Americans—electric fan, stereo record player, and a small TV—hers could have been the house of any big-city "tea-girl." It had homemade curtains, a worn dinette, and walls adorned with religious calendars, cracked plaster, and geckos.

"You'll want to see Mother," Lan said over her shoulder, heading for the back door.

"Mom's here?" Now it was my turn for big eyes. My heart began to pound. I put Tommy down with Lan's little boy, Eddy. Clad only in a torn T-shirt, he stared at my sons suspiciously as they began exploring the house.

"Of course. She's doing laundry. She comes over all the time to help with the housekeeping. I'm a working girl, Bay Ly. And if you think you're going to roll in here on a red carpet and—"

She started to tell me how I was still her little sister, her subordinate in every way, but I tuned her out and focused entirely on a little gray figure a dozen yards away, ragged and wet as the clothes she sloshed in her bucket.

"Mama Du," Lan said flatly, "look who's here."

My mother squinted into the sun, sheltering her eyes. Her face was as wrinkled and dark as a moldy quince—yet more beautiful to me now than Leatha in all her makeup.

"It's me, Mama Du," I squeaked. "Bay Ly!"

"Oh," she said blankly, as if someone had just told her the time. "When did you get back?"

My heart sank to my toes. "This morning."

"Well, you look healthy." She wiped the perspiration from her forehead, glanced at the sun, and turned back to her laundry.

I looked dumbfounded at Lan. My sister silently stretched out her arm, palm down, and waved her fingers, motioning me back into the house.

"What's wrong with her, Chi Lan?" I asked. "I've been gone a whole year!"

"What do you expect?" Lan said. "You abandoned her after all she did for you. You went to live in Saigon."

"I went to *America!*"

"She never believed that. I showed her the stamps and postmark on your letters but she couldn't read them and wouldn't believe them if she did. Now she'll never believe it. Who would go to America and come back?"

Tears flooded my eyes but I held them in. When I was little, my big sister sometimes made me cry in front of our mother. I wouldn't give her the satisfaction now.

"So—have you eaten?" Lan asked, finally remembering her manners.

The standard, polite answer among all peasants everywhere would have been "Yes, we've eaten," but, in fact, we had left the hotel without lunch. Even though I couldn't swallow a thing now, the boys were always hungry.

"No. I'm sure the boys would like some *bun ca*" (an old-fashioned fish noodle soup).

"Okay, I'll go to the market." Lan put a kerchief around her head and held out her hand, this time palm up.

So much for family hospitality! I gave her a cold look, opened my purse, and pulled out the few piasters she'd need for the ingredients.

As Lan left, my mother came in with a basket of dry laundry, all neatly folded. She saw the boys and dropped it at once, extending her arms under a big, gummy, betel-dark grin.

"Hung! Chau!" She always used Jimmy's and Tommy's Vietnamese names. "Come to Ba Ngoai!"

Jimmy went screeching to the brittle old lady he remembered so fondly and Tommy toddled after, uncertain and wary—good reflexes to cultivate for life in a war zone. She ushered them out back to play and when they were gone my tears broke like a summer cloudburst.

That night, while our mother tended the kids, Lan told me what had happened in the war, to our family, and around Danang since I left. With U.S. forces blockading the North and mining Haiphong, cutting off its war materiel from China and the Soviet Union, and with peace talks making progress, everyone had high hopes that the fighting would soon be over. As had been the case in the war with the French, everyone expected the treaty to redefine a few boundaries, establish some new political rights, and prompt another mass migration of people from one district to another. After that, life would surely get back to normal—or what we remembered as normal during the brief lull between the French and American wars. U.S. soldiers had been steadily withdrawing and business for bar girls like Lan was beginning to fall off, as it already had for the merchants and black marketeers in every city. Like the countdown to the treaty, the days before Lan's American man abandoned her were certainly numbered. I did not get the feeling she was anxious to go back to the rural life. But that was Lan's problem, not mine.

We decided that the boys and I could live in Lan's old one-bedroom Danang apartment, which she sublet to GIs, until Ed came north from An Khe. Its torn-to-hell couch, broken chairs, and on-again-off-again refrigerator were four years older than the last time I'd used them and a bit more weathered, like me. But I couldn't complain. I was glad I had to pay Lan only one week's premium rent before Ed appeared in his dust-covered American sedan to carry me off.

Because Ed had been living in the construction barracks and had not yet found a place for us to live, we decided to leave the boys with Lan and my mother—along with Thanh, the faithful young housekeeper who had worked for me and Ed before we left and who now worked for Lan. Thanh had been elected to tell my mother of my departure for America, an onerous task she peformed better than any sister. Loyalty like hers transcended wages.

The day-long drive with Ed to An Khe was, for me at least, like leafing through a childhood photo album. After America's broad vistas, craggy mountains, and stark plains, I had forgotten how dense and verdant our little corner of the world really was. We passed black-pajamaed girls prodding water buffalo with a stick; old ladies bearing shoulder-poles that would have bent the strongest laborers in the West; and roadside shrines declaring our spiritual connection to the trees and paddies and eternal sky around us. My old reflexes, which had been so embarrassing in America, now seemed perfectly natural—even valuable. I reminded Ed to drive in the center of the road to avoid land mines and to take new roads under construction whenever possible, since the Viet Cong rarely attacked the peasant crews. We encountered several bands of hitchhiking government soldiers but I told Ed to pass them by—they could easily have been cowboys. This time, he did *exactly* as he was told.

We arrived at An Khe around dusk. The only vacancy was at a sleazy bar with small rooms out back, which were used by the local hookers. Our "bungalow" was equipped with a ratty straw mattress and sheets mottled with stains, but we were exhausted and just lay down on top of them in our clothes. As soon as we shut our eyes, the headboard of the bed in the next room began to bang against the wall and Ed sat up, cursed, and lit a cigarette. It was answered soon thereafter by headboards in the other rooms—the mating call of An Khe!—and we couldn't help laughing. I congratulated myself for leaving the kids in Danang and fell asleep, leaving my "third eye" open to watch over Ed.

The next day we looked at a furnished triplex in the country, which was being vacated by one of Ed's co-workers. It was a beautiful place. Our neighbors would be an American ambulance driver, a physician, and a middle-class Vietnamese family with three kids. The house was surrounded by fields and trees, with a U.S. MACV (Military Assistance Command, Vietnam) housing facility, a small hospital, and a Vietnamese high school across the street. A few miles in the opposite direction was the sprawling military base at Qoc Lo 19, the strategic center of An Tuc, now defended mostly by Republican forces because of the American withdrawal. The house had its own well and a communal bathroom, which was very clean, but what I liked most about it was the small pond, stocked with fish, near a coconut grove that reminded me of the area behind my father's house at Ky La. Ed saw me fall in love with the place so he rented it on the spot.

We went back to Danang to retrieve the children. Little Thanh, a girl about my size but with a flatter, almost Chinese face that complemented her stocky build, decided to leave Lan and come with us as our maid. It was like old times, but with the war winding down and my own family less than a day's drive away, it promised to be good times as well. Besides, with Ed's long workday and a mess hall at the construction site, my wifely duties would be minimal. Even motherhood took a holiday as Jimmy entered Catholic school and Tommy spent most of his time with Thanh. I had plenty of time to read and catch up on a year's back issues of popular Vietnamese magazines. I renewed my acquaintance with the Buddhist monks whose solace and instruction I missed, and took long walks around the pond with my father's spirit. In every way, it was the paradise I'd dreamed of in America, but never found.

In a few months, though, that paradise became a hell and my life would be changed forever.

Shortly after we arrived, one of my girlfriends borrowed the MACV dining hall to give a party for her husband. Ed and I attended, along with many others. This time, I wore my American clothes; to honor Ed, of course, but also for vanity—to impress the other Vietnamese girls, most of whom were dying to go to America.

At first, the party was pleasant but a little dull. We knew most of the guests already and, seeing them every day, had nothing new to talk about. Later, though, many interesting people from the An Khe base arrived. One was a U.S. Army major named Dante (Dan) DeParma, a military adviser who spoke some Vietnamese already and was learning much more in his assignment. He was Ed's height (I came up just to his chin) and was a little older than Anh, Jimmy's father. He seemed more mature than the American servicemen I'd met before Ed, yet he was handsome enough to capture and hold a young lady's eye. Like Ed, he wore glasses but instead of making him look bookish or elderly, they gave his face a clear-eyed, sensitive aspect—like a physician's. I listened, enchanted, as his soft, melodic voice drifted between English and Vietnamese. With his boyish grin and sparkling eyes, he was more charming than anyone I'd met in a soldier's uniform. I could almost hear my father's voice behind the wit and humor and compassion of his words. After ten minutes with this wonderful newcomer, I felt inebriated. My face flushed red and my heart pounded in my ears. My breath came so fast and shallow I thought I might pass out. I knew, too, that I was in terrible trouble.

I spent the rest of the evening torn between heaven and hell. While Ed and I visited with other couples, my eyes kept searching for Dan. More than once, I caught him staring back at me with an inscrutable smile on his face, and I became more flustered than ever. By the time the party was over, I was a nervous wreck and later that night had to pretend I was getting sick in order to deflect Ed's amorous advances. I just couldn't cope with another man until I'd sorted out my feelings for Dan. I was no desperate refugee now, but a woman with two children who had "been to America." That alone kept me tossing and turning all night.

The next day I came back from market and Thanh told me that an American officer—speaking Vietnamese—had been to the house asking for me.

"Who was it?" My heart jumped, afraid and excited.

"He didn't say. He's going to come back, though."

The next day I was in the kitchen when Thanh answered the door.

"Co Ly dau?" I heard a masculine voice ask. "Is Ly at home?"

I hurried out, beaming. "Hello, I am Ly." I recognized Dan at once. "What may I do for you?"

He didn't answer right away, but just stood there taking me in, as if reassuring himself that I was the person he remembered. I prayed he wouldn't be disappointed, turn on his heels, and leave.

"I'm Dan," he finally said. "We met at the party the other night."

"Oh yes." I offered my hand. "I remember. How are you?"

"I'm very well, thank you." He took my fingers like a gentleman helping a lady across a stream—from someplace she had been to the next place fate or luck or god would take her.

"Listen, Ly," he said, "I don't have much time right now, but I wonder if you could do me a favor?"

"A favor? Of course."

"I'm new at the post. I don't know anyone around here except the GIs I work with. I'm looking for someone who can tell me about An Khe—the local population, what people really think about the war and all of that. The other night, you seemed like one of the few Vietnamese who understands Americans. I just wonder if we might have tea some afternoon—to talk. Maybe you can help me with my Vietnamese. I know it's not so hot!"

We laughed together like people who had known each other all their lives. I felt the minefield of love and honor and duty close in around me.

"Your Vietnamese is very good," I said, "much better than my English. I would be happy to help you."

"Wonderful! Perhaps tomorrow, then? About this same time?"

"That would be fine!"

He took my hand again and it was all I could do to let his go.

The next day—and every afternoon thereafter for a week—Dan and I took tea on our porch. While Thanh served us with a motherly frown, Dan told me about his immigration from Northern Italy as a child (which explained his old-world manners); his wife, who could bear no children; and the American sons they had adopted. In his words I heard no bitterness about his war experiences or at nature for denying him a son, only compassion for his wife and his love of life and living. I told him little about my life before Ed, but much about my misery in America and how I longed for a life of peace in the land of my ancestors. We agreed that, no matter what politicians on either side might say, continuing the war would be madness and that nobody would win if new fighting broke out. By the end of the week, my heart was his and I knew he felt the same, but we agreed to do nothing about it.

I now had to face the consequences of my actions. I was not ashamed of my feelings for Dan—on the contrary, they lit up my life —but I was not proud of them either. If nothing else, they forced me to look my own loveless marriage in the face. I had been miserable in America and had no desire to go back. It was in its way a war zone as lethal to my spirit as the battlegrounds outside Ky La.

Now Dan had come along—to appreciate me for what and who I was, not what I should but could not become. Our attraction was so strong and sublime, transcending even the flood of passion, that the sin of infidelity seemed insignificant compared to the crime of turning away a soulmate. With peace about to bloom in my country, would I be wiser and more pious to return with my children to my "war" in America, or follow my destiny with Dan in the land where my father was buried? It was a question that answered itself.

Midway through the second week, all my doubts had vanished. When Thanh's censuring looks chased us from the house, we took long walks through the grove or just sat by the pond—talking, laughing, or sharing the silence of the day. By the end of the week we were holding hands as we walked and Dan couldn't leave without kissing me goodbye.

At the beginning of the third week, Dan said, "This is pure torture. Eventually you'll be going to the States and I'll be reassigned to God-knows-where. What have we got to hope for?"

"Well, if it makes you feel better," I said, "I won't be going home with Ed. I make up my mind last week. If he wants to stay in Vietnam, that's okay, but I cannot make him happy in United States because I cannot be happy myself. How can Tommy and Jimmy be happy if their *mama du* is so miserable?"

"Will you ask Ed for a divorce?" It was a question and a plea.

"To be honest with you, Dan, I don't know. Ed is a good man. I owe him my life. But he will not want to keep hold of something that is not his."

With that we went on with our lives but continued our chaste little affair. Dan was wonderful with the boys and came to dinner often, sometimes with friends from the base. Ed enjoyed his company, too, and regarded him as a family friend. Even the landlord, who sometimes tended the grounds during the day when Dan came over, smiled and waved whenever we appeared, hand in hand. Only he and Thanh shared our little secret, such as it was, and as long as my maid was assured no vows had been broken, she was content to leave well enough alone. In fact, she came to look forward to Dan's—"the Major's," as we respectfully called him—tea-time visits almost as much as I did.

By spring 1972 the climate in Vietnam—especially around An Khe —began to change. Although the Paris accords had produced the illusion of peace for the rest of the world, nobody in my country was fooled. The faster the Americans withdrew and flooded the land with arms and equipment before the legal deadline which would end that aid arrived, the bolder the Northern soldiers and local VC cadres became. Despite terrible B-52 raids on Hanoi and Haiphong, Northern regiments captured Quang Tri, just inside the DMZ, and seemed to threaten everywhere else. Although they generally avoided the big battles that would have drawn America back into the war, the Communists pressed their advantage in local skirmishes, sabotage, and terrorism that kept everyone on edge.

Abruptly in March, after our first year in Vietnam, Ed was told that he'd soon be transferred—probably to Saigon or Danang, the last bastions of the once formidable American presence—because enemy pressure was too intense.

"You're lucky," our Vietnamese landlord said after I told him the news at the water well. "We've heard rumors that something big is about to happen. This place isn't as safe as it seems."

I put down my bucket, alarmed, and thought of Dan. "What do you mean? What about the big army fort? The Communists wouldn't dare attack it!"

"There aren't as many soldiers around here as there used to be. Without American support, our troops aren't as anxious to fight. Things could get bad very quickly."

That night, Ed's worried expression only compounded my fear.

"What's the trouble?" I asked, hoping he would reveal something about conditions on the American base, and, indirectly, what the future might hold for Dan. "Don't tell me you have bad news too?"

"Yep—I'm being recalled to Saigon. Rumor has it they're going to ship out the foreign workers. And I've got another year to go on my contract!"

"So—you just go someplace else. Or they pay you off, right?"

"It doesn't work that way. The fine print says they can cancel the contract if conditions get too rough. Worse than that, I lose my tax benefits on the money I've already earned if I go back to the States. One way or another, I've got to find a way to finish my contract."

We talked over alternatives during dinner, trying to cheer each other up, but with my mind preoccupied with Dan and the danger he might face, I didn't have much sympathy for Ed's tax problems. Later, after the traffic in the street died down, the crickets and cicadas started their evening concert and I stared up at the bright, full moon. It was a still, humid night of such rare beauty that I couldn't imagine anything going wrong anywhere in the world. A neighbor's dog barked and Ed cursed it. Then, without warning, all hell broke loose.

Explosions came from the direction of the base—then an ear-shattering blast from the MACV building across the street. Dishes jumped and knickknacks toppled from the shelves. A thousand-pound hammer banged on the walls, dropping pictures, which shattered on the floor. All of a sudden the room was filled with dust.

Tommy was nearest so I grabbed him and dived under the table, covering him with my body. Jimmy ran screaming from his bed and squirmed under my outstretched arm, followed by Thanh, who huddled against us. The lights blinked and went out. Explosions flashed white on Ed's awestruck face as he stared, silhouetted, out the window. After a short, tense pause, the din began again, louder than ever, crackling and snapping like New Year's firecrackers.

For what seemed like an eternity, we lay quivering and helpless. I cursed myself silently for being caught unprepared: we had no family bunker—even a stray shell landing nearby could tear our house apart. Worse, the anguish I felt for Dan, at ground zero of the attack, eclipsed any fear I had for myself or my husband, or the empathy I usually felt for my brother Vietnamese who had to endure these terrors daily. It was just one more way the war could drive you crazy.

After twenty minutes, the explosions finally stopped. Working quickly and silently, we packed the things that we could carry—mostly food and water, barricaded the doors and windows (as if that would've stopped anyone), and waited for the dawn.

An hour after the attack, the crickets resumed their chirping. We went to our beds and tried to sleep, but every dog bark and creaking timber woke us up and sent us diving under the table.

In the gray morning light, Ed crept through the eerie silence to the hospital and learned that although the big army post had held, all civilians, Vietnamese and American alike, would be evacuated as soon as possible. A short time later some trucks with MPs appeared and drove us to a small airstrip where a waiting twin-engined transport took about two dozen of us, still dazed and uncomprehending and with little more than the clothes on our backs, to Saigon.

The "Pearl of the Orient"—Vietnam's great, sinful capital, was beginning to fill with refugees from the Communists' sudden offensive, making accommodations tight and everything else even more expensive.

We rented a small apartment and Ed went every day to his employer's office, trying to determine the status of his contract. One day he came back looking very discouraged.

"Well, it's over," he said with a brave smile.

"What over? The war? The fighting?" My heart jumped for joy. Now that we were safe, at least temporarily, I could only think of seeing the Major again.

"No, of course not," Ed sniffed. "My job. The contract's been canceled."

"Well, what you going to do?" I thought surely he'd want to go back to America and we'd have our final battle about our marriage and I'd at last be free to join Dan.

Ed shrugged. "I was thinking about that on my way home. How would you like to live in Canada?"

I frowned. "Canada? Too cold! Too much like Yellowstone."

"We'd only be there for six months. Then we'd go back to San Diego and start over."

I didn't have to say anything. Ed could see I wasn't crazy about his plan.

"You go to Canada first, like you came here first last year. You find a nice place to live, then I come with the boys."

Ed frowned. "I don't like that idea. It's not safe for you in Vietnam."

"That's why I have to stay. I have to see my family one more time. Danang is a big city. I'll be okay. Tommy and Jimmy will be fine.

You go to Canada and do what you have to do. We'll come along later."

Ed knew he had no choice. His company would pay to relocate him, but they wanted his decision soon. A few days later, he handed me an envelope with some money to pay our way to Danang (including Thanh's fare), then back to Saigon for a flight to Vancouver. We kissed and hugged on the sidewalk outside our building and he got into his shiny truck with a couple of co-workers and drove off to the airport. Despite his many kindnesses to me and the boys (not the least of which was saving our lives!), and despite the fact that I genuinely cared for his well-being and hoped he would be happy, I earnestly prayed that I would never see him again.

Jimmy, who understood a lot more than he could speak, asked when we were going to see Ba Ngoai—his beloved grandmother.

"Soon," I told him, hustling them both upstairs. My mind was already buzzing with plans. "But first, we go see your friend the Major in An Khe."

In those days, people got to An Khe two ways: either by convoy from Qui Nhon or by bus after a plane ride from Fleuku. Since most civilians had departed, the Qui Nhon road had been closed, which may have been the government's way of saying it was no longer contesting Communist control in the area. So after a one-hour flight to Fleuku, we joined the crowd at the bus station and I asked around for the time of the next motorcoach to An Khe. A sweaty baggage handler, red with the dust of the area, only laughed at my question.

"You're crazy, little sister. Nobody goes to An Khe. VC are all over the place."

"But I have to get back to my home and husband."

"Then flap your wings. Only the birds get into An Khe."

Birds!

I took Jimmy's hand and Thanh grabbed Tommy and we scrambled back to the airstrip, where small military cargo planes, including helicopters and artillery spotters, swarmed in and out like bees in a hive.

"Look, I've got to get to An Khe," I told the officer, a Vietnamese captain, in charge of QCs guarding the line of Hueys. "My husband is there. I've got to join him."

"No way," he shouted back above the whining turbines. "Even if I had a chopper, I couldn't spare the space. Charlie's all over the place. For all I know, you could be a VC agent!"

Indignantly, I produced my visa and endorsements showing that I had just come in from America and was married to a U.S. citizen. I let him see Ed's picture but kept my thumb over the name. I could see the officer weakening.

"What is his name and rank?"

"He's a major—an American major. His name is—" For a horrible instant I could not remember Dan's odd-sounding Italian name. During those wonderful weeks, I had always referred to him as "the Major" or Dan—I couldn't even picture his name tag, although he had worn it on his uniform every time I saw him. "Demara," I blurted out. "Major Daniel Demara."

The captain led me to the operations shack where he picked up a phone, presumably to call An Khe.

"Nobody's heard of him," the captain said, covering the mouthpiece with his hand. He didn't hang up and I didn't like the way he was looking at me.

I waved and yelled "Thank you!" and got out of there quick. My temper now took over from my anxiety. Here I was, less than a two-hour drive from the love of my life—and he might as well have been on the moon!

Near the airport gate, I spotted a man in bell-bottoms and a flowery shirt leaning against a dust-red car smoking and reading a paper. He didn't look like a cabbie, but those days anybody with wheels was an entrepreneur.

"Bac Oi!" I shouted, "Excuse me, uncle! How much to go to An Khe?"

The man looked startled, not so much at my request as by the two screaming kids and bewildered teenager I dragged in the dust behind me.

"Why, a hundred dollars—American."

"I only have piastres." I rummaged through my purse. Of course, I had plenty of American dollars, but I wasn't about to let him know it. If he didn't kill me and take what he wanted, then the rest of the crowd surely would.

I gave him the piastre equivalent of a hundred dollars—part of which was to have been our airfare to Canada. If my father's spirit was watching what I selfishly did with my husband's money and to Tommy, Ed's natural child, whose life I had no right to risk, he decided to keep quiet—probably out of disgust. Women in love are very formidable, especially to their own conscience.

"And we'll have to go now," the man added. "The government troops have just swept for mines."

"That's okay, we're ready to go."

He looked behind us as if expecting something else. "No luggage?"

"No," I smiled lamely, "just us!"

He was almost as suspicious as the captain, but the hundred dollars was very persuasive.

After stopping at the bus station to check travel conditions, we set out for An Khe, driving slowly and staying squarely in the middle of the road. The driver didn't talk much for the first half hour, just steered nervously, scanning the brush and the road ahead. Then, when nothing happened, he relaxed and jimmied a cigarette out of his pocket.

"You know, the real problem isn't the Commies," he said, lighting up and resting his arm on the window. "It's the damn American patrols. They blast anything that moves. Shoot first and let God sort 'em out, that's what they say." He did not seem to think that having American dependents on board would make any difference to a point man's itchy trigger finger.

Whenever we approached peasants heading toward Fleuku, which wasn't often, we'd stop and ask them about conditions farther on. To the last they advised us to turn around, and my driver always gave me a chance to do so, but I told him to keep going. The once busy road—usually filled with cars, buses, convoys, and motorbikes—was eerily empty, but that wasn't half as spooky as An Khe when we arrived that afternoon. Even the great houses of its few wealthy residents stood empty and boarded up. Its bustling streets were bereft of everything save browsing chickens, stray dogs, and scattered soldiers wearing combat gear and worried faces.

Following my directions, the driver took us straight to our house, which, at least on the outside, looked just as we left it. We got out and I gave him a big tip, mostly to thank the local spirits for protecting us on the road. He drove off quickly, as if the highway was already being rolled up behind him. I smiled and waved to the lone QC (Vietnamese military policeman) standing guard at the entrance to the MACV building across the street. He didn't respond.

Inside, things seemed the same but with a subtle difference. The boys ran after their toys and Thanh and I went to the kitchen to check the food we had previously packed—some rice and cookies and a jar of fresh water. Only after I knew we could survive awhile in the field would I worry about finding Dan. A cool breeze rattled through the window. I began to think more clearly.

Of course—that's what's wrong: the windows are open!

"Boys!" I shouted, "come here quick!" Thanh began stuffing supplies down her blouse and I grabbed a kitchen knife and hid it behind my back.

The boys scampered in and a familiar voice followed them from outside. "Whoa—hold on!"

It was our landlord in a sweaty, half-open workshirt. He wore a military pistol stuck in his belt and a relieved look on his face—almost as relieved as ours. "What are you doing here? Everyone's supposed to be gone!"

"I could say the same about you!" My initial relief turned to caution. Whenever the Communists took over, the landowners were usually the first to go—to underground jails or deep-jungle prisons or simply into the bush for a quick bullet through the head. It was unlikely that anyone associated with Saigon's monied class would stick around without good reason. Could our trusty landlord actually be a Viet Cong agent?

"Well, all this belongs to me, doesn't it?" he waved his hand around the room. "Do you think I'm going to leave it to looters? Right now, they're a bigger problem than VC. Of course, I only have to fire one shot and the QCs come running. But what about you? Why did you come back?"

"Everything I have in the world is here," I said without much exaggeration.

"Oh, I see. The Major?" The landlord raised an eyebrow and smiled.

"Yes. Have you seen him?"

"He came by a few days ago looking for you—"

My heart rose to my throat.

"—but I haven't seen him since. He didn't leave a message."

"How can I contact him and let him know I've come back?"

The landlord stroked his chin, "Maybe we can call him on the MACV radio. They've been very good about helping civilians."

I sent Jimmy across the street with the landlord—mostly to get him out of the way while Thanh and I tried to put our house in order, but also to let Dan hear Jimmy's voice on the radio and assure him it was us. Within a few minutes, a jeep stopped in front of the house.

"Mommy—the Major!" Jimmy cried, as if it was Christmas morning. "The Major's back!"

I ran into Dan's arms and gave him the biggest kiss anyone— including our chuckling landlord and stupefied Thanh—had ever seen.

"Ly—*tinh yeu tren tran chien,"* Dan sighed, squeezing me tight. "Love in a battle zone, eh?"

"I couldn't leave you behind," I sobbed. Tears flowed from us both uncontrollably.

We went inside and Tommy—who missed the comfort of his father and who was worried about his mother and terribly confused and frightened about everything—blurted out "Daddy!" and grabbed Dan by the leg. We laughed through our tears and Dan picked him up and gave him a big hug. Of course, the nickname stuck. From that moment on, Dan was "Major Daddy."

Unexpectedly, the next seven days turned out to be the best in my life. Our passage to An Khe had been uneventful because the Communists had intentionally suspended operations all over Vietnam. Their plan was to gain some advantage then halt just short of provoking a U.S. response. They wanted Americans out of the country for good and were willing to bide their time. Although the South Vietnamese military and vestigial American forces remained on high alert, one warm lazy day ran into another without the slightest hint that the war would resume in earnest. My new An Khe "family" made the most of it.

I told the landlord that Ed and I had separated and Dan moved into the house. Our "wedding night" was as blissful as I ever dreamed of as a young girl contemplating my marriage to Tung, the boy from the neighboring village whom the matchmakers had chosen for me. All that ended years ago with Tung's death on the battlefield. If I had learned one thing from that terrible time, it was that life's first duty is to live. And in the ghost town An Khe had become, our new "family" bubbled life from every pore, from every childish giggle, every shared bowl of rice, every stroll around our pond, every sigh on our wedding bed.

But such is the nature of bliss: it cannot last forever.

The day he moved in, Dan had a special field telephone installed so that he could communicate directly with the base in case of an emergency. In the deep silence of the first night of our second week, the telephone shrieked into the blackness.

"DeParma here," Dan said in a sleep-husky voice. His eyes grew wide in the dark. "Son of a bitch!" He slammed down the receiver.

"What it is?" I asked, rising to my elbows.

"Regulars. Moving in from—"

At that instant explosions began, more distant than the first attack but still too close.

Dan literally jumped into his pants and was almost out the door by the time Thanh and the boys reached our bed.

"Stay put." He cradled his M-16 loosely on his shoulder like a boy going out to hunt rabbits. "Keep all the lights out. I'll be back as soon as I can."

For the rest of the night, we huddled together and listened to the distant barrage. Unlike the first attack, South Vietnamese aircraft now streaked overhead and we knew something big was going on. I sang a little song to calm my sons—and myself. It was "Our Warriors," a tune of praise I learned during the war with the French. Tonight, I sang it like a lullaby.

> Daddy guards the Ngu Hoanh Son mountain,
> Barring the way to the Viet Minh.
> We ourselves wait through the night,
> Beneath the warbirds—
> Beside the tanks.
> We rally at Son Da
> Though the enemy is overwhelming.
> Like fish in the sea,
> We are safe in our dark caverns.

The boys—and even Thanh—eventually nodded off, children sleeping through a summer storm. But I could not. Not only did my worry for Dan and fear about the battle keep me awake, but my conscience hurt me too. I had committed the sin of adultery, if not in my heart, then at least in the eyes of god, my father, and our ancestors. I had taken my beautiful babies and an innocent young girl back into the shadow of death to satisfy my own desire for a dream-happy life.

Now the jaws of the tiger were snapping shut. Through its teeth, I could see nothing but the night.

THREE

Marooned

THE BATTLE for An Khe lasted until dawn—South Vietnamese soldiers and the remaining American support troops against a big force of North Vietnamese.

Shortly after sunrise, we ate a small breakfast. Jimmy strung Ed's portable tape recorder around his neck and began comforting himself with some of Ed's tapes. Soon, a helicopter landed in the grassy field behind the high school and we all ran to the window. "Major Daddy" got out and the kids ran to greet him. I grabbed my purse (which still had the remains of Ed's money so I wasn't about to leave it unattended) and followed. Dan was alive and in one piece!

The man who met us, though, was a dozen years older than the Dan who had rushed from the house last night. His eyes were red-rimmed and tired; his face grimy and unshaven. His voice, shouting above the helicopter's whine, was coarser than a buzzsaw.

"Come on!" he roared. "Get aboard!"

"I get our things." Although we were dressed, we weren't prepared to travel.

"Forget them. No time." His strong hand clamped my shoulder and hustled me across the street behind Thanh and the kids.

We scrambled, heads down, under the singing rotors. Before hoisting me bodily into the aircraft, he stuffed a note into my purse.

"Here," he shouted, "take this!"

The metal floor was hot and the interior stank of cordite and sweat. The American door gunner helped the boys buckle onto a troop seat, where they huddled, big-eyed and silent, while I turned to give Dan my hand. To my shock, he was already outside the arc of the rotors twirling his index finger at the pilot. The engines roared.

"Dan!" My cry was lost in blowing grass and dust. I strained to see him as we lifted off but our home was instantly reduced to a silver speck. The bug-helmeted crewman pushed me back into my seat and swiveled his enormous machine gun into position. This terrified me more than anything because the helicopters usually flew with their guns pointed skyward unless they expected trouble. (The Viet Cong always tried to stay hidden, so they seldom fired on an aircraft that didn't look as if it would fire on them.) Anyway, I knew all helicopters were most vulnerable on takeoff, so I just sat back, tears rolling down my face, and clutched my boys with white fingers.

"Tinh chi dep, khi con dang do," Thanh said into my ear. "Love is most beautiful when it is nearly lost."

After several minutes, the battle zone was behind us and the helicopter had picked up speed and height. I relaxed my grip and looked at the crumpled piece of paper Dan had shoved into my purse. It read: *To whom it may concern: Help this family get out of Vietnam. Reward. Major Dante DeParma, U.S.A.*

A few minutes later we descended, circled a barren field once as if checking things out, then set down next to the highway at Qui Nhon.

"Okay, Missus DeParma," the door gunner yelled, "end of the line!"

He disconnected his cords and straps and jumped out ahead of us, helping me down first, then Thanh and the kids.

"But Saigon!" I yelled, barely able to hear my own voice. "You take us to Saigon!"

The crewman only shook his head, tapped the helmet over his ears and climbed aboard. The pilot revved the engine so we had no choice but to scurry for the safety of the road.

I cursed like a Danang bar-girl. I was livid at the crewmen for dumping us in the middle of nowhere and scared at what might happen next. Somehow, cursing helped summon those instincts and skills we would now need to stay alive.

The highway was jammed with refugees moving south. Like foraging ants, they carried everything they could: suitcases, bundles, wicker baskets, clay pots—even sticks of furniture and other useless items they knew they would have to jettison eventually or barter for food and shelter. I decided first to move against this human tide on the outside chance the buses were still running. My cash would buy us a seat.

Predictably, the bus terminal was a madhouse. Whenever a loaded bus departed, more passengers swarmed on top and threw off the suitcases and bundles, believing human lives made better baggage. When the next bus arrived, people again clambered aboard, indifferent to the destination, so we just went with the flow. The world was now *thoi loan*—crazy and upside down. It was every man for himself.

We boarded early enough to get two seats. Nobody cared where we were headed as long as it was away from the enemy. Whenever we slowed for traffic, bystanders tried to jump aboard. Most were kicked and beaten back by the people clinging to the roof and fenders.

Twenty minutes out of town the bus began to slow. We had come upon a Republican army checkpoint and that usually meant trouble, no matter what the passengers' politics. At best, we could expect a lengthy search for VC infiltrators, weapons, and contraband. At worst—well, everyone knew what that meant.

I was especially worried for Thanh. I was no spring chicken (and, after the last few years, looked older than I was), disheveled, and burdened with sniveling kids. Thanh and several other girls on the bus, though, were in the bloom of youth: stewbones dangling before hungry dogs. Quickly, I dug a bottle of aspirin out of my purse and told Thanh to swallow a handful. She was no fool and complied. Within minutes she turned pale and sickly. I shoved Jimmy's tape recorder under our seat and hoped that no one would notice. Even without paper or pencil, I could always dictate a message if we got into trouble.

The door swung open and the first Republican soldier climbed aboard. He was a sergeant, quite thin, but looked as tough as a mangrove root. The driver complained about keeping his schedule, the dangers of stopping too long, the mechanical delicacy of the bus, but the sergeant ignored him and walked slowly to the rear. His eyes cut left and right. Two more soldiers boarded behind him, backup in case of trouble.

From long practice, we tried to look inconspicuous while not ignoring the soldiers. Be too casual and the sentries would get suspicious or become angry because you failed to show them respect. Be too serious and they'd think you had something to hide. Like everything else in a war zone, success or failure, life and death, usually walked a narrow line.

The sergeant stopped a few seats ahead of us and talked with an older woman. Jewelry changed hands. In the middle of an ominous silence, the soldier behind him turned on a transistor radio. The sound was full blast and the sergeant whirled and the rest of us jumped. The soldier quickly shut it off. The sergeant scolded him, turned back toward us, and moved on. The soldier kept the radio.

When he got to our row, the sergeant looked a moment at Thanh —pale as death, sweating like a horse, choking back her vomit—and kept going. He rustled through a paper bag behind us. A man raised his voice—fist on flesh. The backup soldiers lunged forward and the bus got quiet. The boots shuffled again. It was all I could do to keep from looking. A woman, probably the stubborn passenger's companion, sobbed quietly.

Now I began to fear for the two lovely girls—about Thanh's age, sixteen or seventeen—I'd seen at the back of the bus. Incautiously, I twisted in my seat to steal a peek. The soldiers had paused in front of them; first to tease ("What are you doing on this bus? Does your mother know you're here? Where did you get such a pretty dress?"), then to intimidate ("Haven't I seen you before? We arrested someone like you last week. You're not a prostitute, are you? You know what we do to girls like that?"). I thought they were just going to give them a hard time and leave, when we heard the most terrifying thing you can hear in such a situation.

The sergeant chambered a round in his rifle.

"Okay, get up," he demanded. "You're coming outside."

One teenage girl—almost as pale as Thanh—left the bus in front of the soldiers. They took her to the opposite side of the road, so I couldn't see what was happening. The people on that side of the bus carefully averted their eyes. We waited for the shots.

After an eternity—fifteen or twenty minutes—the girl reboarded the bus. Her clothing was rumpled and dirty, her hair matted with twigs. Muddy tracks—dried tears—streaked her bruised and swollen cheeks. She limped to her seat.

Even before she could sit down, a soldier barked at the driver, "Get this pile of junk out of here!" The engine sputtered. The bus jerked forward. A sigh of relief washed over us like summer rain and I only hoped that Thanh would not choose this moment to throw up. I moved Jimmy away from the window so she could have extra air. When the checkpoint was safely behind us, some older women tended the girl. Her soft sobs—my country's anthem—played in our ears for the next two hours.

Our progress was slow and sundown caught us sooner than expected. Of course, driving at night was unthinkable. We stopped at a "refugee camp" that was no more than an open space where a few roadside vendors gathered to make money from their troubled neighbors. I wanted to spend the night on the bus, glued to our precious seats, but soldiers ordered everyone off. I bought a newspaper at quadruple the usual price and spread it across the ground so we might at least sleep on something dry. Earlier busloads had cleaned out the food, so we went to bed hungry as well as scared and exhausted.

The next morning, the vendors came back and we had some *banh mi sua*—French bread and condensed milk. That would be the pattern for the next seventy-two hours, all the way to Saigon. By day we crammed into the buses, sweating checkpoint after checkpoint. At night, we slept under the clouds, huddled together like dogs to keep warm, until our only snack—priced like a meal in Saigon's finest restaurant—could be taken on the run. To make matters worse, somewhere on the bus, or in between buses, some light-fingered traveler had relieved me of my purse—leaving us only the emergency money I had tucked in my clothes. We arrived in the capital with enough cash to get a room, but not get us to Canada. For us, it was the end of the line.

Even in the few short weeks since we had been there, Saigon's complexion had gotten worse. With most Americans gone, competition was fierce among the bars, prostitutes, and drug dealers. Crime was on the rise and nobody went out after dark. Clashes between QCs, metropolitan police, and hoodlums—many in paramilitary gangs—were frequent. Under such circumstances, we wondered what, if anything, prevented the Communist battalions—which seemed to roam at will in the countryside—from waltzing right up to the president's palace.

Saigon persisted (and would persist, for a couple of more years) like a wheezy old lady too cantankerous to die. Instead of surrendering to her enemies, the city settled into a prolonged death rattle. The old citizens began to leave or isolate themselves behind iron gates and private guards. Newcomers—mostly refugees from the outer districts—took up residence wherever they could and scanned the newspapers for jobs, war news, and personal messages from friends and relatives. Although vacancies soared, rents stayed high, partly because of the inflated wartime economy and partly because few people trusted the government to get things under control. If traditional Vietnamese culture had long ago broken down, the bastardized wartime society that replaced it was now teetering drunkenly on the rubble.

With a little luck and a lot of hustle, I found a vacant apartment in a Korean tenement and we settled in to make our plans. Each day I scoured the newspaper casualty lists, which were always published by rank, beginning with *thieu ta,* Vietnamese for "major." I thanked fate or luck or god every day that Dan's name was always absent.

The other news was not as good. The headlines screamed: "Americans Begin Withdrawing from Vietnam!," "First 40 POWs Will Return to U.S. for Christmas," "U.S. and South Vietnamese in Secret Negotiations for American Troop Withdrawal in Return for More Weapons and Ammunition," "President Thieu Refused to Send an Escort to the Tan Son Nhut Airport to Receive Kissinger and Haig," and the one that for me said it all: "U.S. Has Killed Over 600,000 Vietnamese Civilians."

After another week, the Communist offensive had stopped and another lull began. It was clear to everyone, though, that without the Americans a Northern victory was not only inevitable, it would probably come very soon. I had no choice but to kiss goodbye my dream of staying in Vietnam. When the Communists took over, the ax would fall first on those with ties to Americans and the old regime; next, on those who had betrayed the VC or Northern army in some way; and finally, anyone who profiteered from the war. By this reckoning, I was already a three-time loser. Even with new identity papers easily purchased in Saigon's phony passport bazaar, I would eventually be recognized by friends and neighbors. I would have to leave the country—and do it while I still had the chance. The only two questions were: how many family members could I persuade to go with me; and how would I pay for it all?

Thanh and I decided to divide our forces. Above all, I felt my first obligation was to contact my mother. Now that the fighting had stopped, I told Thanh I would go to Danang if she would fly to An Khe, collect our things, and make contact with Dan. We would meet back at our Saigon apartment in a few days with whomever and whatever we could bring.

I sat opposite my mother's stony face in Lan's kitchen. I told her about Ed—how he was a good man but how our ages and our ways of life were too different to make our marriage work. This didn't surprise her at all, but she was shocked and mortified that I could ever consider taking up again with a U.S. military man. At least Ed had been a civilian! I told her I was unable to contact Dan, that he very likely had been killed.

"In any case, Mama Du," I said, "we've got to think of the family. It's *thoi loan* out there—the end of the world. Soon, the very people who tried to kill us a few years ago will be in charge. Do you think they're going to forget the grudges they've nursed for twenty years?"

"You can always live in the city," my mother said, thinking again like a peasant, although her tears betrayed her true opinion of the idea. "Danang or Saigon—you know very well how to get along in those places."

"No, not anymore. Things have changed. I have two sons now. And if you thought the cities were bad before, you should see them now. Even the countryside has been torn apart. Do you know a farmer anywhere who can still support his family on the land?"

"What will you do in America if everything there is so bad?" My mother sounded genuinely concerned. I'm sure she thought her own life was over.

I sighed deeply, thinking of what going back would really mean. "I will grit my teeth and bear it, Mama Du—for my children, just as you did for yours. I thought my debt of *hy singh* had been paid, but I was wrong. I've already faced my first indignity. I cabled Ed's mother, Mom Munro, the only one of his relatives who understands me, and asked her to tell Ed I need more money—that what he gave me was stolen. Without it, we're trapped. I'm sure he'll send enough for all of us. You only have to say yes, Mama Du and everything will be all right. I'm sure we can be happy in America if the whole family is together."

But my mother had spent so much of her life saying no—to invaders and interlopers and people who threatened her family—that she wasn't about to say yes to "the enemy," even if it would save her.

"My bones belong here, next to your father's," she said. "Ask Hai and Lan and Ba if they want to go, but leave me alone. Whatever's going to happen will happen."

I did ask my sisters, and except for Lan, their answer was the same: "We can't leave Mama Du."

When I put the question to Lan, she only laughed.

"What? You must be joking! Things have been quiet for a month. Or sure, they're fighting in the DMZ and in the mountains near Laos, but the troops haven't got the word. The treaty's about to be signed. The war is almost over. I don't know what you're worried about. Besides, weren't you the one who warned me about America—*two parts sour for every part sweet?* Isn't that what you said? Forget it."

I returned to Saigon with empty hands and a heavy heart. Fortunately, Thanh had fared better. Dan was alive and well and would be coming to Saigon for two weeks leave—Thanh had given him our address. I didn't know whether to laugh or cry or give thanks or curse the heavens. Did I really want to see Dan again only to tell him goodbye?

Of course, somewhere in my schoolgirl heart I wanted to believe that Dan would divorce his wife and arrange for my divorce from Ed, marry me himself, and take me back to live on an American farm —a place I understood, where my boys and the other children we'd have could grow up to be as big, strong, smart, and wonderful as Major Daddy. Despite—or perhaps because of—everything I'd been through, I still wanted to be rescued.

When Dan arrived, though, he quickly dispersed my schoolgirl dreams. After a tearful, passionate reunion, we found a quiet moment to talk about the future.

"I can't leave now, Ly," he said in my father's voice. "My tour lasts another year. You can't stay either. You know how things are going. It's time to play it safe. It's time to take care of yourself and your beautiful boys. Go back to Ed. Make the best life you can. I won't forget you. Someday I'll come for you when we're both free. The war won't last forever."

The war won't last forever. When had it not been part of my life?

Dan stayed with us as long as he could, which wasn't nearly long enough, and used his influence to expedite our paperwork. By now, Ed had gotten Leatha's message and wrote that he'd worked out his tax problems and that we could return to San Diego instead of Canada. He cabled some money, but it was not enough for the entire airfare, given our sky-high rent and the unexpected length of our stay. Fortunately, Dan made up the difference, so I did not have to go back on my knees to Ed. For that—among many, many other things —I was eternally grateful to him.

Dan returned to An Khe and several weeks later, Thanh followed. She never liked the idea of living in America, especially after hearing my stories, and the idyllic world of An Khe, where the truce still held, appealed to her greatly. When Dan offered her a job as his housekeeper (mostly to allow me to leave with one less worry), she accepted with gratitude. Then, on the eve of our departure, fate or luck or god again intervened.

At the last minute, our exit visa was delayed some thirty-six hours on a "technicality"—which meant more "donations" were needed for various office "tea funds." However, while the necessary palms were being greased, I had just enough time to make one last visit to An Khe. I hurried to the Air Vietnam office, booked a flight, and returned later in the day to pick up our tickets.

"I don't know," the clerk said, fumbling around behind the counter, "the damn thing was here a minute ago."

"What do you mean?" I blinked, disappointed and a little suspicious.

"I mean I don't know where your ticket is," he smiled slyly, "You'll have to help me look for it."

Oh, so that's your game! I had a little bribe money left, but not much. I offered him all that I could. "Will ten American dollars help you in your search?"

"That's not even enough to insult me!" he grunted, then grinned the lecherous grin I'd seen a hundred times before. "Anyway, there are other ways you can help."

"No. Oh no. No, no, no, no, *no!*"

"Hey, don't make a scene. It doesn't have to be right now. I get off work in an hour—"

"No, no, *No!*" I was crying now and making such a stink that he closed the window and hung up his OUT TO LUNCH sign. I thought of finding an American MP (the QCs or city police would do nothing) but few were left and by the time I had pressed my complaint the flight would be gone and my last chance to see Dan would have vanished with it.

I went back to the apartment and collapsed on the bed, sleeping or just staring up at the ceiling until it was time to pick up our visa and go to the airport. The first time I left Vietnam I was disgusted with my country and worn-out with myself. My second departure was almost without feeling—except, perhaps, the sense of relief one gets after vomiting or voiding: putting the contents of a bad meal behind you. I was physically and emotionally sick—sick of the corruption, the violence, the worry, the risk. Most of all I was sick with myself: for bringing my sons back into danger; for taunting fortune once too often and walking the tightrope between heaven and hell; for dishonoring my father's spirit by putting my own selfish desires over everything he stood for in his life. I had run away believing I had found the passage to a better life. Now I had come back and found that wherever I went, my troubles only followed. I had discovered— perhaps early, perhaps late in my life (who knows how long one will live?)—that lasting victories are won in the heart, not on this soil or that. Happiness is not a place called America or Vietnam. It is a state of grace. Someone may rescue you; but only you can save yourself.

On July 17, 1972, Ed met us at LAX, grinning from ear to ear. Jimmy ran to meet him, grateful for a familiar face, while Tommy, even though he was Ed's natural son, clung to my skirt and cried. Big crowds reminded him of refugees and he'd seen enough of those to last a lifetime. I wore my contrite and wooden smile like a mask, pinning it in place with thoughts of Dan. It was time to do the penance I so richly deserved.

"Now you save us twice!" I joked, but felt just stupid and guilty.

"What else could I do?" Ed grinned. "You're my family and I love you!" I felt as if I would cry.

The drive to El Cajon seemed even longer than the awful bus ride from An Khe to Saigon. Ed and I talked about the deteriorating war situation and he tried to cheer me up by mentioning the "big reception" his women were preparing.

"Yes, I can imagine," I said, staring glumly out the window.

The first few days back in California were pure hell, but for different reasons than I expected. Mom Munro, whose two guest rooms we occupied until Ed found another job, was characteristically kind and understanding. Even Erma, who was too pleased to have Ed back to do much gloating, was magnanimous in victory. No, my purgatory—as the monks said—would be of my own devising. The boys and I had grown used to sleeping together and continued to do so, partly because eighteen-month-old Tommy still clung to me the way a baby monkey clutches its mother, but mostly because I sought any excuse to avoid being alone with Ed—and not just to evade my wifely duties. Being near him made me feel guilty, terrible, and sick. His tolerance, like the forbearance of his relatives, only made me feel worse. Of course, he was a man, not a saint, and his patience was not inexhaustible.

"Won't those kids ever leave you alone?" he asked one evening several days after we'd arrived. "It's not natural. You shouldn't coddle them so much, especially Tommy." His sexual frustration, bad enough during my absence, was made worse by my virginal presence: I was so near and yet so far.

"Ba bao di ngu mot minh em thoi!" Jimmy barked at his brother unexpectedly, just like a cadre leader. "Go to bed by yourself, you little brat!"

"Khong! Em ngu voi ma! Bieu ong di-di!" Tommy answered back defiantly, "No! I'm sleeping with my mother! Tell that man to go away!"

"Daddy wants to sleep with Mommy," Jimmy continued in Vietnamese.

"Daddy's in Vietnam!" Tommy answered, thinking of Major Daddy.

Of course, Ed didn't understand a word of this, but it made me realize just how much I had confused my precious little boys. I recalled the fable my mother once told me of the wife who made her young son bow before her shadow every night in place of her long-absent husband, and say to the shadow, "Goodnight, Father!" When her husband returned, the man tried to embrace his boy but the son yelled, "You are not my daddy! My daddy visits Mommy when night comes!" Thinking his wife had been unfaithful, the husband beat her and she drowned herself in a river. After her funeral, as the husband lit a candle, the little boy came up, bowed before his father's shadow, and said, "Goodnight, Father," as he had been taught. Instantly, the husband realized his mistake, but now it was too late. For me the story showed how tragedies can happen even though everyone tries to do what's best—all in the name of love.

Ed was angered by the boys' exchange, "Have they forgotten their English already?"

"Just when they excited," I fibbed. Jimmy really liked Ed. He remembered the months of attention he got before Tommy was big enough for Ed to notice. "Look," I told Ed, "you sleep with Jimmy; I sleep with Tommy. Pretty soon Tommy want to be with his brother, then we sleep together, okay?" I pecked Ed on the cheek like a sister.

"Yeah," Jimmy continued to Tommy in Vietnamese as Ed hoisted Jimmy onto his shoulder, "be good, you little moron, and Daddy will buy you toys!"

When they were gone, I hugged Tommy and thanked him for being "my little protector," which must've really mixed him up. I had never been able to sleep with Ed out of anything other than duty, but now, after Dan, sleeping with him seemed worse than infidelity—it seemed a sacrilege.

When Tommy and I were alone, I spoke softly into Ed's portable tape recorder, dictating letters to Dan—some in English, some in Vietnamese, since there were still many thoughts I could express only in my native tongue and I knew Thanh would be there to translate if Dan ran into trouble. In keeping with my elaborate deception, I would ask Ed or Leatha or Erma to mail the tapes for me, since they were always addressed to Thanh, my faithful housekeeper, friend, and "little sister" whom Ed knew and trusted well.

After a while, the awkward "truce" between me and Ed's women broke down just like the Paris Treaty that "ended" the war. Erma and Leatha resumed their criticism of my marriage. Ed, finding little success as an over-the-hill job hunter, began a new "affair" with his cigarettes. Finally, I went with him on his interviews (some of which involved overnight trips to other cities) just to get out of the house and cheer him up after getting rejected. On those few occasions when we did sleep together, I spent less time making love than nursing him through the endless bouts of coughing, fever, and chills that plagued him every night.

Now my only happiness beyond my boys came from the weekly packages I received from Thanh filled with Vietnamese newspapers, magazines, and the love letters from Dan she secreted in their pages. He addressed them to minh oi, my pet name, and wrote how much he loved and missed me and couldn't understand how a wonderful young woman like me could fall in love with a "dumb Wop" like him. He would reminisce about our sometimes idyllic, sometimes terrifying adventures together and closed his letters with glowing promises about the future—how he would divorce Carmine, his wife, and we would one day be together forever. I read the letters so often that the tear-softened paper eventually fell apart in my hands.

Eventually, even Leatha's great patience ran short with the miserable couple who shared her roof. We moved to the nearby community of Santee, not far from Kathy and her husband, where Ed assumed a VA loan on a three-bedroom home in a housing tract so new that even the insects had not yet found their way inside. In a way, the neighborhood's barren landscape symbolized the blank tablet my life had become. I looked forward to filling it with green saplings, life, and hope.

Jimmy was now five and, because of his previous schooling in Vietnam, was ready for first grade. I started American school too, studying English-for-immigrants in the military-style Quonset huts of a nearby community college. Each morning, I took Jimmy to school on a bike Ed bought me. I must have embarrassed him a lot in my traditional Vietnamese dress and peasant hat, reminding him of the "bad old days" when his biggest concern now was fitting in with American kids. Ed baby-sat Tommy while I was gone, and even took him to job interviews, which, being always unsuccessful, left them both in a bad mood when I got home.

At the adult school I began to learn something about the "American melting pot." In addition to immigrants and bored housewives, I met several U.S. military veterans who told me how the government would send them to any kind of school they wanted simply for doing their patriotic duty. I felt happy for them and was again impressed at how well the American government seemed to care for its former soldiers. Also, the instructors were generally kind and patient, the way my father had been when he taught me our Vietnamese customs and traditions, not harsh and short-tempered like most Vietnamese teachers.

After a few weeks of this new routine, I came back from class to discover that Ed had returned from Leatha's with one of Thanh's packages. My heart zoomed—first up, then down like an American roller coaster—when I saw it had been opened.

"So *that's* what you two were up to all those months!" He threw the letters in my face before I could even put down my textbooks.

"What do you mean? What you talking about?" My heart raced. I knew very well what he meant.

"If you love him so much—why don't you go back to Vietnam?"

I picked up the crumpled letters. I guessed one had fallen out of a magazine, or perhaps Ed had discovered it while idly leafing through the pages. Either way, the game was over. I couldn't look Ed in the face. Although I felt proud of my love for Dan, my downcast eyes somehow made my feelings seem cheap and dirty, adding anger to my embarrassment. My sudden flood of strong feelings found no outlet other than tears.

He snatched back the letters and stalked out of the room. I heard him crying in the kitchen. The boys stood big-eyed, dumbfounded. They had seen Mom and Dad fight before, but never like this. To make matters worse, Ed had probably opened the letter at Leatha's, perhaps with Erma looking over his shoulder. Their shaking heads and clucking tongues no doubt magnified the mortal wound I had delivered to Ed's poor heart. I stood hugging the boys as Ed came back into the room.

"I want you and Jimmy to pack," he said thickly, rubbing his red eyes. "I'm sending you back to Vietnam."

I knew I was supposed to feel fear—perhaps beg for mercy—but I only felt relief.

"All right," I sniffed, and in a strong voice that surprised even me, added, "but I want my boys with me."

"No way. Tommy is my son. I won't give him up. Write to your lover boy. Tell him to send you two tickets. I want you out by the end of the month."

I took the letters and went to Tommy's room—the land of exile—and left Ed alone with his grief. I was once again astounded at how much trouble love could bring into the world. Could one person be happy only by making someone else miserable? It didn't make sense. It was not the world my father had told me about, where love conquered evil.

I sat on Tommy's bed for what seemed like hours, reflecting on my life and thinking about Dan. Finally Ed came in and put his hand on my shoulder. It was not the vise-grip of a policeman, but the hand of a stern, wounded father. He gave me a pen and pad of paper.

"What do you want me to do?" I asked.

"Write what I tell you. 'Dear Dan, Please send me and Jimmy a one-way ticket to Saigon. Ed found your letters and is sending us away—' "

"What about Tommy?" I asked, my throat tightening.

"What about him? He's staying here. Finish the letter."

His dictation—the pouring out of his feelings—went on and on, and writing it broke my heart. In one sentence, he would try to be fair and objective ("My husband realizes he is an old man compared to me") only to be vindictive in the next ("but I have repaid his kindness with deception"), and so on. Finally, when he realized the exercise was punishing himself more than me, he stopped. The words in that letter were the last he spoke to me for two weeks.

He mailed the letter and I dutifully packed—keeping Tommy's things handy—and waited for the expected tickets. In the meantime, packages continued to come, and Ed carefully screened them for romantic contraband. When he found a letter from Dan—and there were several—he'd ceremoniously confiscate it, read it silently, curse and shake his head, then put it in his pocket. I don't know which was worse, the pain I felt forgoing Dan's letters or the pain Ed gave himself by reading them for me. Just as the absence of Dan's words made me hungrier for them, so did Ed's feasting upon them only fatten his own misery. In the end, I realized he was torturing himself to death, and torturing me by making me watch. It was like witnessing my father's death all over again.

About ten days after our blowup, the reply to Ed's letter came. It did not include a ticket. Ed handed it over and I stretched it tight between my fingers. Among the words of endearment, regret, condolence, and advice, it said, "You must get a lawyer and divorce Ed. Ed is an old man and married you to take advantage of a young and desperate girl. Do not come back to Vietnam. I will come for you when my tour is finished. Wait for me."

Now I really did not know what to think. I began to feel like a toy smacked back and forth by two strong-willed boys who had forgotten what the game was all about. Ed had not taken advantage of me; *I* had taken advantage of him. He had been understanding, thoughtful, and caring—to me and my fatherless child, whom he treated as lovingly as his own. *I* had rewarded him with infidelity and deception. Dan had stolen another man's wife—repaid his trust with betrayal—but only when that wife had declared her marriage over in every way but the final stamp. Each of us did what we had to do, all in the name of love. Wishing for the best, we could not have done worse. Fighting for love, we earned the same bad karma as soldiers do in war. I couldn't believe this was happening!

"I have been terrible to you, Ed," I said, blowing my nose in a hankie. "I am very, very sorry. I hope you can forgive me."

"I—I tried to be good to you." Ed still sounded dazed, shell-shocked. "I tried to be good to the boys."

"You are a good man." I squeezed his hand. "But I can't love you like I love Dan. I will always care for you, but like a father."

"My second wife cheated on me," Ed continued as if I wasn't there. "That's why I went to Vietnam. I thought if I could find a nice Vietnamese woman everything would be fine. Asian women are supposed to be loyal, aren't they? I just can't believe it!"

I wiped my eyes. "One thing is still true. I'm still a little girl when it comes to love. If you let us stay so Jimmy can go to school and I can take care of Tommy until Dan comes to get us, I will be very grateful and make it up to you somehow. But, if you want Jimmy and me to move out, I have a girlfriend in L.A. You won't have to worry about Dan and—"

"Oh"—Ed waved Dan away as if he were beside the point instead of the focus of our trouble—"I don't hold a grudge against Dan. I *am* too old for you. I know that. The whole thing was a mistake. You see what funny things love does to us old farts, too, as well as you pretty young girls?"

Ed and I got along okay after that. We had finally found in our mismatched loves something the other person could empathize with and understand. By recognizing how far apart we really were, we became closer than ever.

I wrote to Dan and asked that he send no more *thu tinh* love letters out of respect for Ed's feelings. Although I did speak to Dan twice on the overseas line, it was only when Ed was out of town. Ed's only joy in life now was Tommy, who had begun to accept the poor old man once again as his father. Leatha, Erma, and Kathy always loved Tommy too, despite the despicable mother he inherited, so together they provided a good extended family.

One evening, Kathy and her husband, Mike, were supposed to come over and play poker with Ed, but canceled at the last minute because Kathy was sick. It was just as well, because Ed came down sick that night, too—coughing his head off all evening. I put him right to bed, but unlike his other bad evenings, the coughing didn't stop when he lay down.

"I think you should see the doctor tonight—right now!" I said, stern as my mother.

"I'm okay," Ed hacked. "I just have to catch my breath."

"Come on, we go to doctor!" I tried to rouse him.

"Forget it! We don't have medical insurance and doctors are expensive. I'll be okay."

But he tossed and turned and wheezed all night. In the morning, I called Erma and told her the situation. She and Larry came right over and took Ed to the nearest hospital emergency room. The hospital released him hours later and Ed came home looking worse than when he had left: pale and sickly and hardly able to stand up.

"The doctor says he has a bad cold," Erma explained. "He'll be better in a few days."

But a new day came and went and Ed was no better. In Vietnam, I would've burned incense and consulted a psychic to find out what was wrong—spirits often used the illness of living relatives to send messages—but in America, people only laughed when I explained this option. I told them that once, as a child, my father was so sick he could swallow nothing, including his own spit. The herbal healers failed to make him better and my mother went to the village psychic. The witch doctor faced the four points of the compass in turn, and reported that the spirit of an ancient Vietnamese prince had gone hunting near my father's paddy the day he got sick. One of the prince's ghostly arrows had gone astray and was lodged in my father's throat.

"The wound will never heal," the psychic said, "until the prince finds your father and claims his arrow."

So my mother and some relatives helped carry my father to the psychic's house, where he lay for three days. On the third day, he emerged—completely cured but for a dark mottling on his neck which he carried for the rest of his life.

I wondered now if I should take matters into my hands and help Ed in a similar way, but I knew no seers or mediums in America. With a terrible sense of foreboding and helplessness, I watched Ed's skin turn blue and his eyeballs bulge and their blood vessels break as he fought with increasing futility for every breath. I had always imagined that, in old age, good people died *em dem*—peacefully in their sleep—not gasping for air like a carp out of water. Finally, I could stand it no longer and called an ambulance. While they worked on Ed in the emergency room, I phoned Erma and told her to come down. When she arrived, she started to criticize me for ignoring the doctors' advice, then the nurse came in to tell us that the attending physician had been obliged to cut Ed's throat and insert a tube into his lungs in order to keep him alive. Erma shut up, and I did too.

Ed stayed at the hospital hooked to a life support machine, while Erma drove me home to look after the boys. Over the next few days, Erma or Larry Jr. would come to pick me up and drive me to the hospital for a visit. Because I didn't have a license, I was completely dependent on them and they weren't as anxious to have me around as I was to comfort Ed. So I spent most of my time trying to keep my mind on my lessons or cleaning and recleaning the house or planting new flowers, which had now become a cleansing ritual in my new life.

One afternoon, I received a call from Kathleen, Ed's sister, a registered nurse who had come down from Oregon. We had a good rapport and she became the source of much information I couldn't get from the family or hospital staff.

"I think you should come down, Le Ly," she said. "Tonight could be the night."

I gave the kids to a neighbor and called Larry Jr. whose turn it was to take me to the hospital. I arrived about five in the afternoon when the shadows were long on the clean-scrubbed floor. Poor Ed lay in his hospital bed like an old car torn up at the shop: tubes ran in and out of his mouth and arms and legs; sheets and wires were stuffed everywhere; his sunken eyes glowed dimly like headlights on a failing battery. Behind him, a breathing machine hissed like a restless demon, waiting to claim his soul.

I stared into the hopeless, helpless face and told him how much the boys missed him. I told him all the things we would do when he got out, but these were lies because he was never getting out, both of us knew. I could tell the thought of Dan still tortured Ed worse than the fluid that clogged his lungs. He was at the stage of dying we in Vietnam call *tran troi:* the time to lighten the soul. This is the phase of passing in which the soul is still too burdened to leave the body without some effort. The dying person can thus look forward to a lot of suffering until he or she makes peace with old enemies and yields untold secrets and says all the important things that would otherwise be left unsaid so that the soul can depart from life as naked as when it arrived.

All these things I knew very well from my country, having become very familiar with death, but I was unsure what effect the unholy American machines might have on such rituals. Obviously, part of Ed was already dead while part of him was still alive. I was preparing to put the customary red cloth over Ed's face to catch his spirit as it departed, when the nurse came in and, perhaps misinterpreting my gesture, said it was time to go. I went back to the waiting room where Erma and Kathleen and Kathy were trying to sleep and, all of a sudden, Kathleen opened her eyes and stood up and hugged me and I knew that Ed was gone. After a few minutes, a doctor came down the hall, woke the other women, and told us Ed had expired. Everyone began to sob. I did too, catching their grief like a cold, although my own prematurely aged spirit was far from sad. Unlike Ed's other women, I knew that his essence had merely gone back to the well of souls and was even now supping the bright light of eternity—the feast of unutterable joy that had been his due, but had seldom been his salary, in life. *Song goi thac ve*—Life is but a visit; death is going home. Although I knew I would have to get on with the business of living—which meant surviving—as soon as we left the hospital, I gave myself the luxury of pausing a moment to wonder if Ed's and my souls would be linked again—in some other form, on some other planet, in some other epoch—to try again to learn our lessons in love.

Ed's friends and relatives gathered at Erma's to mourn his passing. Larry Jr. and I were among the last to arrive and the living room got quiet as we came in.

"Here, honey," Erma said, handing me two pills. "Take these and go to bed. You must be out on your feet."

I was tired, but not exhausted, and certainly not too tired to ignore my duty to Ed. I wanted to set aside some food from the gathering to comfort his soul, to assure the survivors that I would worship Ed's spirit and maintain a place for it at my *tho chong,* our family shrine. It seemed, however, that role wasn't appreciated by Ed's "real" relatives. I took the pills but didn't swallow them. Instead, I lay down on the bed in Erma's guest room and listened to everyone file out, promising to meet again at Leatha's to resume the wake without having to deal with any of Ly's nonsense.

Nonetheless, I vowed to help Ed achieve *em dem* any way I could. This was entirely possible, even after death, because his troubled soul would hang around the earth until it was *sieu do,* enlightened enough to leave. I closed my eyes and cleared my mind. I imagined him floating in front of me in his shroudlike hospital gown, tubes and wires dangling from his arms like seaweed. I tried to let his spirit voice speak through this apparition, but it got tongue-tied and angry, just as he did in life. This was not the way to *em dem,* but it was a good way to begin the haunting of an unfaithful young wife!

I popped open my eyes. The afterimage lingered a second or two and sent chills down my spine. I went over to Leatha's and asked if someone could stay with me while I tried to go to sleep. Larry Jr. again drew the short straw. I hoped this would not become the pattern by which Ed's ghost worked out its grievances against me, though I deserved it all—and more.

Ed's funeral was in Washington State. He was laid out amid a wall of flowers next to his father. A third plot, I was told, was reserved for Leatha. I can think of no worse punishment for a mother than to see a son die before her eyes, so I began to view Mom Munro in a new light: a soul like mine whose karma must include much suffering from a prior life. She seemed to sense this burden—or at least a new awareness of it—by the way she treated me after the funeral, which was more like a child than ever. I kept avoiding the pills she and Erma tried to give me, since they muddled my mind and, although Ed's ghost continued to frighten me, I wanted to keep a clear head in case he decided to give me a message. More than anything, I wanted to get a Buddhist monk into the house to console the new spirit, but the chance of that, as Ed would say, was less than a snowball's in hell. Between my worrying, lack of sleep, and guilty conscience, I began to look a wreck.

Finally, during the long car ride back to San Diego, Kathleen asked me what was the matter.

"I make Ed die," I admitted in a small voice. "He save me and the boys and I thank him by making his last few years on earth miserable. He lose his job, he get sick, I fight with him about his cigarettes. I cheat on him with younger man. I do all these terrible things—"

"Now look here, little lady," Leatha said severely, "you did not kill Ed, no matter what you say. He was a grown man. He knew what he was doing. He had a good childhood—he lived a good life. He fought for his country with honor and had two beautiful sons with Millar, his first wife. You gave him a third and I know he was grateful for that. He adopted Jimmy and brought you to America because he wanted to—not because you made him. If you found comfort with another man—not that I condone it, mind you—it was because Ed was more a father than a husband to you. What woman can't understand that?"

I reached out my hand and Leatha took it. We both dabbed our eyes. Her kindness was genuine and undoubtedly lightened her soul. I accepted it gratefully, hoping against hope that the soul debt she shed would not be added to mine.

Perhaps that was Ed's ghost plan for revenge beyond the grave: to keep me tired and baffled and helpless until I went crazy. Anguished spirits are not famous for their compassion. Ed's ghost might be the distillation of all his bad karma. I would have to proceed very carefully with such an entity in my house—but I really had no choice.

The women continued to talk about my future as if I wasn't there. Kathleen thought I should get a job and begin dating immediately so as to find a new father for Jimmy and Tommy. Leatha didn't like the idea of my running around with other men while her son was still warm in his grave. But she did agree that three years, the traditional Vietnamese hiatus between marriages, was too long.

I didn't tell them, but their discussion reminded me of an old Vietnamese parable about a poor woman with so many children that, when her husband died, she sat by the grave fanning the moist dirt so it would dry more quickly and thus appear to potential suitors to be the requisite three years old. As fate would have it, a prince came riding by and asked what she was doing. She confessed and he was deeply touched by her honesty. When the prince got home, he feigned death in order to judge his wife's reaction. Instead of creating a noble fiction like the peasant woman, who had a need to remarry quickly, the wealthy wife began nailing shut the prince's coffin herself so that he couldn't return from the grave and frighten away her suitors. The prince's retainers, in on his little conspiracy, freed him immediately and he popped out proclaiming, *"Thuong thay cho ke quat mo, get thay cho ke cam do dong dinh!*—Love for the one who fans the grave, hate for the one who nails the coffin!" He divorced his fickle wife and remarried the woman who honored both her children and her nation's customs.

Nobody in the car asked about my own prince—Dan—and his pledge to come and claim me when his Vietnam tour was over. Perhaps they didn't put much stock in the promises of American soldiers. Of course, my own experience with such men hadn't fared any better. Only time would tell the character of my prince. In the meantime, I could only "fan Ed's grave" and try to get on with life.

Ed's son Ron and his wife, Kim, whom we had visited in Las Vegas, came down to see how I was doing. I told them I was fine, which was mostly true. My trouble with Ed's ghost was something they could do nothing about, so I never mentioned it. When their questions turned to Ed's will and the whereabouts of his other papers, things took a different turn.

"I've tried to get my father's files," Ron said, "but Erma won't let me have them. I want to see if he's left anything to our side of the family—and to make sure you get what's coming to you."

"Don't worry about me," I said. "I have two arms and two legs. The boys and I will get along fine. Ed did enough for me while he was alive. I will not ask more from his family."

"But you don't understand. If Dad wanted you to have something, you should have it. We should all respect his last wishes."

I was flattered that Ron might be concerned about us, but I could sense he was concerned for himself and his brother, too. The last thing I wanted was to get in the middle of a family squabble over Ed's estate.

"You know," I said, "everybody thinks I married Ed for his wealth, but we have very little money while we married. Mom Munro is making our house payments now, and I tell her I pay her back when I can. I owe her three months' payments already."

"That just goes to show you, Ly." Ron was very insistent. "You should hire a lawyer. As Dad's wife, it's your duty."

"Please—let your poor father rest!" I said. "The boys and I will get along fine without a lawyer. That is not the Vietnamese way."

"So—you'll get along on welfare and food stamps?" Ron knew that Leatha had, in fact, already suggested we sign up for "our benefits, our rights."

"Maybe. And I will get a job."

"You're dreaming." Ron laughed bitterly. "What skills do you have? What education? This isn't Vietnam. You can't support yourself by wheeling and dealing on some street corner. And do you know what housekeepers make? Not enough for one person to live on, let alone three."

Of course, Ron was right, and I was beginning to wonder if the same survival skills that had brought me this far would be able to take me further. Still, my ability to earn a living in America didn't change what was right. I never bothered Erma about Ed's papers. I never knew what was in his will.

That night, as the children fell asleep beside me and I was nodding off, Ed's ghost came back for its first visit in weeks. He was still dressed in his hospital gown, but at least the wires and tubes were gone. He held his arms out to embrace me.

"No! Go away!" I shouted and covered my head with my blanket. "Please—you're frightening me. Don't come any closer!"

He pointed a long, ghostly finger at his neck, as if something were caught in his throat.

"What is it?" I asked. "You choking again? Something caught? You have something to tell me?"

The sad old eyes lit up. He pointed to the boys, then again at his throat.

"I'm sorry," I said earnestly, "I really don't know what you want."

The spirit didn't get angry this time, but it evaporated, impatient. The next day, I told Mom Munro, since she seemed to understand me best, and in Vietnam a mother never rests while the spirit of a deceased son is still at large.

"It was all in your head, Ly," she said. "People in our situation often hallucinate."

"I swear to god, it is the truth!" I couldn't believe this otherwise spiritual old woman couldn't accept the facts.

"Well," she patted my knee, "let's just keep this between ourselves, okay? If word gets around that you're seeing ghosts, they might take the kids away from you, and who would be better for that? Besides, Ed never believed in that mumbo-jumbo. You said yourself he didn't want any fuss made over him after he's gone—the way you offer food and money to your father. It's time to be sensible and put all that stuff behind you."

Oddly enough, Leatha's advice gave me just the insight I needed. I agreed that it was past time to put all the nonsense behind me and simply to do what had to be done. As soon as I left her house, I put a framed picture of Ed up on my father's shrine, lit some incense, and offered him a bit of Top Ramen (Ed never liked rice, even the sweet white sacrificial kind) and a bit of spirit play money—the first offerings I had made since his funeral.

That night, we slept the profound sleep of three—or was it four? —untroubled souls at peace.

Although Ed's ghost was appeased, those early months on our own were very hard for me and my boys. Although five-year-old Jimmy and two-year-old Tommy had experienced many terrible things, they did not yet grasp the full meaning of death. They missed Ed terribly and asked constantly where he was. Once, I answered in English that he was "in heaven," which I did not pronounce properly, so they ran pell-mell to the kitchen to look for him in the oven.

Sunset was the loneliest time for all of us, so instead of sitting alone in an empty, haunted house, I took the boys for evening strolls around the neighborhood. Through the picture windows, we watched our neighbors' cheery lights snap on and saw them gathering for dinner. As the sun sank lower and the air turned chill, I held my boys close and sometimes cried. Like the setting sun, I could feel darkness at my heels. We walked until our legs gave out, then ran home as fast as we could and jumped into bed, huddling, taking in and giving each other warmth, until we fell asleep.

After a while, I got up the courage to ring the nearest doorbells and introduce ourselves. I said we were neighbors coming by for a visit, but we were usually greeted with odd looks and lame excuses— or booted out as salespeople, religious freaks, or panhandlers. Even on the warmest nights, I never felt so cold.

Once, we met a man in Bermuda shorts watering his lawn and struck up a conversation. I learned he was a Vietnam vet who had recently been stationed in Danang. Of course, my heart leapt and I asked him about the old neighborhoods and news from the front. I also asked if he could direct me to the nearest Buddhist temple so that I might engage one of the monks to help us settle the restless spirit of my departed husband. He gave me a queer look and disappeared inside. I thought he was putting on long pants for a proper visit, but when he never came back, I went up to the door and rang the bell. The young woman who answered said only, "My mother is gone and my father is sick." I figured that poor man had enough problems, so we did not disturb him again.

About this time, I began looking for work as a housekeeper, the only marketable skill I had. As in most American suburbs, though, Santee's public transportation was almost nonexistent. I soon realized I would have to learn to drive in order to get to work. I passed the written test with flying colors, but was stuck for a vehicle on which to practice for my driving examination. Fortunately, Erma had been over recently and asked if I would consider selling them Ed's pickup truck, which was too big for me to handle.

"Of course," I said. "I need the money for a smaller car."

"Well, we don't have the cash to pay you all at once. And if we took out a loan, we'd just end up making the bankers rich. Why don't we pay you a little each month for the next few years until the truck is ours?"

"But then I have no money to buy a little car!" I protested.

"Well," Erma wrinkled her nose, "think it over. At least it's better than nothing. Besides, it'll keep the truck in the family."

By now, Erma knew which of my buttons to press, so without thinking, I blurted out, "Okay, if it will keep it in the family."

Her husband Larry offered to drive the truck to a local dealership for an estimate and I said okay. After Larry explained what we wanted, the appraiser gave it the once-over and said, "If you were going to trade it in, I'd give you four thousand on the spot. But, if you want cash, the best I can do is twenty-six hundred."

Until Larry explained it on the drive home, I didn't understand why the dealer had quoted two prices. What difference did it make if we bought another car—wasn't it still the same truck? As a result, I was disappointed when Larry told Leatha afterward that we had agreed on $2,600 as a fair price. It seemed to me that if we had sold the truck to the dealer, I could've driven away in a nice little used sedan and maybe even put some money in my pocket. Of course, the truck wouldn't have "stayed in the family," so that plan was out. What I didn't realize was that Larry and Erma weren't just trying to get Ed's truck for good terms and a low price—they also didn't trust me with money. All they could see was me getting skinned by some salesman and losing both the truck and the cash I would need for my children, especially Tommy.

Fortunately, that situation, too, was improving.

Not only did Larry and Erma keep up their payments, but Ed's social security checks now started to arrive and I was able to take my family off food stamps and save a little bit besides. After six months, I was not only able to pay Mom Munro what I owed her for the mortgage, but purchase a used Chevy Vega on a note cosigned by a friend. It was a poor little car—lime green and a little rusty—compared to the other family vehicles, but it was beautiful to me. Jimmy, Tommy and I tooled around San Diego like the little kids we were, going to drive-in movies and parks and the big drive-through zoo up in Escondido or just hanging out at the shopping malls when there was no housekeeping to do.

My first real employment break came when I was hired to care for a twenty-two-year-old paraplegic named Don who had been injured in a traffic accident. I had seen plenty of broken young bodies in my time, almost all of them from war, but it seemed unusually cruel for fate or luck or god to rob a young man of his legs in such an unnecessary way. In any event, my first-aid training with the Viet Cong and hospital training with the U.S. Navy in Danang served me well. After a lengthy interview with his parents (who thought that a pretty girl would do as much to restore his health and spirits as a conscientious nurse) the job was mine.

The money was good—$2.50 an hour, the highest I'd ever made— so I quit school and worked for Don full time with as much overtime as I could get. Don was a very understanding employer and let me bring Tommy to work—and even Jimmy, in the summer, when school was out. After Don's morning bath and breakfast, we'd often spend the day at the park or at the beach. He became good friends with the boys and we talked for hours about this and that, steering clear of subjects that depressed him, like sports and cars, and focused on topics that made him happy, like music and nature. Looking back, the reward of seeing Don's soul bloom from the gnarled old root his body had become was better, in many ways, than any paycheck.

After three months, Don joked that if he ever recovered the use of his lower body, he would ask me to marry him. I told the story to his parents, thinking it would encourage them, but they only shook their heads. In addition to his paralysis, apparently, Don was terminally ill. Unlike me, the best future he could hope for was measured in months.

I couldn't take another death so soon after Ed's, so—despite the good pay and friendship—I gave them my notice and went back to work as a maid. It was just as well.

At the end of the summer, 1973, I received a letter from Dan. Major Daddy was finally rotating stateside. In a few weeks, he would be coming to San Diego.

Dan's flight arrived at three on an August morning, but that didn't matter. I had been unable to sleep for days. I arrived at the airport early, which proved a wise precaution. I couldn't figure out how to raise the pole that guarded the parking lot (I didn't know you had to take a ticket) so, assuming the airport was closed, I drove around in tears. A policeman finally stopped me and, after seeing that I could walk a straight line and touch my fingers to the tip of my nose, escorted me to the proper terminal.

Dan deplaned looking rumpled and tired but he was to me the most beautiful sight in California. We returned to the house (the boys were spending the night with neighbors, so we had the place to ourselves) and tumbled into bed, doing what long-lost lovers do best. His kisses were like water on desert sand: I drank them in and begged for more. The memory of his embrace had been the only force that had kept my little world together. I showed him, as much as I knew how, the whole universe of love. When we finally slept, it was—for our first time together—without the fear of bombs and bullets.

In the morning, I proudly took Dan on a tour of my little domain: our well-scrubbed house, new-used car, and yard filled with vegetables, flowers, and herbs (looking more like my mother's Ky La garden than a typical suburban backyard). Dan already knew about Ed's death and the full- and part-time jobs I had taken to augment our social security. He praised me for what I had accomplished. For the three days he was with us, he made us feel like a family again: people with a future as well as a past. Then, the morning of his departure, the bombshell finally hit.

"You know, I still have to divorce my wife before we can be together," Dan said solemnly, though not as solemnly as I heard his words.

"Didn't you write to her?" I asked. "Didn't you tell her about us?"

"I didn't have the heart. Remember—I haven't seen her for over two years. I thought it would be better to tell her in person. These things take time, Ly. They're never easy. It can cost a lot—not just money, but my reputation. If I have some time, I can minimize the problems. In the meantime, I want you to quit those terrible jobs and spend your time in school. I want you to improve your English and become an American citizen. Vietnam is finished, you know that. The Communists will take over soon and you'll never be able to go back. This will be your new home—our new home. I want you to make the most of it."

He boarded his plane, promising to come back as soon as his divorce was settled. Although my experience with such promises was poor, Dan was the love of my life. I set my natural worry aside and did as I was told.

Jimmy had now turned seven and clamored to join the Cub Scouts like the other boys in his class. I was not pleased to see these little men march around in their uniforms, but what they studied in their "dens" was similar to what village boys learned in Vietnam—how to make things with their hands and to respect Mother Earth—and the friends he brought home from school were clean and respectful. I went along with the program. Although he had forgotten most of his English while we lived in Vietnam, he was now reading and doing arithmetic with the smartest kids in his class. In this, and in the way he took care of his little brother, I saw much of my brother Sau Ban.

Although the older child looking after the younger is common in Vietnam, it was apparently not the custom in the United States. Because Jimmy was so responsible, I felt no qualms about leaving him in charge of Tommy while I ran to the store for groceries. Once, however, I returned to find a police officer getting out of his car in our driveway.

"What is wrong, officer?" I asked, alarmed, although I could see my boys playing peacefully in the middle of our yard.

"We had a call from a woman complaining of child abuse at this address." He slid his baton into a ring on his belt with a menacing hiss.

"I—I don't understand." I stood taller and watched my accent and tried to look and sound very American.

"The lady making the complaint said you leave your children home alone—unsupervised all day. Is that correct?"

"Heavens no! I just go to get milk and chicken for dinner!" I opened the top of the shopping bag. "Here, take a look. You want to stay and have supper with us?"

The policeman glanced at the house, saw that the kids were all right—obviously well dressed, clean, and well fed—and shook his head.

"No, thank you. We seem to have been misinformed." He got into his squad car and left.

I watched him drive away, then gave the evil eye to the neighborhood. I knew the lady next door had a teenage daughter. Maybe she was angry at me for not hiring her to baby-sit—but I just did not have the money to pay for "protection" on these brief trips to the store. For people who were so hesitant to open their front doors in friendship, they sure seemed anxious to keep an eye on me from the back!

I did use baby-sitters, of course, mostly when I went to the local community college, where I was spending a lot more time. There, I began to meet the first few of what would eventually become a tidal wave of Vietnamese streaming into the country. A couple of these new acquaintances invited me to go dancing, to discover the San Diego "singles scene."

"Come on, Ly," one pretty, wealthy girl named Huong told me after class. "You act like an old maid! Don't let those two kids slow you down. Boogie while you're young. That's what life is all about!"

Well, I didn't know about that, but I agreed that my life for years had been one long cycle of taking care of other people: of men, little kids, old ladies, cripples, and wealthy homeowners. Like most of my new Vietnamese friends, Huong was married with a husband who supported her and had only one child to mother. She had little to do with her time but play cards, take classes, and keep herself looking pretty. Still, I thought American rock music was too loud, and the crazy, jerky dances reminded me of Danang bars, places I'd just as soon forget. Besides, I was still pining for Dan, to whom I considered myself engaged.

"Ly, you're such an idiot!" my girlfriend exclaimed whenever I mentioned his name. "Wait for a soldier and you'll wait forever. Even if he gets a divorce, what makes you think he'll come back for you? How can you compete with all the other girls in America? Remember, when a man gets divorced, especially after an unhappy marriage, it's like getting out of jail. Do you think he's going to rush to put himself back in handcuffs?"

Although I knew Dan and I had something special, I had to consider the facts. Our love was intense, but so was the war going on around us when we met. I was also well aware that people said and did lots of things in a combat zone they often regretted later. Besides, who was I in America—or even in Vietnam—but an ignorant farm girl and widow with two sons? And didn't Dan himself suggest that I go back to school? Was that a hint that I might not be good enough for him anymore? I remembered how Ed ogled the brassy American "chicks" at the shopping malls and concluded that, in his right mind, no handsome young American would settle for a puny, dark-haired, dark-skinned "foreign imitation" of the real American thing.

So I went dancing. At first, my experiments at socializing "the American way" failed miserably. In San Diego, most of the men at the clubs we visited were sailors, so it was just like the bars in Vietnam, except here I had to pay a cover charge and buy drinks (always Coke or Seven-Up—I still couldn't stomach alcohol because of my ulcer) instead of sell them. Some men were obnoxious and some were polite. One named Floyd—whom I saw several Saturdays in a row—even called Erma to say he wanted to marry me. He knew Vietnamese customs were different, so he went to what he thought was the closest thing I had to a U.S. mother. Unfortunately, although Floyd was nice, I had no desire to marry him, even if Dan hadn't been in the picture. Erma's enthusiasm for his proposal, however, tipped her hand, which was to get me remarried and out of her hair as soon as possible.

"But he's such a nice man, Ly," she said over the coffee she and Leatha had especially arranged for me to share. "I really don't see why you're waiting."

"I'm waiting for the man I love!" I replied, incredulous that she would even ask after the debacle with Ed. Floyd was no grandfather, but he was in his midforties—closer to Ed's generation than to mine.

"Ly, you're such a dreamer!" She clucked like a mother hen. "Listen to me: the Major was just another American who got lonely in a foreign land and decided to take up with a local ding-a-ling. Now that the war's over—for him at least—he doesn't need you. He dumped you, Ly! Wake up and smell the coffee! He's not coming back!"

Of course, the same thing had occurred to me, but thinking it and saying it were two different things.

"Besides," Leatha added, patting my knee, "you're running around too much. This new crowd you're with—it's not a good thing. They're not good people. You need to find a man and settle down. Think of Ed's son. Think of your boys."

I wanted to remain polite but I saw no reason to meekly accept what they said. If being an American meant taking responsibility for yourself, it also meant you could let other people know it.

"Okay, I think of the boys. I think of them every day. I think of them more than you do, okay? I am their mother. I wait for Dan, but I see other men too. *I* choose who I marry."

They murmured their agreement and saw me to my car believing they had won some kind of victory; and maybe they had. Dan hadn't written in a long time and although he had promised to return one day, that day seemed as far away as ever.

Although I found more work as a housekeeper, I decided that neither my scholastic nor my social life should suffer. This put pressure on the boys, who saw their mother less and less, so I began to feel guilty. December rolled around and I tried to make it up to them by celebrating a kind of Super Christmas—Christmas and Tet rolled into one—buying presents and sacrificing, feasting and fasting, partying and praying. Tommy was still too little to make sense of any of this, and Jimmy tried valiantly to explain his crazy home life to his normal American classmates. However, we had love and we had each other and that made up for a lot.

Two weeks before Christmas, 1973, another Vietnamese friend named Linda took six of her girlfriends, including me, to a country and western bar to celebrate her birthday. I had always enjoyed American country music because its nasal twang reminded me of Oriental tunes and the crowds at "cowboy bars" were usually friendly. Midway through the evening, a handsome, gray-haired man —a little younger than Dan and not so thin—came in alone and Linda tapped me on the shoulder.

"There he is, Ly," she pointed him out. "There's the man for you!"

"He is very good-looking," I agreed, but I had seen handsome men before and they all started to look like Dan before the evening was over. "It's your birthday, Linda. You go dance with him."

Linda went to the bar and before long they had struck up a conversation. Good, I thought, now she'll have a good time and forget about matchmaking for old maid Ly!

The newcomer came over with Linda. "Hello, Ly" he said pleasantly, having been told my name and god knows what else! "My name is Dennis—Dennis Hayslip. Your friend says you've been looking for the right dance partner all night. Do I qualify?"

My girlfriends laughed and I smiled lamely and gave Linda a dirty look.

"Nice to meet you, Dennis, but I don't dance," I said.

"Oh, come on," he insisted, "there's nothing to it. Even cowboys can dance!"

He was very persuasive and very cute—like a cuddly, protective teddy bear. The hand that lifted me from the chair was very strong.

A moment later we were slow dancing and trying to make ourselves understood over the music.

"Where are you from?" I asked, knowing that nobody is born in California. They all come from somewhere else.

"I just got in from Cleveland." He smiled a dazzling smile. "Ohio, you know. A good state to be from!" He wasn't Dan, or even a close imitation, but something completely different.

"So," I said, "you going to live here? Or just visit?"

"This is my new home," he said with conviction. "But I've got no friends or family. I know good girls like you are careful about giving away your number, so here's mine." He borrowed a waitress's pen and jotted down his number on a matchbook. "Call me when you can. I'd like you to show me the city."

"Well, I don't know. I have two little boys—"

"That's okay. I love kids—really. I hope I can meet them." The music stopped and everyone clapped and shuffled back to their tables. He held my hand longer than was proper but let me go just before I could object. He pulled out my chair like a gentleman. "I hope you'll call soon. I'd really like to see you again."

Dennis left and my girlfriends crowded around to hear what he was like: did he smell good or have bad breath and what did he do for a living and was I going to see him again?

"No, I don't think so. I really want to wait for Dan," I told them. Everybody booed and Linda took the matchbook and stuffed it deep inside my purse so I couldn't "accidentally" forget it.

The next morning, Huong called to say she was giving her own birthday party for Linda on Sunday at her house. She said it would be the perfect opportunity to get to know Dennis better—and expose him to the kids—without risking "a regular date."

I hemmed and hawed, but soon realized I had no reason to say no and every reason to say yes—if for no other purpose than to get these amateur *mai dong* off my back.

I called Dennis that afternoon and he accepted my invitation. He picked us up at a local supermarket (after the Floyd incident, I was much more careful about showing new men where I lived) and we spent the afternoon like an old married couple: him attending to me and the boys without making a big fuss; me being considerate of him without all the silly first-date jitters. The boys enjoyed his company and I admit I liked having a handsome man around again—treating me like someone special.

After the party, everyone went out of their way to tell me how well they thought Dennis and I looked together, like furniture in a new house, and pointedly asked when I was going to see him again.

"This is the man for you," Linda said, repeating the password of the day. "Don't let him off the hook."

"I don't know about that," I tried hard now to separate the man from the aura he brought to my life. The two were not the same. "He's very nice but my heart still belongs to Dan."

"Oh god!" Huong exclaimed. "Dan again! *Lam me say*—When are you going to let that loser go?"

"Duong dai ngua chay biet tam, nguoi thuong co nghia tram nam cung ve," I answered. "On a long road, even good horses will run away, but a faithful lover will come back if it takes a hundred years."

Everybody groaned.

The next Saturday, I met Dennis downtown and we took my car to go sightseeing. We returned late at night so, instead of driving all the way back across town to get his car, which would have exhausted the kids, I gave him some blankets and invited him to use our extra bedroom for the night.

"I really appreciate that," Dennis said. He made no pass at me or made me feel uneasy at all, "I had a wonderful time. Your boys are really great. That's because they have a great mother!"

The next morning I got Jimmy off to school and Dennis and I talked for hours over coffee. His family had immigrated to the United States from England—just like the Munros. He said that when he was six years old, his father had died in an auto accident and, unaccountably, a chill ran down my spine. Despite the burden of five kids—Dennis, his two brothers, and two sisters—his mother never remarried but supported them on her own as a waitress in a roadside restaurant. He also said he came from a very religious family, which was refreshing to hear in a country where holidays meant mostly food, football, and fooling around. He used to be a deputy sheriff in Ohio, which made me feel safer, too. I asked why he had come to San Diego.

"I just got divorced," he said, making an unpleasant face. "My ex-wife and I fought over our boy. He's ten—a good kid. You know, he reminds me a lot of Jimmy. Anyway, she got custody and I just couldn't take it, so I came to California to start a new life. I'm studying computers. They say Southern California is where it's all going to happen, so here I am. And here you are, too."

He took my hand—the shy handclasp of a village suitor. After our chat, I did the dishes and drove him back to his car.

Dropping him off, I said, "My sister-in-law has invited the boys and me over for Christmas dinner. Would you like to come?"

Dennis brightened at once—the talk about his divorce, unsuccessful job search, and the upcoming holidays kind of depressed him—and he accepted. Naturally, he was a big hit with the Munros, bringing small gifts for everyone, loads of toys for the boys, and impressing Erma and Leatha with his good looks and good manners.

"Ohhh, I approve of him!" Erma beamed, as if she'd been asked.

"He's so good with the children," Leatha chimed in, completing my suitor's résumé. "Don't let this one get away!"

After Christmas, Dennis spent a lot of time at the house. He had no local relatives and I felt sorry for him being alone. Also, having him around kept my own friends quiet about my love life, which was worth any inconvenience—not that Dennis was a burden. He pitched in with chores and baby-sat the boys while I went to work and school or did things with my girlfriends. Besides, Tommy and Jimmy needed a father figure and benefited as much from Dennis's attention as he benefited from having surrogate sons to raise. He even encouraged them to call him Daddy, which surprised me and delighted them. From every perspective, it was a perfect friendship—but not a romance.

One day after a picnic with the kids at Balboa Park, he took my hand and said, "Ly, things are really looking up for me. I love you and the children very much. I'm very close to getting a good job downtown. I will soon be able to support you and give you and the boys everything you deserve. Will you marry me?"

I had been half expecting his proposal for weeks, but had yet to come up with a gentle way of rejecting it—without rejecting him.

"Well, I'm happy and surprised you think so much of me. But I don't know you that well yet. And there's a lot you don't know about me. Like I tell you before, I'm in love with someone else. I like you a lot, Dennis—really, I do—but I don't think we can marry."

"You're still thinking about that army guy?" Dennis lost his dreamy smile and leaned back. I suspected there had been some conversations about Dan behind my back.

"Yes," I admitted, feeling a little silly. I knew what he was going to say about army boyfriends before he said it. "He's getting a divorce from his wife."

"I see. And he calls you all the time, does he? Writes letters every day? Helps you and the boys with money?"

In truth, my beloved hadn't phoned since well before Christmas and his letters were even less frequent.

"He thinks about me. He cares about me. He doesn't have much money. Like I say, he's going through a divorce."

"I see. So this man who never writes or calls and sends nothing to help the kids and who may or may not be getting a divorce still keeps you dangling on a string—keeps you from getting on with your life, is that about it?"

"Dan loves me," I said, feeling my eyes get wet. "He will come back."

"Right. I bet you believe in Santa Claus, too! I can't believe you'd listen to a man who's already proved he can't be trusted! After all, didn't he cheat on his wife when he took up with you?"

His words struck me like a hail of bullets. Dan was no saint, but he was guilty of nothing I hadn't done myself. Dennis seemed to know a lot about anger, but as a student of love he was even worse than me. As his accusations against Dan piled up, I began to notice something more than jealousy in his voice. He spoke with a terrifying *righteousness*—all blood and thunder. I had known many kinds of religious men in my life, dangerous as well as the compassionate, and his words began to make me nervous.

"You can't trust these army guys, Ly, you just can't trust them. Any of them." He finally paused for breath. "I should know. I was one of them."

"You were in Vietnam?"

"No, Korea. But believe me, we played the same games with the poor Korean girls. They meant nothing to us. We used them and just walked away. Nobody pays any attention to promises made in a war zone. Only suckers believe in Santa Claus!"

For some reason, I thought of poor Judy in her ratty trailer up in Orem, Utah. Maybe by standing fast and refusing to let her man go, she thought her own Santa Claus would come home. Maybe she was right.

I told Dennis I would need time to think. I got up and walked around the meadow while he cooled off and watched the kids. I found I couldn't argue with anything he or Erma or Leatha or Linda or anyone had said about fickle American soldiers and their merciless affairs with Asian women. But neither could I deny what I felt in my heart. I came back determined to play out my hand.

"I know what you say about army men"—I sniffed back my tears—"but I have to let go and let fate or luck or god do whatever it's going to do. I love Dan, but you are my best friend. The boys and I love to spend time with you. I don't want you out of my life, even though I can't marry you. If you can't live with that, then I understand, and it would be better for you to just go. Better for me, better for you, better for the boys."

To my mild surprise, Dennis only shrugged. He was clearly unhappy, but I could tell he would be nearly as persistent as I was in getting what his heart desired.

"Well," he said, slapping his thighs, "one way you could help me stay in your life is to let me borrow your guest room until my job comes through. My rent is paid through the middle of January, but after that I'll have to move on. I'm willing to help out, of course—keep the place up and baby-sit. That is, if you'll have me."

"Of course you can stay." I felt so relieved that we weren't going to talk about marriage anymore that I would have granted him anything. I gave him a big smile and wiped away my tears. "You're a good man, Dennis. Good things are going to happen for you. I'll do what I can to help."

Dennis moved in on the fifteenth and I have to admit, it was good to have him there. I felt safer at night and, because we didn't sleep together, I didn't even have to fear the return of Ed's ghost.

One morning, though, the mailman delivered a crisis.

"It's from Dan," Dennis said, holding the envelope up like a dead rat after bringing in the mail. He tried to sound chipper, but I could see the tension growing in his face. I was excited, of course, but wanted to keep things low key. I turned my back and ripped open the envelope—food for a starving woman! The letter was short and sweet, and I read it quickly. I knew Dennis was concerned about what it said, so I invited him to sit with me at the table so we could discuss it.

"So—Major Wonderful is coming to visit?" He grinned but his eyes were angry. "Isn't that great?"

"I think so, yes," I said. "I kind of hoped you would be happy for me."

"Look, I'm not your brother, Ly!" Dennis said bitterly. He got up and started pacing around the kitchen. "And I'm not just some kind of handyman or baby-sitter—" He was getting very frustrated and could hardly talk. "I—I don't want him here. I don't want him in the house!"

You don't want him in the house? Whose house do you think this is?

I forced a smile. Two of us in the same condition—excited, disappointed, angry—would not make things better. "I'm sorry you feel that way. I have been waiting for Dan to come and see me for long time—"

"Well, you'll just have to wait some more! Believe me, Ly—there'll be trouble if he comes. *Big* trouble."

"What do you mean?"

"I mean I *love* you Ly! I love the boys. I don't want him coming between us!"

"But I love Dan. You know that. I tell you up front. That's no secret. Now what you talking about—there's going to be trouble? I don't understand!"

"I just mean there's going to be trouble if he comes around here." Dennis stalked the floor now like a caged tiger, wringing his hands, rubbing the back of his neck. I had seen the symptoms a hundred times in GI bars: just before punches were thrown. "Just call him and tell him not to come and everything will be fine."

Once again, things were getting sticky and dangerous and out of control all because of *love*—that terrible four-letter word! It defied all understanding!

My first priority was to get Dennis to calm down, so I said I would think everything over and let's get on with our day. That night, I called Linda—not just because she was the most levelheaded of my girlfriends but because, as a former bar-girl herself, she was likely to understand my dilemma. Besides, I felt she was partly responsible for injecting Dennis into my life. If a team effort got him in the door, a team effort could boot him out the window.

"So what's the problem?" Linda asked after hearing me out. "You've got two guys crazy for you—every girl should be so lucky!"

"This is no joke. Dennis is really acting strange. I think he could really make trouble."

"What do you mean—take a swing at Dan? Try to hit you? Do something to the boys?"

"I don't know. Maybe none of that. Maybe all of it. I just don't want to take a chance."

"Then forget about Dan, okay? He's just coming back for a roll in the hay."

"That's not true. He says we're going to talk about the future!"

"Oh sure. Then where was he during the holidays—with his wife and children, right? At least Dennis is *here,* Ly. He loves you and wants to take care of you and the boys. And he's a hunk—so what more do you want?"

I decided that what I wanted most was peace of mind—no trouble from anybody over love or divorce or violence or war or anything. I didn't want Dennis to think he had bullied me into getting his way, so I called Dan the next afternoon while Dennis was on an errand. I almost melted when I heard his voice on the line, but I steeled myself for what I had to do.

After some pleasant chitchat—as if he had never been gone and had written all the time and had lived up to all of his promises—I said, "Look, Dan, I have a big problem. A man—a good friend—has fallen in love with me. He's in the house—no, it's not like that. He just a good, good friend to me and Tommy and Jimmy. But he goes crazy when I tell him about you. I honestly think he will hurt somebody if you show up."

Dan asked a little more about "this guy" and how we really felt about each other and exactly whom he had threatened to hurt. After a while, he simply sighed and said, "Do what you want, Ly. It's your life. But this Dennis character doesn't own you either. If you want, I can come up and have it out with him, but I don't think that would change things."

"What do you mean? What about your divorce?"

"I told you, it's just not that easy. It's not like selling a car or a house you don't want. It involves the courts and money and people's feelings. I've also got to think about my career—command and staff college and making colonel and all of that. It's going to take some time. If you can't deal with that, I understand. Your first job is to take care of yourself and the boys. If you don't want me to come, I won't. It's that simple."

We were both quiet for a while, then I said, "Okay. Well, it probably best, then, if you don't come. At least until after I get Dennis to leave. He's a good man, but I don't want him to go crazy over this. I don't want anything to happen to you. If I lose you, then I have nobody, right? Then we do everything for nothing, right?"

Dan didn't answer. Eventually he said, "Ly, my other line is buzzing, I've got to go. Keep in touch, okay? I still want to know how you're doing."

"Okay. I love you," I felt cast off and lost at sea.

"Okay, me too," Dan said and hung up.

The next day, Mom Munro and Erma came over unannounced. Perhaps my secret network of supporters had gone to work, instigated by my call to Linda. Perhaps they had something else on their mind.

They strolled in, looking distastefully at the signs of male occupation—big tennis shoes by the door, shaving kit in the bathroom, beer and hard liquor in the kitchen (I didn't drink at all and Ed had drunk very little, but Dennis made up for us both). I offered to make tea but they said they couldn't stay long. Erma glared at my little Buddhist shrine in the corner.

"I'm not sure I approve of your putting Ed's picture up by that heathen altar," she sniffed. "Oh, I understand your people's belief in such things. You're free to worship as you wish. It's just that—well, Ed was a Catholic. We're all good Catholics. There's just something wrong about burning incense in front of a Catholic man's picture. In fact, that's why we're here. We'd like to have all of Ed's—our family's—pictures back, if it's not too much trouble."

"You want his pictures back?" I was shocked. It felt like Christmas in reverse—very odd for such good Christian ladies.

"Yes. We feel we've intruded into your new life more than we should. You have a man in your house now and you certainly don't need us—the family—getting in your way anymore."

"Mom Munro"—I felt my throat tighten—"you want Ed's pictures too?"

She sniffed into a hankie. "I think it's for the best, dear. After all, you have Dennis—a new family—to look after you now."

"Yes, Dennis is responsible for you now." Erma forced a smile. "Of course, we still care about you and the boys. I've thought about taking the money we're paying you on the truck and putting it into a trust account for Tommy. That way we can be assured Ed's son will have the things he needs—money for an education—when he gets older. But we haven't decided anything. Jimmy, of course, will still be your responsibility."

Dazed, I collected as many of Ed's things I could find—including Jimmy's favorite tape recorder—and stuffed them in a box. I couldn't believe they still didn't trust me with my own money and possessions —even old photos. "Here you go, Erma." I tried with all my might to keep compassion, not bitterness, in my voice. "I truly hope this makes you happy."

They headed for the door. "Of course, you don't need to call us anymore if you have problems. I'm sure you and Dennis can work everything out between you from now on. Goodbye, Tommy." Erma blew a kiss and waved. "We'll see you again soon. Goodbye, Ly. Good luck with your new life!"

Chong chech ra nguoi dung, I thought: In Vietnam, "The daughter-in-law is a stranger on her husband's death!" It appeared to be a universal custom.

Mom Munro didn't say anything, but gave me a big hug and patted her eyes with a hankie before following her daughter to the car. As things turned out, Larry's truck checks would keep coming, and Erma called later to apologize if she hurt my feelings. She thought I would like to know that Ed's pictures had made Leatha very happy. All things considered, it was probably a very good trade.

That night, I told Dennis everything that had happened: about my call to Dan, Dan's canceled trip, and how Erma and Leatha had come by to reclaim Ed's possessions a whole year after his death. Dennis poured himself a scotch and smirked.

"See? I told you that army jackoff wasn't man enough to fight! I guess you can see now who really loves you and who is full of shit!" Dennis had never sworn before—at least in the house in front of the kids. If this was how he acted "in victory," I would hate to see him get really mad. Nonetheless, I had something more to say. Perhaps his good news about Dan would help him take the bad news a little better.

"I guess you're right." I swallowed hard. "Anyway, I was wondering today how your search for a job was going? I hope you get good news soon. You must hate to put up with all my silly things and have to baby-sit little kids all the time. Do you think you will be able to get a new place pretty soon?"

Dennis looked at me blankly. "You haven't heard a word I've been telling you, have you, Ly? I love you! I want to live with you! God *damn* it!" He slammed the table, picked up his bottle, and went to his room.

Immediately, I began to feel sorry—to think I had been too blunt and hurt his feelings. After all, Dennis wasn't responsible for Dan or my troubles with Ed's women or even the employers who seemed to like everyone but him. His only crime was trying too hard and loving me too much. I was condemning him for that?

I rushed down the hall and tapped on his door. I could hear him talking to himself inside the room, plus a little *click-clack* like he was opening and shutting drawers or latching a suitcase. Maybe he thought I was kicking him out right now—which I wasn't. I couldn't believe how cruel I had been!

I knocked again, louder, and cracked the door. "Dennis?"

His suitcases were still in the closet. All the drawers were shut. He sat on the edge of his bed, whiskey glass on the nightstand, twirling the cylinder of a shiny revolver.

FOUR

The Day Heaven Fell

GUNS AND MEN!

I slammed the door on Dennis, grabbed Jimmy, and ran into Tommy's room. I pushed the lock button and wondered what to do next.

It didn't occur to me to call the police because, in Vietnam, domestic problems were nobody else's business and violent husbands were part of almost every marriage. Also, not being an American citizen, I couldn't imagine the police taking the word of a pitiful immigrant over a red-white-and-blue, gun-loving American, particularly one who used to be a policeman himself. I didn't even think to call a friend because it was very late and I was afraid of being impolite. I didn't even know Dennis liked to drink so much until he brought liquor into the house, like a security blanket. I didn't even know he had a gun until that moment.

Although the kids didn't know what was happening, we had spent enough time huddled together in the middle of the night for them to realize something was wrong. The anxious seconds turned to minutes and minutes into hours. I know I dozed off because all of a sudden the black outside was light.

I shook Jimmy awake and told him to get ready for school. I crept into the hall. Dennis's door was open. His belongings were in place but his bed had not been slept in. On his pillow I found a hand-scrawled note. It repeated all his arguments about Dan and how unfair I was and how unfair life had been and how he had decided finally to do something that would make everybody happy because they would never have to deal with him again. I looked out the kitchen window and saw his car was gone.

I flew to the phone. I called Linda and Huong and even Erma to see if they had heard from Dennis.

"See what you caused?" Linda said. "He was so nice to you and the boys and look how you repaid him!"

"You should just be thankful he loves you so much," Huong said. "Pray you haven't killed him!"

"I don't know how you do it, Ly," Erma said. "I suggest you call the police and let them handle it."

No matter whom I called, they seemed more anxious to blame me for what might be happening than to help me try to prevent it.

I dropped Jimmy at school and with Tommy squawking in the back, drove around looking for Dennis. I went first to all the places I thought might appeal to him as suicide spots: the local bridges, parks, the cowboy bar where we met—places that had meaning for us both. Then I stopped at the local police station (I could always communicate with Americans better in person than over the phone) and told them the situation. The desk sergeant was sympathetic but said they couldn't do anything unless a crime had been committed. Had Dennis threatened me with the gun? No. Did Dennis's note actually say he was committing suicide? No, just that he would "do something" to make us feel sorry for the way we treated him. The sergeant said that could mean anything, including just dropping out of sight for a while to make us worry.

Tommy and I drove around for the rest of the day. When school was out, I picked up Jimmy and drove around some more. After a while, I gave up searching and just thought about how much trouble my love for Dan was causing so many innocent people. How could something so good lead to so many bad things?

We returned late that night to find Dennis's car in the driveway. The man of the hour was passed out face down on the lawn in the back. I smelled the alcohol from a dozen feet away so I decided to let him sleep it off. I put the kids to bed and made a quick search of Dennis's room and his car to impound the handgun, but with no luck. I only hoped it wasn't tucked into his pants and ready to go off —like the other dangerous weapon men seemed so anxious to use on the women who displeased them!

Later that evening while I was reading in the living room, Dennis came in. He looked contrite, like a spanked puppy, so I swallowed the angry remark I wanted to make. Instead, I asked if he was feeling better and he smiled and said yes. He apologized for "going a little crazy" and said the thought of losing me was too much for him to take. I wanted to tell him that in order to lose my love, he must possess it first. I never considered us anything but good friends, regardless of his secret desires. However, I thought it would be wiser to let things cool off. We could resume our discussion about him getting a job and moving out later. Unfortunately, that discussion never took place.

In October 1974, Dennis received a job offer from the City of San Diego based on a referral from Huong's husband. Dennis was thrilled, of course, and the good news launched a weeklong celebration. He treated me and the boys and our friends to a night on the town, gifts, and—best of all—a happy face. Although he still drank socially, he cut way back and he busied himself preparing for his new job. He was like a new man and I just couldn't spoil things by kicking him out, especially when the reason for doing so seemed so distant—like another bad dream. This only gave my girlfriends more ammunition in their campaign to make Dennis and me into a couple.

"See what you nearly lost?" Linda pointed out one day over lunch. Like everyone else, she was treating Dennis's "recovery" from depression as if he were a returning POW. "All he needed was a little support until his luck turned around."

What Linda and Huong overlooked was the fact that I still didn't love him. Even if I was forced by circumstances to put Dan out of my life, at least for the time being, I had no power to get Major Daddy out of my mind. As it had been with Ed, a sexual relationship with Dennis—in or out of marriage—just seemed sacrilegious.

So life went on. The TV and newspapers were full of Watergate. I never paid much attention to it—South Vietnamese politics was so full of scandal and corruption that I just couldn't see what the shouting was about. Nearly all of the U.S. forces were withdrawn from

Vietnam. The U.S. draft ended in 1973, and with it the civil distur-
bances that seemed to annoy Americans as much as the war itself.
The Paris Treaty went into full effect and Washington "declared
peace." The next year, of course, President Nixon resigned and his
replacement, President Ford, proposed amnesty for America's Vietnam War deserters and draft evaders. Although Dennis thought it
was a terrible idea, I secretly applauded it and said a prayer for this
enlightened new U.S. president. Only by ending the war in people's
hearts, as well as on the battlefield, could it ever be truly over.

So it was that with my old and my new worlds one step closer to
the peace and tranquility I longed for, I accepted Dennis into my bed.
I did this partly out of loneliness, to see if I could put the memory of
Dan behind me for good. But mostly I did it to remove the thick
blanket of sexual tension that had begun to envelop my little home.
As long as he thought himself a failure, Dennis had no trouble
respecting the rules I had set. Now, with a paycheck of his own, he
began to feel like "the man of the house," with all the rights and
privileges he thought should go with that role.

Although sex with Dennis was easier than with Ed, it was for me
still duty, not love—or even pleasure. I knew that sleeping with
Dennis—crossing that important threshold—was not the smartest
thing to do, but it seemed the least of several evils. I could send
Dennis packing, but after accepting him this long, the risk of another
outburst of drinking and violence just seemed too great. I was also
reluctant to rob the boys of the father figure they needed so badly—
he really did love the kids. In any event, Dennis's contribution to our
household expenses allowed me to save a small amount of my housekeeping money as an emergency fund. I made up my mind that I
would never again be caught in a crisis without enough cash to bail
myself out.

Unfortunately, such a crisis already loomed on our horizon, and no
amount of money was going to make it go away.

In the spring of 1975, television began to show the tortured
breakup of my native land: burning cities, refugee buses fishtailing
along dirt roads, interviews with somber South Vietnamese and
American officials who tried to put a positive face on the Republican
collapse. Part of me wanted to believe their lies were true—not because a continuation of the war would be good for Vietnam, but
because it was at least a situation my family had learned to cope with.

But when I saw the Soviet-made North Vietnamese tanks roll by China Beach, once a stronghold of the American presence, and the ragged, malnourished Viet Cong prisoners released after years of confinement by the South—I knew the war was all but over. With one side finally ascendant in what had been a struggle of inhuman proportions, I couldn't believe that the victors would offer the losers anything but hell.

"I bet I know some of those people," I said, commenting on the crowds of farmers, kids, and old people who had gathered along the roads south of Danang to cheer (or just sullenly watch) the advancing Northern armor. "I wish the camera didn't go so fast."

Dennis answered like a good American. "If the Commies take over Danang, your friends won't be around for long. Remember the massacres in Hue after the sixty-eight Tet offensive? Even if the Commies don't kill them, we should nuke the whole goddamn country. Better dead than red!"

I realized Dennis's blood was up, so I didn't remind him that my mother and sisters would be among those charred skeletons grinning from the rubble. He didn't realize that the Viet Cong were often merciful to Central Coast villagers—their own kinsmen, many of them secretly favoring the North, although nobody knew what Hanoi's regulars would do. *Dinh chien, dinh chien,* I chanted under my breath, like the mothers in the newsreel—"The war is over, the war is over." I knew the people beside the road weren't cheering for the troops, only celebrating the fact that the fighting had stopped. If the terror of the police state was yet to come, at least their endless trial by combat was over.

I began to wonder what the end of the war would mean to each member of my family.

My mother and eldest sister, Hai, oddly enough, were probably safest of all—at least for the time being. Ky La was a poor rural village, decimated by the war, and nobody would bother them much until old scores were settled in the cities. At least my mother would have a chance now to learn what had happened to her relatives, including my eldest brother, Bon Nghe, who would assume my father's role as patriarch. Nobody had seen or heard from him since 1954, when he was conscripted by Hanoi.

Of more immediate concern was my sister Ba, whose village husband had also been conscripted and shipped north. A few years later, Ba had been forced to marry a South Vietnamese policeman, Chinh, to keep him from sending my father to a Republican prison. I also worried for my niece Thinh, a girl slightly younger than me who had been a good friend while I grew up. Her husband, Bien, was in the South Vietnamese Navy, which at least offered a chance of escape since Danang was a big port and Bien had access to ships.

The fate of Anh, Jimmy's father, and his aristocratic wife, Lien, was another matter. As a rich industrialist, he would be high on the list of state enemies. I actually received some letters from Lien, who was grateful that I never made legal troubles for Anh over my pregnancy. She told me that Anh had a brother in Minnesota and I could see their thoughts turning to their exile in the States.

But mostly I worried for Lan, the sister I knew best, having spent the last few years before I met Ed in her company, learning the tricks of the black market and bar-girl trade. *Ban than cho de quoc My,* the Communist inquisitors would call her: "She who sells herself to the American empire." To make matters worse, she had two Amerasian children—*mau ngoai xam,* "carriers of foreign aggressor blood." The Viet Cong and Northern Communists really hated people like her— and me—since we betrayed our countrymen and gave our bodies to American soldiers. To the very puritanical and righteous socialist leaders who would take over the government, the necessities of war, of just surviving, would be forgotten in favor of a moralism so strict that normal people couldn't have observed it even during peace. Try as I might, I could not imagine a future for Lan in Vietnam that would be anything but painful, bleak, and short.

On March 28, 1975, the TV news showed a red flag with a single yellow star being raised over "the White Elephant Club" beside the Danang River. I was secretly amused that the Northern army had chosen this spot—familiar to everyone in Danang—to hold their symbolic flag-raising ceremony. More than just a well-known government building, it was a tony meeting place for high-ranking South Vietnamese and American businessmen and officials. The Viet Cong had tried for a decade to infiltrate the place—to assassinate bigwigs or blow it up—but had failed every time. Now, as a symbol of fat-cat capitalism and "U.S. imperialism" as well as Southern rule, its downfall must have been especially satisfying to local cadremen.

This typical Viet Cong preoccupation with political as well as military objectives made me worry most. Both rumor and public records would show that I had "defected" to the United States and the local cadremen (who already had a grievance against my mother and plenty of other reasons to resent my family) might see my actions as the straw that broke the camel's back. All it would take was one accusation by a jealous neighbor—that my relatives were spying for me and sending information about Vietnam to the United States—to bring the ax down on their necks. Not only had I put my family through hell while I was there, but it seemed now that I might yet be the death of them, although I was five thousand miles away.

Naturally, I prayed often that all this wouldn't come to pass, but my prayers seemed impotent. I wanted and needed to do more, something brave and decisive to help my relatives, but every road seemed blocked.

Except one.

On April 19, 1975, I received the following telegram, in Vietnamese, from Lan: PLEASE HELP. ALL THREE OF US WILL BE KILLED BECAUSE OF CONG LAI [my Amerasian children].

I began to cry—both from terror and relief: terror at the obvious danger Lan was facing; relief because I finally knew she was alive. Even better, the telegram had been sent from Saigon, which was still several weeks, if not months, away from Hanoi's legions. I also had the information—the excuse and the documentation—I needed to get involved in her rescue.

I read the telegram to Dennis and he exploded. Although he hadn't served in Vietnam, he hated Communists everywhere and Lan's telegram and the exodus of Vietnamese only seemed to prove what he had been saying all along: that the VC and Northern army weren't supported by the people. In a moment of weakness, though, he volunteered to do what he could to get my family out.

I asked him to call the State Department (he was, after all, a government employee as well as a man and was certain to get more cooperation than I would) and ask how we might get Lan and her boys evacuated. Unfortunately, the machinery that had gotten America so heavily involved in the war—the State Department, the military, the CIA—now backed off like frightened children from the fire they had started. They said we would have to take Lan's inquiry to the Immigration and Naturalization Service, the INS, just like any other foreign national seeking asylum. The fact that each day's delay was a lifetime for refugees made no difference. We would have to "go through channels."

And those channels were already clogged. Tens of thousands of other Vietnamese were trying to get out via American sponsors and while we slogged through the swamp of paperwork and dead-end phone calls, I received more heartbreaking telegrams from Lan— each more urgent than the last. One thing we did learn from the INS: because I was not a U.S. citizen, if I left the United States to help Lan get back there was no guarantee I would be allowed to return myself. Since I had made a vow after An Khe never to put Jimmy and Tommy in harm's way again or to take any risks that would leave them motherless, this seemed like the final blow. I cabled Lan, telling her I could not come personally, and she wired back: TRY PETEY BAILEY IN NEW JERSEY.

Peter T. Bailey (called "P.T." or Petey by those who knew him) had been one of Lan's boyfriends in Vietnam and had always treated her son, Eddie, kindly. If anyone outside the family had a reason to help, it would be Pete. He had not answered her letters or wires, but a stateside phone call had never been tried.

"Hello, is this Mr. Bailey?" I asked when a male voice came on the line. I had been given his number by long-distance information.

"Yes. Who's this?"

"The Petey Bailey who worked for the navy in Danang? Who had a Vietnamese girlfriend named Lan?"

I actually heard Petey choke. Maybe he thought I was Lan.

"I was in 'Nam, yes. Who's this?"

"This is Le Ly, Lan's sister. You probably don't remember me—"

"Oh yes." The voice tried to sound pleasant. "How are you? *Where* are you?"

"I am in Southern California. I live here since 1972. So Petey, you probably wonder why I'm calling you, right?"

After a pause he said, "It's probably about your sister. I hear things are pretty bad over there."

"She want to come to the United States, Pete. She's afraid of the Viet Cong—for herself and her sons. You get her letters? Her telegrams?"

"Yes, but there's nothing I can do. I can't go back—I have a life here now. And even if I could, I don't have the money."

"That no problem." I tried to sound optimistic. "My husband passed away and I have some cash—"

"It doesn't matter. I can't go."

"But what about Lan's sons? The VC will kill them when they take over!"

"I feel terrible about that, Ly. I feel terrible about what's happening to your country. But I can't do anything about it. I wish I could. I wish you both good luck. I hope things work out for you and Lan. But please don't call here again."

He hung up, leaving me with a heavy heart and no plan. We were back to square one.

After more days of unreturned phone calls to the INS, I received a desperate telegram from Lan. She said this would be her last message: she was running out of time and money and had to save what little she could for a last-ditch effort to escape.

I crumpled the telegram and bawled like a baby—Lan's spoiled baby sister who had shared with her so many adventures and horrors over our too short, too terrible, too wonderful lives together. I just couldn't bear losing her. Not this way! For the last two months, my life beyond the telephone, TV set, and Lan's telegrams had barely registered. I hadn't been able to eat or sleep and even my periods had dried up. If my family wasn't going to survive the war, I apparently wouldn't either.

Dennis put his arm around my shoulder. "Don't worry, Ly," he said softly. "If there's no other way, I'll go."

At first, I couldn't believe what I heard. "What do you mean?"

"I mean I will go to Vietnam and bring your sister Lan and her sons to the United States—if that's what it takes to make you happy."

"Make me happy!" Now I really couldn't believe it. "You are saving my life! Saving Lan's life! How could I ever repay you?"

He smiled. "Can't you think of a way? I already have."

I was confused. I had already given Dennis everything I had to give—my body, my house, the love of my boys—what else could he want?

"I want you to marry me when I get back," he said. "That's my only condition."

"Well, you take my breath away." That was no exaggeration. I felt as if I had been punched in the stomach. "I guess I need to think about that."

"Sure. But don't take too long. It takes time to get a visa and who knows how long your country can last."

Ta phai hy sinh—more debt of guilt and duty! My father used to say, *"Cuu mot nguoi tren duong gian hon ngan nguoi duoi am phu"*: it's better to save one life on earth than one thousand souls in hell. Now I knew that he was right, especially when that life was my sister's: my father's—and my own—flesh and blood.

"Okay," I said finally. "That is a fair price to pay."

"It's not a price, Ly." Dennis kissed me. "It's your future. Dan's out of your life forever. It's time you and the boys shared that life with me—officially."

Dennis worked like a man inspired. Since January, he had been employed by the U.S. Customs Service. As a GS-5, his pay wasn't great, but it gave him an inside track in renewing his passport and expediting a Vietnamese visa. With equal determination, I cleaned out my life's savings—almost ten thousand dollars, which I had set aside for my own old age and the boys' education—and gave it to Dennis. I was used to trusting fate or luck or god for my salvation. Now, through dire necessity, I would have to add Dennis to that list.

When Dennis's visa was approved on the grounds he was a "missionary" going into the country to "save a life," I called all my Vietnamese friends and asked if they wanted to send husbands and/or money with him in order to bring their own families out. To the last, they all refused.

"He's crazy to go there," Huong said, although she, too, had relatives in danger. "And you're even crazier to risk losing him."

In the end, I felt almost as bad for Dennis as I did my family. Here he was, going into a war-torn capital on the verge of collapse—into a country he didn't know with a language he couldn't speak—all to bring out a woman he'd never met with kids who were not his own. His prize was the hand in marriage of someone who did not and could not love him—but what was all that to Dennis? He was desperately and foolishly in love. Hadn't I taken similar foolish risks to be with Dan?

With Dennis on his way, I sent a telegram to Lan, telling her that a man named Dennis Hayslip would meet her at the Embassy Hotel in Saigon in two days. I did not tell her he was carrying money, since the chance was too great that the message would be intercepted and read by an opportunist, a corrupt official, or worse.

This thought rekindled all my old wartime paranoia. Since he now possessed my life savings, I could imagine Dennis simply "skipping town" with my sons' future. I also imagined him getting blown up as he got off the plane or being ambushed in the street by cowboys. I knew he might be torn apart, too, by a mob of ordinary citizens simply because he was an American. The newsreel in my head was worse than the one on TV.

I also fretted over my duty to Dennis's family should the worst happen and he not come back. How would I explain to his mother, a solid midwesterner like Leatha, that her son had been killed on a dangerous errand for a fickle Vietnamese girl who had already buried one husband? How would I feel if Jimmy grew up to run a similar "errand" for a woman who was not his wife and who did not return his love? The whole situation was awful, terrible, and unavoidable. It was like the war itself.

Of course, my bad stomach picked this moment to show how much it shared my worry. I couldn't keep anything down and, on several occasions, was in too much pain even to stand up straight. As the days wore on, I tried to keep track of both Dennis's progress as I imagined it, and the actual course of the war. TV news was like a countdown—it was only a matter of time before Saigon was blasted from the face of the earth!

To make things worse, four-year-old Tommy and seven-year-old Jimmy (who tried to help by not fighting and by doing chores, like washing the dishes—which I always had to repeat anyway) asked periodically "Where is Daddy?" I could only point to the TV and say, "With Ba Ngoai—Grandma." Who knew if it was true?

Finally, the situation in Vietnam was so bad that the State Department put a phone number on the screen where relatives of servicemen and Vietnamese citizens could receive detailed information. When I finally got through to the number, all I heard was a recorded voice saying that all communications between the United States and the Republic of Vietnam had been interrupted, including airline flights.

I slammed down the phone—knocked it off the table—and cursed through my tears. If Lan and her boys lived, she would owe it to her Phung Thi grit and guile—not my puny effort. Dennis was never coming back. For the first time, I felt sympathy with the U.S. military officers who had been forced to send novices into combat—boys on a man's mission—in the name of some higher goal. There was no higher purpose than survival, and right now, for virtually everyone I cared about, that goal seemed far away.

I added pictures of Dennis and Lan and her two boys to my little shrine and lit incense and cooked sacrificial rice and burned paper money and paper clothes and prayed sincerely for their souls once an hour, every hour, as long as I was awake.

Finally, the cramps in my stomach became excruciating. I could no longer stand up. I curled over my knees and lay on the floor, watch-

ing the shadows come and go—praying, cursing, thinking, mourning. My boys cried for food and lay beside me like little puppies
around a dying she-dog. I could not remember the last time I had fed
them. As if drugged—locked in a dream—I crawled to the phone
and dialed Linda. *This is Ly. You must come over.* After seconds or
hours or days, she appeared in my smoky living room, beside my
blazing altar, blaring TV, and terrified little kids. She took Jimmy
and Tommy to a neighbor's. She drove me straight to the hospital.

In the sterile green room, I told the cat-eyed doctor through my
tears about everything that troubled me—overwhelmed me—half in
English, half in Vietnamese, just like my life. My story was part
medical history, part family history, and part deathbed confession. I
had no idea how much he comprehended, if anything, and I really
didn't care. He gave me a thorough examination and a shot to calm
me down. He said I should stay in the hospital at least overnight to
get a good night's sleep—my first since "my husband" had been
away. Then, as the shot took effect, he smiled and told me something
he hoped would give me pleasant dreams.

"Have a good sleep, Mrs. Munro. You and that little baby you're
carrying are going to need it!"

Another child—just what I needed! And a soon-to-be-fatherless
child at that!

While they ran tests to confirm my pregnancy, the hospital staff
worked hard to keep me quiet so I would not miscarry. They
wouldn't let me watch TV, so I had a chance to think things through
and communicate with my higher self. I consulted with my father
and Ed and other ghosts who visited me, from time to time, during
dreams and deep meditation. I had been trusted once again as the
repository for a soul in transit. In one way, it was yet another burden
on the narrow shoulders of one who had already showed herself
unworthy. From another perspective, though, it reminded me of who
I was: Phung Thi Le Ly. It confirmed for me my role in life—at least
as I understood it. It gave me, perhaps, one last chance to show the
power of love over hate.

Despite my doctor's advice, the first thing I did when I got home
on April 23 was to turn on the TV. President Ford was giving a
speech in New Orleans declaring that the war was "finished"—not
won or lost, but stopped like a hopeless argument. Two days later,
Republican President Thieu abandoned Saigon and four days after

that, General "Big" Minh took over the government. Most pictures now came from the U.S. naval vessels offshore: horrifying shots of rescue helicopters ditching at sea (there was no place for them to land) or empty helicopters being thrown from crowded decks to make room for new arrivals. I watched these pictures closely, hoping against hope to see Lan or Dennis, but after a while all the refugees looked the same: bedraggled, terrified, *Vu lan*—spooks.

The few TV pictures we got from the mainland were even worse: people climbing the fence of the U.S. Embassy on Thong Nhat street, defying MPs with batons and rifles, while the "cherry picker" helicopter lifted the chosen few from the roof.

On April 30, a North Vietnamese tank crashed through the gates of the Republican president's palace and parked rudely on the lawn. The tank commander waved his arms and grinned like the defiant teenager he probably was. If the war had been "finished" a week before by the politicians, it was now finally over for the people. I sighed the sigh of ages—a chill wind from the mountain of corpses my homeland had become.

I got out my address book.

I called everyone I knew: to share my relief, to share my tears, to get information, to rejoin the human race.

Sadly, what little news they had to share was bad. Nobody knew anything that hadn't already been on TV. Communications were still down and all flights in or out of the country had been stopped for the foreseeable future. Vietnam was sealed like a tomb.

Even worse, American television began to look elsewhere to amuse its fickle audience. When Vietnam was mentioned at all, it was by politicians and analysts. Americans don't like losers and Vietnam was one story people had heard more than enough about. Fortunately, local newscasters couldn't turn a blind eye to the thousands of refugees arriving daily at Southern California ports and airports—especially Camp Pendleton on the coast just north of San Diego. Watching them mill around by the surf, U.S. troop ships in the distance, was like an eerie replay of the marines' first landing ten years before at China Beach—but with all the actors reversed. Having failed to bring American peace to Vietnam, the marines were now bringing peace-starved Vietnam to America. I was not optimistic about the reception—or the life—these refugees would find, but I knew it would be better than the one they left behind.

Almost three weeks after Dennis left and a week after the South had fallen, I had resigned myself to facing life alone. Consequently, when the doorbell rang late one night, I assumed it was *the* telegram —a message from the State Department or military or Red Cross or Dennis's church that would finally confirm his fate.

"Who's there?" I asked through the door.

The answer was not "Western Union" but a child's giggle.

I opened the door onto my sister. Lan looked exhausted and as old as our mother, but beautifully alive. Her two little boys crouched behind her.

"Troi oi!—Oh my god, I can't believe it's you!" I hugged her rag-doll body as tight as I could and she hugged her little sister and we both started laughing through our tears.

"Where's Dennis?" I hugged the boys and looked behind her. In the darkness, the man of the hour was dutifully unloading their bags from the cab that had brought them from the airport. I ran out— immodestly in my nightgown—and hugged him for all I was worth. In the porchlight his face was unshaved and gray, having seen a decade of life crammed into the last ten days.

We took our reunion inside where I woke the boys and reintro-duced them to seven-year-old Eddie—the Vietnamese cousin they barely remembered—and four-year-old Robert. The boys looked ne-glected and underfed, which was understandable, but nothing Amer-ica couldn't cure. More disturbing was the fear in their movements, as if, like timid rabbits, they couldn't trust the shadows around them. They referred to Dennis deferentially—reverentially—as *Ong My,* "Mr. American," even when he wasn't in the room.

While the kids got acquainted with American toys and bathrooms, I took Lan on a quick tour of my American palace. My own previous reaction to everyday American luxury was mirrored in her face.

"Everything is so nice—so beautiful!" Lan said in Vietnamese, afraid even to touch the light switches. "Dennis must be very wealthy. He treats you like a queen!"

"Oh no—this is all mine. Dennis works, but aside from paying part of the mortgage and some household expenses, I pay for every-thing. Anyway, to Americans, all this is nothing special. I'm better off than some, but not as rich as many."

I could see that Lan, if unwilling to believe me, would at least suspend her judgment in this strange land where everything—in-cluding the customary big sister/little sister relationship—was upside down. Too excited for sleep, I asked them to sit around the table and tell me of their escape. I told them how terrible the pictures of the fall of Saigon looked on TV.

"The pictures were nothing," Lan said, brushing aside my three weeks in hell. "Everybody in authority ran away at the end of March. President Nguyen Van Thieu split with six tons of gold and left a recording for the troops to stand and fight alongside him, can you believe it? Many times I'd have given a month's pay to see a real policeman—even a corrupt one—but everybody who served the Americans was looking for the door. In the last few weeks, the cab drivers, *siclo* drivers, laborers, shopkeepers, the angriest refugees— they ran the city. They used the anarchy to strike back at the people who lost the country—the government soldiers, bureaucrats, and any Americans stupid enough to be hanging around. Dennis barely made it out alive."

"Did you find Lan okay at the hotel?" They looked as if the question was ancient history.

"Oh yes," Dennis said. "The cab driver tried to rip me off and we got into a scuffle. He was a little guy, but he had a knife."

"But you okay now?" I looked him over.

Dennis laughed. "Hey—I used to be a cop! Anyway, Lan got a crooked lawyer to draw up a phony marriage certificate. He said it was the only way a Vietnamese national could get out of the country. Problem was, even that bastard tried to hold us up. After we paid him, he waved the certificates at us and asked for more money. I told him to piss off and left, but Lan stayed to negotiate. The asshole finally got her to transfer everything in her bank account to his name. It wasn't a lot, but it was everything she had."

"Not quite. I still got some gold out of the country," Lan said proudly. Of course, Lan was no different from other Vietnamese refugees. Gold, like a child, was their future. Later I would learn that some Chinese businessmen made a killing that spring meeting the refugee planes and boats and buying smuggled-out gold for half the market price. Nobody in this world is ever so pitiful that somebody somewhere won't try to take advantage of him!

"How much?" I tried to sound impressed but was really quite angry at them both. After all, Dennis still had over half the ten thousand dollars I had given him to pay for their escape. Getting nabbed and tossed back for smuggling contraband after all he had risked seemed the height of greed and folly.

Lan beamed. "About a half-dozen twenty-four-karat gold leaves. Dennis wore them in his boots."

"So, then you got your visas to the U.S.?" I asked.

"Yeah, after we got the marriage certificate, we didn't have any problems," Dennis said. "The Commies were so close that the State Department figured no American would jerk them around. They wanted me out as badly as I wanted to leave. Lan and the boys were just baggage."

"So when did you actually leave the country?"

"April twenty-eighth."

"My god—two days before they took the city!" I slapped my cheeks.

"That's what they tell me," Dennis shrugged. I was relieved to know they had been out of danger during those last desperate hours, then recalled how sick I had made myself during those same few days. "You probably know more about what happened after that than we do," Dennis concluded. "We got shipped to Guam, then finally got a plane to Pendleton. It was just like being in the goddamn army again."

"So why didn't you call?"

Dennis and Lan exchanged blank stares. "To tell you the truth, it didn't occur to me for the first few days. I mean, we were okay— we'd made it. The rest was just getting home. When I finally did think to call, there were either no phones or the lines were too long or some other damn thing. Anyway, we're here now and that's what counts."

"So—you two are married?" This tactic was not part of the plan. I had assumed Dennis would simply bribe their way out or buy phony missionary papers or something like that. I smiled a congratulatory smile, half waiting to be told that the union had been consummated and both newlyweds liked the arrangement and that I would not be held to my end of the bargain.

"Only in the eyes of the State Department," Dennis said. "That means we'll have to show an annulment. If worse comes to worst, we can always drive down to Mexico for a quick divorce."

"Well, all this is quite a surprise." I forced a smile, letting out one long breath, then taking in another. "Now I have a surprise for you!"

Dennis was ecstatic to hear he would be a father; not just because he liked children, but because he believed that a child would draw us together—perhaps even make me love him as much as he loved me.

We got on with daily life. Lan received her green card but when she tried to change her name by claiming an annulment without proof, the INS took it back. Dennis made arrangements for their Mexican divorce.

Like me, Lan had to learn to be an American. I showed her how to use the dishwasher, the clothes washer and dryer, garbage disposal, and the other indispensables of American homemaking. I gave Lan one bedroom for herself, a real luxury in our country. All the boys shared the second (although Robert usually slept with his mother), and Dennis and I shared the third. Although Eddie was Jimmy's age, he still had nightmares about the war and, when he wasn't screaming in terror, was screaming for his mother. I realized all Vietnamese women treated their firstborn sons like kings, and Lan and I were no exceptions. But Jimmy's quick acceptance of American-style independence made Vietnamese son-coddling seem archaic and more than a little useless. In fact, this was the first of many instances in which my own Americanization—much further along than I had dreamed—was magnified by my sister's example. However, this realization didn't upset me. On the contrary, since I observed all the important Vietnamese holidays and traditions, I felt these changes only made me a better person—a woman with two cultures instead of one. Not everyone agreed.

After a month or so, when Eddie was settled in school (where he began learning how not to be a prince) we drove down to Tijuana and got in line at the American "divorce mill." Needless to say, Lan's and Dennis's was not the only interracial marriage-of-convenience being annulled that day. The place seemed full of Caucasian men and Oriental women, more than a few of whom were Vietnamese. Right up to the last minute, I kept telling Dennis and Lan what a fine couple they made and (secretly to Lan) didn't she feel more comfortable in America with a legal husband? But Dennis was adamant and Lan still had ideas of getting back together with Petey Bailey. The divorce went ahead.

That same day, July 21, 1975, my marker was called in. Before the ink was dry on their divorce decree, Dennis and I obtained our marriage certificate. As it turned out, no respectable U.S. institution would acknowledge our Mexican marriage, so a year later we went to

Las Vegas and did it all over again at a little wedding chapel. I recited the strange sounding English-Christian vows and the hired witnesses clapped, but the tears in my eyes were from anything but joy.

The months rolled by and our odd extended family put its roots down farther in American soil. The boys became the best of friends and relished telling people they each had three brothers, two mothers, and one father. While Jimmy and Tommy helped Lan's boys with their English, Eddie and Robert showed them how to make musical instruments and toys out of aluminum cans and other junk they'd grown up with in the poor streets of Saigon and Danang.

Not everybody appreciated this mix of cultures. Jimmy and Tommy had gotten used to turning their backs on catcalls of "chink" and "gook" and so forth—but Eddie and Robert had not. More than once they came back from a neighborhood "day of play" with black eyes and bloody noses.

Eventually, all the boys took steps to hide their true heritage: that they were of the "enemy" race their friends' fathers and older brothers had fought against. Sometimes this was as simple as telling people they were Hawaiian or Mexican. Sometimes the contrivance took a little more thought, and was bought at a higher price. Once, Jimmy's teacher told his class to write a brief autobiography. He "interviewed" me and asked me to tell him everything I could remember about his early years, which I was happy and proud to do. When he was finished, he read the completed paper to me and I was moved to tears as I heard my own recollections woven together with my son's with such innocence and clarity.

A few weeks later, at parents' night at his school, I met with his teacher and asked many questions about how America was educating my child. The teacher pointed with pride to a wall covered with student autobiographies. I looked for Jimmy's and couldn't find it. I asked the teacher where it could be—my son had always been very conscientious about his school work and I remembered well the evening we spent evoking our memories of his young life.

The teacher shook her head and said, "You know, that was the only assignment Jimmy never turned in!"

Lan continued to talk about P.T. Bailey. At first, I told her to forget him, just as my friends had tried to get me to forget about Dan. Like Ed, Petey was an older man and a civilian contractor, not military. But unlike Ed, he liked to spend money, which was one reason Lan never pressed him too hard for marriage—it was unclear who would be supporting whom. Now, in her loneliness, Lan was talking herself into believing that Petey would be different in the United States—especially if they were married. In fact, the more Lan isolated herself from American society, the more she romanticized Petey. Since she didn't have a job and was making no effort to find one, I began to agree that having a man take her and the two boys off my hands might not be such a bad idea.

But *not* P.T. Bailey!

In this case, "Mother Ly" knew best. I did not want to see my sister spoil her new beginning by making the same bad choices I had. I put my foot down. I told her all this talk about Petey had to stop, no two ways about it.

So Lan invited Petey for a visit. He was just as I remembered, but now, of course, much older. He was tall, very thin, didn't talk much, and smoked even more than Ed. If he had any money, it was not apparent from his clothes or personal habits. He dressed poorly and rarely volunteered to pay for anything, even the expenses of "his woman" when we went out, which was seldom and only to McDonald's.

Because Petey had been out of work since he returned from Vietnam, he was in no hurry to end his visit. After a month, our three-bedroom house, just right for me, Dennis, and my boys, now looked like a refugee camp. Dennis's salary and benefits were some help, but what was left after his withholding and various bar tabs was barely enough to make ends meet. With a household of seven living on the income of one uneducated Vietnamese housekeeper, some social security, and a debt-ridden civil servant, we could not get by forever.

One day, I tried to talk about this with Lan, which was tricky. In Vietnam, I had been her worthless little sister and when our parents finally shamed her into taking me in—an unwed teenage mother on the run from the Viet Cong—she began a reign of terror that still gave me chills to think about. Although I knew we must talk candidly about Petey and her getting a job and place to live, I didn't want to enrage her because I didn't want to get socked, which was not entirely out of the question. So I waited until Dennis's day off, then coaxed him into lounging around the house—within earshot—while Lan and I worked things out over coffee.

"You know, Nam Lan," I said in Vietnamese, using her family

number name (sister "number five") and trying to sound very deferential, "you are very lucky. When I arrived, I didn't have any gold leaf to help get me started. I was like Ed's daughter and a little-nothing fly to his relatives. With your money and good English and experience as a nurse's aide, you can get a good job and rent a nice place to live. You can sell your gold and put the money in the bank to get interest and use a little to buy your boys nice clothes for school instead of having to borrow Jimmy's and Tommy's and—"

"Okay, I get the point." Lan got up, went to her room, and returned with two sheaves of gold from the stash she kept under her mattress. She tossed them down in front of me. "I didn't know you were so poor. If you were so poor, you shouldn't have brought me from Vietnam—you know why? Because now you're responsible for me. That's right! You and the Americans. You Americans turned me into a refugee, so you can just damn well pay for it! That's how I feel. But I'm no miser. If you want my gold—here it is, all I have in the world. Spend it on clothes and hamburgers, I don't care."

"Please—I don't want your gold. It's just that Pete—"

"Oh, that's very nice! Now you're going to complain about Petey, eh? Well, what about Dennis? You took him in when he was down and out. Why don't you give Pete the same chance? My god, Bay Ly, Dennis doesn't even make enough to support you, and he *has* a job! How can you complain about Petey? Anyway, Dennis signed papers in Vietnam that he would be responsible for me in the United States. Maybe you should talk to him and make him live up to his promise."

Our "discussion" got no better, but at least I didn't get punched. Dennis looked in briefly, waved, then ambled out to his favorite bar. Lan stalked off to her room and I spent the rest of the morning crying until I had to get ready for work.

Of course, not every discussion with Lan was about money or our current problems. We often reminisced about our family—especially the years before and at the beginning of the American war. People forget that life is hard for peasants even during peace. Natural disasters—typhoons and droughts—can take their toll as surely as bombs and bullets. In peacetime, however, such tragedies are easier to accept as acts of god. We talked about working in the moonlight when the rice paddies got too hot; about steering our water buffalo around with a stick, as if it were a little duck instead of a thousand-pound ox. We talked about making mud houses and taking warm-rain baths and playing card games at Tet. The more we talked, the more our memories and tears flowed out of us and dissolved our sisterly troubles.

"Remember, Bay Ly," Lan said, "when I was working for that rich family in Saigon and our brother Sau Ban came to visit? I filled him up with leftovers from the master's lunch and talked about this and that, then Sau Ban hugged me and said he was being sent far away and didn't know when he'd be back. In those days, everybody knew what that meant—he was being sent to the front, but I thought he'd been drafted by the government. I was afraid to press him for details, but I saw Hai a couple of weeks later and she said he had joined Uncle Ho. If I had known he was going off with the Viet Cong, I would've tried to stop him. The family I worked for was very rich and influential. I know I could've persuaded them to help him get a desk job or something—safe in Saigon away from the fighting."

The pain in Lan's voice revealed another side of her soul—the loving big sister to everyone in our family except Hai, who was the eldest and sort of "above it all," more like another parent or aunt than sibling. I had forgotten that Lan had taken care of Sau Ban, just as she had taken care of me, in the earliest years of our lives, while our mother worked in the fields. Bon Nghe was closest to her in age, but he was a boy—and the eldest boy at that, the bearer of our family name. Our parents had poured every ounce of love and concern they possessed into his care and well-being, leaving not too much for Lan, who had to stay home to take care of us kids or work in the fields herself, often for hire in our neighbors' paddies.

One time when Lan and Bon Nghe were out tending our cows, French shells began to fall. The cows scattered and Bon Nghe went one way while Lan went the other. Bon Nghe made it home and explained what happened, but Lan never showed up. Our parents didn't go looking for her for several days, after which Lan made it back on her own. My mother always excused their delay on grounds that they assumed Lan had been killed, but I don't think that carried much weight with Lan. When she was fifteen, our mother sent her to Danang to help support the family. Of course, as an ignorant farm girl, she was given only dirty, menial jobs and was constantly abused by her employers. She says she understood our mother's reasons, but she probably felt as if she had been kicked out—as if her value as a daughter was measured only by how much money she could send home. We never discussed it, but I think this was one reason Lan became a loner—the black sheep of the family—at least in the years before I could claim that title. I always tried to remind myself of this before I got too righteous about anything she said and did.

By mid-November 1975, time had cured some of our odd, extended family's ills—but aggravated others.

Pete Bailey got a year's contract in Greenland and promised to send monthly checks to help Lan and the boys get established in America. I helped Lan find a job as a nurse's aide at a hospital not too far away. On the negative side, my pregnancy was starting to show and it was only a matter of time until we would have to convert Lan's private bedroom to a nursery. We would have to have another *cai va voi nhau*—sisterly argument—but this time I took matters into my own hands, to give Lan's better nature a gentle push.

"Look here!" I beamed one day, showing Lan a shiny new set of keys. "Look what I have for you!"

"You changed the locks?" Lan grunted. "You're kicking Dennis out? Good."

"No—don't be silly. They're keys to a new apartment I've rented for you and Eddie and Robert. It's only a few miles away, isn't that nice? We can visit whenever we want. And it's a short walk to the hospital where you work—you won't even have to ride the bus. You'll love it. I've already stocked the cupboard with a month's supply of food."

"So—we'll starve after one month. I can't believe we're having this discussion again, Bay Ly. You want more gold—to rob my boys of their future? Go ahead, take what you want!"

There was no use trying to reason with her, since her reasoning was so peculiar and didn't admit another point of view. When all else failed, she relied on the fact that she was my elder sister and my senior in all family matters. Since it was questionable whether any other members of our once proud and happy family survived the fall of the South, that fact alone was usually enough to win the argument.

Except today. Today Dennis and I were going to play hardball, but in a sporting way.

Lan often went with me to pick up the boys after school. Today, instead of taking everyone home, I simply drove Lan and her sons to the new apartment. It was an older building in an older neighborhood (not as nice as our tract in Santee, but it was all I could afford) and still much nicer than the nicest place she had in Vietnam. I arranged to have Dennis meet us there—partly for security, in case

Lan made a scene, and partly to show that we meant business, that it *was* a family decision: a decision made by my new American family, husband and all.

Lan got out looking shocked and numb, as if she were going to her own execution. I led them on a tour of the two-bedroom, kitchenette apartment. It was furnished with old, knockabout furniture, but nothing Lan couldn't replace after a few months' work or a few checks from Petey. For a woman who, six months before, couldn't have gotten odds on her life, it might as well have been a suite at the Ritz. We left them wandering through the rooms and promised to return with their things, which we did, that same afternoon.

Fortunately, Lan's purgatory didn't last long. Within the year, Petey returned, true to his word, and they were married. I was not thrilled with their chances for success, but who was I to talk? Lan was happy, and because of that, so was I.

Now it was Dennis's turn to make waves.

Dennis was deeply religious, and I had made the mistake on more than one occasion of sharing with him my mystical visits with Ed. At first, he discounted them as figments of my imagination, my heathen culture.

"If you threw away that stupid shrine," Dennis remarked, "you'd stop having these silly hallucinations."

He was right, of course, but for the wrong reason. If I destroyed my ancestors' spirit house, they would abandon me, but our problems would only get worse. Still, Dennis agreed that "funny things" went on in our house; things even his Western education and Baptist upbringing couldn't explain.

One afternoon as I was putting our dishes away in the high American cupboard and Jimmy was eating a sandwich at the kitchen table, I opened a cupboard door and was instantly blinded by a shaft of light. It darted left and right, then disappeared.

"Cool, Mom!" Jimmy shouted, drinking his milk. "How'd you make that light snake?"

He was so used to oddities in this land of technological miracles that it didn't even occur to him to be scared.

"You saw it? You saw it too?" I felt my heart pound in my ears.

"Sure. How'd you do it?"

I told Dennis later about our "magic trick" and he took me seriously enough to ask Jimmy what he saw. Dennis came out of the boys' room puzzled, but unconvinced.

"Jimmy saw *something*." Dennis shook his head. "It was more than a reflection or anything like that. I'll be damned if I can tell you what it was. Maybe static electricity."

Not too long after that, while I was reading in bed waiting for Dennis to turn in, he appeared in the doorway, pale and sweating.

"Son of a bitch!" he gasped—not in anger but amazement.

"What's wrong?" I got up. "You sick? You want some water?"

He wiped his face with a towel. "You won't believe this—or maybe you will. I just saw Ed!"

"Of course. I see him all the time."

"You don't understand. *I* saw Ed—standing ten feet in front of me! It was like a color slide: click, he was there, click, he was gone. Christ, I've never even seen the guy except in a snapshot! But there he was. I'll tell you one thing"—Dennis shut the door as if that would be any barrier to hallway ghosts, "we're getting out of this house!"

On December 19, 1975, not long after Dennis had his vision, I gave birth to Alan—my third son by as many men. Like all my boys, he was a beautiful baby, bringing into my world with Dennis a sweet dollop of love where before there had been only the thick crust of duty. Dennis was so proud of this new little man who bore his name that he allowed that name to be extended to my other two sons as well, although he never adopted them formally. It takes more than a name to make a family, but at least we had a start.

Once again, when Dennis made up his mind to do something, he couldn't be stopped. He fell in love with a big five-bedroom, two-story house on a San Diego cul-de-sac and used the equity from my Santee house, plus his own VA loan, to take possession in March 1976. I questioned our ability to make the payments, which were much more than those for Ed's house, but Dennis was buying an exorcism, not just a roof over our heads. For him, the cost of his own peace of mind was no object.

Although for Dennis the new house was a move up, it was for us a move backward. Santee was a navy community with many working-class families. Our new San Diego neighborhood, however, was mostly white collar, so the people were more reserved and not too interested in this ex-GI and his Oriental wife. In Ed's world, I had at least been an exotic decoration. On Dennis's new block, I was no more welcome than another Asian gardener.

We did one thing right, though. I hired a Vietnamese geomancer to evaluate the house. In the East, thoughtful couples won't move into a home until an astrologer has studied its aspects: the alignment of its front door and which way the bed should face and so on. The man we hired came for his interview in the old Santee house. He sniffed the interior suspiciously as soon as I let him in.

"How long have you lived in this house?" he asked.

"About four years," I answered.

"And your sign? Wait—don't tell me. *Ky suu con trau"*—he scratched his chin—"another water buffalo, eh? I'm surprised you and your husband are still together. Your door faces the sunset. Hasn't that ever bothered you?"

I thought about all the evenings I had sat in the front yard staring at the setting sun, hoping for some miracle that would take me home, or at least make me feel at home in this strange place called America.

"No, I don't think so," I lied.

"Hmph. Well, think about it."

I offered him some tea. He asked about Ed's sign and I told him I thought Ed had been a cat or a rabbit.

"You should've paid more attention, my dear. It sounds like he was *man thap hon*—a man with a lower destiny. Perhaps his mission on earth had been to bring you from Vietnam. When it was over, he had no further function, so he died. The universe is very economical, Mrs. Hayslip. People think they can do whatever they want with their time on earth. Where do they get such silly ideas?"

I agreed, and pointed out that since our time was so precious, we probably shouldn't waste any more of it in the house we were leaving, and analyze instead our new home. He agreed, but not before finishing his tea and cookies.

The geomancer walked through the new house like a city building inspector, taking measurements and checking his compass.

"The kitchen's okay," he said, squinting at the walls like an exterminator, "but the front door will give you problems. I suggest you remodel as soon as possible and have it open onto the sunrise."

"That really won't be possible," Dennis said, struggling to keep from laughing. "The house costs enough already. We can't afford any big changes."

"Suit yourself. It's your happiness we're talking about, not mine."

The astrologer made some additional comments—things we couldn't do much about, and suggested that if I wanted to say some conciliatory prayers, he would give me directions to a Buddhist temple that was not too far away.

My heart jumped. I had been looking for a proper place to pray on high holidays and, even more important, to consult with priests and monks about the things that troubled me. Now this funny little man had presented me with just what I'd been seeking. My generous tip beyond his nominal fee surprised him, but it was still much cheaper than a new front door.

The little Buddhist temple had been established by expatriate Vietnamese, donating whatever they could to gain a spiritual foothold in this strange new land. Although most of the money had come from wealthier immigrants, the temple was sparse: less a sign of rich-man parsimony than traditional Buddhist asceticism. At one end of the empty hall was a shelf with a contemplative stone Buddha. Around it was arrayed smoking incense and plates of offerings—mostly withering fruit and stale cookies. Like most temples, even the walls smelled of incense, a reminder of ever-present divinity. What I liked best, though, was the constant drone of the caretakers' chants and the sound of the *mo* and *chuong*—the wooden knocker and metal bowl which were beaten like drums and cymbals to summon certain spirits and ward off others. The monks themselves could have come from any Saigon street corner: barefoot, saffron robed, shave-headed men who always greeted you with a smile and a prayerful bow. Because they spoke no English, they were totally dependent on their sponsors for news of the outside world as well as food or money deposited respectfully in their *binh bat,* little begging bowls. Over the coming months, I would make myself a fixture around the place.

The demands of setting up our new household were many—getting the kids settled in a new school; planting the front yard to look like our neighbors', and tilling the back to look like a farm (with bananas, guavas, bamboo, lemon grass, mint, and all kinds of vegetables); and meeting our neighbors, Pat (a blond "surfer chick") and her husband, Mike, a sympathetic Vietnam vet.

When I wasn't working at home, I was visiting the temple. The monks (whom I called *su,* or "master") appreciated my knowledge of the old traditions and desire to learn more. Before long, even the *Hoa Thuong*—the chief priest—started calling me *phat tu,* "my child," which is both a term of endearment and acknowledgment of my special status as his student. I even had the luxury of using one of our extra rooms as a "temple room" for my ancestral shrine and a bookcase that soon overflowed with literature about religion and philosophy, Eastern and Western. The tension between these instincts of mine—to observe my family's traditions while trying to understand new ideas—and Dennis's low tolerance of anything beyond the Christian gospel quickly led to difficulties even the geomancer had not foreseen.

At first, we tried to be even-steven about things. Dennis came to my temple a couple of times just to see what it was like. I didn't force my beliefs on him any more than I had forced them on Jimmy or Tommy. Like my father before me, my only instruction to my children would be by my example. If they became curious and asked questions, I would be glad to answer. If they did not, that was fine too. Thus has spiritual education always gone forward in the East: novices asking the master, not the teacher demanding answers. In matters of spiritual sustenance, the *su* learned long ago that it was not only foolish, but harmful, to force nourishment on someone who was not hungry.

Dennis's approach—and that of his church—was considerably different. Because the congregation was half Oriental, services were conducted in both English and Mandarin, and the associated Bible school had a playground that was open to the kids all week. The playground was one reason Jimmy and Tommy liked the church better than the temple—even when it came to religion, Americans were better at marketing their product! But in place of the Buddha's message of transcendence and reincarnation was a nonnegotiable demand that we sinners renounce Satan and get on with Christ's work. One particularly adamant evangelist was a pretty young college student named Janet, who boasted Chinese ancestry. She asked me after one church potluck if I would like to meet with her the following Thursday to study the Bible. I was always impressed with scholarship and said yes enthusiastically. I invited her to come by about lunchtime.

I did not know what to cook for a good Baptist. Dennis and I had entertained both Occidentals and Orientals from his church and had argued about every dish. My Western-style meals always had a kind of "soy-and-ginger" flavor and my Vietnamese food was often deemed unpalatable—and sometimes poisonous.

"Besides," Dennis once said, holding up a piece of *banh tac* (rice wrapped in banana leaves) with obvious disgust, "our church friends don't like the idea of eating the same kind of food that you offer to the devil."

"Offer to the devil! What you talking about? Buddha is *not* the devil!"

"Well, he's a graven image—a golden calf—read the Bible and you'll see. Anyway, they feel wrong accepting the hospitality of a pagan—you know, somebody who doesn't believe in God."

"But I *do* believe in god!"

"Not their God—*our* God—the Lord our God in Heaven."

That sounded a lot like *Ong Troi*—Mr. Sky. He and Mother Earth are the parents of everything. But I thought it was unwise to point this out just now.

"Buddha was just a man," Dennis continued. "You can't worship just a man."

"I don't worship him, I only offer prayers and respect. And there are many Buddhas, not just one—"

"What about your burnt offerings? Isn't that idolatry—worship of the dead?"

"What about your funeral flowers? Aren't you worshiping the dead with them?"

"That's different. You don't understand. You really need to study the Bible."

I didn't know how different our customs really were, but at least we agreed I was too ignorant to tell him the facts about his own religion. I wanted to learn from Janet, not debate her. I decided to prepare a big lunch using mostly American packaged foods, so Janet wouldn't get sick, but I made some Vietnamese dishes, too. She arrived right on time, a half hour before noon, sporting a big leather-bound Bible with lots of pages marked by ribbons. When she saw me, her pretty sienna lips parted like Moses' Red Sea.

"Hello, Janet," I said, "it's very good to see you. Please come in."

She did so, taking off her shoes, impressing me with her knowledge of our customs. She looked into the kitchen.

"So much food!" she said. "I hope it's not all for us."

"Don't worry, the boys will finish what we don't eat."

"Well, I was also worried about time." She looked at the watch on her delicate wrist. "Do you mind if we start our lesson while we have lunch?"

I thought we were going to have a discussion—questions and answers—like the ones I had with the monks. American "lessons," I had learned in community college, tended toward one-way conversations, from all-knowing teacher to stupid little students. I didn't think that was the way the universe was built, so it did not seem to be the right way to talk about the cosmic god. But I also did not want to be impolite, so I said, "Yes, of course. Why not?"

While I dipped an egg roll in *nuoc mam* fish sauce, Janet said, "First, let me explain about God. He is the Father of us all and created us to love one another, and to love Him most of all. He is so perfect, though, that He cannot tolerate any sin around Him."

"But Pastor Chun say we are *all* sinners," I interrupted. "Does that mean no Baptists go to Heaven?"

"Oh, no," Janet laughed, "that's why God sent His only begotten son, Jesus Christ, to earth in order to show us how to live a sinless life. He then caused Jesus to be crucified so that the rest of us could be saved. Do you understand so far?"

I wrinkled my nose and shook my head. She talked some more about how God could not, apparently, forgive me directly, but only if I professed my belief in His son. It all seemed so complicated—like the procedure for getting passports rather than getting into Heaven. After a while, she gave up on theology and told me about her Buddhist family in rural China and why she converted to Christianity.

"Like you, Le Ly, my parents and some of the other villagers were Buddhists and often left food offerings outdoors by their family shrines. One day, when I was a little girl, we had a terrible drought in the hills. Some tigers came into the village and attacked people, but only those with food by their houses. All the Christian families were saved. The missionaries said it was a sign from God and I believed them. Everybody in the village converted after that."

Although I was moved by Janet's sincerity, I didn't know whether to laugh or cry at her story. I was an old hand at reading animal signs, but it was unlikely that the cosmic god would send tigers to disprove his own existence. This inconsistency in so important a family legend did not seem to disturb her.

We finished our meal talking about the other strange (if secular) differences between Asia and America. Then Janet decided it was time to go.

"Shall we meet again next week?" she asked.

I wasn't sure where these sessions would lead, but Dennis seemed happy I was having them, so I said, "Yes, of course. Why not?"

About this time I met a Vietnamese woman named Huyen at the

temple. Like me, she was married to an American but had free time
to devote to charity. The first time I went to her house, I was surprised to find it was in a poor neighborhood with weedy yards, cars
without wheels in driveways and wheels without cars hanging from
tree limbs for the local kids to play on. I banged on her flimsy
aluminum screen door, afraid I had overdressed for the occasion, but
she gave me a royal greeting.

"Khoe khong Chi Ly—How are you, Sister Ly?" she said, bowing
her short-cropped head politely. "You probably wonder why I've
asked you here!"

"Not at all." The house was dark as a movie theater and I pulled
off my sunglasses. It was summer and she had no cooler. All the
shades had been drawn to keep out the heat. "I always enjoy our
visits."

"Well, this one is very special." She called out for three boys,
eleven, thirteen, and fifteen, who arrayed themselves by height. I
knew they weren't hers because she told me she had only one daughter, Rose—a girl as pretty as her name—whom I had already met.
She went down the line, "This is Anh, An, and Hiep—the man of
the family. They are my late sister's children. My brother-in-law can't
raise them, so now they are mine."

They were good-looking boys, although, like so many refugees still
flooding into the United States, they had not yet learned to smile. I
mentioned this to Huyen, mostly as a joke to loosen them up, but she
agreed.

"They're very unhappy here," she lamented. "Look at this house—
it's so small! It's like living on that terrible boat they took to escape
Vietnam. And I only have one small daughter, so who can they play
with? They need a better place to stay, where they can learn about
America."

I guessed where the conversation was going, but I didn't mind.
Our new house was too large for the five of us, and Dennis always
said he liked big families. I volunteered to take the boys on a regular
basis, including several nights each week—provided they got along
with my kids, which they did, swimmingly, at first meeting. Jimmy
and Tommy had Caucasian friends at school, but they still felt more
at home with the Oriental kids at Dennis's church. Having Huyen's
nephews in the house was like moving the church playground to our
backyard!

The new boys spoke very little at first, even when I addressed them in Vietnamese, but they snapped to for all sorts of chores, showing they came from a thoughtful, disciplined family. They were polite to the point of formality, saying *da thua di,* "Yes, Auntie," which was the Vietnamese equivalent of "Yes, ma'am." They also preferred Vietnamese food, which was considerably cheaper than meat-heavy American meals. This pleased even Dennis, who agreed they could stay as long as they liked. This was the crucial ingredient for Huyen's next request.

"The boys like your family—good!" she said. "Maybe they have a future. I'm told I cannot apply for welfare because they are my sister's children, so their life with us would be poor. The only way for them to get a good start is to find sponsors for the foster parent program. The state will pay their expenses, but you must provide the love. Do you think you can do it?"

The love part was no problem, but I had some concerns about the paperwork. To qualify as foster parents, we had to have blood tests (for drugs and diseases) and give our fingerprints to the police. Two social workers, including one of the foster children's race, had to come out and inspect our house—to see that we could shelter and feed the kids properly. In Vietnam—at least before I left—each of these steps was an opportunity for corruption. I was very worried that we would be compelled to pay fee after fee and donate to various administrative "coffee funds" before we could earn a foster parents' license. But my fears were unfounded. The authorities seemed delighted to place at least a few of the thousands of homeless Vietnamese children who were swamping their resources. A week or so later, Anh, An, and Hiep moved in to begin their new lives as Americans.

For the first year, everything went well. The State of California paid the newcomers' medical bills plus a little over two hundred dollars per child (little Anh received less), so we were able to make ends meet. Dennis was moved to the second shift at work, which meant he got a little more money and was gone from two in the afternoon until midnight. He slept late, rising after the kids had gone to school, so he hardly ever saw them except on weekends. He busied himself with lots of "man hobbies," which was all right with me. I didn't, however, appreciate his gun collecting. He seemed to buy a new one every month: shotgun, hunting rifle, or handgun. And his motorcycles seemed more dangerous than the American warplanes that used to streak above my village. I got shivers of fear just looking at his big cruiser. He also started drinking, not too much but at the wrong times—alone after a fight with me or after a bad day at work.

Unfortunately, Dennis splurged on our first Christmas with the foster kids and money got very tight. Since I paid the bills each month, I was astonished at the big balances he ran up on our credit cards, particularly since I never took my cards out of the drawer and Dennis, like Ed, never went anywhere without them. Gas and electricity and automobile costs had all gone up since the fuel crisis of the middle seventies, and we now used more of everything because of our bigger household. I finally told Dennis that our high living couldn't continue. He inspected our checkbook.

"The new kids eat too much," Dennis said with a frown. "Buy less meat and more peanut butter. And forget about McDonald's and new school clothes, at least for Anh, An, and Hiep."

"I can't do that," I protested. "The state has certain rules. The foster kids are supposed to get clothes and entertainment like the other boys."

Dennis grunted. "You Vietnamese really stick together, don't you? Still taking advantage of the Americans! Whose side are you on now, anyway?"

His attitude had changed. He was wary of all the boat people and hated them for taking American jobs. He was shocked at the Khmer Rouge's "killing fields" and saw in Vietnam's invasion of Cambodia "just another domino falling." He was upset by Watergate and cynical about his government.

Religion, too, was no longer a comfort. The Baptist and Catholic sponsors insisted that all Vietnamese refugees join their church, including the Buddhists. This caused the local Buddhists to react strongly to prevent conversions, so the old religious wars that had troubled the Vietnamese soul for decades began afresh on American soil. All these big problems converged on our little house and took their toll on everyone. As the old Vietnamese saying went: *Gop gio thanh bao*—Small winds gather to make a tempest!

I had to admit that I spent a lot of time with the new boys. They still preferred Vietnamese to English and hearing it reminded me of home and made me feel better. They also needed a lot of love and counseling, and there was no substitute for the many hours of sympathetic listening I had to put in. Because of this, Dennis began to feel neglected.

"I'm on the family's side," I said. "But these poor kids have had such a hard time already. We just have to follow the rules. I see the monthly bills. You spend money for guns and for your motorcycle, but—"

"Leave my things out of it!" Dennis slammed the table. "Those guns are an investment. They go up in value—they'll pay for Alan's education. And the bike gives me the only freedom I have in this place. Working on it relaxes me, okay? So just leave my stuff out of it."

Dennis walked away and poured himself another glass of scotch: his usual way of ending an argument.

But our financial problems couldn't be ignored. When we couldn't cover our monthly bills, I went back to work as a housekeeper and, whenever possible, as a private nurse's aide. One of my clients was an elderly man named Charlie who had been paralyzed after a stroke. He had been a "gun nut" in his younger days and I drew him out on this subject whenever I could, hoping to get some insights into what made Dennis tick. Sometimes, Charlie said, he used to go hunting for food, but usually it was to kill for the sport of it: to disembowel the animals and mount their heads and skins for trophies—just as some French and Koreans and Americans had done to villagers in my country. I couldn't understand how men—how anyone—could view such brutalities as sport. Even if they didn't commit such acts themselves, just keeping the guns that made them possible seemed an invitation to more atrocities. Having been through what I had been through, I knew I could never be rational about firearms or the men who loved them. More important, I saw no reason to be.

Meanwhile, my Bible "education" wasn't exactly paving my way to Christian Heaven. After a few awkward sessions, I looked for reasons to put Janet off, until we met less than once a month. When Dennis and I became foster parents, I told her I would have no more time for "lessons," although I promised to keep reading the Bible on my own, consulting Dennis when I had questions. In reality, I read the Bible less and spent more time with the Buddhist monks, who, more and more, seemed to be the only people who understood me.

"You have a nice family, a nice house," my favorite teacher said one day after I had unburdened myself of all my problems. "And your husband is faithful and never beats you. How many rich women can say the same thing?"

"I know I should be happy with my life, master, but I feel I am being pulled down when I must move upward."

"You are still paying *nang nghiep*—soul debt—and heavy karma, *phat tu*. Whatever is disturbing you, there is a reason for it. Learn from it. The road to nirvana is never broad and safe, but always winding and treacherous. The best bowl of rice is the one for which you have worked the hardest, isn't that true?"

He used my agreement to make that road a little twistier.

"You are good with children," he said. "Perhaps they will be your salvation. *O hien thi lai gap lanh, nhung nguoi nhan-duc troi danh phuc cho*—Blessings and luck come to those who are kindhearted."

I thought for a long time about what that comment meant. It would be many years until either Jimmy or Tommy was old enough to help support his family financially or in any other way than the normal joy of being a kid. It then occurred to me that the same psychic energy and skills I was applying to clients like Charlie, who were hopelessly bogged down with *nang nghiep* themselves, might be better applied to little children who could benefit right away from my spiritual sense. It seemed to me that by increasing my commitment to the foster children program, I would hasten my own salvation.

Fortunately, our reviews by the social workers had always been A+. Almost as soon as I applied, we were approved for two more parentless Vietnamese refugees. Our total kid-count now came to eight.

As my master promised, the happiness these children brought our household quickly balanced our spiritual and emotional ledgers. Dennis was pleased because what I lacked in Christian knowledge I made up for in Christian charity—which won him praise from his congregation. What they didn't know was that I needed these stray kids as much as they needed me! One woman who worked for National Semi-Conductor was so impressed with my confidence and spirit that she offered me a job with her company for considerably more than I was paid to take care of Charlie. Of course, I took it in a flash. With a little luck, the extra money would repair our family checkbook the way the foster children were rehabilitating my lost and lonely soul.

Then, just as my happy little world looked brightest, the cosmic god spread his shadow across the light.

FIVE

Too Much Left Unsaid

LIKE THE SYMPTOMS of a terrible disease, the signs of our impending disaster accumulated slowly.

At National Semi-Conductor, I went to work on the assembly line making circuit boards. With the extra money, I was able to put Alan in day care and assist Hiep, who had just got his driver's license, in purchasing a jalopy so he could commute to his own part-time job and help me run errands for the kids. For the first time in a long time, my problems seemed resolved. I gave my attention to exploring my new world at NSC.

Two types of women worked on the assembly line—all Vietnamese. The first were *nha ngoi*—"tile-roofed women"—who came from privileged families in Vietnam and left only because of the Communist takeover. These women tended to hang around together, play marathon sessions of *tu set* (a pokerlike card game), and brag about how many maids, cars, and designer dresses they once had had. A few even cheated on American welfare to keep from spending their stash of gold and jewelry. Although all of them had lost much after the war, they still had more than most.

The rest of us were *gai nha la,* or "thatched-roof girls": poor, uneducated farm girls who knew nothing of the city, or knew it only as housekeepers, tea-girls, or prostitutes.

The job of putting colored resisters into circuit boards was so tedious and boring that both groups found time to gossip and tell stories. Although I always felt more at home with the country girls, their conversation held no surprises, and often depressed me. Like patches from the same torn quilt, we all missed the family love, religious rituals, holidays—but not the dangers—that had formed the patterns of our lives.

Like other Asian immigrants, especially Chinese and Koreans, these Vietnamese had a special way of helping each other in the midst of an alien culture. Mistrustful or ignorant of Western banks, they staked one another with funds for new enterprises in what they called the "money game" or *choi hui.* Very simply, each "player" put the same amount into a common pot, then those who had some money-making idea submitted a bid to the group—how much she was willing to pay to use the pool. Naturally, the person who offered most got the pot for that round, then everyone anted up again (including the "winner," although she couldn't make another bid until everyone had a turn) and the process was repeated, usually once a month. The person needing the money least (that is, the one offering the lowest bid in all previous rounds) got the final pot for free—a reward for staying in the game and helping everyone else. As a result, *choi hui* was touted as "a game that everybody wins"—which was true provided the enterprise earned enough money to pay back the pot plus the promised return.

Several people asked if I wanted to join the next *choi hui* pool starting up, but these players all had husbands and bigger incomes, so I was reluctant to get involved—although I could see how such a self-help club might prove very useful later on.

With Ed's social security benefits and the foster children's check, I was now making as much as Dennis but even that was soaked up every month by our blossoming expenses. That's why the news six months later—that most of us new hires would be laid off at the end of a big government contract—only made me question the wisdom of my own work ethic. I was a hard worker and didn't cheat the company or the government. I didn't pilfer company goods and resell them. It seemed unfair, therefore, to fire me.

So I went back to housekeeping and began looking for another invalid to care for. I also spotted more credit card receipts for guns, ammo, and motorcycle accessories in the monthly bills. I also saw a down-payment receipt and other paperwork for a parcel of land in Idaho. I didn't know much about that state except that it was as barren as Utah and we had no business buying land there when we could scarcely afford our too big home in San Diego.

"Are you still bitching about money?" Dennis shouted when I had the bad judgment to show him our overdrawn checkbook. "I told you how important my investments were. Look, if it makes you feel better, the land is for our retirement. I'm going to take the boys up there and teach them how to hunt and shoot. They should learn what it takes to survive—to protect themselves."

"What?" This thatched-roof girl blew up like a hut in a hurricane. "You will *not* teach my children to shoot! I see too many guns in my life! Killing is no way to protect anything! I don't even want guns in my house! If you want to go out, take the gun with you and don't ever come back!"

Dennis only shrugged. "I'm sorry you feel that way, but the guns stay. If you don't like it, you can go. It's a free country. But don't *ever* tell me to get out of my own house again!"

Dennis never exploded right away; he always smoldered first, feeding his hates the way maggots eat festering flesh. He walked to our dresser and pulled out a revolver. "Look at it, Ly. One day it may be the only thing that stands between you and a threat to your life."

"Threat? Threat from who? *You* the only person who waves guns around here! You the only person who drinks and shoots!" It was a stupid, if true, statement and I regretted it instantly.

"Not from me, from burglars"—the heat rose in Dennis's voice— "from dinks who slip back in here after you've wined and dined them to take what they've seen. To take care of that stupid, fucking *Major* if he's ever dumb enough to show his face around here!"

Dennis shoved the gun under his belt and went off to have a scotch. I slammed the door and sat on our bed crying in disbelief.

Dennis's clergyman, Pastor Bob, was a tall, big-boned man with a hairpiece. I knew we were supposed to confide in him with our problems, but I could never quite trust a man who was afraid of something as natural as a bald spot—our Buddhist monks had no problem shaving their hair completely off! Nevertheless, I poured out my heart to him and he listened respectfully: about our money problems, Dennis's guns and attitude toward the foster kids, and our increasingly vain attempts to make our two shores meet in the middle of the wide ocean between us.

Afterward, Pastor Bob tented his fingers and said tranquilly, "You know, Le Ly, I've already spoken to Dennis about many of these things. I told him I would pray for your family and asked that he try harder to accept Christ into his life. He said he would and things are already going better for him. Have you considered joining our church? I don't mean just Bible studies and coming to Sunday service, but being baptized? It will wash away your sins and make you a happier person."

I sat there thunderstruck. I had come for help—personal and spiritual—and all I got was an advertisement!

I told Pastor Bob I didn't think our family had enough time left to let God solve our problems in His mysterious ways, so he gave me the name of a marriage counselor in Mission Valley just north of San Diego.

"She's a woman." Pastor Bob winked. "Sometimes it's easier to talk to someone like ourselves."

I was not encouraged when the elevator to "Mary Ann's" antiseptic new third-floor office opened onto a brass-lettered sign that read CHRISTIAN FAMILY COUNSELOR. In Vietnam, spiritual and family advisers went out of their way to be just like us: not like doctors in a hospital. In America, it seemed, people were trained to think that solving personal problems was beyond their capacity—something ordinary people just couldn't do. Perhaps that was why America's divorce rate was so high. The helpers were asking regular human beings to do things they believed only high priests and doctors understood.

Mary Ann was about fifty: slim, blond, blue-eyed, and dressed like a Macy's salesclerk instead of a lab-coated doctor, which made me feel a little better. We went to her well-appointed office and sat at a coffee table like friends.

She asked me about my background, so I gave her what had become the standard, sanitized American version of my story. Experience had shown that ordinary Americans, especially women, were only confused and alienated by my wartime experiences. They were usually sympathetic, but just didn't understand. Men could not get past their anger about the war and women felt only pity. This did not leave us with much common ground for building a relationship or solving problems. With Mary Ann, I concentrated mostly on my experiences in America, hoping for some womanly insights. She asked if I had a boyfriend.

"No, but there is someone I think about when I feel very bad or very good." I looked at the carpeted floor. Although I was innocent of infidelity, my heart still belonged to Dan.

"I see. And does your husband have any girlfriends?"

Actually, that had never occurred to me—although it was apparently the first thing most American wives worried about when they had problems with their men. I suppose part of me almost wished Dennis would find a girlfriend: somebody to take the heat off me and keep him away from home when he was in a bad mood. I answered, "No, not that I know of."

"How about your sex life?" she continued, probing into what she obviously thought was the quicksand of most American marriages. "Is your husband satisfied with you? Does he ever complain about anything?"

"Not in the bedroom. I'm always there for him, whenever he wants me. Our problem is about guns and money and the way he treats me and thinks about the Vietnamese. He brings all the big world's problems into our little house and I don't know what to do about it."

"Well, as far as the gun problem goes"—she touched my arm like an understanding sister—"you say Dennis used to be a policeman. Guns are a part of his life. You come from Vietnam. It's natural for you to be afraid of them. But you're in America now. Things are different."

Yes—in Vietnam I never had a family member wave a gun in my face! But she was the doctor and I was paying for her advice so I kept quiet.

"Now, about the way he treats you—what church do you go to?"

"Sometimes I go with our boys to Dennis's Baptist church, but mostly I go to a Buddhist temple." Although just saying the words relaxed me, they made her very concerned.

"Well, maybe that's part of the problem. Have you ever thought about giving up the Buddhist temple and spending more time at your husband's church? You know, when people accept Christ into their lives, many wonderful things can happen."

I sat back in my chair while she repeated Pastor Bob's advertisement for Christianity and suggested that I might go shooting with Dennis to get over my fear of guns, perhaps even ride on the back of his motorcycle—the big black warbird!—to share the things that were important to him. When the appointment was over, she led me to the door and said, "Think about what I said, Le Ly"—she gave me a little hug—"and keep up the sex!"

Sex, guns, and Christ! Was that all Americans cared about? I went straight to the temple, where no appointments were needed.

"You must advise your husband that all life is sacred to you," my *su* told me. "Tell him you believe that nobody should kill—not even kill animals. It only creates bad karma. I can't tell you what will happen, *phat tu,* only that everything happens for a reason. Discover the cause, act properly, and the effect will follow you into your next life. If you want to go on to a higher plane, you must trust your feelings and act upon them."

Unlike the counselor's advice, the monk's words made perfect sense to me. I stopped fighting with Dennis but I also stopped thinking I had to do things his way. I simply left the room when he got his guns out—to clean them or show them to visitors—and encouraged the boys to do the same. I made the minimum payment on bills involving guns and motorcycles and just let the credit card balance grow. It was not a solution, but it was a lifeboat I could use until our marriage was refloated—or sunk from all its holes.

I dropped Mary Ann-the-Christian-counselor and, after much persuasion, took Dennis to see Joseph, a clinical psychologist recommended to us because he had been in Vietnam. He was a thoughtful, curious little man with two small bumps on his bald head that looked like devil's horns. But he had a more balanced view of things and became, for me at least, a valuable mentor.

Joseph's big concern was Dennis's love affair with guns and his use of liquor to "calm down." This, Joseph said, only depressed Dennis further. Joseph was also alarmed to hear that Dennis owned eight guns, with more arriving every month. He suggested to Dennis that if his guns were really investments, he wouldn't mind locking them up in a storeroom or gun club if it made his wife feel better. It was not the advice Dennis wanted to hear. He clammed up and said nothing more for the rest of the session, which was his last with "Dr. Joe." At least somebody besides me was the focus of his anger for a while.

In late 1979, during one of Dennis's drinking sprees, Joseph had me take all his guns to the local police station, where Dennis later had to go personally to pick them up. This only made Dennis believe that

Joseph and I had teamed up against him, but it felt good to have a smart and resourceful person to turn to when things got out of hand.

I also had another good break that bought me a little more time—time, I hoped, for things to work out on their own. I was recalled to work at NSC.

The first lunch hour after my girlfriends and I returned as "furloughees" was like a company picnic. Everybody brought food to celebrate and we hugged and cried and laughed like a family reunion. I thought I didn't have any good stories to tell, so I just listened to the others talk about their adventures over the past few months.

"You know, we wouldn't be here at all if it wasn't for that big new navy contract," one of my girlfriends said. "We should be here for at least another six months—maybe longer." I hadn't really thought much about what NSC made. I imagined our components were used for TV sets and radios.

"What are we making for the navy?" I asked.

"Bomber systems, I think," she answered. "Who knows? Who cares?"

"You mean we're making parts for bombers that fly off and kill people?" I almost choked on my noodles.

"I suppose so. But there's no war on—that's why business is slow. At least other countries buy this stuff—West Germany, Korea, you know."

I shuddered. The tough and remorseless ROK—Republic of Korea—troops came to our village during the war. Life and death had no meaning to them. Making components for their war machinery—for *anybody's* war machinery—would do little to reduce my soul debt in this life. Worst of all, I was astonished to think that, by simply accepting a job that was good for my family, I might be doing something harmful to all life on earth. By helping my children, I could be damaging my soul.

This killed my appetite and I left the group to sit alone under a tree. I got out my copy of the *Tu-Ke Tinh Tam,* the Buddhists' "bible," which was distributed by my temple. One girlfriend saw me and jokingly called out, "Look at Cu Ly—Old Maid Ly!" The nickname stuck. For the rest of the time I worked at NSC, I could no longer idly gossip with my co-workers—my fellow conspirators and criminals. Like the wounded souls who arrived on the refugee boats, I forgot how to smile.

One lunch hour while I was reading under the tree, a girlfriend named Thoa came up and said, "Cu Ly, if you take all that stuff so seriously, you ought to consult a soothsayer to see when you're going to become a Buddha!"

I knew she was joking, but it made me a little angry, "I don't want to become a Buddha. I just want to learn how to be a human being, okay? Besides, I don't know any fortunetellers. If I did, I would contact one tomorrow and find out how my family is doing in Vietnam."

"Oh, that's no problem," Thoa surprised me by saying. "You should go see Ba Thay Boi. Lots of the girls consult her—about their kids, marriages, how much money they're going to make, and all that. I don't believe in that crap myself, but the people who do swear by her."

Thoa was a "crackerjack" as Ed would say: a sharp girl and kind of a hustler, but her heart was pure and I trusted her as a friend. I phoned the number she gave me that night and made an appointment for the soothsayer's next free evening.

Ba Thay Boi was about Lan's age but looked twice as old. Whether it was because of a hard life or braving the withering winds of the spirit world year after year I couldn't say, but her house was a museum of the occult. Some of her props were for show—like the reading crystals that nobody but gullible round-eyes believed in. But the books on her shelf—the *I Ching* and dogeared Chinese horoscopes—told me she took her unusual calling very seriously. We got down to business at once.

I asked for a reading, telling her nothing about myself or my problems. Like an American doctor examining a new patient, she looked carefully at my palm, read some tea-and-herb leaves, and asked me to shuffle a deck of cards with a hole in the center, which she then arranged in a pattern. With all the evidence before her, she consulted some charts and finally looked me in the eye.

"Your biggest problem will not last much longer," she said with great certainty. "Your luck will change when the weather is wet and cold. A game will be involved—but it will go too far and that person will never come back. Your task is to stay out of the way—to be patient—and do nothing you will regret. After the dark clouds pass, you will be bathed in golden light and everything will be made clear to you."

The way she made her prediction chilled me, but on the whole, it seemed positive. Cryptic though it was, I interpreted it to mean that by this winter, Dennis and I would quit all our game-playing—as I had already started to do—and the person he had become (bitter, sullen, intolerant, possessive) would give way to the man who originally loved me and my boys and rescued Lan. My job was simply to do the right thing: to let go and let god run the universe.

The first thing I let go of was my job at NSC. I had decided to go into business for myself, just as I had done in Danang when my future seemed most bleak. At least when I was working on my own I called my own shots, was dependent on no one, and could look my father's spirit in the eye and hold my Phung Thi head up high.

My plan was to open a small deli. It wouldn't cost much and all I needed could be had through the "money game" at work. Because of my club and snack-bar jobs in Vietnam, I already knew how to do everything: deal with produce jobbers, keep my customers happy, keep track of the day's receipts, and what I didn't know my more experienced friends were willing to teach. The foster kids were big enough now to look after Alan and one another, so I went ahead and made all the arrangements.

I ante'd-up my two hundred dollars and successfully bid on a pot of five thousand dollars to buy an existing business in a low-income neighborhood that was filled with people like me: immigrants from Asia—mostly Laos and Cambodia—and Mexico. In the front I displayed Oriental food, which I knew would be popular because it was plentiful and cheap, and in the back I had a little kitchen for cooking and storage.

It took me a couple of weeks to get the place going. I continued to work the same hours I'd had at NSC, partly to keep Dennis from knowing I had quit my job, which would certainly have started a fight; but mostly to give me time to show him I had something to replace it with. I was sure he would be proud once he saw my little business, since he was always trying to get me to "think like an American."

"Absolutely not!" Dennis shook his head when I finally told him —showed him—what I had accomplished. "I absolutely forbid it!"

"But why?" I was more than disappointed—I was astounded. "What can we lose?"

"What can we lose? I'll tell you: our house, our cars, the boys' school money—everything! What if the potato salad goes bad and people get sick? What if somebody slips on the floor and gets hurt? They'll sue us for everything we've got. You don't know Americans like I do. They'll sue at the drop of a hat. Besides, you're just a dumb immigrant. The lawyers would skin you alive."

"Then we'll buy insurance!"

"No way. That's just more money out of pocket. You've got to close the place right now. Today."

"But we'll lose all the money I borrowed!"

"It's better to lose a little now than a lot later on."

"But other Vietnamese own stores!"

"Yes, because they're refugees and the U.S. government helps them—backs their loans. You're not a refugee. You've got a white husband behind you and there's nobody to protect me if you get into trouble."

I couldn't believe what I was hearing. Caution was one thing but paranoia was another. He was always talking about "free enterprise" but now the concept seemed to terrify him. I told him I would think about what he had said, but that I would operate the shop until I could at least pay back my friends.

The next morning I got up to find that my little green Vega was gone. Dennis had taken it, knowing I couldn't drive his Ford Pinto, which had a stick shift. I got Hiep, bless his heart, to drop me off at the shop. That evening, Dennis was angry that I had gone to the shop without his permission. "The best insurance," he said, "is to keep the damned place closed!"

The next morning both cars were gone and Hiep had already taken the kids to school. I took the bus—transferring three times—and walked the last mile to the shop on foot. Even then, the store was open in time for lunch. When I returned (somewhat late, but the kids had already started dinner), Jimmy asked, "Why is the car parked three blocks away?"

"You've seen the car?"

"Yes—it's in the alley behind our school. Why did you leave it there?"

I stormed out of the house and retrieved the car. When I got back, Dennis was just turning into the driveway. He got out and slammed the Pinto's door.

"God *damn* it!" he screamed. "Who told you where the car was?"

"The boys found it by accident." I stayed in the car with the window partway up. I didn't want him to reach in and wring my defiant little neck. "Why did you hide it?"

"You know damn well why!" He stalked into the house and had some scotch for dinner.

The next day, the Vega was in the driveway, but it wouldn't start. I had to take the bus again. That evening, I asked Hiep to take a look under the hood and he said the battery terminal had been unplugged.

I asked Hiep to take the kids to a movie, even though it was a school night, and waited for Dennis to come home. This whole "musical cars" game had gone far enough and it was time for a showdown.

"Why do you treat me this way?" I asked. I tried to sound concerned, not angry, which was difficult. "I know you don't like the deli, but what happens if one of the kids gets hurt and I have to come home and take them to the hospital?"

"Hiep has a car." Dennis went at once for his scotch.

"But Hiep goes to a different school and has a job. He's not a parent or even a guardian. Besides, I don't think Hiep has anything to do with this. I want to know why you play this silly game with me."

Dennis tossed back his first glass and poured another. "Because I'm tired of the games *you* play, Ly. Yes, you and your Vietnamese friends. You're with them all the time. You plot against me and all Americans. I know the way they use the system once they get here. I've seen the way you favor the Vietnamese kids over me. Don't you think Alan and I deserve the same attention as those damned boat people? You spend too much time running around going to your temple and plotting to take advantage of me and the system. I think you should stay home and take care of me and the house. That's why I play the car game. I know it's the only way you'll get the message—and it works."

Dennis grabbed a pencil and began drawing on a paper napkin. He tossed the napkin down in front of me: a little cartoon of Buddha on a toilet with monks kowtowing to him.

"There—that's what I think of your temple. Buddha is shit!" He stormed into our room and slammed the door.

Every night his temper got shorter. Whenever I would complain about something—even little things that had nothing to do with him, like a long line at a gas station or a rude salesperson—Dennis would say things like "Then why don't you go back to Vietnam and swing from the trees and eat bananas?" When he was talking on the phone to a friend, he might say, "Never marry a Vietnamese bitch. She'll take your money and shorten your life!" When we'd see a news clip or documentary on TV about Vietnam and I would comment on the beautiful scenery, he would say, "Then you should've stayed there!" He even sent money to Oral Roberts, the Christian magician he loved to watch on TV, and asked him to "pray for my heathen wife who is possessed by demons." He got back a small cross and a picture of Jesus which he kept with him all the time—even under his pillow, next to his gun.

I once made the mistake of telling Dennis at such a moment that I was thinking about writing a book about my life in Vietnam—to try to explain to Americans what it was like to grow up in a village and what the war meant to ordinary people in the countryside. He only laughed.

"You? Write a book? You can't even read the Bible!"

"I can write a little bit, and what I can't write in English, I can write in Vietnamese and get translated. People think they know who the Viet Cong were, but they really don't."

"I'll tell you this: you start talking about the VC and the Commies over there and they'll take away your kids. You're even starting to piss me off about it, so just shut up, okay? Forget about your stupid goddamn book and fix dinner."

I fixed his dinner, but I also started writing down what I remembered about my family and life in the village. The text was all in longhand on yellow pads and in Vietnamese, so Dennis, if he ever found it, would think it was just a letter. It became a lifeline to my past and, I also realized, to my future as well. Even if nothing came of it, the project kept my head above water whenever Dennis tried to push me under.

I hoped Dennis would get over his peevishness, at least long enough to let me pay back the debt on my deli. But he never did. He escalated the car game by taking my keys and then my cash until it took nearly as much time to discover and correct the morning's sabotage as it did to commute and open the store. Finally I turned the shop keys back to the landlord and told him I could no longer stay in business. Between the rent penalties and forfeited deposits and loans I couldn't repay, I figured I had lost about ten thousand dollars. Dennis was unimpressed.

"So, who do you owe the most money to—Vietnamese?"

"Yes," I answered. "My friends from NSC."

"Well, they were no friends to you. All they did was break up your family. Without them, you wouldn't have gotten into this mess. We should sue them for damages."

After months of waiting for Dennis to snap, I came unglued myself.

"What are you talking about? It's not them, it's us! I try to build something for our family and you keep tearing it down! I can't take it anymore, Dennis—I just can't take it! I don't have a car! I don't have any money! You call the foster home program and have all the checks mailed to you at work so I can only use what you give me. What am I supposed to do? *What am I supposed to do!"*

The room spun and the knot in my stomach tore up through my heart and into my head and banged around like the clapper in a bell —a big temple bell, a bigger Baptist bell—louder and louder and louder and louder.

I woke up in a hospital bed. I knew at once I had been drugged, because my limbs didn't respond the way they should and the weight on my soul seemed enormous—immovable. Mumbling in the haze I heard *Mr. Hayslip* and *don't worry* and *nervous breakdown* and *what did she have for breakfast* and *ulceration* and *well, I don't know about that* and *go home and we'll call you in the morning.*

Somebody took my hand and I thought it was Dennis and tried to pull away but it was the doctor. I clutched tight.

"All right, Mrs. Hayslip," the boyish doctor said with a pleasant grin. "Why don't you tell me what this is all about?"

So I did.

Dennis didn't come to the hospital the next day, probably on doctor's orders, but he picked me up on the third.

We didn't talk much on the drive home. Dennis asked contritely how I felt and I said I was fine but my throat hurt and I didn't feel like talking. When we got home, the house was empty.

"Where is everybody?" I asked, startled. "Where are my boys?"

"My mom flew in from Ohio to pick up Alan for a visit. Jimmy and Tommy are at Pat and Mike's. The social workers came and got everybody else. Things will be nice and quiet for you now. You'll get a lot of rest."

I staggered upstairs like a zombie. It was as if a giant artillery shell had landed on my house, wounding me and blowing everyone else to kingdom-come. Only Dennis—the man with the guns, with the big black bomber—was unscathed. In fact, he acted as if he had won the battle.

I couldn't sleep so I went back down to help Dennis fix dinner. Halfway down the stairs I heard him on the phone, so I stopped.

"—No, Mom, I don't want Alan back. Keep him there. Don't worry, I've already called the realtor. The house goes on the market tomorrow. No, she's not okay. She's really messed up. I guess it was the war or something. Yes, you were right. Yes, yes. I know. Okay. I'll call you soon—"

I tiptoed back upstairs and collapsed onto the bed. I didn't know what to do. I obviously couldn't trust Dennis, or even talk things over with him anymore. He was making all the decisions by himself, even the ones that affected me, my children, and my property. Perhaps the court or the hospital had given him the right to do that—I didn't know. I only knew that I had to think of some way to get my kids back and get my life in order.

The next day, Jimmy and Tommy came home, which made me feel a lot better, but I still didn't know what to do about Alan. A few hours after Dennis had gone to work, his niece called from Ohio. She was a little older than me and although we had only met once, in 1978 when we had driven East to meet most of Dennis's relatives, she seemed like a nice, responsible girl.

After asking how I was, she said, "Ly, I have to talk quickly, I'm calling from a pay phone. You've got to come and get Alan. He cries for you all the time. I think what Dennis is doing is wrong. This isn't the first time he's pulled something like this. He tried it before with his ex-wife and Victor, his son. I don't think anybody here will cause you trouble, but you've got to do something fast."

I thanked her and called "Dr. Joe," whom I hadn't seen in several months. I told him about the deli and my nervous breakdown and what was going on with Alan. Joseph told me exactly what to do.

First, I called an airline and got a round-trip reservation on the next flight to Cleveland and a one-way child's fare for the return flight landing in Los Angeles, not San Diego. I didn't have enough money for the tickets, but doing something positive to solve my problem made me feel a lot better. Then I got together all the papers —birth certificate, photos, my passport, and marriage certificate— that proved Alan was my son and put them in an envelope. Next, I called some of my Vietnamese girlfriends and tried to raise cash for the ticket.

"Can I pawn my wedding band with you for six hundred dollars?" I asked Luan, who did a lot of that sort of thing. "You've seen it. You know how nice it is."

"I don't have that kind of money right now," she said, and told me to try so-and-so.

Either nobody had any money, or word was out that Le Ly Hayslip was a bad credit risk. I finally talked a neighbor into lending me four hundred dollars on my ring, and decided to pin my last hopes on Lan who, I figured, still owed me a favor.

"Lan, this is Ly," I said on the phone, trying to sound like a mature and responsible adult instead of a needy little sister. "Dennis finally cracked. He sent Alan to his mother's in Ohio. He's planning on leaving me and wants to keep our son. I've got to go get Alan. I've been able to raise most of the plane fare, but I need two hundred dollars more and someone to watch the boys. Can you help me?"

"I can watch the kids, but I can't lend you any money. Petey and I have all we can do to meet the payments on our house. Anyway, I don't think he'd like it. Remember the last time we talked about money? I can't believe you'd ask that question!"

Good old Lan—as predictable as the seasons, the tides, the stars in the sky! While she chewed me out about how mean I had been to her, I wondered if she remembered how she had got to America. *Cuu vat, vat tra on, cuu nhon, nhon tra oan,* my mother used to say. "If you want gratitude, don't save a friend—save an animal!" She was right, but Lan was right, too. I never should have called.

I phoned my neighbor again and came up with enough valuables from our overfurnished American house—costume jewelry and appliances—to guarantee the rest of the airfare.

I dropped the boys at Lan's and caught the red-eye to Ohio before Dennis got home from the evening shift.

The flight gave me a much needed chance to catch my breath. America's terrain rolling beneath the wings seemed endless—as green and brown as the ocean had been blue and white on my flights across the Pacific.

Upon arrival, I took a cab directly to the city's police headquarters and presented my credentials and my complaint. Thank god Joseph had been busy. He had made dozens of calls and testified to the authorities in California that as a "licensed mental health professional," he believed Dennis was unstable and potentially dangerous. Fortunately, Dennis's record in Ohio spoke for itself. He had a history of child kidnapping from his previous divorce. He had also been involved in a serious assault with his first wife's boyfriend and was hospitalized as a result. Although Dennis had been a fellow peace officer, the local police agreed to support the request of their sister agency in San Diego.

Three squad cars with a pair of officers each went with me to "Grandma Hayslip's" house, where we arrived about noon. They told me to go to the door and see if the residents would voluntarily return my child. The policeman in charge said they would come running in case of any problems. They got out of their cars, pistols at the ready.

I did as I was told, with one exception. I did not ring the doorbell, but went right in. "Mom" Hayslip was fixing sandwiches in the kitchen and I scooted right by her without saying a word. I could hear cartoons on the big TV in the living room and homed in on it like a "smart bomb" after a bunker.

My little boy sat on a cushion looking exhausted and miserable. Ghostly TV images danced on his pale face. When he saw me, I thought he would burst for joy.

"Mommy!" He clapped his hands and jumped up.

I grabbed him, pinned him close to my heart, and ran out the way I came in. I brushed by Mom Hayslip, who was too amazed to say anything—but I knew she recognized me. Her heavy footsteps followed me to the porch. On the steps I turned and yelled, "All I want is my baby!"

I got into the squad car but the police lingered a minute in case Dennis's mother wanted to come down and ask any questions. But she knew what was going on and didn't ask. Instead, she ran back inside. Through the window I saw her dialing the phone.

The officers drove us straight to the airport and one waited until we safely boarded our plane. Joseph had told me that by the time we returned, Dennis would probably know what I had done, so I had booked our return flight into LAX and took the train to San Diego. Instead of going home, I took a cab straight to our local precinct and told the police what was going on. I said I was especially concerned about Dennis's drinking and his guns.

Unlike the Ohio police, though, the local officers refused to drive me home. Instead, they said they would ask Dennis to come and pick me up, and interview him before we left. I didn't like the compromise, but it was all they were going to do.

For almost half an hour, I sat in the waiting room and watched Dennis and an officer talk through a glass door. At first, Dennis was angry and belligerent. After a while, he seemed to calm down. By the end of the discussion, he was laughing and joking with the officers—perhaps they shared some "gun nut" stories, who knows? He came out and offered his hand to help me up.

"Come on, honey," he said sweetly. "Let's go home. I'm sure we can work all this out."

The officer put his hand on my shoulder, "If you have any problems, Mrs. Hayslip, be sure to call us first. Don't try and take the law into your own hands."

I didn't reply to either of them but went with Dennis to the car. Inside, his manner changed totally and he didn't say another word all the way home—he just glowered at the traffic.

When we got to the house, Dennis took Alan into the den and locked the door. I was not worried for Alan—Dennis loved him, perhaps too much—and the same locked door that kept me out would keep them in. What surprised me most was my greeting from Jimmy and Tommy.

"Hi, Mom! How did everything go?"

"What are you doing here? You're supposed to be at Di Lan's!"

"Daddy picked us up," Jimmy said. "I asked if he was going to hold us hostage for Alan but he just laughed. He said he loved us and wanted us near him while you were gone. Isn't that great?"

I could've died—but not before shooting Lan myself for giving the kids to Dennis without my permission! What was she thinking about?

The next morning, while Dennis and Alan slept in, I called Dr. Joseph. He was not pleased with the way things had turned out.

"I think you're still in great danger, Ly," he said somberly. "I believe your husband is very ill. He kidnapped Alan once. He may try it again. Normally, I don't advise separation for my patients, but in this case—you should think seriously about living somewhere else, at least until things settle down."

This put me in a quandary. In Vietnam, divorce among peasants was very rare. More frequently, a husband would *bo vo*—leave his wife and live with another woman—but they would still raise the kids together and he would pay what he could to help support the original household. Nobody called lawyers; village opinion was enough to police most situations. Consequently, I didn't know whom to blame for my failed marriages except myself, or whom to turn to next for advice except the temple monks.

"Den nha ai nay sang con nhi," my *su* said when I told him of Joseph's suggestion. " 'The light shines brighter in other homes.' You cannot take your family problems to doctors and lawyers and expect a solution. They think of the fastest cure, which is not always the best —especially in matters of soul debt, which can consume many lifetimes. Do you think these people will care for and comfort and support you when your husband is gone? I know the human heart, *phat tu.* These people you consult are not bad men, but neither is your husband. These advisers seem to help you, but in the long term, they don't. Your husband seems to abuse you, but really, he hasn't. Where are your scars from his beatings? Show me your starving children. Where are the girlfriends he keeps?"

"Go home," the monk concluded. "Do not add to your own bad karma by trying to change your husband's. Help him learn what he was put on earth to learn. You are a water buffalo, are you not? Like the water buffalo, you must labor long and hard and without complaint. That is your character and your destiny."

I left the temple feeling more confused than ever. I couldn't argue with the monk—he was right about eternity. But the doctors and policemen and lawyers knew a lot about solving problems here and now. Perhaps I was becoming a victim of America's need for "instant gratification." Perhaps I hadn't given Dennis the chance I had barely given Ed: to let our lives find a balance of their own. Everything in our marriage, from beginning to end, had been a negotiation: to rescue Lan, to give Dennis a sense of home and family, to keep a roof over our heads, to reconcile our different religions, to nourish my soul in this alien land. The problem was, our deals never worked out, and the bill was coming due.

Despite my better inclinations, I made an appointment to see a lawyer: a woman attorney recommended by a friend.

Miss King was short, very plain, and very tough. Unlike many of my American neighbors and other Caucasian counselors who tried to hide their condescending attitude, she made no secret of her opinion that I was an ignorant little farm girl who should do exactly as she was told.

"Look, Mrs. Hayslip," Miss King said after I had explained things as best I could. "We can do this one of three ways: the easy way, the hard way, or the right way. The easy way—you feel good, I make a lot of money, and you still have all your problems. The hard way— you feel bad, I feel bad, and I still make a lot of money. If we do it the right way, though, you'll feel like shit and I'll still make a lot of money, but at least your problems will get solved. Now which will it be?"

"I guess I want my problems solved—"

"Good girl," she said flatly, shoving some papers across the desk. "You fill these out and return them to me. If you need help, go to a neighbor—I'm not an English teacher. When you're done, we'll get a court order barring your husband from your house."

"Couldn't we just ask him to go nicely?"

"Honey, when you ask someone nicely, you send a Candygram, not an injunction. The son of a bitch has eight guns—a regular Fort Apache, right? You gotta get his attention with superior firepower. You said you wanted to do this the right way, didn't you?"

I agreed and scooped up the papers.

On the day the injunction was served, I took the precaution of taking the kids to Pat and Mike's. From several houses down, we watched Dennis loading his things into an old van he had recently purchased. Hiep was helping him, which made me feel a little better. Hiep was a levelheaded kid and, as a reminder of the old days, Dennis's ability to get along with him was a good sign. After a while, we noticed that Dennis was not only loading his guns, liquor, and clothes, as allowed by the injunction, but a lot of furniture, too, which was not. Mike wanted to go stop him—make a big stink and even call the police—but I said no.

"Let him do what he wants, that stuff doesn't matter," I said. Mike looked at me as if I were crazy—as if I didn't understand what American divorces were all about. He was right. All my Vietnamese instincts ran completely contrary to my American advice. All my actions—done in good American fashion—seemed to betray everything my father had taught me. My only hope was that by doing things "the American way" while keeping the Vietnamese way in my heart, I would somehow wind up doing what was right.

The next morning Dennis's van was gone so the boys and I returned home. I opened the door onto an almost bare house and the kids ran in and the first thing I heard was an echoey "Daddy!" My heart jumped to my throat. Dennis came into the kitchen holding Alan.

"What are you doing here?" I was stunned and glanced at the phone, thinking momentarily of calling either Mike or my lawyer, or even the police.

"It's Sunday," Dennis said, smiling. He had dark circles under his eyes and was unshaved. He sat jiggling his son on his hip. "I came to take Alan to church."

My mind raced. "No, I don't think—"

Dennis was out the door.

"Come on Jimmy—Tommy—" I called over my shoulder and followed, wrapping a scarf over my unbrushed hair.

"What are you doing?" Dennis asked.

"We're going with you."

"No, you're not. You stay here and fix lunch. We'll be back after the service."

I would have laughed if I wasn't so scared and confused. I would have loved to go back in the house, but I swore I would never let Alan out of my sight again until this whole mess had been resolved.

We piled into my car while Dennis put Alan into the front seat from the driver's side, then just stood by the open door. I could see he was angry and wondering what to do next. Mike was on the sidewalk a few houses down getting his morning paper. He called, "Ly—is everything okay?"

Dennis gave him the finger and glared at me though the windshield. "Bitch!" His fist slammed into the glass, cracking it like ice.

We drove in steamy silence to the church, even though none of us were dressed for it. Dennis brusquely led us to Pastor Bob, who took the three boys to Sunday school. When the sermon was over and everyone was filing out, Janet stopped to talk to me. I tried to be polite, remembering where I was, but I tried also to keep one eye on Dennis as he snaked through the crowd toward the playground. Finally, I said to Janet, "I don't want to be rude, but I must go!" and ran toward the back. Tommy and Jimmy were still on the playground with some other kids, but Dennis and Alan were long gone.

I got a ride home and called Miss King's answering service. It seemed like hours before she returned my call. I told her what had happened.

"So—we're going to do it the hard way after all, eh?" I could almost see her head shake in disgust. "Why didn't you change the locks? How come you let him keep the keys to your car? You should've called the cops the second you saw him in that house. He was a trespasser, Ly. He broke the law just being there."

"Okay, all right." I was more than a little disappointed and angry myself. "I was stupid. So what do I do now?"

"Sit tight. When the phone rings, answer it and do what you're told."

An hour later, the phone did ring. It was a police inspector who said my attorney had just reported a kidnapping. He asked if there was any change in my son's status—meaning, had my husband brought him home—and I said no. He asked me a lot of other questions, then told me to stay by the phone, which I did for the next two days. Out of desperation, I called Lan—I knew she wouldn't or couldn't offer much help, but she could at least listen to my worries and comfort me as my sister.

Instead, I got another lecture on how I was getting what I deserved because I had kicked her out of our old house in Santee in favor of Dennis. Now that he was showing his true colors, she said, I should find some other shoulder to cry on.

I hung up the phone and there was little Jimmy staring at me from the hall. He was not so little any more—thirteen years old, with his father's dark complexion, gemstone eyes, and delicate jaw. The world —the era—of his birth now seemed a million miles and a million years away. In his sad, empathetic Vietnamese visage, I saw Hiep and An and Anh and all the other little boat-kids who had, because of my bad judgment and bad karma, now been scattered to the winds. The foster child agency still had them all and wouldn't return them as long as my home life was in turmoil. What right did I have to create my own extended Vietnamese family, my own "village," when I couldn't even keep my natural family together? Once again, in the name of love, I had tried to do my best and made things worse than ever.

The phone rang. I knew Lan would call back—to apologize; to cry with me like a sister. After all, despite her own hard life, she, too, was Phung Thi. I lifted the receiver.

"Ly?" it was a husky male voice. "This is Dennis."

My breath caught in my throat, "How is Alan?"

"He's fine. Do you want to see him again?"

"Of course! I'm worried sick! The police are looking everywhere for you."

"Fuck the police. If you want to see him again, do exactly as I tell you."

I couldn't believe my ears!

"What do you want?" I said quietly. Maybe if I stayed calm, Dennis would calm down too.

"Write a letter to your lawyer. Tell her you're dropping all charges against Dennis Hayslip. Tell her you want the house and all our stuff put into my name. Tell her you're dropping the divorce—Ly, are you listening to me?"

"Yes, I'm listening."

"Get the letter notarized, then take it to Pastor Bob. Tell him I'll call tomorrow morning and ask him to read the letter over the phone. Do it, Ly, or you'll really be sorry."

As soon as Dennis hung up, I called Miss King and Pastor Bob. Both said to do nothing and let the police do their work.

The next day, Dennis called to curse me for not writing the letter and hung up.

After two more nerve-wracking days, Lan called. She said Dennis had phoned and said Alan was fine. She said she couldn't talk now and hung up. A day later, she did the same thing, which was very odd. Usually, she would prolong the conversation just to give me another lecture. It was as if someone was watching her. She called a third time in as many days:

"Ly—listen carefully. This is the first time I've had a chance to tell you. Dennis and Alan are here with me—yes, they're here right now. Ly, he's getting ready to take Alan to Canada. Alan's really upset and doesn't want to stay with Dennis anymore—"

She suddenly changed her voice, pretending she had been talking to a girlfriend about clothes or something, and hung up. Dennis had obviously come into the room. I called Miss King—who again told me to stay put and not try to do anything myself. She said she would call the police. A couple of hours later, she was back on the phone:

"Ly, good news. Alan is safe. Dennis is in custody."

"Thank god!" I sank into my chair.

"The police want to know if you're going to press charges. You know—put Dennis in jail."

"No, no. As long as Alan is safe, that's all I care about. Dennis already has enough trouble in his life. When will they bring my son home?"

Miss King was silent a moment, then said, "I'm afraid it's not that simple. They've taken him to the Hillcrest Receiving Home. That's usually the first step before putting a child in foster care."

"No! I want my son with me!"

"Well, your husband said some pretty amazing things in his statement. He says you abused the children, particularly his son, and even molested some of the foster kids. The police can't take any chances. They figure a foster home is better in cases like this until an investigation can sort things out."

I was crying—heaving—convulsively now. How could Dennis make his own son suffer so much? It was worse than unfair: it was an atrocity.

I composed myself and took some clean clothes and toys to the receiving home. Alan met me with the refugee's look in his eyes and almost got me crying again. He was unwashed and underfed—whether because he couldn't or wouldn't eat during his captivity, I didn't know. As I bathed him and changed his clothes, with the help of an attendant, we noticed little scabs and scratches all over his body.

"How did this happen?" the attendant asked, scowling at me.

"How should I know?" I almost shouted. "He's been gone for two weeks!"

Working through my tears, I dressed my little boy and remembered him *mang nang*—heavy in my belly. I recalled the pangs of his birth—*de dau*—and remembered chewing his food for him *nhai com suon nuoc,* as he was weaned. I was shocked, angered, and insulted at the insolence of men. All the American men I had known—in Vietnam or America—became narrow-minded, petty, and vindictive when they were angry. They didn't know about women and didn't respect them. I couldn't believe such men had ever known a mother's love: the love of the woman who brought them into this world. Such atrocities as I had witnessed in both countries could only be perpetrated by men with no awareness of the sacred origins of life. They considered children—even their own—as no more than weeds in a garden. We called them *vo nghi*—"no conscience" men—and I only now really understood what that meant. They had no idea where they came from or where they were going. They were men who loved their hunting dogs and guns more than their ancestors—and no wonder. They were nothing but dogs themselves.

I came to care for Alan every day and stayed long as I could, often bringing his half brothers. On the day of Alan's disposition hearing, I appeared with Miss King. The hearing officer reviewed the police reports, our files from the domestic relations court, our casebook as foster parents, and transcripts of interviews with dozens of people—including the foster kids, my natural kids, and our neighbors.

Finally, he looked up and sighed. "Mrs. Hayslip, your file shows you've been an exemplary foster parent for five years. But they also suggest that your husband is a very unstable and possibly dangerous man. If I were to release your son to you, how are you going to handle things in the future?"

"I will do whatever you say, your honor."

The hearing officer laughed. "I'm not a judge, but I do have some advice. Get out of the local area. You may not be aware of it, but the police report says they found several firearms in your husband's car when they arrested him, along with some hate notes and some very bizarre drawings of you—presumably made by your husband. Since you declined to press charges, the police dropped the case; but that doesn't mean your problems are over. If you can lie low for a while—stay out of your husband's way, avoid giving him easy targets for his rage—things might return to normal."

I told the hearing officer I would stay with a friend—an old girlfriend from NSC who had always been calling me to visit—in Los Angeles for a while, but neither of us knew if "a while" would be long enough.

When Miss King dropped me off at the house and waited for me to gather our things, my arms and legs felt like lead. When I was growing up, I had to run from bombs, artillery shells, the Republicans, the Americans, and the Viet Cong. I went into exile to save my life and wound up losing that old life forever. Now, I was going into hiding again, and I was double-struck with fear and desolation: first, because of what I didn't know; and second, because of what I did.

Just as I was leaving the house, the phone rang. It was Lan. She told me Dennis had called several times to get information about what was going on: with me, the boys, and the hearing at Hillcrest. She said he bragged about hiring "the best lawyer in San Diego" and how he was going to clobber me and my "ball-busting bitch attorney" in court to win all the boys, the house, the cars, and all of our possessions. Lan thought I would be alarmed but I told her to relax, I felt okay.

At least Dennis was now reaching for lawyers instead of guns and whiskey bottles.

At our first court hearing, two of my Vietnamese girlfriends' American husbands and Pete Bailey testified against me. Although treachery in some form lurks in almost every human heart, I was surprised by this and credited it to Dennis's sharp lawyer, whom I could tell Miss King respected the way one tiger gives way to a bigger one in the forest. Dennis needed to make the case that I was an unfit mother, and my friends' husbands were more than willing to tell the judge how we sat around in our lunch hours talking about ways to beat the American system. Of course, Petey was no family friend either, despite our charity to him when he and Lan needed it. He reinforced Dennis's claim that we Vietnamese women were somehow always "plotting" against him.

In the end, the judge was unimpressed. He ordered Dennis to return my car, give us title to the house, and split with me the furnishings he had taken. More importantly, he gave me custody of Alan, allowing Dennis frequent visitation.

For a while things seemed to go okay. Dennis and I scrupulously observed the judge's orders and even Lan called more frequently. At first I thought she just felt bad about Petey's testimony, especially since the judge didn't believe it. Later though, I found out it was because she was still in touch with Dennis. She owed him a tremendous debt and he was not about to let her forget it, particularly when he saw it as a way of getting through to me.

Lan said Dennis had complained of heart trouble and now walked with a cane, although that didn't stop him from hunting with his guns and riding his big motorcycles. He even dropped in for counseling with the Buddhist monks, which really floored me.

"You should be nicer to him," Lan said, "that's all." I realized she was probably right. At least Dennis was trying.

The next time Dennis dropped off Alan, I invited him in for coffee. We chatted about this and that and he did not seem vindictive or suspicious, just grateful. He said we should help each other "get off this circle of hate" and I agreed, although I did not agree with his method for doing it. Within a year, I received a letter from the Reconciliation Court. Dennis wanted a refereed meeting to see if we could get back together.

By now I had found another computer assembly job. I was hired as a supervisor because of my previous work experience, serious attitude, and because the owner of the company, Kathy Greenwood, took a liking to me. My co-workers this time were mostly Mexicans or Hispanic Americans, Laotians, Filipinos, and a few Vietnamese. For the first time, I also worked with black Americans, and had a chance to relate to them in some way other than as dangerous soldiers. As I got to know them, the stories I heard from these people had themes common to my own experience: dislocation, depression, desperation, as well as the joys of big families and eternal faith in unexpected good luck and in the existence of something bigger than themselves.

I also became a foster mother again—of sorts.

Jimmy's father, Anh, had arranged for his other two teenage sons, Chanh and Tran, to escape Vietnam by boat. After braving pirates and patrol boats on the South China Sea, they were picked up and interned in a Chinese refugee camp on the mainland. They arrived in Minnesota in February 1981, under the sponsorship of Anh's brother. However, the cold weather horrified them and they contacted me. They said their father had always considered me his second wife and they had fond memories of when I was their nanny. They stayed at our house, long enough for Jimmy to get to know his half brothers a little better, then got good jobs and moved on. It was odd how much our worlds had turned upside down—an irony that was lost on them but affected me greatly. When I first met them, I was a war-worn teenager a little younger than they were now. Their father was a wealthy Saigon industrialist who used me to comfort himself, then cast me and my mother aside when nature took its course and I got pregnant. Now they had come to America, as penniless as I had been, to seek refuge in my beautiful home. I had an overpowering sense of motion—of passing from one room to another, or floating from the trough to the crest of one big wave. Where the currents would take any of us after this, who could say, but we were all part of one big cosmic cyclone—the whirlwind of life—and it was dazzling.

I went to the reconciliation meeting armed with plenty of advice—just enough to confuse me, like a man with so many clocks that he never knows the time. My lawyer told me to be cautious, which I was bound to be anyway. Huong told me that "a child without a father is like a house without a roof," pretty much what my monk said, too. My co-workers at Digidyne, Kathy's company, were evenly split. The people from big, happy families thought we should get back together;

those who had been divorced said to leave well enough alone and don't try to resurrect the past.

Once again I felt torn between *tinh* and *nghia*. *Tinh* is love in all its shades, including passion. *Nghia* is the spirit-bond of soulmates. By conceiving a child, Dennis and I had become intertwined with *nghia,* just as I was bound to Ed's spirit and Anh through my other children. Westerners seemed to think that spouses can be shed like old clothes—*vo chong nhu ao coi ra kho gi*—but I wasn't so sure. Soul debt is a burden I had already discovered couldn't be worn lightly.

The reconciliation hearing ended inconclusively. Dennis was so determined to be contrite he actually hit below the belt, promising me title to all our possessions and legal custody of Alan. He even produced the deed of trust to our house, like an appliance salesman waving a contract, and said he would sign it over to me on the spot if I would only take him back. Instead, I asked for a recess to think things over. I went to consult my *su*.

"Master," I said, "my only goal is to break this bond of *nghia* with Dennis as soon and as cleanly as possible. I am willing to accept him as a friend, but not again as my husband. If I refuse his offer, will our bad karma continue?"

My *su* smiled and invited me to share some tea. Usually, this was a reward. Now it seemed like a preparation.

"Phat tu," he said, "there is a yin and yang for everything: good and evil, cause and effect. In the war, you saw many people killed, some of them were babies. Were these people blameless?"

"I cannot know, master." I knew this answer was wrong, since Buddhists believe every effect has its cause. But I could not conceive of a universe where a newborn baby was guilty of anything.

"But you admit that the baby was born of woman—"

"Of course."

"So, you do not dispute this natural fact. Similarly, you must accept the natural fact, the karma, that caused both the baby's birth and its death. You may weep for the slain baby and feel empathy for its suffering, just as you may weep for the soldier who earns more bad karma by killing it; but in doing so you must not disclaim the laws of the universe—the wheel of incarnations—that caused the act. Birth and death, whatever the circumstances, are as natural as the movements of the sun and moon, which we accept without question."

"And my duty toward Dennis?"

"You say he has slapped one cheek—done you a terrible wrong?"

"That is true, master."

"Then offer him the other. Give him a chance to redeem himself. If he fails you again, you will at least have satisfied your own *nghia* while his soul debt has increased."

After Tet, in February 1981, Dennis moved back on what the court referee termed "a trial basis." How long that trial would last was anyone's guess.

Things did not start auspiciously. Dennis's "heart condition" miraculously went away (he attributed it to the donations he had been making to Oral Roberts), although he still found himself incapable of doing much work around the house. Chanh and Tran were back with us and Thoa's kids joined us too, when her business ran into financial trouble. I could see the tension rising in Dennis's face. He didn't get along with Anh's sons, either, knowing who they were, and he soon began complaining again of how I favored the Vietnamese over him. To make himself feel better, he bought more guns and another big shiny motorcycle, not caring what it did to our budget. It was as if he had never left. By the following New Year's, the trial was over—at least for me.

"Dennis, things just aren't working out," I told him. "I think it would be best for everyone if you moved out. Let's not waste any more money on lawyers. Let's stay friends for Alan's sake and our own sakes and get on with the rest of our lives."

A shadow eclipsed his face, chilling me to the bone. "Okay," Dennis replied darkly, "if that's the way you want it. Why should it bother you if I'm disabled?"

"I'll be happy to look in on you and help out if you get sick. I'll even pay your phone and utilities for the first few months until you get a job."

"Oh yes, you'll pay," he snarled. "You'll *all* pay!" and stormed off to his room.

At first Dennis ignored my decision, then paid it lip service but never got around to doing anything about it, so I finally had to call my attorney—a man who replaced Miss King—who filed eviction papers.

"Dennis is a very dangerous man, Ly," the lawyer said. "You made a big mistake taking him back. He's going to fight twice as hard now to hang on. Get ready for some pretty rough sailing."

The San Diego County sheriff served Dennis the eviction notice while the kids and I went to a movie. When we got home, Dennis was gone and most of the house was intact. That night, it started to rain. I stationed myself by the window, guarding my sleeping children and my house, and cried all night as the streets and gutters overflowed.

For the next couple of days, I tried to conduct business as usual. I phoned Lan to see if she'd heard anything, and she said no, and didn't elaborate, which meant she was probably telling the truth. None of my friends had heard from Dennis either, including the ones he had recruited for the hearing.

The weather got worse. As the rain persisted, so did my feelings of pity and later, remorse.

"I'd even let a stray dog in from the rain," I told Kathy one night on the phone. "Something has happened to him, I'm sure of it."

"Get hold of yourself," she said. "A dog can't go to a motel or friend's house. He's a big boy. He can take care of himself."

On March 3, 1982, the kids got out of school early and Jimmy called while I was still at work.

"Mom, there was a business card stuck in the door for you. The note on the back says you're supposed to call the guy as soon as possible."

"Who's the card from?"

"Umm—Detective Scott."

"A policeman?"

"Yeah. From Homicide. Does that mean somebody got killed?"

"Just give me the number, sweetheart." My fingers were trembling so badly I could hardly hold the pencil. My mind flew to the people Dennis might harm: the kids, Jimmy and Tommy—no, they were home, thank god. Little Alan—why would Dennis ever harm him? He was at day care. I would check on him as soon as Jimmy got off the phone. But if the trouble had been there, certainly someone would've called—they had my number at work. My mind buzzed with other possible victims: Lan? Petey? They had helped Dennis all along, why would he harm them now? I couldn't think of anyone except myself he might hate enough to kill. Maybe Detective Scott was calling to warn me of a death threat. That had to be it.

"Detective Scott, please," I told the person who answered.

"This is Scott," a no-nonsense voice responded.

"Mr. Scott, this is Mrs. Hayslip—Mrs. Dennis Hayslip. You left your card on my door this morning."

"Oh yes. Ah, Mrs. Hayslip—is anybody there with you?"

"Well, yes, the people I work with."

"Good. Well, I've got some bad news for you, Mrs. Hayslip. I'm sorry to inform you that we found your husband dead this morning. He was sitting in a van—Mrs. Hayslip?"

"Yes, I'm still here."

"He was sitting in a van in an alley behind the First Southern Baptist Church on Luna Street in Clairemont."

My god—that's by the Sunday school playground! I must've driven by that spot a dozen times. How could I have missed him?

"What happened?"

"He was in the front seat reading a newspaper and having a drink. Looks like he was burning some charcoal in the back to get warm and, well, with all the windows up, we figure he was asphyxiated. It happens when the weather gets cold, Mrs. Hayslip. I'm sorry."

I started to say something, but my throat was too dry.

"Mrs. Hayslip—can you drive or get a ride home? I'd like to meet you there, if that's possible."

"Of course. I'll be home in half an hour."

I went to Kathy's office. I must've been white as a sheet, because she got up and walked over as soon as she saw me.

"Ly—are you okay?" She took my hands.

"He's dead," I sniffed. "They found him dead."

She held me a moment. I felt like crying—really letting go—but couldn't. The tears glistening in my eyes were as much in anger as sorrow. *He didn't need to do this!* My thoughts now were completely with Alan: how he would take it, how this would affect him. In the back of my mind, too, were the spiritual consequences: Was the soul child tainted by the mistakes of the soulmates? For that matter, was Dennis's death really a neglectful accident—a spiteful man drinking and carelessly trying to stay warm in an airtight little place—or was it suicide? Perhaps that was what Detective Scott wanted to talk about.

My lawyer and the detective met me at the house. Alan was still at day care and I didn't want to pick him up and deal with his shock and anger and grief until I understood the story myself. Detective Scott handed over Dennis's personal effects—his wallet, watch, and other small items taken from the van. Along with the van's registration was another legal paper: Dennis's eviction notice.

The story made local TV and radio news for a few days, then faded away. The reporters always identified the victim as "a man recently evicted" or "forced from his house" by his wife. The *San Diego Union* carried an article on Dennis's death—"Man Found Dead in Van Next to School Playground." The reporter interviewed the teacher who had found him.

"I saw him sleeping in the van. He goes to this church so we all know him. I saw him again the next day and came out and knocked on the window. He didn't answer so I went to get the pastor. We came out and couldn't wake him so we called the police."

I couldn't help but wonder if Dennis parked there just to get a glimpse of Alan as he came and went from the playground. Barricaded in his van, a house on wheels, Dennis had become the ultimate soul-in-transit: observing the land of the living from the outside in; an alien in his own neighborhood as I had once been. At that moment, reading the newspaper account, I felt closer to Dennis than at any time I had known him. I broke down and cried the cry I had put off for days, months, and years—the one that had been welling up inside of me since I had first come to America.

Alan was too shellshocked to get everything out of his system right away. He was a sensitive boy. Despite all the bad luck in his life so far, he had been spared the crucible of war that so deeply etched Jimmy and Tommy and gave them the perspective to handle such tragedies—not easily, perhaps, but with resilience. He would adjust to the reality of his father's death in time and in his own way. He was, after all, the grandson of Phung Trong.

After Dennis's body had been preserved and dressed at the mortuary, I visited him alone. Kneeling on the ice-cold floor, I held on to his coffin and cried—the last tempest of tears and sobs he would get from his partner in *nghia*. I asked him to forgive me, although I didn't know then—and still don't know—how I could've done things better. His spirit had no answers, made no reply. Too much had been left unsaid between Dennis and me, and only now, after the shouting was gone forever, could our dialogue begin.

Funerals are a man's best epitaph. The church handled all the arrangements for Dennis's memorial service and the only Caucasian to attend was Pastor Bob. The rest were Chinese parishioners and my Oriental friends from work. Lan showed up, but Petey stayed home —boycotting a tragedy I think he and Dennis's other friends believed

I caused. To Dennis's credit and theirs, all our foster children came. It was curious but somehow comforting to see the little church filled mostly with the very people Dennis was convinced were plotting to destroy him. Somehow, that gap between what Dennis thought and how things really were made a better eulogy than the pastor's luke-warm speech.

Dennis's family did not attend the San Diego service. They wanted the body shipped to Raymond, Ohio, so he could be buried beside his father. I agreed. Dennis's sister said that Dennis had phoned shortly before his death and said I would be sorry that I had evicted him. That was already true enough, but it cast his schoolyard vigil in a more sinister light. Perhaps he intended to do more than gaze wist-fully at his little boy. However, such thinking only perpetuated the circle of hate, so I put it out of my mind.

Alan and I accompanied his father to his last resting place, chang-ing planes three times, making a gloomy, stormy trip even more exhausting. A hearse met us at the airport and took us to the mortu-ary where Dennis's mother, brothers, and sisters had gathered. Den-nis's first wife and his other son, Victor, didn't show up, although they had been invited. Everyone was dressed in business suits and talked quietly among themselves. Nobody paid any attention to the casket, which I found very odd, especially in contrast to a Vietnamese funeral, where the body is the object of everyone's attention and grief. For that matter, I didn't see much distress on anyone's face except Dennis's mother, his sister, and Alan. As I said, funerals are all about truth, no matter what is said.

The motorcade to the cemetery was eerily quiet. In Vietnam, we beat drums and chant and burn incense the whole way to the gravesite. In America, as it was with Ed's funeral also, bodies passed into the underworld like thieves slipping into the night.

As Dennis's coffin was lowered into the ground, I felt two very strong emotions. First was the ancient sadness I felt at Ed's funeral: the regret of unpaid soul debt which I knew would follow us into the future.

The other was a gradual euphoria. More than the lightness of a lifted burden, it was the same quiet, transcending joy I eventually felt after my father's death, when he began to visit me in dreams. Then I learned that I would never be alone in life, that only by letting go would I have the capacity to reach for more. Now, having made and lost two soulmates, I felt ready for my next stage of growth. Like the little hand that grasped mine by Dennis's grave on that cold Ohio day, I knew that transformation would one day result in something strong and grand and wonderful.

PART TWO

Finding the American Dream
(1983–86)

SIX

Stirring the Melting Pot

BACK IN SAN DIEGO, I felt like a motorboat revving my engine while still tied to the dock. Dennis's short, angry life had slowed my search for myself in America, and I was still having trouble getting rid of the extra baggage. I was an explorer without a compass: a missionary without a mission. One minute I felt elated and energetic, the next I was awash in tears.

Compared to my condition when Ed died, though, I was worlds ahead. Then, I was a wide-eyed, ignorant immigrant whose only assets were her will to survive and the love of her children. Jimmy and Tommy got over the shock of Dennis's death fairly quickly, because they had already been through a lot and were happy to find some peace. Alan, though, who was not only the main object of Dennis's affection, but of our conflict, took it a lot harder. Before, he was a happy-go-lucky kid. Now, he was somber and pensive and spent most of his time in his room, listening to bedtime stories Dennis had recorded. At times like this, I wanted to hold him extra close, but he often turned from my affection. His sullen glances struck my heart like arrows.

Some Chinese parishioners from the Baptist church took turns staying with us, as was the Oriental custom, for our first few days of mourning. With their support, I went back to work a week after Dennis's funeral. People there were kind. They were concerned about my health and gave me the space I needed to get well. Unfortunately, one woman who had counseled me to throw Dennis out made a very disturbing remark. It would haunt me for the rest of the year.

"I hope Dennis left you something to get by on," the woman said, fiddling absently with her circuit board the way a village gossip weaves a basket.

"What do you mean?" I asked.

"You know—an estate, life insurance, all that."

"I don't know if Dennis had any insurance. He barely had enough money for food. Anyway, I don't want his money. It brought us nothing but bad luck. I just want to put everything behind me."

"Well, hon, you'd better have your lawyer check it out. If you don't get the dough, the State of California will—or some greedy relative. How's that gonna help your boys?"

I wanted to tell her to mind her own business, but I had tangled enough with "the American system" to know that she was right.

That evening, Jimmy and I unpacked Dennis's van, which had been sealed since the police investigation. Inside, among a lot of other papers we couldn't figure out, was a million-dollar "double indemnity" insurance policy on my life, along with newspaper clippings about mass murderers and men who had killed their families—even an old *TV Guide* with a couple of shows circled that dealt with spouse abuse and serial killers. I was so horrified I couldn't speak and although my first impulse was to trash them before the boys could get a look, I decided that my lawyer should see them first.

He took much longer to riffle through the files than I expected. "This is pretty spooky stuff," he said, although I didn't need a lawyer to tell me that. When he got to the legal papers, he said, "Well, there's at least one silver lining: you now own your house free and clear." He explained about mortgage insurance and "the death of the principal breadwinner," although, in that case, the wrong person had probably died. "Also," he said, "the police reported the death as a vehicle-related accident, so your automobile insurance owes you some money, too. Wait a second—what's this?"

He pulled out a legal-size, blue-bound document folded like an accordion. "Well, I'll be damned. It seems Dennis had a hundred-thousand-dollar government life insurance policy—with his sister Janet as trustee. Alan and Victor are shown as joint beneficiaries. Look—here's your signature on the bottom. Don't you remember signing this?"

"No." I told him the truth. I had signed a lot of things Dennis put in front of me. Most of them were so confusing I wouldn't have known what I was reading anyway; and if I questioned anything, it usually caused a fight.

"Well, it doesn't matter. Under the circumstances, I think I can get the policy turned over to you. Do you want me to give it a try?"

"No—I don't want the money. It's tainted—bad karma. I know you think that's silly, but I believe it. I would rather Dennis's sister gets the money than fight over things anymore."

The lawyer leaned back in his oversize chair and gave me that "amused parent" look I had grown so used to. "That's very noble, Ly, but how does Alan benefit if his aunt keeps most of the money for Victor? If she's trustee, she can use it any way she likes. Don't you think Alan would be better off if you controlled his share?"

I felt myself being pulled back into the swamp of Dennis's life. Although I really and truly didn't want anything more to do with Dennis's money or possessions, I realized the time might come when Alan would appreciate my forbearance. I gritted my teeth and said yes. A few weeks later, I got a call from Janet. After asking politely how the boys and I were doing, she got right down to business.

"Ly, I got this awful letter from your lawyer. It says you want to be made trustee for the policy he set up for his sons. That's not right, Ly. If Dennis wanted you to administer the funds, he would've named you in the policy. In fact, he specifically said you *were not* to act as trustee. You even signed it, saying you understood and gave up any legal claims. Now—here you are, pulling a stunt like this! Why don't you respect Dennis's last wishes and leave things the way they are?"

"Because I know what is best for my son," I answered. "I cannot rely on you or the insurance company or the banks. I could not even rely on Dennis when he was alive! I spent the last two years trying to protect Alan from his father! But please—do not worry. I don't want to control all the money—just the half that belongs to Alan. Victor should have his money, I agree, and you are welcome to that. I only want what is best for my son."

"Okay, Ly. I don't want to fight over this, either. I'll agree to give up trusteeship for Alan if you can find a lawyer who will take my place and be co-trustee with you. Have him draw up the papers and I'll sign them."

She hung up and although I felt justified in everything I said, I still felt sad and unsettled. I did not want my relationship with the Hayslips to go the way of my relationship with the Munros. I believed in the power of families to help kids grow up, and felt bad that Tommy had been lopped off like a thorny branch from the American side of his family tree. Maybe in his maturity he would find some way to rediscover his roots among Ed's family, but the precious years lost in between would never come again. I did not want this to happen to Alan—yet here we were, drawing battle lines on legal papers, pitting Alan against his American half brother. It seemed as if a garden with even a sliver of "Vietnamese bamboo" was doomed to wither on this side of the ocean.

Even with no bribes to pay, justice can be expensive. Because of the divorce and other legal bills, not to mention the cost of two funerals, I was paying out everything I earned each month with creditors lining up for more. Thao's children came back to live with us as well as Anh, the youngest of my original foster children, and Chanh, Jimmy's half brother. This only increased our monthly expenses, but the happiness I found in a crowded house more than made up for the cost.

My lawyer wrote everyone to whom we owned money, asking them to give me a little time after Dennis's death to straighten out his affairs. Most of them expressed their condolences with dunning letters and threatening phone calls. When a husband dies in Vietnam, people leave the widow alone while she pulls herself together. Unless they do, the family risks falling apart. Without the family, no debts get paid. Now, I had to settle not only my debts and our joint debts but Dennis's private debts as well: not just his lawyer (I was supposed to pay for all the trouble he caused me?) but previously hidden expenses from Dennis's "other" life—his one away from the family.

The worst were the credit card people. When Dennis signed up for the cards, they treated us like royalty. "You need more money?" their letters would say. "Fine—just spend more and we'll increase your credit limit." Dennis was happy to comply. When one of them called to complain of Dennis's high unpaid balance, I could only laugh and tell him, "You think my dead husband owes *you* a lot—think of the soul debt he has incurred in the afterworld!" I began to explain the

Buddhist principles of karma but the dunner hung up and never called back.

When things looked worst—when our family debt stretched out for months and months beyond my income—I comforted myself with the story my father told me when I was about nine, about money and its true value.

"There was once a hard-working farmer, Bay Ly, in a village very much like ours."

"Was he as hard working as you and Bon Nghe?" I asked, thinking nobody could work as diligently as my father and oldest brother.

My father laughed. "He made us look like idlers! He did not lift a finger unless it gained him something and his hands were always busy—that's how hard he worked! Of course, he owned many paddies and employed a great many poor villagers, all of whom he expected to work as hard as he did but for a fraction of the reward. Consequently, people looked on him as very mean and cruel, which he never understood, since he worked harder than anyone and gave jobs to people who would otherwise go begging.

"Anyway, his wealth increased over the years, and he built a great house which he filled with gold and jewelry—the things you buy when you already have too much. Still, he traded sharply with each vendor and paid his laborers no more than the going wage. In his eyes, people were valued like beans in a market—worth no more than what a clever bidder would pay.

"One day, the man fell terribly ill and his sons gathered around him.

" 'Father, I will call the greatest physician in the land to come and cure you,' his number-one son said.

" 'No,' the farmer replied, 'I have worked hard all my life. It is time now for me to rest.'

" 'But our lands will perish without you, father,' his number-two son said. 'Come back and show us what to do.'

" 'Rubbish,' the farmer replied. 'I have already shown everyone what to do by my example. You will all get along just fine without me.'

" 'Then let us hire the best stonecutter in the land to carve a huge sarcophagus so that your body may rest forever with your treasure,' his number-three son said.

" 'No,' the farmer replied, coughing his soon-to-be last breath. 'Just find a hollow log and use that for my coffin. Cut holes for my two arms so that my open palms can dangle. Parade me three times around the village so that people can see I carry nothing to the grave, then bury me in our ancestral cemetery. Disburse my treasure to those who have served me best, not neglecting the villagers most in need.'

" 'But father,' the sons cried together, 'why should the richest man in the village be buried like a pauper?'

" 'Because I want everyone to see that you can't take your treasure with you. *Vac tien ra ma mac ca cai chet*—Shall I take my money to the grave and bargain with death? All we have after passing is our soul, which can travel to its next life only if it is unburdened. I want them to see that the true wage of hard work is not money in a treasure house, but the health and happiness of the friends and family you leave behind.'

"So saying, the farmer died and his sons did as they were told but also took it upon themselves to build a temple in his honor where the farmer's soul is nourished even to this day by the thankful prayers of later generations."

"Do you want Bon and Sau Ban to build a temple for you after you are gone?" I asked my father.

"No, little peach blossom," he said, handing me my hoe and gently swatting my bottom in the direction of the fields. "A poor farmer's church is his paddy, and like the wealthy farmer, we must be about our business."

Like rice seedlings, planted row by row, my resources slowly grew. Alan and Victor split Dennis's insurance benefit, which gave them each a nest egg for education and emergencies. The mortgage insurance gave me the choice of paying off the house or receiving a lump-sum payment. I took the money, since the monthly payments of $375 were quickly looking like a bargain in California's heated real estate market.

The "death van," as I thought of it, was paid off by Dennis's auto insurance, but I couldn't bear to keep it one minute longer. I ran an ad and sold it to the first caller. We fared much better when the "accidental death" portion of the auto insurance was settled: a check for forty thousand dollars, which I used to satisfy the rest of our creditors.

With my worldly debts paid, I turned my thoughts to the things I owed the spirit domain. I had avoided the Buddhist temple since

Dennis's death because I felt bad for disregarding my monk's advice. True, I had taken Dennis back, but my patience ran out after a single year—a drop in the ocean to the cosmic god. Still, I wanted to mend those fences.

My *su* received me graciously, as he always did. Instead of lecturing me on my responsibility for Dennis's death, he simply asked if I "wanted to do anything for the temple"—penance for whatever was still troubling me. I said yes, and was given a list of chores: from the menial—sweeping up—to the more significant, stuffing envelopes and helping with the temple's outreach program. Since I now had some extra cash, I made a larger than usual donation with the hope that some of it would go into improving the shrine, which was the centerpiece of every temple and the way visitors gauged the health and generosity of the local Buddhist community.

Word now began to pass in the Vietnamese community that the Hanoi authorities were letting individual packages get through to needy families. I began sending "care packages"—boxes of good American clothing, food, and drugstore medicine—to Tinh, my niece in Danang, who I figured had the best chance of any relative to survive the Communist purges. She had also been used by various branches of our family to keep in touch, so if anyone knew how to reach my other relatives with gifts, supplies, and letters from America, it would be her. My relief packages went unacknowledged, but still I persisted. *Co cong mai sat, co ngay nen kim*—with perseverance, one can whet a piece of iron into a needle.

Thinking about Tinh and my family gave me the courage to dig out the notes about my childhood I had transcribed on lined paper a few years before. I didn't know how long our money would last and I would have to go back to work, so I decided to use this rare "vacation" to finish what I had started.

The task was much bigger than I supposed.

Because of my third-grade education, writing was tedious: making marks on paper was laborious enough in my tortured longhand, but thinking of the right words to say was even more difficult. A villager's vocabulary focuses on getting through the day, saying our prayers, and gossiping, rather than on discussing big ideas—so I spent more time looking up words in my Vietnamese-English dictionary than I did actually putting them on paper. Fortunately, the wheel of life had turned far enough to give me an unexpected ally.

Jimmy was now a fifteen-year-old handsome teenager. Like many of our race, he looked more youthful than his years, except in the eyes, which had seen more than they should. He was intelligent and worked hard in school. And he was my son, which meant he had my father's heart. Jimmy, I decided, would be my collaborator and teacher.

When I was studying for U.S. citizenship, Dan had encouraged me to take all the necessary classes and then some. Ed was indifferent to my education, but was glad to see me happy. Dennis thought anything beyond my Bible education was a waste, and said so often. I was a poor student in things that required memorization and rule-following, like English grammar. I was a good student, though, in subjects that seemed useful—such as citizens' rights—and legends from American history.

I particularly liked the stories about Abe Lincoln. I was fascinated that America had waged its own civil war, just like Vietnam. Although I never dared mention it in class (because the war was still going on), Lincoln reminded me of Ho Chi Minh. The highest goal for both men had been to hold their country together, even if part of it wanted to break away. Both Uncle Ho and Honest Abe saw that, in the long run, a divided house must fall. America should thank its stars that its great civil war lasted only four years (instead of five times that long for mine), and that the last living memory of it has long since passed. Many of those suffering souls are no doubt back among us, reincarnated with new lives. Some are still struggling to learn old lessons; you can feel it in the soil. Every old battlefield is hot with frustration and unexpended hate, even in the dead of winter.

My favorite teacher was an old woman who struck me as the very image of a *Nico* or *Su mau*—a female shaman or wise old godmother. (Gender makes no difference to the nearly perfect souls that inhabit such bodies. They are about to ascend to a higher plane of existence, so they are indifferent to earthly preoccupations like sex and ambition.) I visited this teacher often after class to hear stories about her youth and the tribulations of an earlier age in America, when everyone was so poor even the economy was depressed and the United States was not yet the world's policeman. I also told her stories about my family and the history of Vietnam. Eventually, we visited each other's houses and I considered her one of my best American friends. She astounded me one evening, though, when, as I was leaving, she took my hand and *thanked* me for taking the time to teach *her* so many things. It was the first time anyone but my boys had ever suggested that I knew anything worth knowing. For me, like my American instructor, teaching was as natural as learning.

So Jimmy became a very proficient student of my life, although I had to ease him into this occupation gently. To prepare the way, I bought him a Commodore computer.

"You're getting pretty good with that keyboard, aren't you?" I smiled a proud mother's smile.

"Yeah, I can really whip out my papers now. Thanks."

"Then you'll have free time to help me with my notes and stories." I held up a box half filled with writing paper. Jimmy's face fell.

"Gee, I don't know, Mom. I didn't take typing at school. I sort of learned on my own—" I could see he was in a hurry to get to the mall and feed quarters to the computer games, or was today his day for baseball? "Maybe I can do it tonight."

"Okay, so you do it tonight and won't watch TV?" I could tell he hadn't thought the deal all the way through.

He put down his jacket and picked up the first page of the manuscript. "Why are you doing this anyway?" He could not conceive of anybody working so hard over something that wasn't "due next Wednesday."

"It's a book—*my* book! *Tram nam bia da thi mon, ngan nam bia mieng hay con tro tro*—Stone wears out in a hundred years, but words can last a thousand! It's the story of how I grew up in Ky La and what happened during the war and how you were born in Danang. Yes, you're in it!"

With more enthusiasm, he dug deeper into the stack.

"Where?"

"Well, you'll have to wait and see, won't you? You have to work your way to it."

In the end, he agreed to help his mom in her daunting task. I think the only reason he promised to do it—besides reading what his mother had to say about him—was because he thought I'd never finish it. Ignorant farm girls don't write books. What Jimmy didn't realize was that this was my—our—"treasure house." As my father told me, we must be about our family's business.

Part of that business was to learn more about business itself. Because I now had some assets—a house and some cash—to manage and never had to think about such things before, I took a course in business administration. What I lacked in professional polish, I made up for in experience—on the Danang black market, in my abortive but very instructive venture into the deli business, as a production line supervisor. When it came to sizing people up and figuring out how to get something done and make a little money in the bargain, I was first in my class. While the other students studied the book and talked to the professor to get good grades, they often came to me when they thought about starting a real business. Which is not to say that I was unimpressed with American business education. In Vietnam, it would have made a very good scam!

The thing I disliked most was the way my teacher made business seem like a dog-eat-dog affair, which in my experience (even in the black market) it never was. The most successful people I knew spent a lot of time earning the trust of those on whom their success depended. I learned early that it was better to make a small profit from many customers—and have those customers come back—than to rip somebody off and spend the rest of your life looking over your shoulder. (*An it no lau, an nhieu tuc bung,* my mother used to say—Eat a little to feel better; eat too much and feel a bellyache!) That's not to say that you shouldn't be aggressive about getting what you want; only that "looking out for number one" really means getting *everyone*—customers, partners, employees—to want you to succeed as well. I used to call my professor's shortsighted advice "the class on being selfish." Of course, America was the world's economic colossus and my home country was very poor, so who was I to talk?

I applied the best of what I learned to my volunteer work at the temple, which is where I now spent most of my free time. With their minds always on the next world, the monks needed plenty of help in this one. I always looked at it as an investment in my soul, with principal and interest paid in my next life.

Jimmy and Tommy spent a lot of time at Dennis's old church. I understood why. The big white church gave them the kind of American family life I couldn't. They were now going to regular services and joined Bible study groups of their own, some of which met at our house. Despite the sometimes overbearing zeal of people like Dennis and Janet, and what I felt to be the misdirected spiritualism of their holy men, I bore no ill will toward the Baptists. Although their theology seemed a little loony (their compulsion to "convert heathens" without a hearing, for example, seemed like holding a trial wherein only the prosecutor was allowed to speak), the people who believed it were fundamentally good. As the monks assured me, god knows his own face even when others can't recognize it.

I only became uncomfortable when my boys, one day, decided I had to convert to Christianity to escape the flames of hell.

"Don't you know that the only way to salvation is through our Lord, Jesus Christ?" ten-year-old Tommy said.

"Why do you worry so much about changing other people?" I asked.

"Well, if you knew the world was going to end, wouldn't you want to save as many people as you could?" Jimmy replied.

"Well, the world ends for everybody one day or another; some sooner, some later. What difference does it make if it ends all at once? That's just more work for god, but if he wants it that way, it's fine with me."

"Mom—" Jim said disgustedly. "You're missing the point."

"No, I don't think so." I was sorry now that I hadn't made more of an effort to instruct them in our traditional family beliefs the way my father had instructed me. Perhaps just giving them the example of a weird old lady chanting by a smoky shrine was not the way American kids learned best. We would actually have to talk about things.

I said, "Suppose the three of us are driving in a car and it goes off the road—"

"Then Tom must be driving!" Jim socked his brother on the arm and I hushed them up.

"No, really, suppose the three of us go off a cliff and god has to decide which of us to save. Who would he choose?"

"He would save the people who believed in Him," Jim said. "Me and Tommy."

"He would not save me?" I tried to look hurt.

"Do you believe in Jesus Christ? Do you accept him as your Savior?"

"No, but I know I am one of god's children. I worship as I was taught and try to live a good life. Why would he be so mean to me just because my paperwork wasn't in order?"

"Mommm!" they whined in unison.

"You see, I believe natural law carries the seeds of all religion: mine, yours, Dennis's, Ed's Catholic family's—everyone. Men have found a hundred little ways to get the details wrong, but god needs just one way to be right."

"I don't understand," Tom said.

"Well, when you come to me and ask me to believe in Jesus, I ask you, 'How do you know Jesus is your lord?' and you say, 'Because

God says so.' Then I ask you, 'How do you know God says so?' and you say, 'Because Pastor Bob told us.' So I ask, 'How does the pastor know?' and you say, 'Because he has studied the Bible.' And who wrote the Bible? 'Learned men,' you say, 'who have heard the word of God and seen His miracles.' So, I conclude that you are asking me to believe in Jesus because other men say so. Wouldn't it be better to listen to god directly—to see his miracles yourself?"

"You mean like Jesus walking on water and all that stuff?" Tommy said enthusiastically. "Sure, but that happened a long time ago."

"No, I mean miracles that happen every day: babies being born and birds squawking across the sky and dreams at night. That is how god talks to us. To me, those are real miracles worthy of a cosmic god and we are all part of them. You agree—it's easy to believe in god when you see the miracles yourself, right? I tell you I see them every day. Therefore, it is easy for me to believe in my god, no matter what others think or say. From what you say, though, the Baptists believe God reveals himself just to a few people and the rest of us have to take it on faith. That is faith in *men,* Jimmy and Tommy, not faith in god."

"So who would God save when Tommy wrecks the car?" Jimmy asked, a little less certain.

"I'm not god and I'm not a Baptist." I chucked his chin. "You tell me!"

My business and religious interests collided one day in the form of Tuy, a girl I met at the temple. She came in on a busy day and had the monks shave her head in front of everyone—a big act of atonement. By shaving her head, we Buddhists believe, she emulates the condition of a newborn baby, who comes into the world with only its karma from another life, not the new soul debt created by recent mistakes. It's a way of signaling the cosmic god that you're willing to start over and not repeat the same error—an act that makes everyone feel better, even if the sinner relapses. I was glad to have witnessed it and went over to thank her afterward. We got to talking about our backgrounds.

Apparently she too had been married to an older American worker in Vietnam. Like me, she also had marriage problems and got very sick. Although she didn't tell me what she had done to shave her head (and I didn't ask—that would have been impolite), I got the feeling it had to do with bad choices and men, things I knew something about. Tuy said that, as part of her new life, she was thinking about opening a jewelry shop. I told her I was studying business and hoping to find a way to invest the small amount of money I came into after my husband died. We agreed that neither of us felt comfortable doing business with the rapidly growing Vietnamese community: they were all sharp, experienced business people and a little cutthroat. We felt we would be taken to the cleaners. However, we were impressed with each other and Tuy asked if I would like to see some samples of the kind of jewelry she planned to sell.

We met the next day (she was wearing a wig now, so her sin was between her and god) and she showed me a bag full of lovely diamonds, jade, and pearls. She said she had bought them from Vietnamese refugees "just off the boat" and my heart sank. Still, she swore she had paid a fair price for each, the most she could afford.

"I just need a little more cash to open the store," she said. "And I've already found the perfect location. Do you think you would be interested?"

"Well, the jewelry is very nice, but I just want to take things easy for a while. I really can't afford the risk."

"What risk? I'll let you hold these pieces as collateral. They must be worth at least seventy-thousand dollars retail." Her face then clouded up. "Le Ly, you're my last hope. My husband won't help and he's turned all our friends against me. He doesn't want me to succeed —to be anything on my own!"

That sounded familiar enough to make my own eyes water.

"Okay," I said. "All right. I can give you forty thousand—just about all I have. I'll keep these jewels in my safe deposit box. I know you are a good person inside. I know you are serious about turning your life around. I think it would be good for me—for my soul—to do what I can to help you."

She thanked me effusively and, true to her word, her little shop was open in a week. Like a proud mother, I saw in her effort the reborn "daughter" of my own little dream—the Oriental deli—that had been smothered by Dennis in its infancy.

Unfortunately, Tuy faced other problems. Everything that could go wrong did—not all because of her own bad judgment and inexperience, but bad luck and bad timing as well. Not long after she opened, she called in a panic.

"Ly, I need the jewels!"

"What? You mean your collateral?"

"Yes. I can't pay my wholesaler so he's stopped delivery on my stock. Unless you let me sell that jewelry, I won't be able to pay my rent!"

I thought for a moment, wondering what my business instructor would do; but the blame for losing the cash was mine as a not-so-careful investor. I realized that what I had *really* been trying to purchase was heaven's favor by giving a sinner another chance, and that I had accomplished. To keep her jewels on top of that, after she had tried and failed would simply have added to my own moral debt.

"Okay," I said finally. "I'll bring them by."

Of course, I never saw my money or the jewelry again. Tuy's husband had been right, she was just a bad business person. It taught me a valuable lesson, though: don't judge other people's experience solely by your own. To Tuy's credit, she made periodic attempts to pay me back—a hundred dollars here and a hundred there—but I've never expected to see my forty thousand dollars. The last I heard, she was working as a masseuse and had been arrested—I was afraid to ask what for. I certainly did not want my money so badly that she should break the law to get it, so I sent her a note telling her not to worry about it—I would get along just fine until she was back on her feet.

If she shaved her head again after this fiasco, nobody at the temple knew it.

I decided on a different strategy to protect and multiply what money I had left. Twice burned, I was afraid to start another small business, so I attended some investment seminars hoping to find an answer. At one seminar, I learned that "common stock" represented ownership in a company and that you could buy it without having to manage the business or suffer all the hassles. Since bigger companies issued most of the stock on the market, it was possible to buy "shares" in big established corporations—the best of all worlds!

I became a stock junkie.

I bought shares in entertainment companies that made glamorous American movies. I bought stock in high technology firms, like the company I used to work for. I became "part owner" of giant corporations that cranked out products every American seemed to need. Whenever one of their ads was on TV, I would call the boys over and squeal, "Look! Your mother is part owner of that big company. Isn't that great!" Eventually one of them asked that if I was part owner, how come we didn't get their products for free? I told the boys they were too young to understand business and sent them back to their homework, but it seemed like a pretty good question.

Of course, by this time, the "Reagan recession" was over and the economy was on the way up, so just about every stock did well. In less than a year, I made a five-thousand-dollar profit and had the self-confidence to try to put my old life completely behind me.

Since Dennis's death, I had wanted to leave the neighborhood. The boys spent a lot of time with church people and, at their impressionable age, I wasn't sure everything they learned from them was healthy—too much intolerance and blind faith in angry men. I also didn't feel comfortable working in the yard where I could feel the eyes of my neighbors on me. I could almost hear the mothers cautioning their daughters: "There, you see what happens to you when you worship false idols and kick out your husband? Look how lonely she is—a poor black widow!"

In a way, they were right. I kept in touch with Lan, who had now opened a secondhand clothing store in El Cajon, but we had less and less in common. Always a bit aloof, she never really applied herself to becoming an American and, I suspect, always thought my eyes "were becoming too round." I occasionally went out with Kathy and my friends from Digidyne, but I had trouble warming to the singles scene. I was ready for something else—a true new beginning.

After a little searching, I found a new, smaller house I liked a lot. I discovered that if I liquidated my stock portfolio (which now matched my original $40,000 nest egg) and borrowed $20,000 against my house, I would have the $60,000 needed for the down payment and could service the monthly mortgage on *both* places by renting our big old house.

"That's a good plan," my banker said, looking at the figures I jotted down, "but what happens if you can't rent the first house? You'll need to show us another source of income. Anything will do. Just bring in a pay stub and I'm sure your loan will go through."

This was very disappointing because by this time I was deeply absorbed in writing my book and had neither the energy nor inclination to go look for a menial job just to satisfy the banker. I wondered who could help me out without making a big deal of it. Against my better judgment, I called my sister Lan.

"Look, this house is a good deal," I told her. "Home prices are going up fast in California. Unless I trade up now, I will be priced out of the market. If you give me a letter saying I work for your store, I will cut you in on part of the profits. We can't lose."

"Oh?" Lan asked. "What about the law? You don't really work for me. I would have to say I pay you something. I wouldn't want you to come back later and demand money based on that letter."

"Don't worry, I wouldn't be doing any work—"

"Oh, that's very nice! Money for no work?"

"No, no." I knew Lan was toying with me but I tried to hide my frustration. "It's just for the banker. Just a piece of paper for his file. He already said he wanted to lend me the money. It's just a formality."

"But it's still a lie. I don't want to lie for you, Bay Ly. It's not right. It's as if we were back in Danang—"

"Yes, exactly! And we did lots of worse things in Danang!" I was starting to get angry.

"But this is America." This was an odd argument coming from Lan, but I listened. "I thought the old ways made you angry, Bay Ly. You're always going on about the corruption in the South. Well, here you are trying to do the same thing in America. If you're not careful, you'll wind up going to jail—or being deported. Is that what you really want?"

I hung up, mad as could be. But as I cooled down, I realized Lan was right. How easy it was, with a little knowledge and the smell of a few dollars in your nose, to cut corners, to take the easy path, to add new debt to your soul even as you put money in your pocket. *Especially* as you put money in your pocket! I called the banker and told him I couldn't go through with the deal. I should've called and thanked Lan, but I was still her baby sister and just couldn't lift the phone.

My interest in real estate brought me into contact with many people: brokers, investment advisers, businessmen. I met one developer who, in addition to being very professional where finances were concerned, was personally very kind, and interested in me and my family. His current project was a custom home development in Escondido, about thirty minutes north of San Diego. He said that with residential real estate values growing faster than the population in San Diego County, home prices even in the outlying areas were ready to take off. Getting in on the ground floor in this new neighborhood, he said, would accomplish both my objectives: to invest in a brand new area and start a brand new life.

When I finally saw the development, the reality was even better than the dream. I fell in love with a two-story five-bedroom house with a sunken living room, a family room, and a big kitchen. After a few calculations, we figured that with rents so high now and demand so great, I would be able to cover both the old and new mortgages with money to spare. I applied for financing and waited for the other shoe (my lack of a backup pay stub) to drop, but it never did. Because of all my equity, the paperwork went through without a hitch. *Than tai go cua*—Lady Fortune had finally knocked on my door.

Of course, feeling prosperous and being prosperous—spiritually— are two different things. I went to Los Angeles to hire the only available *Ong Thay Dai Ly*—an astrologer who reads earth signs and could give me the auspices of the house. On the long drive back to Escondido, the short, husky psychic explained the foundation of his craft.

"The Chinese zodiac goes back many thousands of years, little sister," the round-faced shaman said. "When the Buddha was leaving earth, he called the animals to bid him farewell. One of these animals was a rat who saw a big elephant browsing by the roadside. 'Come on, Mister Elephant,' the rat squeaked, 'we must hurry to say good-bye to the Buddha.' The elephant simply shoveled up more hay and said, 'You go, little rat. I am too big and important to rush. The Buddha will wait for me.' But the Buddha didn't, and the first twelve animals to arrive were rewarded with their own namesake year, forming the twelve signs of the Chinese zodiac. First was the rat, followed by the ox, tiger, rabbit, dragon, snake, horse, sheep, monkey, rooster, dog, and boar. Everyone born in a given year takes on certain qualities of the namesake—the "animal" that lurks in the human heart. You say you were born in the Year of the Ox, which is the Water Buffalo in Vietnam. That means you are dependable and patient—a tireless worker—but you can be stubborn. You respect tradition but this can sometimes lead you into prejudice. You are romantic but love often makes you the fool—am I right so far, little sister?"

I blushed because it was as if the astrologer were looking into my soul. I only hoped his spirit sight would be clear enough to discern the pitfalls and stumbling blocks in the home that was to be my fortress for the future.

We arrived at the site of the almost completed house around three o'clock. Like the first geomancer, he circled the structure compass in hand, noting which doors opened in which direction. He also dug in the earth, tasting it the way a chef tastes dough, and rolled it between his fingers. Inside, he consulted his celestial charts and tables. When he was finished, he took me into the kitchen.

"Here is your only problem," he said solidly. "Notice how your front door lines up with the back door in the kitchen. Everything that comes into your life the front way will go out the back: men, money, happiness, you name it. I suggest you build a wall across the opening or at least block the door—put a bookcase against it and always keep it locked. Other than that"—he rolled his charts—"I suggest you move in on the eighth of July between ten and twelve in the morning. Bring fruit, flowers, a bucket of water, a dead chicken, and plenty of incense and paper money to burn: these are the things you'll need to propitiate the spirits of earth, water, and your ancestors. It's also a good idea to invite a few homeless spirits, too, since you were a child of the war. Put some of the food on the floor, too, so that the crippled spirits can feast—everybody always forgets about them. If you like, I can come back and help you with the formal blessing."

"Yes," I said, "I would like that very much."

When the house was finished, we moved in like a colony of ants: one stick of furniture, one carload of belongings at a time. About halfway through our two-week-long effort, I spent a night alone in the house just to enjoy its quiet and sense of peace. My dreams, for once, were my own: no Ed, no Dennis, no nattering relatives, no war ghosts—nobody but the entity called Phung Thi Le Ly. I enjoyed it immensely.

Our new household was decidedly smaller. Thao's children went back to live with her (Escondido was too far for their mother to commute) and, similarly, Anh and Chanh wanted to stay in San Diego near their friends. Amidst our new neighbors (who, in a new development, were all newcomers themselves) in a new community, we felt like pioneers. The only things we'd have would be the things we made for ourselves, and we knew our work would be good.

For the next few weeks, the boys and I landscaped the yard and I installed custom curtains and miniblinds, sparing no expense for this investment of a lifetime—*song phai co cai nha, gia co phai cai mo!* I got a carpet as lush as Leatha's. My developer friend, our first guest, estimated that the value had already increased by $25,000 since I first made my offer, almost a year before. This was the America we had dreamed about in Vietnam. This was the America I yearned for when I arrived with Ed: a place of my own, steeped in beauty and good karma; hospitable to flesh and spirit, promising security in old age, leaving me answerable to no one but myself.

The day finally arrived for the *Ong Thay Dai Ly* to formally bless our house. I had carried out all the preliminary rituals and acquired all the materials he said we would need for the ceremony and the convocation of household spirits. He arrived from Los Angeles with two companions.

"These are your associates, brother?" I asked respectfully. "Acolytes? Your disciples-in-training?"

"No," he answered absently. "This is my brother-in-law and his neighbor. They want to go to the San Diego Wild Animal Park when we're finished. They've never been there."

The four of us gathered near the den's walk-in closet where my Buddhist shrine was set up. Jimmy and Tommy weren't entirely sold on my beliefs, although they respected them a little more. In return, I tried to keep my religious paraphernalia out of sight so their school friends wouldn't think their mother was too weird. It was a nice idea, but it didn't always work.

I put unblemished fruit on the altar, along with smoking incense and a recording of chanting monks—in stereo—one of the best applications of American technology I had seen. We drew the drapes and made the room as dark as possible. I lit as many candles as I had and their perfume quickly mixed with the incense to give the place a surreal quality. Our souls relaxed and prepared us for our encounter with the incorporeal world. In his role of medium, or *xoc dong,* the geomancer produced a mystic slate, like a Ouija board, and placed it in front of us. He began chanting with the record and we all closed our eyes.

After a short time he said, "The spirits are here." Then he got quiet; then giggled like a little kid, which really startled me. "Oh, there are so many of them! I can't believe it! And high spirits, too— very elder ancestors. And outside, there are many more—younger, lower ones who want to come in but can't. Oh, this is marvelous!"

Suddenly, the *xoc dong* broke the circle. In his normal voice he said to me, "Ly, why don't we build a little altar for the lower spirits in the dining room. It won't take but a minute, and we should be polite. There really are a lot of them. You might like to know that Ed and Dennis are among them."

As quickly as I could, I put some offerings on my dinner table along with a very fine ceramic Buddha.

We resumed the séance and the higher spirits had their say. Unfortunately, it was in the language of a superior plane and we understood none of it, but after a half hour of mumbling, chanting, and jerking in his chair, the *xoc dong* came out of his trance—very thirsty —and pronounced my ancestors extremely pleased with their new spirit home and the work I was doing in America.

"My work?" I was genuinely puzzled. "What work is that?" I couldn't believe my ancestral spirits could be particularly proud of my ill-fated deli and Tuy's bankrupt jewelry store. "What is the work that pleases them so much?" I asked again. But the *xoc dong* didn't say.

"Now I have a message for you from Dennis," he continued. A pained look came over his face. "He's standing back—he's a little shy. He doesn't want to come into your new house. He's not used to his new world. No, that's not it. He's bitter—yes. But he forgives you. He is a student of the other spirits and is learning from their wisdom. He wants—he asks—for you to take his soul to the Buddhist temple. He says, 'Place me in the temple.' He also tells you to lock your door always—"

"Which door? The kitchen door? The kitchen door is sealed."

The medium looked very pained now and I could tell he wanted to break contact. Dennis could do that to you.

"He says he will watch the house. He says he will watch your house—until you put his soul to rest in the temple—" The medium's eyes popped open. "Well, that's it." He wiped his forehead with a handkerchief.

"Are you sure that was Dennis?" I asked. "He was a very strong Christian. He swore that if he died, he would not come to visit me like Ed. I'm surprised he even talked to you."

"Dennis is surprised now about a lot of things." The *xoc dong* drank some more water. "We humans can see just beyond the end of our noses, eh? But spirits can see everything. In life, we see in three dimensions. After death, we see in dozens. It takes some getting used to."

"But he'll be angry if I take him to the Buddhist temple. He hated that place."

"Not anymore. Trust me—he's very uncomfortable where he is. He senses the warmth of the temple. He wants to be soothed. He's like a sailor all alone in a small boat on a vast, foggy sea. He is lost and the temple is his only beacon. In the temple, his soul will receive the instruction it needs. As it finds peace, so will your living family— his descendants—find peace."

That night, I couldn't sleep. Although I was gratified that my ancestral spirits had followed me to this new place, I was still perturbed about Dennis. I knew that angry spirits were very temperamental and had to be handled in just the right way. I wanted Dennis to find peace, but I didn't want to inflict *hau qua*—the curse of a bad ghost—on the monks and congregation at the temple. I felt I was in a terrible quandary.

The next day, I drove to the temple and told my *su* that I wanted to perform *Qui y*—the ceremony for anchoring a lost soul. I apprised him of the dangers, which he knew very well. To my relief, the monk agreed with the *xoc dong* and added that I would be paying off a good deal of soul debt by helping to guide a lost spirit to the path of enlightenment. He told me exactly what I must do.

That evening, I prepared a soul feast—vegetarian dishes and rice —for Dennis's spirit. I brought the food and framed photographs of deceased members of my family to the temple shrine, then got down on my knees and stretched my arms out over my head. I named all the lower spirits who had died away from home and whom I now wished to be comforted in the temple: my brother, Sau Ban; my father, Phung Trong; my first husband, Edward; and my second husband, Dennis. The monk then asked the three "spiritual jewels" —Buddha, the Enlightened One; Dharma, the Teacher; and Sangha, the Highest of High Priests, Keeper of Mysteries—to accept these lost souls into their infinite facets. The monk then placed the photographs in the inner sanctum among the resident souls.

And that was it.

I thanked my *su* and made a generous donation to the temple, although this wasn't strictly necessary. The monk said goodbye, but in a way that was strange—both happy and sad—and gave me a benediction I hadn't heard before: *"Le trao hoc vi."*

During the long drive back to Escondido, I mulled over the wisdom of what I had done and found my soul getting light, my feelings more buoyant, with each passing mile. By the time I parked in my garage and crossed back into my dream house, I was so lighthearted that I might well have floated above the carpet, as airy as one of my spirits.

I got down my Vietnamese-English dictionary and looked up the monk's benediction. It was the phrase used to congratulate students when they graduated from high school or college. The word was *commencement*. It meant the end of one great thing and the beginning of something grander.

SEVEN

Pursuit of Happiness

AFTER DENNIS'S FRETFUL SOUL was put to rest, I found greater peace in every other part of my life.

The boys did well in school and expanded their interest in religion from Baptist dogma to include the teachings of Buddha, karma, and the natural order of things. Jimmy, in fact, found in this philosophy the God of Einstein as well as the Christian God of Abraham. Our debates became discussions and all four of us learned a lot more about *dao lam nguoi*—how to become a human being.

I worked even harder on my family's history, although now that I approached the story of my own teenage years, the memories brought cold sweats, cramps, and tears, like a mother's hard labor. Because putting the manuscript aside even for a day was much easier than going on, I began to doubt my will to finish it. Yet I persevered. How could I not? I had a million lost souls behind me: pushing, wailing, singing a joyful chorus at every completed page.

One day while I was loading my car with groceries, mulling around this memory and that, I spotted an unusual little store across the street called the *Philosophical Library*. Although I had never studied "philosophy" as it is classified by American colleges, I had often been told by instructors and classmates that I had a "philosophical turn of mind." I couldn't help but wonder what a bookstore devoted entirely to my turn of mind would be like.

Instead of shouting best-sellers and coffee-table books of warplanes and bikini-girl calendars, the walls were adorned with spiritual posters: fantastic cloud cities, lush jungles, eclipsing moons, sorcerers, and images from both the Western and Eastern zodiacs. Along with Buddha statues stood racks of packaged herbs, incense, healing crystals, and tapes of soothing music. Instead of shelves lined with dust-dry books by dead European authors, there were lively volumes on Taoism, Confucianism, Buddhism, Hinduism, and both amateur and professional guides to astrology—most written by people with Oriental surnames. As Jimmy would later say after seeing the store, "Gee, Mom, looks like you died and went to heaven!" He was half right. When I finally came back out, all my frozen foods had melted and the fruit had sprouted leaves.

The little shop became my second home. I attended the many lectures and seminars held at the store and bought every tape they had for sale and borrowed or rented those that weren't. I made friends with the owners, the staff, and the customers. For some of them, the bookstore was an introduction to a "new age" in Western thinking about spiritual and religious matters. To me, it was like meeting old friends and family. Best of all, this discovery came at a time when I needed it most, when my spirit was almost drained dry by the confrontation with my own war memories. Before, I didn't believe Americans could care about the spiritual life of my people. Now, after seeing America's new awareness firsthand, I decided that to tell the story of a Vietnamese family without its soul would be like giving stillbirth to a baby: a lifeless imitation of what god and nature intended to be vital and complete. As I studied, I went back to my self-appointed task with new energy and hope.

Some of my "library" friends lived in Rancho Bernardo, an exclusive suburb filled with almost wealthy people, many of them retired. During one of my visits, my friends and I ate at a new Oriental restaurant called the Royal Eagle. The food was good but the servers were young and inexperienced. They had trouble meeting the needs and expectations of Rancho Bernardo's older crowd. Coincidentally, one of the waitresses had worked with me at NSC in San Diego. Alone on a return visit, I spoke to her as soon as it was convenient.

"Thuan em—Sister Thuan!" I met her by the busser's station. "How are you doing?"

"Chi Ly!" she responded, "It's been a long time!"

We chatted only a minute or two—I didn't want our reunion to make the service worse. It was almost six o'clock, and diners were arriving in a steady stream.

"Tell me," I asked, "who owns this place? Do they have a manager?"

"No, no manager. The place just opened. Kenneth—the owner—is trying to save money. Would you like to meet him?"

"Very much!"

She disappeared into the kitchen. Maybe Thuan thought I wanted a job as a waitress and had visions of our gossiping during breaks like the old days. I had something different in mind.

A young, thin Chinese-Vietnamese man came back through the swinging doors. His shoulder-length hair bulged beneath the state-required hairnet; his face was coated with perspiration above a soy-stained apron.

"Hello," he said pleasantly, offering his hand. "You are Miss Hayslip? My name is Kenneth. What can I do for you?"

"Ong chu, please call me Ly. Your restaurant is very nice"—I gestured to the lucky red wallpaper and gold trim—"very beautiful."

"Well, thank you very much! We're doing the best we can. I hope you're not interested in a job. I can't hire anyone else until business picks up. Maybe later in the year—"

"That's why I wanted to talk to you. I would like to work for you, but not as a waitress. Take a look." I stood back and let Kenneth's own operation make my point. "Here it is, the beginning of supper rush, and people are turning away because of the long line by the register. The retired people who eat early are trying to pay their checks while the people getting off work have to wait for tables. Your waiters and waitresses are bumping into each other trying to seat people and take orders and serve food and run the cash register and handle the take-out and nobody's coordinating anything. I'll bet half of them don't know enough English to read the menu! You don't need more servers or cooks, Kenneth, you need a manager: somebody who can get your people to work together as a team and give your customers professional service."

Kenneth shook his head, "I try to keep an eye on things from the kitchen, but—I don't know. Managers are expensive and this is a family business, you know? Still, if you want to fill out an application, I'll let you know when business gets good enough for me to interview you for—"

"No," I smiled at him. "I don't want an application, I want you to watch me!"

I was dressed in a nice *ao dai* anyway and had nothing to lose, so I thought I'd give Kenneth an audition. I went straight to the half-dozen people waiting inside the door, introduced myself to the first couple, thanked them for coming, grabbed a pair of menus, and showed them to the nearest clean table for two. I went back to the register, checked out an elderly customer and his wife ("Thank you for bearing with us," I said with a smile. "This is our grand opening. I hope you will become our regular guests"), seated another pair and signaled a busser to begin clearing a table for a party of four. After a couple of minutes, the logjam by the register was cleared and I went back to Kenneth.

"See?" I grinned. "All it takes is a little coordination—knowing what to do and thinking ahead. And a little show business!"

Kenneth scanned the tables—all smiling faces and quiet conversations. Servers and bussers came and went without colliding. "Come inside," he said, taking off his apron. "Let's talk."

Before Kenneth could give me his well-rehearsed (and, I'm sure, very sincere) speech about how little he could pay a hostess/manager, I relieved him of his anxiety.

"Look, Kenneth," I said, "I don't want to work for wages. I've done that already. Let me show you what I can do for two weeks— just like tonight—for free. After that, let's sit down again and talk about my compensation."

Because my short-term costs were zero and the benefits I promised were immediate, Kenneth jumped at my proposition. For the next two weeks, I came in early and went home late. I learned the names and favorite dishes of many customers and remembered them when they returned. I made friends with the food servers and helped them adjust their schedules to get the hours they wanted. I helped clear tables and realigned several sections so we could get to and from the tables easier with less noise and fewer accidents. I spent as much time as I could with the kitchen staff, sharing praise from the customers and joking with them about everything from the peculiarities of American taste ("You know that guy at table twelve actually eats ketchup with his egg rolls!") to the mysteries of the clipper machine, which our young dishwasher operated with as much pride as the captain of a 747. Absenteeism dropped and repeat business soared. Daily receipts climbed. Many of the customers began asking for me by name and thought I owned the restaurant.

When it came time to discuss my compensation, Kenneth was less concerned about how much I would cost than how much I had shown my services could pay.

"Okay," I said, "I will give you three choices. "I already said I didn't want wages and that's still true. You may pay me a salary if you wish, but I warn you, it will be high. I would much prefer to work for a percentage of the day's receipts or, even better, to work for a percentage of the profits, as a co-owner. That way, my pay is based not only on how much money I help bring in, but on how well I help you to hold down costs. That way, we make money together, right? What do you think?"

Kenneth could see the wisdom of my offer, but he was still the "proud parent" of a fledgling business and I could see it was too soon for him to consider taking on a partner. Instead, we negotiated a modest salary with a sales incentive, which suited me fine. I told him that, under such an arrangement, I could work only the lunch and dinner rush hours—eleven to two and five to nine—and he agreed.

Meanwhile, I kept working on my war memoir: dictating story after story to Jimmy, who dutifully typed them into his computer. These sessions were very emotional, particularly when it came time to talk about adventures Jimmy shared, but was too young to remember. I still cried at the mention of my departed father and brother, whom I still mourned and prayed for daily, and my mother, whom I hadn't seen for more than thirteen years and missed beyond measure. When things were going good and neither of us wanted to stop, Tommy became responsible for meals and brought us tea and snacks. When the going got tough or we broke down in tears, little Alan would bring the tissues, which we stocked like pencils and paper. A day didn't go by that I didn't gather my boys into my arms and cry out of relief that the war was over. Often I grieved that they would never know the Vietnamese family life I loved and feared I would never see again.

By the end of summer, 1985, Jimmy and I had completed three hundred pages, which to me seemed bigger than an encyclopedia: a mouse giving birth to an elephant! Although it was only a fraction of what I wanted to say, it was enough to test the publishing waters.

From the reference desk at the local library, I got a listing of all American publishers and sent out a hundred copies of my rough draft. After a few weeks, the replies trickled in. Some were curt and businesslike, and made me feel sorry for wasting the publisher's valuable time with my stupid ideas. Some said they liked the idea of telling a Vietnamese peasant woman's story to Americans—to give identities to the "faceless" Asians who once crowded their TV screens —but Vietnam "really wasn't our thing" or "isn't very hot right now." Others thought its time had yet to come ("We need the benefit of historical perspective that another generation will bring"). Well, I didn't have time to wait for the next generation. If history had taught me one lesson, it was that each generation must learn for itself what love, war, child-rearing, and universal law are all about. Unless people took it upon themselves to share what they had learned, each country would never be anything more to another than colors on a map. One reply—"It would be hard for our readers to accept because the subject matter is based on the viewpoint of enemies who killed our people in war"—only made me more determined to get my side of the story published.

After six months of watching me work hard to learn the food service craft, Kenneth made it clear that he was not ready to admit a partner. I would have to satisfy my proprietor's dreams—*lam chu tu minh,* to command my own destiny—elsewhere.

"I've decided to open my own restaurant," I told Kenneth one day after my shift. "I'll give you a couple of weeks to find a new hostess and manager, if you want to replace me, but I've already applied for a second mortgage on my house and withdrawn twenty thousand from the bank. With that and a little luck, I think I can start a business of my own."

He looked a little disappointed, but not surprised, then brightened. "I don't suppose you're looking for an investor—?"

I brightened too. "You know of somebody?"

"Sure. Me! I know what you can do. I'm sure you'll be successful at anything you try. You understand why I can't give away part of this business now—but if you're willing to take on partners, I'll be happy to participate in a new one."

We talked another hour, my excitement growing by the minute. Kenneth didn't have a lot of ready cash, but he knew people who did. He also had a wealth of ideas, experience, and contacts. What about menus and food preparation? No problem—Kenneth had trained a good chef who was itching to run his own kitchen. What about start-up costs and renovations? Kenneth had friends in the construction business who did great work at good rates. I left feeling lucky to be the Royal Eagle's hatchling instead of an extra "mother."

Along with Mr. Ho, our third partner, Kenneth and I signed the lease for five thousand square feet of preapproved space in Temecula, Riverside County.

I put about fifty thousand dollars and three months' hard labor into getting things started and we opened the doors of the Hollylinh (Mr. "Ho," Le "Ly," and Kenneth "Linh") Restaurant on schedule with assets of over $150,000. We tried to strike a balance between traditional Chinese decor and California ambience: tropical fish and glass-topped tables in place of the usual red pillars and porcelain dragons. We ran into the usual problems, though, when it came to staff. Most of the Chinese or Vietnamese who were willing to work for restaurant wages were "FOB" (fresh off the boat, as Jimmy's school friends liked to say), and knew little English and less about American customs. We hired eight workers in this category, and I decided to try something radical in order to speed their learning. What made my plan especially satisfying was that it relied on nothing more than an age-old Vietnamese custom

In Vietnam, restaurant owners were expected to be very paternalistic with their employees. If you treated your workers like family, it was thought, they would respond in kind. "Good parents" deserved "good children," so considerate, generous bosses were usually rewarded with loyalty and hard work. Stingy or cruel bosses, on the other hand, often created "lazy" workers, or worse. As one saying went: *"Giet nguoi bang muoi"*—A bad cook kills the customers!

Our problem was that the eight workers we hired all shared a two-bedroom apartment in Los Angeles and the restaurant was in Temecula, where few Orientals lived. Kenneth offered to rent them a similar apartment in Temecula, but I couldn't imagine "happy work-ers" living four to a room, especially in the "land of gold." I offered to let all of them live in my house and commute with me to work, which pleased them enormously (especially after they saw my dream house!) and completely baffled my partners. However, the compro-mise made sense, so that's exactly what we did. In my house, we spoke English all the time and watched TV, where they learned about American lifestyles and attitudes. At work, everyone cooperated and immediately applied what they learned.

Of course, I knew this could not go on indefinitely. If our crew had any ambition, some would soon seek better-paying jobs or go to school. I didn't really want to run a permanent halfway house for immigrants anyway.

The solution was for the partners to invest in another house a few minutes from the restaurant and allow the employees to live in it rent free. This not only solved our housing crisis, but created an excellent store of cash for growth and emergencies. Because I had the money, I made the down payment and the title was in my name, although the restaurant made the monthly payments and had a claim against the future equity.

I remember sitting down at my kitchen table to catch my breath on the day we closed. I now owned three houses in and around a major American city and a third of a growing business—no mean feat for a *meo con* kitten so scrawny at birth that the peasant midwife wanted to choke me and throw me away! My sons were healthy, happy, safe, and well on their way to becoming young men their grandparents in both cultures would be proud of. And (although I still collected rejection slips) my book was ripening on its vine along with my bank account.

Was there anything more a woman like me could want?

One day at the Philosophical Library I saw an ad for a spiritual retreat in the town of Harmony Grove—a tranquil place, surrounded by elfin forest in the mountains between Escondido and the sea. Since I knew location made a big difference in spiritual matters as well as real estate, I visited the town as soon as I could. To passing travelers, Harmony Grove might be just another hamlet. To me, it was nirvana —a supermarket of psychics, mediums, and soothsayers.

The first swami I consulted was Paul, a handsome, softspoken young man about my age. If Jesus had been a surfer, he would've looked like this blond-haired namesake of his disciple. Like the Baptists' conception of Jesus, too, Paul never smiled.

On the morning of our appointment, I met him in a rough-hewn cabin. It was sparsely furnished with a single wooden chair, which he occupied, and a couch by the window which was meant for me—psychiatrist and patient. Unlike a Western psychologist, though, he would do the talking and I would ask the questions. Like a good monk who meditates before engaging in any spiritual activity, Paul wanted us to relax. We both closed our eyes.

"Feel the sunbeams on your skin," he said in a soothing, hypnotic voice. "Its yellow light turns your warming flesh to butter. Ever softer, more relaxed. As your body gives way, your mind becomes clearer. As your mind clears, your soul rises from the murky depths to the surface of a crystal pond. Its energy pours forth and rides the light beams to every part of the room. I open myself to the energy of your spirit, to its knowledge of past and future . . ."

We sat in silence for several minutes, then he said, "I see you at the base of a mountain, Le Ly. You are tired from climbing, yet your journey has hardly begun. I see you climbing: slowly, but with determination. The lower slope is steep with jagged rocks. Farther on, the slope begins to flatten, the rocks become smaller. Each stone you touch becomes a flower. Near the summit, flowers are all around you. People at the base of the mountain cheer and reach up with their hands. The mountain is not in the United States. The sunlight on the mountaintop is pure—no clouds—"

I opened my eyes to peek at the guru. He pinched the bridge of his nose and frowned, as if, by looking, I had thrown static into his vision. I closed my eyes and let the warm sunlight carry me off again.

"I am writing a book," I said. "Will it be published?"

He sighed. "Yes. But not soon. It is a milestone on your path, but it is not your destination. It lies half again the distance you have already climbed."

I calculated quickly, trying not to disturb the channel again. It was now 1985 and I had been in America thirteen years. It had been ten years since the fall of South Vietnam and my absolute cutoff from my family, the time when I really felt I stood "at the base of my mountain." Did he mean my book would be published in 1990?

"Do I have a companion on this climb?" I had three soulmates so far, two of whom, Ed and Dennis, were dead and another, Anh, who was locked away in Communist purgatory. As a woman, I wanted to know if I was destined to end my days alone, in the company of spirits, or in the cradling arms of a flesh-and-blood man that I could love and call my own.

"I see a very old man—"

My heart sank. Ed? The prematurely aged soul of Dennis? The vision of yet another older man who would marry me and begin another endless round of *hy sinh?* I could not bear to think so. "Is it my father?" I asked.

Paul shifted in his chair. "No. No, this is someone much older. Very much older. His time on earth, hundreds of years ago, most of the 1500s. He smells of herbs. He says he was a medicine man."

"And he will join me on my journey? On my climb? When?" This was an intriguing, unexpected development. I tried to remember what I had learned in my books about transmigration of souls.

For the first time, I heard the hint of a smile in Paul's voice, "He has been with you a long time. Always, in fact."

My god! Who is this person—this guardian spirit? "What does he want from me?"

"You will become a healer, just as he was in his lifetime."

"You mean a doctor? A physician?" This didn't make sense.

"Your healing art is not of the body."

"Who is this spirit? Who was the man?"

Paul was silent for what seemed like an eternity—ten or fifteen minutes. I heard his chair creak several times, as if engaged in an energetic, wordless debate. As much as I wanted to open my eyes and see what was going on—to see, perhaps, if there was an apparition in the room—I dared not for fear of breaking the channel.

At last Paul said, sounding a little exasperated, "He will not tell me. He says you will find out in the proper course of things."

"Then why is he communicating with me now? Why haven't I heard from him before? Why hasn't my father told me about him?"

"Your father is on a much lower spiritual plane. He says his connection to you goes back much further than your parents. And this is not the first time he has communicated with you. You have been visited by him in prior lives. He says that you will discover his identity only after you have accomplished your mission in life."

Questions began to tumble out of me: What, exactly, was my mission? I knew I had many karmic lessons to learn, but which were tied to my destiny—my purpose for this incarnation? And what did he mean that my healing art would not be "of the body"? Was I supposed to become a *nico,* a Buddhist nun, and renounce the world and concern myself only with spiritual matters? That didn't seem likely. By now my conscious energy was so high I knew I had narrowed, if not shut completely, the door on my psychic channel. I looked over at Paul who was sitting easily in his chair. Contrary to my expectation, he did not look tired or worn out by the experience, but refreshed.

We discussed the possible meanings of his reading and I visited other gurus in Harmony Grove as well, but the message was always the same: I was to lead a crowd in a long, hard climb. I was to practice the healing arts but not as a doctor, medicine man, or nun. Somehow I must find a way to be in the world but not of it. Like the flowering stones in Paul's vision, I must find life and color where before there had only been flint and darkness.

I returned from Harmony Grove with absolutely no idea what to do next.

Jimmy, eighteen, was at the nearby University of California, San Diego. It seemed as if the only time I saw him now was when he got tired of Big Macs and came back for a home-cooked meal—and maybe to do a little work on the manuscript. He never talked much about his studies (what did I know about computers anyway?) but his grades showed he was doing well.

Tommy was fifteen and took up with a crowd that thought school was not so hot. One day he came home and said, "Some army guys came to the school today. The recruiter's speech was really neat. What would you do if I joined up?"

I grunted. "If you go to jail, I'll bring you rice every day. If you join the army, I won't even bury you when you get killed. Does that answer your question?"

Gratefully, he took his restless energy out on the wrestling team, which made it as far as the state championships. He had to skip meals in order to keep his weight down and qualify for a lighter division, which upset me a lot. Why live in America if you can't eat everything your mother cooks?

Alan's life was much calmer. His closest friends came from a nice Filipino family with traditions a lot like ours. He never got into trouble and had pretty much climbed out of the dark hole into which he'd descended after his father died. As his older brothers found their way further into the world, we became the best of friends.

The time I didn't spend with my boys or at the Hollylinh restaurant, I spent in our yard—a compulsive gardner. On sunny days, I planted flowers and hoed weeds and plucked vegetables and turned and watered San Diego's dry earth. I sang half-forgotten songs from my youth as vivid images of my father's cement-walled, thatch-roofed house and my own bamboo bed and my mother's well-swept kitchen floor danced through my mind. As I hosed down my driveway I remembered taking showers on the cement pad by our well and pouring buckets of water over our plough ox to rid it of mud and flies. With a closetful of fine American shoes, I went barefoot so that I could imagine the loamy soil of China Beach, and I wore my ragged black pajamas instead of fancy sundresses. After a while the nodding trees became my father, Phung Trong, and my brother, Sau Ban, working beside me in the paddies. At the end of the day, when the sun was setting, I felt the urge to go home—not to my American mansion, but *home* to Vietnam, where my aging mother, sisters, cousins, and the bones of my ancestors called with increasingly urgent voices.

It had been thirteen years since my final escape from the war. My mother was nearly eighty and even under the best of circumstances (and rumors and letters from Communist Vietnam told only of the worst) she had only a few years left. Few people except diplomats, lawmakers, or military men had ventured into the country since 1975, and most of those were on official government missions to account for MIAs or press various claims arising from the war.

Tears and wishes had sustained me many years in America, but they had not brought me one step closer to my mother's door. If I was going to do anything about it, I would have to disregard a host of naysayers and give it everything I had.

I decided to start at the top. I sat Jimmy down at his computer and dictated a letter to President Ronald Reagan.

"Mommmm!" Jimmy complained. "You can't start a letter to the president, 'How are you? I am fine.'"

"Why not? That's how we do it in English class."

"Never mind. Just tell me what you want to say and I'll do it the right way."

What I wanted to say was that I had to go back to Vietnam. I wanted President Reagan to understand that the Vietnamese people —almost all Asians—feel strong bonds with their families overseas. I wanted, *needed,* make a pilgrimage to my village to say goodbye to Mama Du, my "mother of the breast," before she died. I didn't care about politics. I didn't know anything about communism or democracy and never had. I felt sorry for everyone who had been harmed by the war, on either side. But I was just one person. What I cared about was comforting my mother in her old age, helping my family with a few goods from America, and praying at my father's grave. Couldn't this great U.S. president help a little Vietnamese woman visit her family?

Just to be certain, I had Jimmy write similar letters to California's governor, senators, representatives, and the mayors of Escondido and San Diego. I made appointments with the local politicians and hand delivered my letters. I carried a copy of my President Reagan letter with me at all times just in case fate or luck or god brought me in contact with someone who could help. It was also a talisman, a constant reminder of my objective.

It also occurred to me that Dan might be able to help. I had last seen him in 1973 and last heard from him in '76. Those letters that Ed didn't burn were later destroyed by Dennis, so I didn't even have Dan's "last-known" address. I wrote to the Defense Department, saying that I was Colonel Dante DeParma's lost Vietnamese wife, which, in a sense, was true. I had his social security number and some photos of us together with Tommy and Jimmy and the note he had given me during our helicopter evacuation from An Khe, so my credentials were better than the typical refugee tea-girl looking for an American sugar daddy. I thought it was ironic that the note that was supposed to help me get out of Vietnam might now somehow serve as my passport the other way.

I received a surprising response: Dan's address in Korea. It was almost Christmas, so I scrawled out a brief message on a greeting card and put it in the mail. I almost fainted when I received Dan's letter in return.

In cramped handwriting showing his years, he said how happy he was to hear from me after all this time. He had divorced his first wife, as he had promised, but remarried shortly after we broke contact— about the same time Dennis and I were getting married in Mexico! He said he still regarded us as his "Vietnam family" and wanted to keep in touch. I had to remind myself that my mission was to go to Vietnam, not Korea to take up again with Dan, but his support seemed to make it easier than it would have been even a few months before. Although I believed our original soul connection remained, I think Major Daddy would have been pleased to see that the confused, love-hungry young girl at An Khe had ripened into something else.

About three months after the start of my letter-writing campaign, I gave in to my girlfriends' protestations that I was again taking life too seriously and went with Kathy Greenwood for a "girls' night out." We spent most of the time chatting at a quiet piano bar and I realized they were right—I had needed a break. I went to the restroom and when I came back, Kathy was talking to a dignified gray-haired man at the adjoining table. She introduced me as I sat down.

"I understand you want to go back to Vietnam," the man said, smiling the indulgent smile I'd seen on the faces of dozens of officials over the last three months.

"Yes." I tried not to sound too cynical. "I want to see my poor old mother before she dies—and try to make amends with the family I left behind when I came to the United States. I'm not having much luck, though."

"Why not? Who have you talked to?"

"Just about everybody. Here—take a look." I pulled Jimmy's letter to President Reagan out of my purse. Although it didn't start with my ESL niceties, it made my case well enough. The man's indulgent smile faded.

"Well, I can see you're serious about this," he said, taking a pen out of his shirt pocket. On the back of one of my business cards he wrote a Vietnamese name and title. "Here, give this fellow a try."

"Who is it?" I asked.

"The Counselor to the Vietnamese Mission to the UN—the United Nations in New York."

I looked at the name, assuming the man must be an expatriate Republican—one of the high officials who still maintained a liaison with the American government hoping for the day they could return to power in our country. "How do you know this man?" I asked.

The man smiled. "I do business with the UN from time to time. My mother used to live in New York. But I was always on the road and didn't see her for years. When I finally returned for a visit, she had already died. I don't think that should happen to anyone."

On Monday, the United Nations operator routed me to the Vietnamese Mission. It was answered by a man with a thick accent.

"Hello," I replied. "Do you speak Vietnamese?"

"Van a, Chi muon hoi gi a—Yes, of course, what does Sister want?"

I continued in our native language. "Brother, I am Vietnamese, too, and want to go home to pay my respects to my mother before she passes away. She is seventy-eight years old and I don't think she has much more time."

"Certainly, I understand. Why don't you go?"

"I don't follow you." For a minute I thought this fellow was joking.

"I mean, why don't you book an airline ticket and go?" he said. "Who's stopping you?"

For a "counselor," I couldn't believe how stupid this man was! Didn't he know about the war? Surely an ex-official would know about the Vietnamese Communist government and America's official policy of "no contact"! I assumed I would have to educate him.

"Who's stopping me? Well, for one, I am a U.S. citizen now, and the Hanoi regime controls the South. If I go there, the government could throw me in prison or send me to a re-education camp. And even if they let me out, the U.S. government might not let me back in. I've talked to a lot of refugees and many American officials. The whole problem is with the Communist government."

"Sister, do you know who you're talking to now?"

"Well—no, not really."

"You're talking to a Communist. I am a representative of the Socialist Republic of Vietnam. We have a small Mission here in New York to coordinate relations with the United Nations and the United States. We hope one day to have full diplomatic recognition, but—"

I hung up the phone.

My hands were shaking so violently my pencil clattered to the floor. I sank back into my chair. The last Communist—*Cong San*— I'd knowingly talked to was at a graveside—my grave!—after my kangaroo trial with the Viet Cong. My warder, Loi, a village youth who had become a VC fighter after the Americans arrived, decided on a more terrible punishment than the merciful bullet in my head. Instead, he and his comrade, Mau, raped me and forbade me to return to my village, beginning the years-long odyssey that would eventually bring me to America. Now, like a vicious, dormant disease, the chills and fever of those years swept over me again.

With trembling fingers, I lit incense at my shrine and said several prayers. I wondered what to do next. If the police were monitoring the Communist's telephone lines, they would surely trace the call and come here next, probably in the dead of night like the Republican and American VC hunters and blow my brains out. I called my sympathetic girlfriends and asked what they knew about Hanoi's UN Mission. All knew less than me. Like it or not, my determination to revisit my homeland was turning me into an expert on matters I'd just as soon let molder in the grave. But what was I to do? What was the alternative? Just give up?

After a week without a call from the FBI or CIA or army intelligence or any officials from anywhere, I got the nerve to try again. I talked to the same man, Sy Liem, so I had a chance to apologize; I also learned I was not the first expatriate to panic on the phone when the identity of the other voice was made known. In fact, I felt like a member of a pretty exclusive club: the first wave of *Viet Kieu*—Vietnamese expatriates lost and lonely in foreign lands—wanting to re-establish communication with their families.

We spoke for half an hour, clearing up my misconceptions about what the UN Mission was for and gaining each other's confidence. He was not a double agent trying to snare people who had former links to the VC and I was not a right-wing "hit lady" trying to set him up for a kidnapping or assassination. He also told me a lot about conditions in the country without the usual gloss of Hanoi propaganda: the poverty, the disease, the lingering effects of the war. Even if only a fraction of what he said was true, the Communist government seemed a bigger menace to itself than any right-wing exiles or American hawks could ever be. Finally, we got to the real purpose of my call.

"So, if you really want Viet Kieu to come and visit," I said, "where do I begin?"

"First," he replied, "you must write a letter telling us when you want to travel, how long you want to stay, and where you want to go. After we've received your request, we'll send you an application for a visa. You don't need U.S. government permission to leave or return to the country. Just book your ticket into Bangkok, Thailand, then make your reservations to Ho Chi Minh City or Hanoi from there. There's really nothing to it. We'll send you a list of the things you're allowed to bring into the country. We know you want to take gifts to your relatives, but we don't want to spoil the market for our own workers' goods and services."

Liem made it sound easy and fun, like a vacation to Acapulco, but I had my doubts. I didn't tell him too much about myself in case the phones were tapped; I had spent too many years playing both ends against the middle to quickly identify myself with either the VC or American factions. The best policy would be to stick to the simple truth: I was a homesick Vietnamese who, having had some good luck in America, now wanted to share that good fortune with her relatives. Beyond these simple facts, what more was needed?

I wrote my letter, burned some incense, and prayed.

One evening, not long thereafter, I learned that the University of California, San Diego, was holding a writers' conference in La Jolla. Knowing I could leave no path untrodden, I sent in my application along with a sample chapter of my story and, just as I waited for the Vietnamese UN Mission to approve my visa, I marked time for the organizers' response. With Tommy and Alan involved more and more with school and friends, I spent a lot of time at the restaurant, anything to stay busy and keep from worrying about my manuscript or my trip.

Business at the Hollylinh was better than ever. Although I wasn't there every day, I quickly developed some "regulars" who asked for me by name and with whom I always spent a little extra time sharing stories about my childhood and adventures during the war.

For like-minded customers, my conversation sometimes turned to spiritual matters. Sometimes, just for fun, I would read their fortunes from their palms or in a deck of cards. At first, I did it as a joke, answering their questions—"Will I be rich? Does my boyfriend love me? Will I marry soon?"—in a lighthearted way, making sure not to mislead anybody or make anyone feel bad. The question the women asked most was "When will I find Mr. Right?" I could only respond that I was still looking too and couldn't help them out!

Sometimes, though, I got very strong sensations from a palm or from the unusual way a deck of cards was dealt. Then the funny business stopped and I would tell them that I really wasn't qualified to tell fortunes. But everybody would egg me on so I just did what I had seen other psychics do during many seminars, consultations, and séances: I let myself be open to the feelings they were having. Even in the bustle of a busy restaurant, you'd be surprised how intense and specific some feelings can be. Only much later would I learn that this, in fact, is how most psychics get their start; not from schools or tutelage with a master, but by plumbing the depths of their own intuition and thinking a lot about what certain feelings and images seem to mean.

Eventually, word got around that "Miss Ly" was, at the very least, an entertaining psychic and, if the stars were right, the conduit for some very interesting insights. Although I didn't perform on cue and never charged for my services, I was flattered by the attention and always tried to follow the professional psychic's ethic: first, never divulge really bad news, particularly feelings of impending death or serious illness, because you could be wrong; and second, always qualify your precognitions as things that *might* happen, not something that's inevitable, because that, too, was the truth. If people didn't realize they alone were responsible for their lives and the consequences of their actions—including good or bad karma—they had no business consulting a psychic, whose messages could always be misinterpreted.

One day a group of five came in for lunch and asked for Miss Ly. They were all Caucasian, well dressed, and very lively and intelligent. We talked a little about Vietnam, past and present, and they asked for a reading, which I gave each of them in turn. Everything was lighthearted and fun and they left full and happy. A week later, an article about Hollylinh and its proprietor, the "fascinating Miss Ly Hayslip," appeared in the local newspaper. The group had been reporters, including a restaurant reviewer. The article was so favorable that reservations flooded in from surrounding towns and I was obliged to make appointments for people who demanded psychic readings with or without chow mein.

It also put Hollylinh and Ly Hayslip on the map for a very different sort of customer as well.

A week or two after the article appeared, another group of men came in, but these were not well-dressed, happy reporters. They were all my age or slightly older and dressed like workmen. Some had beards; some walked with a limp; and all had the furtive, uncertain glance I had come to associate with angry soldiers. I sat down at their table—a little out of place in my makeup and *ao dai,* but the ice was quickly broken. One of the men said they were all Vietnam veterans who were curious about "the other side." Despite their cumulative ten or twelve years "in country," they all admitted they knew next to nothing about the people, land, and culture they had gone so far to destroy. They also knew that I had firsthand experience with the war, which their wives and girlfriends could never understand. They were hungry, they admitted, not for noodles and rice but peace of mind.

We talked a little more about their experiences in " 'Nam" and I told them my impressions as a stranger in America. We laughed as they tried out their rusty Vietnamese in thick American accents which, to Vietnamese ears, always sounds like lyrics without the music. A couple of them asked for palm readings and I kept things light, although the electricity in their hands was enough to scorch my fingers.

Word spread and more and more veterans sought me out for information, comfort, companionship, and solace. Of course, not all vets who came through my door were interested in putting the war behind them.

"We shouldn't have pulled out until all the MIAs were accounted for," one angry man said. He was not speaking for his group, but I could see traces of his feelings in their eyes. "And we should send every one of those damned boat people back where they came from!" In a different voice, with a different face, he could be Dennis. I thanked god that my husband's spirit was safely at rest in the Buddhist temple, where it could recuperate and learn instead of floating on boiling clouds of hate. Some other vets were angry about the way they had been treated when they returned: by their government, the Veteran's Administration, the public, even their families, who had shunned them as if they bore some contagious tropical disease.

As I listened to their bitter stories, I became aware that, like the other vets, they knew little about the enemy they still hated with such passion. They had few questions, but plenty of answers, although their curses seemed hollow and unsatisfying even as they were spoken.

To these bloodied and worn-out souls, I could only offer my father's advice: *Lay thu lam ban, an oan xoa ngay*—Turn enemies into friends and your hate will yield to joy. Forgive yourself, forget the sins of others, and get on with your life. It was easy to say but very difficult to show, particularly since my own wartime feelings had been rekindled by my growing desire to return to Vietnam. Beneath the spiritual serenity I tried to project was a cornered little animal who, fangs bared, was ready to fight for her life.

One veteran, Gary, came in by himself. He had read the article about me and talked to some of his buddies who had been to the restaurant. He said he published the *Rancho News* and wanted to do a serious feature story about my views on the war, Vietnam vets, and life in America. He asked if he could send a female reporter to do an interview, but I said I wasn't sure. I told him that women hearing my story either got swamped with pity and wanted to mother me or they are so turned off by my experiences that they pulled away and couldn't deal with it.

"Either way," I said, "you would not get a very good article." He thought a moment, then decided to write the piece himself.

We spent the next afternoon in my office reliving the worst years of my life: my brothers' conscription by Hanoi; the formation of Republican and Viet Cong "youth brigades" in our village (we kids were required to join both!); my torture by the Republican army, and my trial and rape by the Viet Cong; my mother and I in exile in Saigon; the birth of Jimmy out of wedlock and my years on the Danang black market; and my American jobs and boyfriends before Ed appeared and saved me. For the first time in front of any American, including my husbands, I told everything that had happened to me.

Unfortunately, Gary wasn't much interested in my fonder memories: of village life between the wars; of my family and the love of life we found in the midst of death and hate—all the things that kept me going and gave my life its purpose during those terrible years. In telling only half my story, he revealed the cause of my beliefs but not what I had learned. I was afraid the article might further disturb troubled souls who had not achieved even this modest level of enlightenment.

My fears were well founded. The article hit our local community like a bombshell—nobody could read it without strong feelings. Many people called or stopped by to express their empathy and even to apologize for their country, which was completely unnecessary and was a total misreading of what my life had been about. The negative reactions were even stronger.

"We don't want to eat food prepared by some damn Viet Cong!" one veteran shouted outside our restaurant. He had made a scene inside and a couple of waiters and our chef had asked him to leave. "We should go back and nuke every damn Communist! People like you shouldn't be here!"

He stalked off and some of the staff worried that he would come back with a gun but I didn't think so. He wore his hatred like a suit of armor and armor is defensive—it protects what's weak and does not threaten the strong. I had stood and listened to his angry outburst without protesting. I looked him in the eye and nodded that I understood, even if I didn't and couldn't agree with him. After all, he was not trying to convince me, just make me as angry and afraid as he was. The best defense, I felt, was not to be steel, but sponge—to soak up whatever bile he threw out and ask for more. Only the unvented steam kettle explodes. The man who wants you to live in fear threatens death. The man who wants you dead simply kills you. We had both suffered much in the war and now he, too, realized that was a kind of bond.

Still, my partners and our employees were concerned.

"Even if that guy doesn't come back," one waiter said, "what if somebody else decides to firebomb the place, or shoot at us as they drive by?"

The fact was, lots of people didn't like the idea of someone with a past association with "the enemy"—however oblique—living and prospering in America. Kenneth said I was endangering the business with all this talk about my past and I couldn't disagree. They decided to change our ads to stress that we were a *Chinese* restaurant, not Vietnamese, and that was true enough. But I couldn't promise that I wouldn't say anything more about the war or my feelings about Vietnam and America. In fact, unlike the rest of them, I was more anxious than ever to hear from the disgruntled, troubled vets. Their picture of the world was too important and widespread to ignore simply because I didn't agree with it. Whether it was post-traumatic stress, bad karma, or just sour grapes, I felt I had to learn more about these sad, angry, terrified men and, in doing so, learn more about myself and my purpose in this life. Besides, I was writing a book. Now more than ever people needed a vehicle, a reason, to look past the war and desolation to understanding and forgiveness. I had to be about my father's business.

Being hostess, manager, and floor show eats up a lot of time. On a typical day I would leave home at ten A.M. and not return until midnight. Jimmy was still away at college, and Tommy and Alan were in bed by the time I got home. I had a full and successful life— economic security, fine sons, and lots of friends—but something at my very core was still lacking. It was as if my fancy Escondido house, looking great from the outside, was completely unfurnished within. I was preoccupied with discovering the mysterious "mission" Paul had prophesied and I felt in my bones that it now had something to do with these troubled Vietnam vets. Some already said they felt more healed after an hour with me than after ten years of conventional therapy. But even that didn't seem right. Any wisdom I had came from my heart and intuition, not great learning and great deeds.

What uncommon "mission" can there be for such a common person? I couldn't begin to guess.

I was also lonely. With my boys finding their lives more and more fulfilled outside our home and the memories, both good and bad, of Ed and Dennis fading, I felt the need for someone with whom I could share my life. I was also getting very anxious about my relatives —particularly my mother—in Vietnam. As the chances for a visit to that country gradually moved from impossible to probable, I began to worry that some sort of "cosmic countdown" had started: a race pitting my own initiative and ingenuity against the forces (disease, poverty, old age, oppression) threatening those I loved.

In February 1986, I received a call from Sy Liem in New York. He said my visa had been approved for a two-week visit during Tet— Vietnam's big New Year's celebration.

For a full minute, I was too overcome to speak. Fortunately, Mr. Liem continued: "Your visa will be good for three months, so you don't have to pack your bags right away. Take your time and make sure you want to do this. In the meantime, we will send you a list of rules and regulations for your visit. When you've decided and bought your ticket, just send us a photocopy of it."

I thanked him as best I could, hung up, and sat down. Now I knew the meaning of the saying "Be careful what you wish for, you just might get it!" My fondest desire was on the verge of coming true. No more dreams and wishful thinking. As Ed would say, it was time to fish or cut bait.

I was willing to endure some risks to return to Vietnam, but how much risk was too much? Was I willing to risk never seeing my sons again? Was I willing to risk bringing danger to my relatives? Despite the affability of their UN representative, I knew the local cadremen and commissars could be very nasty and emotional when it came to dispensing "people's justice" to a returning black-sheep, black-market "traitor" and the family who gave her comfort and support. Just where did my risks end and those of my loved ones—inflicted on them without their consent—begin?

At the end of my soul-searching, I was left without a hairsbreadth of difference between the forces of caution and the forces of growth and change. Like a pupa in a silk cocoon, I was trapped between the safety of my gilded American cage and my primal instinct to break free, spread my wings, and fly.

At work, I tried out the concept of the trip on Kenneth.

"I have good news," I beamed. "They've approved my visa to go to Vietnam! Now I can visit my mother!"

Kenneth sighed and shook his head. "Are you sure that's the right thing to do? Are you sure they'll let you come back?"

"Of course I'm not sure," I said, as if it didn't make any difference. "I don't have the luxury of being sure. For that matter, I could be killed in a traffic accident on the way home tonight. The only way to be safe is to stay home, and my mother will die and I'll never see her again. I'll never have the chance to tell her"—even the thought of it choked me up—"that I love her and miss her and and will make sacrifices for her when she's gone and—"

"Okay, all right." Kenneth put his arm around me like a big brother. "I just want you to be happy with your choice—to know what you're getting into. We all want to see you come back in one piece."

Another employee, a Vietnamese waiter not too long in America who had a hair-raising escape still fresh in his mind, grunted. "The UN Mission must think you're a Communist. Why else would they let you in? To spy on them? To spread discontent? More likely it's to grab you and put you on trial. Or just send you straight to a camp—that's more their style. I think it's a stupid idea."

He gave me the number of someone he termed a "high official" in the old regime who had spent many years in the re-education camps before his escape. "Give him a call," the waiter said, "he'll tell you what to expect."

I rang the number as soon as I got home. The man answered my request for information with a long silence, then said, "As soon as your feet touch Vietnamese soil, they'll place you under arrest. They'll take you to a small cell and leave you there to think and worry. You'll have no food, water, or toilet facilities. The air will be so thin and hot you'll think your lungs will burst. Then, if that doesn't kill you, they'll bring you out for beatings and torture. They'll tell you to confess your crimes and retell your life's story from the Communist perspective. When you've confessed to loving your family and worshiping god and honoring our old customs and traditions, they'll indoctrinate you to the new social order. If you do everything they tell you and sound sincere and are very lucky, they may move you to a work camp where, if you don't starve or die of disease, you'll at least be able to sleep on a mat and use a regular latrine. Or they may just take you out and shoot you. Their brand of communism has nothing to do with politics. It's about owning people's souls."

His words bore into my head like the barrel of Loi's rifle beside my grave. I still knew virtually nothing about communism, and this man painted it as an evangelical religion more severe and dangerous to nonbelievers than the Crusades or the Inquisition. And I already knew too much about Christian crusaders!

One of the cooks who had legal trouble in America said, "Forget about the Vietnamese: they're nothing compared to the feds. The U.S. government has been fighting Communists for years. They especially hate the Vietnamese Communists for winning the war. If they don't yank your citizenship and deport you, they'll make your life here miserable. The FBI will think you're a spy and the CIA will try to get you to spy for them the next time you go abroad. If you don't cooperate, they'll call all your friends and customers and employers and spread lies about you until you do. Believe me, I know how they operate!"

One waitress, a young woman, had other fears. "Even if the Communists let you go and the U.S. lets you back in, you'll have hell to pay with Little Saigon. I've heard of people getting their houses bombed and shops set on fire just for *talking* about going to Vietnam. If you actually do it, people will assume you're Viet Cong. They'll never leave you alone. You'll be fighting the war all over again. Is that what you really want?"

The war all over again! That's exactly what was happening to me with my own people—the paranoia, the endless second-guessing and gut-twisting fear that no matter what you did, it would be a fatal mistake to somebody. And my friends were caught up in it as well, becoming *chup mu*—suspicious busybodies. Fear was making them belligerent or fatalistic, worried that a friendly smile or handshake would be misconstrued as complicity with "the enemy," whoever that might be. If I learned nothing else from my first twenty years on earth, it was that wars weren't waged just with guns, tanks, and bombs, but with the human heart.

Finally, I turned to my monk for guidance. After laying out all the warnings I had received, I put the question to him, "What do you think? Should I go or should I stay?"

He smiled and said, "I will answer your question with a question. If your house were on fire, and you could only save one person, who would it be: your child, your husband, or your mother?"

"That's easy," I said quickly, "my child."

"Ah. That is the mother's choice. Do you think Buddha would have done the same?"

"What do you mean?"

"I mean, you are thinking like a Westerner, not a child of the cosmic god, the god of our motherland. Remember, our highest duty is *nang tinh*—loyalty to our ancestors. You can marry another husband and conceive a new child, but it is impossible to replace your maker. To choose a descendant is to play at being god yourself. To choose the one who made you is to honor god, the maker, above all else—including husband and children. The world can be painful, but pain is cruel only if it is unjust. How can anyone accuse you of cruelty or injustice if you act in accordance with our highest natural law?"

"So you advise me to do my duty to my mother? To go to Vietnam even if it puts me and my son and my other family at risk?"

"I advise you only to look into your heart and do what you know is right. *Trong cay nhan, hoi qua tat*—A good seed bears only good fruit."

To my surprise, I left the temple with a sense of calm and resolution. Although my father's spirit had been unusually quiet since my séance with Paul, I believed I heard his voice in the words of the monk.

I went directly to my travel agent and made reservations for a flight to Bangkok departing one month hence.

The UCSD writers' conference came and went. I don't think I was a very good student. I met lots of people, including editors, agents, and writers, and received suggestions on my manuscript. But I could not apply any of it—at least not right away. I was caught between heaven and earth, between my spiritual and human responsibilities. Yet I had chosen a path. Sometime between now and the middle of April I would either sink into the mud—*troi trong*—like a sinner swallowed by the earth never to be seen again, or enter the rarefied heights of "Paul's mountain."

I consulted my lawyer, Milton Low, now a family friend, and he advised me to get my affairs in order. This meant writing a will and leaving last-minute instructions for the disposition of my property, debts, and children. I also had to contact the State Department in Washington, D.C., for last-minute advice and information. The first was easy; the latter, harder than it looked.

The man on the phone in the State Department was courteous but discouraging.

"As you probably know," he said, "we have no formal diplomatic relations with Vietnam. We have no embassy in their country and they have none in ours. American citizens are forbidden to travel directly into Vietnam from U.S. territory or possessions, and American companies cannot trade with or do business with the Communist government. If anything should happen to you, there's little or nothing we can do to help. The best we could do is file a protest through the United Nations, but they have no formal power to intervene in such matters. For your information, two U.S. citizens are currently being detained by the Vietnamese government. We've been trying for several months to get them released—or at least to have a third party, like the Red Cross, admitted to assess their condition, but so far with no luck. I can only give you the same advice we gave them: be very careful about what you do, whom you associate with, and what you say."

I mulled over his advice and began to pack. The first decision I made was to realize that the trip was not an all-or-nothing proposition. I could and should approach it in phases, like a mountain climber assaulting a high and dangerous peak. Between each step, I would give full ear to my rational and intuitive powers. I would have several days in Bangkok, for example, to check things out at the Vietnamese Embassy while having my visa stamped. The idea of assertively, but not recklessly, pursuing my objective gave me new courage and peace of mind that, I'm sure, only bewildered my friends.

"I never knew Ly was so brave!" I imagined them saying; but what they really meant was "How could she be so stupid?"

The UN Mission gave me a list of things I could bring into the country. Most severely proscribed were useful items like bicycles and sewing machines that Vietnam made itself and for which they would brook no foreign competition. My younger girlfriends (many of whom were too young to remember the war) thought I should bring in luxury goods—knickknacks and fancy electronic appliances—which were simply unobtainable in the primitive Vietnamese economy. I thanked them for their suggestions, but stuck to practical things like medicines, tea, children's garments, black fabric for home-made work clothes, and even some sweets—things that would make my relatives' hard life a little more bearable. Most of these things I bought in Orange County's Little Saigon, partly to help the local immigrant merchants, but also to indulge my sense of symmetry: American goods going from Vietnamese hands in America to Vietnamese hands in the motherland. The more I shopped and packed and planned the happier and more confident I became.

When everything was just about ready, I thought I'd have one last psychic reading—to check on my family, primarily, but also to see if anything had changed within me. I treated myself to the services of Mr. Vu Tai Loc, the seer everyone in Little Saigon said was the best in the business. I remembered his name, too, from "Big" Saigon, where his startling visions and the accuracy of his predictions were legendary.

He lived in a nice, middle-class neighborhood and greeted me at his door smiling and bowing like a monk, although he was dressed in a sports shirt, slacks, and sandals. His gray head had seen fifty-five years of this incarnation, but he looked infinitely older and wiser—mostly because of the long hair growing from a mole on his chin. Westerners always marvel at this venerable Oriental custom—leaving a mole whisker untrimmed—but it is a tradition that goes back millennia and is worn as a badge of wisdom, like the lotus growing from the Buddha's navel, a symbol of universal knowledge gained over many karmic cycles. He stroked the hair serenely as we talked at his dining table. His house was dark-shaded and smelled of incense and ginger.

"Pull back your hair, child, so I can see all of your face" was the first thing he said after we sat down. He studied me carefully, the way a gem-cutter appraises a stone, and started right off—no preliminary meditation or incantations. "You are going *di xa*—far away— that much is certain."

"Yes." I was amazed. "I'm going to Vietnam to see my mother. How did you know?"

Mr. Loc smiled and stroked his whisker. "You would be disappointed if I did not know, isn't that true?" His face darkened. "Anyway, I advise you against it. The time is not yet right."

I could have fallen through my chair. This was not the news I came to hear. "But I already have my ticket. I've got my visa and bought presents and made arrangements for my children and everything. How long would I have to wait before the time was right?"

Mr. Loc closed his eyes. "I see the number *forty-two*."

"Yes?" I asked hopefully. "Does that mean forty-two hours or forty-two days?"

The seer shrugged. "Perhaps it means forty-two months, or until your age is forty-two."

"I don't think my mother can wait five years until I am forty-two!"

"Your mother will be there for you, don't worry. Your psychic fount flows with energy for your journey. Its bright colors hide the darker shadows. Where you see only the joy of a reunion and the clear air of understanding, I see a ruined temple."

"What kind of temple?" I was shocked by the image.

"I see a ruined temple," he repeated. "The image is very clear. Make of it what you will. In America, some people think of their wealth as a temple; others think of their bodies. Some people worship at temples completely unknown to them until the day they die."

Perhaps his vision spoke of my big Escondido house and the "temple of consumption" it had become in my quest to make it a perfect American home. Did a home really need fine furniture and expensive carpets and elegant drapes? Wasn't my father's poor house in Ky La, with its cement walls and thatch roof and dirt floor the finest home I had ever known?

"Could it represent my business? I own a restaurant, you know, and two rental houses." Maybe he meant the federal mint—the temple of money shown on dollar bills and stock certificates. "How about my investments?"

"The ruined temple used to be quite grand, yes. You must not neglect your business if you expect to retain it. Do you have partners?"

"Yes, two of them."

He leaned closer and took my face in his hands. He brushed away some hair and studied me deeply, then said, "This is not good. You must be first among equals. You are *cao so*—highly destined—and cannot be burdened with the interests of a lower plane. That may sound cruel, but it is true. It applies to husbands as well as business partners. You must be the leader; always on top. For you, compromise is capitulation and since you carry the fate of others in your hands, your victories are shared by many. You are *nguoi gieo nhan*—a seed spreader. Your job is to scatter and plant the seeds. It is the duty of others to tend and harvest them. If you leave now, the seeds you have recently planted will die, no question about it. I say again, you should postpone your trip. Tend to business, which means buy out your partners or sell your interest to them, and wait for forty-two."

I mulled over the seer's advice on the long drive back to Escondido. Mr. Loc's reputation was unimpeachable. Everyone who consulted him and followed his advice had prospered. Everyone who ignored it was soon sorry. But now, my trip had assumed a life of its own—the energy of a boulder rolling downhill. It could be stopped, but only with great force; and then, what would I gain? According to Mr. Loc, nothing more than I already have. I had to ask myself: Was my duty to my mother, as the monk described it, worth the hardship a loss of wealth would bring my sons? Universal law and my own feelings said yes. Without my mother, I would not exist and neither would that wealth. If my temple had to burn, I should at least save from its ashes the one who made me. During the war, I had abandoned my village when my father needed me most, and he died while I was gone. If Mr. Loc was wrong in at least one detail, and my mother died before I was forty-two or forty-two months rolled by or whatever, I would never forgive myself. I might save my treasure but I would lose my soul. I decided that I would not commit the same sin twice.

A few days before I was to leave, I assembled my three boys, Anh's children (Chanh and Tran), my sister Lan, and Milton, my attorney. I told them that I had finally and irrevocably decided to go and that raised the very real possibility that I might not come back. I told them I was not careless of my life or my duty to my sons, but that I had a higher duty to my mother. If they could not understand that now, I promised they would in time.

I also told them that I did not want to overvalue my own life. I admitted that I had contributed to the death of my two husbands. If those poor men hadn't married me, they might still be alive. Their estates—social security and insurance and real estate—became the foundation of the wealth we now enjoyed. I had done so many things wrong in my life that sacrificing what was not really mine to begin with was a small price to pay for doing something right. Nonetheless, I gave Milton the power of attorney over my assets, to be administered to the benefit of my sons until Jimmy was old enough to manage the money himself.

"If I am not back on April fifteenth," I told Milton, "you are to sell my interest in the restaurant and put the money into safe investments.

Lan is my first choice to take the boys as guardian, but if she cannot or will not do it, you should help the authorities find them a good foster home."

Lan said she would be happy to take the boys, but I had learned from experience in this quarter not to take any chances.

"That's fine," I acknowledged, but added firmly, "Lan will care for the boys, but Milton will mind the money."

"What about Tran and Chanh?" Jimmy said. "They're of legal age. Why can't they be our guardians?"

Anh's sons were hard-working, level-headed young men and, although I loved my sister and wanted my sons to grow up with their natural family, I couldn't help but think that, with all the history between me and Lan, they might be better off with Jimmy's half brother.

"What do you say, Milton?" I asked the lawyer. "Would the court have problems with that?"

"Not if you state in writing that that is your preference, and the boys agree, and Chanh and Tran are willing to accept the responsibility."

Lan looked disappointed, but I felt relieved and so did the boys. Milton and I spent the rest of the evening going over my assets and liabilities.

The next day, I phoned the *San Diego Tribune* in a last attempt to get current information about conditions in Vietnam. I had met a *Tribune* columnist at the writers' conference and knew they had an editor who stayed on top of the latest developments in Southeast Asia.

It turned out he had very little information but wanted a lot from me.

"To tell you the truth," the editor said, "I don't know anyone who's been there recently. If you're willing, I'd like to interview you before you go and after you return. I know our readers would be interested in your impressions."

Despite my misgivings about the previous newspaper article and the tempest it created, I felt a little better knowing a big newspaper was keeping its eye on me—would be watching for my return—so I said yes.

The reporter they sent was a young man about thirty—far too young to remember much about the war. I served him tea and we talked all afternoon about my experiences growing up, the things that happened to me during the war, why I was going back to Vietnam now, and what I expected to find. I told him there was a chance, however slight, that I might not be coming back, and he praised my courage, misunderstanding completely that such a "sacrifice" was to me no sacrifice at all, but the duty of a daughter who had been for too long lost and lonely in a foreign land. When the interview was over, I promised to keep a journal—pencil notes and tapes—of the trip for use in a second interview when, and if, I got back. He thanked me for the tea, promised the article would be published soon, and, just before getting into his car, suggested I cancel the trip.

I spent the next few days with last-minute packing and saying goodbye to friends. I had two big boxes of gifts and a small suitcase for myself even though I couldn't imagine bringing back my clothes when they would be like gold to my female relatives. My girlfriends cried and I cried too, although I knew a few of them called me *noi doc*—clever liar—behind my back. People still couldn't believe that anyone who had safely escaped Vietnam's hell on earth would ever want to go back. Perhaps they thought I was going to spend two weeks in Bangkok and would return with tall tales and a nice tan.

The day before I was scheduled to leave, the *Tribune* published the story. It was a fair article, which, unlike the earlier piece, did not emphasize the sensationalism of my adventures over my recollections of peace and family life and my quest for love and forgiveness. However, from midmorning through the rest of the day, the phone did not stop ringing. At that time, I was listed in the directory and everyone with an opinion about my life, good or bad, wanted to tell me about it personally. Consequently, I answered only the first few calls and by evening unplugged the phone just to have some rest. I didn't need any last-minute doubts or recriminations. I was satisfied with my decision and was ready to move on.

Jimmy, Tommy, Alan, and I had a quiet dinner that evening. We were all aware that this might be our last meal together, so we all took our time and just enjoyed being together. Jimmy had decided to cut classes and drive me to the airport. Alan wanted to see me off, too, so I gave him a note for school. Tommy was red-eyed all evening, but refused to cry. He went to his room early "to study," then went to sleep. He said he could not afford to miss school and would not go to the airport. I think he was having trouble accepting my decision. He had seen too much sadness in his short life—losing his own father and then his stepfather—and was in no mood to see his mother follow in those footsteps. He preferred anger to unbearable sorrow and the rest of us understood.

That night, I stumbled through foggy dreams until I came to the front door of our old house in Ky La. My father was sitting on his haunches, finishing a smoke. For some reason, I couldn't approach him closely; something held me back. But I could hear him and feel his presence.

"You're doing the right thing, little peach blossom," he said, exhaling smoke and mist. "You've done well for yourself and your children. Now it's time to do something more."

PART THREE

Taking the Long Road Back
(1987–92)

EIGHT

Journey of a Thousand Leagues

THE JET that took me across the Pacific to Vietnam did more than change days at the International Date Line. It plunged me into another age when my homeland and soul were younger. After rediscovering my past by encountering my country's present *troi dat doi thay*—after heaven and earth *had* changed places—I was on my way back to the future.

I had no idea what that future contained. I only knew that it would be nothing like my previous years in Vietnam or America.

First and foremost, my duty to my mother had been fulfilled, but not without surprises. Communist Vietnam was not at all as its supporters or critics described it. I expected to find a country reined in by jackbooted police and tanks on every corner. I did not expect to find, as my frail but steadfast mother and aging sister Hai had told me, "the war still going on" in the hearts and minds of everyone there, with the issue still in doubt. Crushing paranoia infected every person, including every member of my family—and eventually myself. I expected to find a very poor country, like Mexico. I did not expect to see people still begging and starving in the street; old and young deformed by explosives and chemicals; Amerasian kids (some now young adults) wandering like lepers in a land that hated them solely because of their parents; and hard-working people of moral strength and talent—like Jimmy's father, Anh, and my own brother, Bon Nghe—reduced to poverty, their skills misapplied by a bumbling central government.

On the other hand, I did not expect to hear officials in that government candidly admit their problems, as they did at a supper Anh had arranged for our mutual enlightenment. Having gotten so used to saying no after forty years of sacrifice, the Northern regime had forgotten how to say yes to new ideas—to clear-eyed, if risky, proposals to make life better for the common people. Now, they acknowledged that Vietnam could not survive as a "pariah" nation. To feed its people, to heal them and to make the land itself whole again, it would have to extend its hand in friendship to its once hated adversary, the West—the United States in particular. Having outlasted a faltering America in an ungodly war of attrition, the Hanoi government found itself no match for America at peace.

So where did that leave me, Phung Thi Le Ly Munro-Hayslip— whoever she was and whatever she was supposed to be?

When I arrived in Vietnam I had a strong sense that I needed to return to my "mother of the breast" and the motherland that bore me in order to start my life again—to go "from low tide to high tide" as my mother once said. Surprisingly, the one who put me on a new course for the next cycle of my life—the one in which I would "climb mountains and turn stones into flowers" and "teach what I had learned"—was Anh, Jimmy's father. He became like a spirit guide from my old life to my new one. We spoke very earnestly and for long hours at his sister's house in Saigon. His mandate was simple:

"Em Ly, you must help people overcome the pain of the war—to learn trust where they feel suspicion; to honor the past while letting go of it; to learn all these things so that they, in turn, may teach. Only this way can the circle of vengeance strangling us be changed into an ever expanding sphere of enlightenment."

I told Anh that although I may have come from a luxurious "castle" in the West, like the legendary Siddhartha Gautama, to have my eyes opened by the harshness of life in postwar Vietnam, I was no "Buddha" such as he became. I was, at most, a simple farm girl who felt uneasy around politicians and businessmen and their big plans and bigger ambitions. How could I cure Vietnam's ills when I had so much trouble preserving my own little family?

Anh then asked a startling question. "Even if you've had nothing but trouble with love, has that ever stopped you from loving?"

I could only answer, "No."

"Well then," he smiled. "Don't let the shortness of your arm keep you from reaching out. As I heard you tell your brother, Bon, 'Nothing happens that is not imagined first.' If you want to help our people, start with their hearts and minds, then healthy souls and bodies are sure to follow."

I mulled over Anh's advice on the flight back to Los Angeles, where I was greeted by all three of my relieved and smiling sons. After a little homecoming talk, during which I relayed my disappointment at not being allowed to return to my village (I met with my family in Danang), I tried out some ideas on my boys on the long drive back to Escondido. "Jimmy, your father wants to help Uncle Bon and me build a clinic for my old village, isn't that something? Maybe someday you can go back and meet him; maybe help them get Vietnam back on its feet. The land is so beautiful but the people are so poor. Maybe you'll build lots of clinics and . . ."

I chattered like a monkey, but the boys seemed happy just to hear my voice. When they had been quiet too long, though, I asked, "So, what's been happening while I was gone?"

They looked uncomfortably at each other and Jimmy, who was driving, finally said, "You got a call from the FBI. They want to talk to you when you get back."

"The FBI? My goodness—what about?"

"They wouldn't say. They just wanted to know when you'd be back." Jimmy gave me an impish smile. "Looks like you're in trouble again!"

We laughed but I could feel my jet-lagged heart sink. After doing absolutely nothing to help me visit my family, the government now had some great interest in where I had been and what I had been doing. It was just like Vietnam again, only worse, because I didn't expect this in America! Then again, perhaps I was letting my paranoia take control of me once more—an easy reflex after even a few days in the "people's paradise." I decided to let my higher consciousness take charge and not cross any bridges before I came to them, even ones guarded by the FBI.

The house was as big and beautiful as I left it—the litter of three young men paled after the squalor of even the best houses in Danang. I felt happy and lucky and guilty all at once—what a difference an ocean makes!

Within an hour of my return the living room began to fill with curious neighbors and well-wishers including my lawyer, Milton, who was relieved to know he did not have to execute my emergency plan, and Lan, who had trouble believing I hadn't just gone to Thailand for a vacation. By the time I had told the story of my trip a dozen times, important things began to stick in my mind: the epidemic of paranoia infecting the people is unimaginable; the crushing war-and-soul debt the Vietnamese pay every day is beyond belief, or even cosmic justice. I did not try to convince my American friends about how lucky we were because even I wouldn't have believed it myself until I had returned to see modern Vietnam.

The next day, Agent James Treacy called from the FBI to make an appointment.

He was tall, with hair as dark as his somber suit. He was very polite and introduced every question with a friendly comment, like a banker getting ready to turn down a loan application. His calling card said FEDERAL BUREAU OF INVESTIGATION in big, bold letters, like the credits to a TV crime show starring JAMES H. TREACY, SPECIAL AGENT. I knew very little about the FBI—only what I saw on television and from the forms Dennis had to fill out for his job with the Customs Department. On the other hand, I knew a lot about the *Cong An Chim,* the South Vietnamese secret police. During the war, if Cong An knocked on the door, you were wise to climb out the window.

"Please come in and have a seat," I said, showing him to the living room and offering him green tea. "This is the first time I've talked to the FBI. Please excuse me if I'm a little nervous."

"Don't be," he smiled pleasantly. "How was your visit to Vietnam?"

"Wonderful! Of course, the country is so poor—you wouldn't believe it! Have you been to Tijuana? It's worse than that. By the way, how did you know I went to Vietnam?"

He smiled. "We read about it in the *Tribune.* We get lots of information from the newspapers, just like everyone else. I wouldn't be bothering you now except it's our policy to interview anyone who returns from a Communist country." He pulled out a notebook and pencil just like a reporter. "Now, could you tell me how long you were there?"

"About two weeks. I stayed in Bangkok a few days both coming and going."

"I see. Did you visit your relatives?"

"Oh yes. I saw my mother, my brother, my two older sisters, and my niece."

"They're all okay?" He sounded like he was genuinely concerned. Maybe he had brothers and sisters in some faraway place.

"Yes, they're fine, thank you."

He made a little note. "Vietnam's a long way away. As you know, the State Department prohibits direct travel there. Who helped you get into the country?"

"Nobody in particular." I showed him copies of the letters I sent to U.S. government officials, including his boss, President Reagan. "As you can see, I wrote to just about everyone, but people either didn't answer or they tried to discourage me from going. Finally, I met a gentleman by accident at a bar and he gave me a name to call at the United Nations—the Vietnamese Mission—and they obtained my visa."

"Do you remember the man's name?"

"Oh no. Like I say, we met very casually, by accident."

"Would you recognize him if you saw him again?"

I sighed and stared at the ceiling. "Well, he was tall and distinguished looking, I remember that. He had gray hair and wore a dark suit—like yours—but three-piece, like a businessman's. He was very soft-spoken and said he came from New York. That's about all I remember."

Agent Treacy wrote furiously, then asked, "Did he say what he did in New York? Why was he in San Diego?"

"He told me all that, but I forgot. Sorry."

"Was he alone or did he have companions?"

"I think a couple of people were at his table, but we weren't introduced and I didn't talk to them. Kathy and I were busy—"

"Kathy?" Agent Treacy brightened. "Who's Kathy?"

"Kathy Greenwood. She's my old boss and a good friend."

"I see. Could I have her address and phone number?"

I was now getting very uncomfortable with this whole thing. Agent Treacy was too much like the local cadremen and village "watchers" who used to control our behavior with sly questions and innuendos. Their specialty was asking the same thing over and over again to different people until inconsistencies began to surface.

"Mr. Treacy—"

"James," he said smiling. "You can call me James."

"James—I don't mind you coming into my house to talk about my visit. I know you are concerned about terrorists and spies and drug smugglers and I'm happy to do my part. I just don't like giving you all this information about people who have nothing to do with my trip. They are just friends and acquaintances. I don't think it's right for me to get them involved in all this."

"Involved in all what, Mrs. Hayslip?"

I took a long breath. *It was starting again!* I clammed up.

James put down his pad and pencil. "Look, Mrs. Hayslip—Le Ly —I believe we need to find out more about this man who helped you. He might be just a friendly citizen, as you suggest, but he might also be a Communist spy. I mean, don't you think it's funny that a man who *just happened* to have the information you needed *just happened* to be at the bar that night? Believe me, this is exactly how those people work."

"Okay, all right," I said. I gave him Kathy's home phone number but wouldn't tell him where she worked or any more details about anything. "You'll have to ask those people directly for the information you want." My tone wasn't very friendly.

Agent Treacy put away his pad. "Okay. I think I have enough to work with." He got up and I escorted him to the door. "May I call you again if I need more information?"

"Of course," I said halfheartedly, "but I don't really have much more to say. You seem like a nice young man. I believe you are sincere about what you believe and how you do your job. I just want you to know that I will not spy for anybody, okay? Not for the Vietnamese, not for the American government, not for anybody. You see, I'm thinking about doing humanitarian work for my people— not for the Communist government, but for the people, like the Red Cross. That means I must return to the country some day. I do not want either side to mistrust me. I must work hard to remain impartial."

"That's a fine idea, Mrs. Hayslip," Agent Treacy said. "But you must also realize that lots of other people don't feel that way. My job is to see that our country isn't harmed, even inadvertently."

After he was gone, my paranoia kicked into high gear. I thought about the forms I'd filled out in Vietnam before and after I married Ed—information attesting to my background and character to get into the United States. Checking one story against another was an old police technique for ferreting out people who had something to hide.

I was particularly concerned about my brother, Bon Nghe. I was sure I had identified him on those old forms as KIA or MIA (which he may well have been—nobody had seen him since 1954!), implying, but not really saying, that he was a Southern soldier. I didn't volunteer to Agent Treacy that Bon had an estimable war record with the North, and was now a responsible Communist official in Danang. No doubt Agent Treacy would begin a tedious cross-check of my answers with my State Department and Immigration files. Perhaps he would even "shadow" me as I drove around town—to see if I had any illicit rendezvous with the mysterious man from New York. He might even tap my phone. In wartime Vietnam the government used to read and censor mail, so even my personal correspondence might make a quick detour to the Federal Building downtown before it finally arrived in my mailbox. And, of course, my manuscript lay scattered around the house in easy view of anyone—from FBI agents disguised as utility repairmen "looking for gas leaks" to burglars creeping around in the night. What would a surreptitious reader think about my tales as a teenage Viet Cong conscript? For that matter, how could I be sure that anybody I might meet in the future wasn't an FBI agent or someone on their "enemies" list? It was incredible! For the last two weeks in Vietnam, I knew I had been "supervised"—sometimes from the next seat in a car or a bus or at a restaurant table; sometimes from a distance by a hazy figure with binoculars—and it didn't bother me at all. I expected nothing less from a war-worn, paranoid, totalitarian government. Now, back in the "land of liberty," I was somehow presumed guilty of something I did not do and hadn't even been charged with!

After a day or two, I returned to work at the Hollylinh. The staff and partners and most of my regular customers greeted me like a returning astronaut—with teary kisses, hugs, even flowers. I was moved not only by their affection but their obvious acceptance and understanding of what my trip really meant: that the door kept closed so long between Americans and Vietnamese was now opened at least a crack. The example of my one small step back onto my native soil could be seen as a giant leap for so many souls in pain. I spoke—perhaps too freely, since I didn't really have a plan—about trying to raise money for a clinic in Quang Nam, hopefully near Ky La, to help peasants harmed by the war.

Not everyone agreed.

"You've got to be careful, Ly," one waitress said while we were relaxing after my shift. "Everybody's smiling and laughing now, but some of the staff are convinced you must be a Communist. After all, why would the Vietnamese government let you out?"

"That's silly," I said, being silly myself to think that simply because I was fortified with the truth everyone else would see it, too. "They let me out because they have no reason to keep me and every reason to want me to come back. They want all Viet Kieu to come home and help develop the country."

Kenneth was also disturbed, but for different reasons. He showed me the ledgers from the last few weeks.

"Look at this, Ly," he said dourly. "The restaurant lost three thousand dollars while you were gone. People came in and asked for Ly, and when we told them you were gone, they turned around and left. You've got to forget all this crazy talk about building clinics, at least for a while. You've got to think about the business."

The problem was, for the first time ever, I *was* truly thinking about business—my *father's* business—my life's work, in fact. I told the waitress to tell the skeptics not to worry, that I was the same Ly they had always known. I told Kenneth that I would try to spend more time at the restaurant, particularly during rush hours, but I couldn't promise anyone that my first trip to postwar Vietnam would be my last.

Under these conditions, daily life just dragged. My increasing dissatisfaction with things showed on my face and in my words. My dreams, like the window of my Vietnamese touring car, were filled with gaunt-eyed Amerasian kids, crippled beggars, and starving farmers. The bills that had stacked up during my absence now multiplied like rabbits. Tenants in my San Diego rental moved out and I had to replace them fast to keep up with my insatiable mortgage and insurance payments. My portfolio of other investments demanded more of my time. Kenneth now "rode my bumper" to make up for losses caused by my absence, and the nice, wealthy retirees I used to entertain with songs and fortunetelling now seemed grotesque— overfed and overprivileged parasites hoarding and wasting food and medicine and shelter that could have kept thousands going for months in Vietnam. I was losing my perspective—and my ability to smile.

Even worse, my own household was beginning to show the strain of keeping up with our rich, materialistic lifestyle. On my trip, I envied my niece, Tinh, whose children would help each other get ready for school and eat all their meals—sometimes only a bowl of rice—together. They would come home in the afternoon, bow to their parents (Bien was a barber who had a shop in the front of their house), and say, *Thua ba ma con di hoc moi ve*—"Greetings, mother and father, we're home from school!"

Now, back in the United States, my own son Jimmy—conscientious, independent, and hard-working, like "Grandpa Phung"—was taking his toughest courses in computer science and working part-time; he seldom called home, even for money. Tommy's high school counselors called plenty, though, to complain that he was still tardy or cut too many classes. Even little Alan, who had only recently come to terms with his tragedy, started doing poorly again—withdrawing into himself, ignoring his friends, showing little interest in academics or the big wide world around him. This was not good for a growing, thriving young spirit. On the contrary, it was all too typical of graying, dying souls. Not only had I become a harried "capitalist," I had lost my touch as a mother.

As the demands of the material world increased, my will to keep up with them diminished. I would come home from the restaurant and sit at my desk trying to sort through the mountain of bills and paperwork. Tasks that before my trip took ten minutes now took an hour. Sometimes I would fall asleep at the desk and wake up with a terrible headache or backache. Other times, I would stretch out on the couch and not attempt the long climb up the stairs to my bed.

Like it or not, I had become *danh loi,* a slave to my wealth. I had reached the oasis of glittering treasure for which every poor peasant yearns. But I found that after tasting security and comfort and excess luxuries of every kind, their sweet syrup was as dust in my mouth.

And now Agent Treacy was on the phone again, asking for another interview.

On the day of our appointment, I took the morning off and caught up on my reading in spiritualism and philosophy. I listened to new-age music to calm down and prepare for whatever would come. Agent Treacy wouldn't say what this second interview was for, so I could only assume he had checked my background and run into discrepancies. If the holes in my story were big enough, I might not even be home to make dinner for Tommy and Alan. Even in America, it seemed, you could be asked to *come to a meeting*.

James was polite as always as I poured him some tea. This time, he came armed with a thick manila folder, which he carefully laid on my coffee table like a loaded gun.

"I looked through your visa and marriage application from 1969," he said. "I couldn't read most of it, so I'll have to ask you to help me out."

He produced his trusty pad and pencil and I knew I was in for a grilling. Even if most of my file was in Vietnamese, the FBI could undoubtedly have had it translated. It was clear that he intended to trap me with my own story: to see how well a comfortable, naturalized citizen's recollections matched the statements of a terrified teenage mother sixteen years before.

"First of all, how many brothers and sisters do you have? I'm afraid the record isn't very clear on this."

I gave him the capsule history of my family, including my wayward "Hanoi brother," Bon Nghe. He wrote furiously in his book. One's first instinct in a war zone is to try anything that works, but I resisted the urge to make up stories I thought he wanted to hear. I recalled what I had heard before I left about the officials in Communist re-education camps forcing you to write and rewrite the story of your life—your "political errors"—until failures of memory and contrary opinions looked like criminal guilt. I stopped worrying about what I said sixteen years ago and said only what I knew was true today. Oddly enough, the simple truth worked just fine.

When he was satisfied with my past, Agent Treacy inquired about my future.

"Have you contacted the Vietnamese Mission since you've been back?"

"Yes, a couple of times," I replied, surprised he didn't just listen to his tapes of my telephone conversations—unless, of course, the line wasn't tapped. "The first call was to thank them for helping me see my mother. The second was to ask for information about what I could do to help Vietnam recover from the war."

"And what did they tell you?"

"They said that because the U.S. does not officially recognize the government of Vietnam, I would have to make my contributions through private channels. They sent me a list of charitable organizations currently operating relief programs in Vietnam, and lists of medical and educational and industrial supplies they need most. They said that if I decided to do anything on my own—we had talked about building a small health clinic in my home village—I would have to have the proposal cleared by the government. I told them I wanted to meet some of the UN staff, just so I would know who I was dealing with before I got other Americans involved." I gestured around the living room. "I live in a nice house, but I'm far from wealthy. I will have to depend on outside donations to get the job done. And there is still a lot of corruption in Vietnam. I would feel personally responsible to see that the money wasn't wasted, or went to the wrong people or was spent for other purposes."

"When will you meet with the UN representatives?"

"Not too soon. I've got a lot of problems to clear up first—with my business and my kids."

"Did the people at the UN Mission ask you to do anything for them—any favors—even innocent things, like carrying papers back and forth?"

"No, they did not ask me to be a courier or spy or anything like that. They did ask for one thing, though—" I covered my mouth with a hand to squelch a giggle.

"What was that?"

"They wanted me to sing some songs to them over the phone. I told them my father had taught us lots of humorous songs about the Viet Minh and Viet Cong and Republicans and Americans during the war. I think the men in New York were a little homesick. I heard them laugh and shout around the office for the other employees to pick up the extensions. I felt like Bob Hope entertaining the troops." I laughed out loud. Agent Treacy managed a sick smile.

"So, have you decided to go ahead with your clinic?"

"I've decided to look into it. I already know that I need permission from our government to build anything over there. The State Department must grant me a license and exemption from the law that prohibits 'trading with the enemy,' although you would think that they, of all people, would know the war was over."

"Well, be very careful when you deal with these people, Ly," James said as he closed his notebook. "Communists are very tricky people. They'll make believe they're your friends, then suddenly, pow—you're in way over your head. And once they've got enough evidence to incriminate you, you belong to them. I know. I've seen it happen before—to servicemen, businessmen, even housewives."

He picked up his big folder and I escorted him to the door.

"Well, you don't have to worry about me," I said, a little irritated at having to say it. "I'm an American citizen now and that means a lot to me. America has been very good to me and I'm not about to betray her. But I am also a daughter of Vietnam and its people are my brothers and sisters. They need my help and I really don't think either government should stand in the way of my giving it to them. You know, we have a saying: *An trai nho ke trong cay*—When you pick fruit from a tree, remember who planted it. I owe my life to both countries. I want each to be better places—to get over the war and get on with life."

"That's a lovely thought." James smiled and shook my hand. "We'll talk again."

I knew he was right on both counts.

As soon as he left, I picked up the phone and called the Vietnamese UN Mission. By now, it was late in the day in New York, but Mr. Tan, to whom I had spoken on my last call, was still in the office.

"*Chao anh Tan,*" I said, trying to sound cheerful. "Hello Brother Tan. This is Sister Ly in California."

"Oh, Chi Ly. How are you?"

"Just fine. I'm calling to let you know that I had another meeting with the American FBI. They are very interested in the Vietnamese I talk to in the United States. I think they're afraid you want me to spy for you or something. I just want you to know that the purpose of their visits have been to question me. So far they have not asked me to spy for them and if they do, I will say no—the same as I would say to you. For me the war is over."

Mr. Tan laughed. "It's over for us, too, Chi Ly. Feel free to tell them anything you want—about us, about what you saw in Vietnam —everything. We are trying very hard to establish good relations with the U.S. government. We understand their concerns and know they have a right to inquire into these matters. We only hope they do not cause you and others to lose your will to return to Vietnam and help us out. So tell them the truth and tell them everything. When they see they have nothing to worry about, they'll leave you alone, I'm sure of it."

Mr. Tan's words encouraged me and I said, "I'm very glad you feel that way because I would like to schedule a meeting for us to talk in

New York. I want to tell you about the plans I have in mind to help the people of my village. Could we meet sometime in the next few weeks?"

"Of course." It was now Mr. Tan's turn to sound pleased. "Just let us know when you'll be in town and I'll make some time to see you."

To thank the guardian spirits—the *am binh,* or "death soldiers"— who had escorted me on my journey, I decided to sacrifice a whole roast pig (a very pious and generous offering among villagers) on my family shrine. It was only the second time in my life that I had made such a gesture. The first time was as a teenager in Danang, when my chances for leaving the country looked bleak. The spirits looked kindly on my offer and a week later, I met Ed and the cosmic machinery was set in motion that eventually took me to America. Now, I would make another grand sacrifice, this time with the idea of getting my charitable work off the ground.

I couldn't get a whole pig at Safeway, so I asked my girlfriend Hong to pick one up at a Vietnamese grocer's on her way to join us for Vietnamese Thanksgiving. While I waited, I decorated my altar with flowers and fruit and burned incense and ceremonial money and spirit clothing.

But the appointed time came and went, and Hong was nowhere to be seen. After two hours I called her house and was told she had left with time to spare for the forty-five-minute drive.

A couple of hours after that, I was beside myself with worry.

I was about to call the police, fearing an accident or worse— perhaps an ambush by someone in Little Saigon who knew her hostess was a "dirty VC sympathizer"—when the phone rang. It was a woman who had stopped to aid Hong when her car broke down on the freeway. She just wanted me to know that my friend was all right and would be a little late.

Shaking with relief, I went to the altar and asked the spirits to return tomorrow for their "feast." I then went for a walk in the sunset, chastising myself for letting my imagination run wild. The new course I had set would be full of opportunities for wrong think- ing and panic. If I gave in to each of them—or even to more than a few—I would not only fail in my new mission, I would go crazy, and could easily forfeit my life. What I needed most was clarity—of purpose and of vision. I knew that would not come without a price.

Shortly after Hong and I celebrated our belated thanksgiving, I met privately with Kenneth in his office. He was happy that restaurant traffic had increased again. Since we were now making at least enough money to break even, he couldn't understand why I was unhappy.

"I can't work here anymore," I confessed. "I'm always thinking about Vietnam—what I can and should do to help. In Danang and Saigon, outside restaurants like this, cripples and beggars line up for food all day long. The scraps we throw away daily could feed those people for a week. It just isn't right. Before I came home, Anh and I were eating at a small restaurant and I finally told the manager to serve whoever was waiting out back a regular meal and put it on my bill. He gave a dozen people a feast and it only cost me five dollars. *Five dollars!* Here, I work like crazy and all I get for my troubles are more bills and more worries and headaches. Am I really so much better off with two houses instead of one, or three houses instead of two? Where does it all end? When I'm in the hospital? When I'm dead?"

I told him the story my father had told me of the rich farmer who asked to be buried in a hollow log.

"I feel like that rich farmer, Kenneth. It's time to tear down my treasure house and give something back to the people who helped put me on this life's circle."

"Look, Ly"—Kenneth shifted uncomfortably in his chair—"you know I don't really believe in all this spiritual mumbo-jumbo. I mean, it's a nice show for the customers and maybe there's something to it, but I'm a businessman, all right? It's just not where I'm coming from. But I know you mean well. You're my partner and you've helped my family earn money and I respect that. If you don't want to be in the restaurant business anymore, just say so and I'll find an investor to buy you out. To tell you the truth, some of the staff think you've hung around too long as it is. They're afraid that all the publicity surrounding your trip will put us in danger. Here, take a look at this."

Kenneth opened a drawer and withdrew an article from the *Los Angeles Times*. It was about a Vietnamese man in Little Saigon named Tran Khanh Van who was shot and seriously wounded during my trip because he talked openly about helping the people of Vietnam. I didn't read the details—the businessman wanted to supply Vietnamese schools with computers or something like that. I'm sure Kenneth envisioned my name, and maybe his own, in the headline.

"You know who did this, don't you?" he said. "The Chong Cong

—the Vietnamese right-wingers. The Khan Chien and Phuc Quoc organizations actually run around in black pajamas and sandals and practice small-unit tactics at Camp Pendleton—yes, the CIA trains and equips them! They plan to keep the war going on in people's hearts and minds. They want the Communist government to have more, not fewer, problems. They want to lead an insurrection or invasion. If a Vietnamese doesn't support them, they assume he or she is Communist and burn their home or business. Their youngsters form gangs—South against the North, can you believe it? It's *ma cu an hiep ma moi*—old ghosts come back to haunt the new! That's why they stopped this poor fellow, and why they may try to stop you. Nobody likes the way you've been holding hands with the FBI, either. A lot of people came into this country on false papers or with illegal gold and jewelry and they want to stay as far from the police as possible. Like I say, Ly, I think you're a wonderful person and I applaud what you're trying to do, but my restaurants and employees don't need this kind of trouble. We're just trying to get by, eh? And do the best we can."

Get by and do the best we can. How often I heard and thought those very words during my last few years in the war zone. Everybody yearned for peace so much that they came to the United States—often at great risk—and then promptly forgot the reason for their journey. Buddhist temples have sprouted everywhere but we still don't listen to the temple bell. It was as if none of us had left home! Hadn't we learned anything from the war?

"Okay, brother Kenneth." I put my hand supportively on his arm. "We agree. If I learned one thing on my trip, it was that I have no right to endanger the ones I love simply by trying to help them. You have my permission to find a buyer for my part of the business. I'm sure you will set a fair price. I'm going to New York in a couple of weeks to find out if this whole idea of building a clinic is a real possibility or just a daydream. If it looks realistic, I'll want to move very fast."

"Good," Kenneth smiled and winked. "A moving target is hard to hit!"

Just before I left for New York, my old friend Agent Treacy called and asked if I would be willing to chat with his State Department colleague—someone named Christopher Mayhew. Naturally, I said yes, mostly because saying no wouldn't discourage them and would only make them more suspicious. I also realized I would eventually have to do business with the State Department to get waivers for the medical equipment and supplies I hoped to ship to Vietnam.

Agent Treacy's visits were now becoming routine. By the time he rang the doorbell, punctual as always, I had green tea and Chinese cookies waiting by the sofa.

I shook hands with Mr. Mayhew. "I didn't know my family reunion was so important as to bring you all the way from Washington," I said with a smile.

"Any American contact with the Socialist Republic of Vietnam is important, Mrs. Hayslip," he replied pleasantly. "Believe it or not, your government truly does want better relations between the two nations. We depend on people like you—who take the initiative and go ahead of the diplomats—to tell us what to expect, and to let us know how we can help."

"Well, that is a pleasant surprise!" I gave James a kinder look. Perhaps I had been too harsh on the young policeman whose biggest sin, like my brother Bon Nghe's, was being too straight-arrow in his job.

I showed Mr. Mayhew the same trip photos—of my family, crowds of Amerasian kids, shots of various hospitals—that Agent Treacy had seen on his last visit. He riffled through them quickly. His questions, like his examination of the pictures, were cursory. For a man who wanted to help the Vietnamese people, he didn't seem very interested in their problems.

"Tell me, Mrs. Hayslip," Mr. Mayhew said finally, taking off his eyeglasses, "did you see any military installations over there? Any tanks or aircraft—anything like that?"

"No—just the old American planes at Tan Son Nhut."

"How about troops in the streets? Artillery pieces? Jeeps?" They both had their note pads out now.

"No, only street policemen. And maybe a few jeeps."

"Jeeps, you say? Were they Russian or American?"

"Well, I don't really know what a Russian jeep looks like. They looked pretty new, though; not like the old GI jeeps I remembered from the war."

Mr. Mayhew looked up at James. "Could be Soviet." He turned back to me. "How about Russian soldiers? Who was riding in the jeeps—Vietnamese or Europeans?"

"I really didn't notice—"

"When are you going back?"

"Well, I have an appointment next week in New York at the UN Mission. I hope they will tell me how I can return with some relief material for my village—you know, medicine, bandages, maybe an incubator for the little babies—"

"If you decide to go, please give me a call." Mr. Mayhew presented his card. "There are a couple of things I'd like you to do for us—in the interest of better relations, of course."

I stared blankly at his card. Somehow, it was more intimidating than Agent Treacy's. "What sort of things?" I asked.

"Oh, strictly routine—things we ask of every citizen who goes into a country that's closed to us diplomatically. We're primarily concerned about Soviet involvement. Our satellites can tell us a lot, but they're no substitute for a good pair of eyes on the ground. We want to know if you see any Soviet weapons or troops. Any installations for their soldiers or sailors or Russian warplanes at the airports."

For a diplomat, Mr. Mayhew began sounding a lot like a spy. "I'm sorry, but I think you misunderstand me. If I go back, it will be to see my family again and to take whatever supplies I can to help my village. I really won't have time to go looking for that kind of information, and wouldn't want to do it even if it was allowed."

"Of course, I understand." Mr. Mayhew raised his hands. "No problem. Perhaps you can find somebody in Vietnam, then, who'd be willing to do that for us. Perhaps a relative or a friend. Somebody who trusts you. Trust is a hard thing to come by between Vietnamese and Americans, isn't it? I'm sure you know somebody over there who shares our goal of better relations—somebody who would appreciate having a little bit better life."

I couldn't believe what I was hearing! *No way* was I going to get somebody to spy for the State Department or CIA or the army or whoever sent this guy!

"I don't think that would be possible." I stood abruptly, signaling that the meeting was over. "Nobody in my family can read or write. They're just simple peasants."

Reluctantly, my "guests" stood too. James said, "I understand you traveled into the country with a gentleman from Norway, a representative of the UN's technology training mission, is that correct?"

My god, he's talking about Per—the kind European who befriended me in Bangkok when I got cold feet about going into Vietnam. His compassion and quiet strength was the only thing that got me on that airliner and through a foul-up in Vietnamese customs. What could they possibly want with him?

"Yes, I met a UN worker, that's right," I said cautiously. "Why do you ask?"

"No particular reason," Mr. Mayhew said. "Did he offer you any money to work for him?"

That was the strangest question yet! "No, he was just a good friend to me—very kind and compassionate. What on earth is all this about?"

Mr. Mayhew smiled brightly. "Oh nothing. Nothing at all!" At the door, he extended his hand, which I shook tepidly. "Thanks very much for your cooperation, Mrs. Hayslip. I hope we'll be hearing from you as your plans progress. Oh, by the way, I think I know of somebody who would be willing to pay your travel expenses—"

"You mean someone who would donate my airline ticket?"

"Something like that. For that matter, he might even be willing to donate some money toward your medical equipment. That kind of gear is awfully expensive, you know. Of course, you would have to bring back the information we talked about. That's what interests him most."

"That's enough!" I shouted. "Look, I am nobody's spy! I will not spy on Americans and I will not spy on Vietnamese! Who do you think you're talking to? Stuff like that almost got me killed when I was a kid! I'm not going to get involved with it again! To you it's just a big game, but to people like me it can get out of hand and is a matter of life and death. And your coming here like this, over and over, doesn't help at all. When I wanted to go visit my mother, nobody at the government would even talk to me. Now that I plan to go back, you want to pay me to do your dirty work. Well, I won't, do you understand? So please don't ask me again!"

Mr. Mayhew had wilted against the door. Agent Treacy, though, didn't seem surprised.

"I'm sorry, Mrs. Hayslip," Mayhew said. "I didn't mean to upset you. But facts are facts. Vietnam is a Communist country. They may have treated you fairly, but even as we speak they are killing people in Cambodia. They have invited the Russians to come into their country and occupy all the installations Americans built. Our satellites show Russian ballistic missile submarines going into and out of the harbor at Cam Ranh Bay. Now, you may not think that's important, but your government does. Our job is to keep this nation safe, Mrs. Hayslip, to protect even the citizens who don't agree with us."

"Cong san, Tu ban—" I stopped myself, took a breath, and began again in English. "You remind me of my brother Bon Nghe. Always suspicious. Never willing to take a chance and trust the other side. Don't you see? You both say the same thing, just in a different language!"

I did not see Mr. Mayhew again. The more I thought about him and about my brother the more frustrated I became. Why couldn't worldly men like Mayhew see the warmth of the Vietnamese people as well as the cold steel of tanks and missiles? Why couldn't brother Bon admit most Americans were good people just like most Vietnamese—that everybody *wasn't* trying to steal his country?

That night, I chatted with my father in a dream.

"Well, Bay Ly, you've done it again, haven't you?" he said.

I liked these dream encounters because I was always very young again—never older than I was at his death—although I remembered everything that had happened since then, too.

"What do you mean?" I asked.

"Why, you're caught in the middle again, aren't you? The Americans think you work for the Vietnamese and the Vietnamese think you work for the Americans. What are you going to do?"

"They're foolish. All they think about is the war."

"True, but the hungriest child deserves the most food, isn't that right? *Mot mieng khi doi, hon mot goi khi no:* A bowl of rice means more when you're starving than when you're satisfied. You shouldn't turn your back on anyone who's troubled, little peach blossom. Angry hearts are as much in need of healing as the sickest beggar in Danang. The beggar is healed when his belly is full but wounds of the soul take much longer to mend."

"But how can I serve both the needy and the angry? Half want peace and the other half want war!"

"Build a center, Bay Ly—a place where both sides can come together, where the homeless and crippled can come to rebuild their bodies and their lives and the angry can make peace with their souls. Make it a place where *everyone* is welcomed with open arms, even if their wounds are hidden from the eye. Tell me, what would you be willing to pay for such a place?"

"Why, it would be worth everything I have, Father," I cried, "and more!"

"Then you have named the price. I will send two *am binh* to protect you: the one at your left arm, a soldier; the one at your right, a monk. But only your feet can find the right path. Prepare yourself for a long and winding road."

Shortly before my departure for New York, I received two more messages that would change my life.

The first was a letter from Per, the Norwegian technology adviser I had met on my way into Vietnam. He was responding to a letter I had written to his business address, asking for advice about relief work in Vietnam: what supplies were needed most, which officials to deal with and which agencies to avoid. He replied with a list of individuals he trusted and the names of international agencies and associations that could help me develop fund-raising contacts. Best of all, he mentioned he would be in New York—at the United Nations —during the same dates as my trip. I dashed off a letter with my itinerary including times that we could meet. Through Per, I could see a whole new world of humanitarian resources opening up beyond my little circle of friends in San Diego.

I also received a phone call from Dan.

He sounded very old and distant and I felt like asking some personal questions just to make sure the voice belonged to the man I remembered. He also sounded very anxious. He said he was on the mainland for a few weeks—in Washington for a military seminar and was calling between sessions to ask if I would fly East and visit him—to share the few days' leave he would have when his seminar was over. I told him god was still looking after us—I would be in New York anyway and would love to come down after I had finished my business.

We said goodbye and my brain began to whirl. I wondered first why Dan had chosen to call now, after all these years. We had communicated sporadically since my card to him in Korea. I knew he was now a lieutenant colonel and that his career with the army had been very successful. He had served with distinction in fourteen Asian countries and was now living in Hawaii. He spoke not only Vietnamese but Mandarin and Korean, which meant he had more than a passing acquaintance with Asian culture. His eleven-year marriage to Tuyet, a Vietnamese woman, had produced two children (in addition to the two he and his first wife had adopted). The language of love in our letters had cooled considerably over the years. We talked less about finding peace in each other's arms and more about making peace with the real world life had presented us. We were no longer two lost souls starving for love in a war zone. We were mature, middle-aged people with separate lives, hopes, and desires. A reunion with Dan would be nice, but I could not understand the sense of urgency in his voice—for me to come all the way to Washington when a stopover in San Diego on his way back to Hawaii would have served just as well. Still, as my mother used to say, *Tinh cu khong ru cung toi*—Lost love always finds its way home.

My meeting with Mr. Tan in the fancy UN building was more like a visit to a kindly family physician than to a high diplomat. He was mature but not elderly, and still "war thin"—bony like so many of his countrymen. He speech revealed a fine education and his etiquette showed fine parents. I gave him a short letter that described my modest plans for a health clinic near my native village. By this time I had decided that it would be best for me to provide the equipment and expendables—medicine, X-ray film, bandages, syringes, and so on—from the United States and to provide funds for construction materials if Vietnam would provide the labor. I also hoped to arrange for a few volunteer physicians and nurses to go over, too, but so far I had no commitments. I had no financial statements or working schedule or lists of patrons. I just wanted to show the UN representatives that I was sincere, capable, and uninterested in playing politics on either side.

Mr. Tan read my letter carefully, then said, "I am pleased with your desire to help, Chi Ly. I will forward your letter to my superiors in Hanoi. In the meantime, I advise you to work with the U.S. State Department. No materials can be shipped until you have obtained the necessary waivers to the laws restricting American trade. I warn you, though, it will be difficult. Yet even if you fail, your actions will be noticed by the politicians who make American policy. Eventually, if enough Americans feel and act as you do, these needless barriers will be dropped and your village will have its clinic and more, I'm sure of it."

I was a little deflated as Mr. Tan showed me out. I'm sure he regarded me as another well-meaning housewife with a little cash and spare time whose big plans would shrink quickly once the going got tough.

My meeting with Per was more encouraging because he knew

many more ways to skin a cat. Per's solution, like the advice I had received from others in San Diego, was to work through established organizations that already had permission to perform humanitarian work in Vietnam. This made sense, especially since I was a little nobody and big organizations like the UN and Red Cross had money and staff and connections in high places. Still, I was mindful of what Mr. Thay Vu Tai Loc—the famous psychic—had told me in my latest reading. My fate was to lead, to spread the seeds, so that others could follow and cultivate what I had planted. Giving plans and money to big organizations to do the work fate had assigned to me just didn't feel right. Still, Per's encouragement alone was worth a million dollars. I knew his ideas and the list of resources would be invaluable later on.

With business behind me, I had the luxury of feeling like nervous little girl on the short flight to Washington, D.C. I hadn't seen Dan in fourteen years. I knew from his letters and telephone voice that he had changed—as I had. Overcoming false expectations can waste a lot of time and cause a lot of heartache. It would be far better, I decided, to encounter Dan afresh, with a clean emotional slate, than to overload him with baggage from an era—a war and a life cycle—so long past.

The shuttle bus from the airliner deposited me at the terminal and after struggling with my carry-ons to the concourse, I spotted Dan standing tall and straight as a flagpole in his dress uniform.

I dropped my bag and we embraced like old friends rather than lovers. As curious as I was, I avoided staring into his face, but took in the wrinkles, gray temples, thick eyeglasses, and sagging chin through shy glances as we walked to get my luggage.

"How was your flight?" Dan asked, not above a little peeking himself.

"Sad," I said. "I sat next to another Oriental woman and all we did was talk about our families. At least I've seen my mother one last time, and this lady was very jealous of that. But how have you been? You are as handsome as the last time I saw you!"

"It's the uniform," Dan joked. "I'm still the same dumb Wop you remember. How are the boys?"

"Jimmy's a computer whiz in college. He's helping me with my book. Tommy's in high school—he likes chasing girls and playing baseball more than going to class. Alan's doing okay in elementary school, but I think he's a little lonely. He deserves a better home than the one I'm giving him now."

"I still think they have the greatest mother in the world," Dan said as if he meant it. "And one of the greatest-looking. You haven't aged a day—really!"

We found his rental car and started the long drive to his hotel, talking about old times and avoiding what was really on our minds: what our lives would have been like if we had stayed together and what, if anything, the future held for us.

After dinner, I began talking about the great comfort I had discovered in my studies of the spiritual world, but I could see Dan tune me out. This surprised me, because, with his great knowledge of the Orient and decade-long marriage to a Vietnamese woman, I would've bet he had developed a deep appreciation of this all-important side of our nature. In some ways, I felt again like the ignorant little farm girl he first met in An Khe. In other ways, though, I felt like a monk myself: old maid Ly who had finally transcended her earthly cares—at least the small ones. I knew most Americans, even the very religious ones, pooh-poohed spiritualism and Eastern philosophy because they worshiped at the shrine of science. They couldn't acknowledge the possible existence of a more-than-rational world—a flip-side to the universe, as hidden to the five senses as the inside of the atom. It all made perfect sense to me, which was why people like Dan never quite knew how to handle my enthusiasm for it. To them, I was just a gullible peasant and always would be.

Dan offered to let me share his room and save on hotel expenses. I was grateful for that and said I would take the couch. I could tell he was a little disappointed that we would not sleep together, but he was still a gentleman and said an old soldier would be more comfortable on the couch than a pretty lady, so we swapped. It was a queer way for two old lovers to spend the night, but it was the only way that felt right.

The next day Dan went to his seminar at the Pentagon and I treated myself to a quick tour of my adopted nation's capital. All the grand monuments and sprawling buildings stood in sharp contrast to the shoestring memorials (often made with salvaged materials, like U.S. artillery casings) and dumpy offices used by the Vietnamese government. I was especially impressed with the enormous statues of Thomas Jefferson and my favorite, Uncle Abe Lincoln, who stared down at me like a Buddha, all-knowing, and a little bit sad because of what he knew. These men were heroes, of course, so it was okay to make them larger than life; but they were also politicians, which meant compromising and hurting some people in order to help others. From this perspective, religious statues seemed much better, because the monumental size reflects the immenseness of the viewer's own spirit. I could only wonder what people like Dan felt when they stood before the big statues of conquerors and generals—shrines to earthly power. Perhaps their awe was the closest they would ever feel to true spirituality. If so, it was a poor imitation of one of life's best things.

After Dan got off work, we walked to the Vietnam War Memorial, which vibrated with psychic energy. I was not surprised to learn that a young female Asian architect had designed the monument. To me, it embodied the dark spiritual connection between heaven and earth that the war was all about. We walked slowly down the enormous family headstone: U.S. servicemen and women killed in the war. I shivered as a spirit voice called, *"Lanh leo co don qua*—I am cold and lonely, why am I here?" I answered silently, "Because it was your karma." I looked down at the flowers arranged neatly all around the wall and silently added, "At least your family has remembered you." I wondered if Americans realized how much this great memorial resembled a Buddhist shrine.

I stopped and put my fingers on one of the names. I wondered if I had talked to or seen this man during his tragic, one-way visit to my country. I wondered how many of these men had made love to dark-skinned, dark-haired Vietnamese girls and left their seed to bloom as the gaunt Amerasian kids who had stared at me on my visit. What would the children say if they could be magically transported to Washington to encounter their fathers at this shrine? I couldn't help but think that both souls would find a little peace.

I also wondered how much longer and taller and sadder this wonderful monument would be if the names of *all* the people killed in the war were added—the millions of Vietnamese, including civilian women and children. It would remind us that war is only a factory for building bad karma and reinforcing blind vengeance—not some kind of athletic field for showing patriotic prowess. The spirits inside the giant statues of politicians would never allow such a monument to be built, of course. With such a terrible truth staring them in the face, no men born of women could ever again order their sons off to war.

After seeing the wall, Dan and I had a quiet dinner, although my heart was anything but still. The more I wanted to talk about my feelings, the more Dan seemed to withdraw. To him, matters of the spirit were best left to the chaplain. Giving and following orders was part of military life—he accepted death along with his GI paycheck. As much as he loved children, his own and mine included, he would not hesitate to send them into battle even if he knew they would return only as names on a wall. "That's life in the military," Dan had said on more than one occasion. "That's how we are trained: to kill or be killed."

I got so discouraged with my "soulmate" that I could think of nothing more to say. After I had been quiet a long time, Dan forced a smile and said, "So—what are you going to do now that you're out of the restaurant business?"

"I am thinking of starting some kind of organization to help my people in Vietnam." I tried to keep it simple and businesslike—no spiritualism—just organization and mission, terms Dan would understand.

"Hey, that's great! I know the Vietnamese want all the help they can get. You know, my wife visited her family not long before you did. Her uncle is a physician trained in the North. If we had known you were going, we could've given you some pointers."

"No kidding! Tuyet went back to Vietnam? Even though you are a high-ranking army officer?"

"Sure. My background had nothing to do with it. She just wrote for her visa and went."

"And she didn't get any calls from the State Department or the FBI?"

"No, why should she?"

I was silent again, but this time in puzzlement. My first impulse was to accuse the government of racism—of harassing me because I was Vietnamese; but Tuyet was Vietnamese, too. It didn't make sense.

"Well, anyway," I continued, "I'm trying to finish a book about my life and my family. If I can tell Americans what life was like in the villages, they'll understand the war better and some may even feel like helping."

"That's very admirable, Ly. But how are you going to support yourself and the boys while you do that?"

"Tommy and Alan still get a little cash from Ed's and Dennis's social security. I'll make some money when my share of the restaurant is sold. Besides, I still have three houses in Southern California, although the rent just pays the mortgages. I have some money in stocks and bonds, too, and I still have title to that silly property in Idaho Dennis bought. Maybe when I'm an old lady I'll move up there and grow rice and sweet potatoes!"

Dan's face lit up. "How much do you think all your assets are worth?" He got out a pen and turned over a cocktail napkin.

I was pretty sure what my Escondido house was worth, but I could only guess about Dennis's land and our old house in San Diego. And we hadn't owned the house in Temecula (which we used as an apartment for Hollylinh staff) long enough to have much new equity. I hadn't checked the value of my portfolio, either, although my broker kept calling and asking me to invest in one scheme or another. I made the best guesses I could, erring on the side of not-too-much, and Dan added them up.

"My God, Ly!" He whistled. "You're a millionaire!"

The bottom line on the napkin read "$1,300,000."

I was speechless. Everyone joked about American millionaires but I never guessed I was among them. My cash on hand was too puny to feel wealthy—I almost always came up short on monthly bills. To me, the houses were security for old age, when I couldn't work anymore—like rice paddies full of grown sons and daughters.

"Well, here's to that little farm girl from Ky La." Dan raised his cocktail glass. "You've come a long way, baby!"

I answered his toast with a grin, but my mind was racing ahead, wondering how Escondido's "newest millionaire" could use her sudden wealth to realize her dream for her people. After a minute or so in the fog, I realized Dan was speaking. "I'm sorry—what did you say?"

"I said now that you're a lady of means, you should have a man to look after your assets."

I shrugged. Somehow, inviting a man into my life seemed like the last thing I ought to do. "I don't know. I seem to be doing okay."

"Sure, right now," Dan was more animated than I had seen him since our reunion. "But what happens when you get preoccupied with your organization? What happens when you want to spend more time in Vietnam, or travel on the fund-raising circuit, or go on radio shows to talk about your book? What will happen to Tommy and Alan with no parent around to guide them with their problems?"

These were all good questions and, to be honest, I hadn't thought about any of them. I'd somehow imagined that I could raise money and get equipment and supplies and coordinate transportation and write my book and do all of that from my house. What did I need besides my shrine, my kitchen, and a telephone? But Dan was a man of the world—feet planted in reality, not spiritual outer space. I couldn't ignore his advice.

That evening we sat together in Dan's room, shoes off, in our bathrobes, talking like old married people. With some hesitancy, Dan admitted that his life with Tuyet had not been the bowl of cherries he had led me to believe.

"To tell you the truth, Ly," he said, "that's why I invited you to D.C. I wanted to see you again, to help me make up my mind about leaving Tuyet. The children are the only reason we'd stay together, but I'm beginning to think that would be a big mistake."

Dan cradled his head on my lap. I stroked his silver-streaked black hair and really felt sorry for him, and also for myself.

"You know," I said, "I was jealous of Tuyet all these years— married to the only man I ever loved while I wasted my life with Dennis. I let him bully me into marriage. If I had been stronger, you would've married me, not Tuyet, and you would not have these problems. *Toan thien toan my*—Both our lives would be perfect."

We fell asleep in each other's arms, just like fourteen years ago at An Khe, before Viet Cong rockets disrupted our paradise forever.

The next day was the last day of my visit and Dan decided to make the most of it. After more sightseeing, he drove me out to a picturesque point by the Potomac and brought a chilled bottle of champagne and two plastic glasses out of the trunk. My stomach was churning—I was already beginning to miss him—but I didn't want to spoil his mood.

"What's the occasion?" I asked, accepting a cup.

"In five years," he began, "I'll retire as a full colonel. Between now and then, I'll have my choice of assignments—I'm thinking of Indonesia or Malaysia. The army will provide me with nice quarters and a houseful of servants. I'll have big parties and entertain diplomats and businessmen from all over the world. After that, I'll take a civilian job that's been offered to me for more than a hundred and twenty thousand dollars a year. So here's the deal. You want to help the people of Vietnam and I want to help you. If you live in Asia, it will be much easier for you to visit Vietnam and control the resources you provide. If you have a good man to watch over you and your boys, your mind will be clear and you'll be able to concentrate on your mission. That's what I'm offering, Ly. I want us to pick up where we left off. Tuyet and I are finished. *Anh yeu em nhieu lam minh oi*—I still love you. You are the only woman I want in my life, but only if you still want a big dumb dago like me!"

I hugged him hard, spilling my champagne. "Of course I still want you! I have wanted you all these years. Maybe god has made us wait so that we could each learn our lessons about marriage first—so this time we could get it right, eh?"

He hugged me back and we kissed like teenagers and he finished his champagne and mine as well.

"Of course," I said, "I must discuss this with my boys. Their life is in America now. They may not want to leave California."

"Don't worry." Dan's enthusiasm was boundless. "I'm stationed in Honolulu. It's just like San Diego, only better: prettier beaches, prettier girls—and all the Big Macs they can eat. The boys will love it."

Everything was moving so fast, I was literally out of breath. One minute I was a lonely widow trying to keep the world from running me down; now *duyen den!* I was a bride, with the whole world spread out before me.

"What shall we do first?" I asked. A thousand details crowded my mind.

"First, you should move to Hawaii—right away, before the end of the summer. That way, the boys can start school in the fall semester and we can be together while we plan our wedding and new life."

"Well, I can't just pick up and go. It will take a bit of time."

Dan smiled. "I've been in the army twenty-five years, Ly. Everything I need, everything that really counts, fits into one duffel bag; that, or right here—"

He placed his hand over his heart. I kissed him again.

"Anyway," he concluded, "I'll pay for everything. Get a property manager to rent your houses. Put the things you don't need into storage. Tuyet and I recently sold some investment property so I'll send you thirty thousand dollars as soon as I get back. Will that help you settle your affairs?"

I could think of no reason—practical or otherwise—to say no to Dan. We returned to the hotel and celebrated our honeymoon early. It was the closest thing to that golden week in An Khe I had yet experienced. I was secure. By going back to Vietnam and returning, I had completed the first great cycle of my life. I had discovered my life's mission and was making ready to fulfill it. My boys were healthy and on their way to becoming fine young men and good Americans —a credit to their Phung ancestors. Now, I would marry the love of my life and, like Lao Tzu's famous traveler, take the first step on my "journey of a thousand leagues" to be at his side. I had finally paid off my debt of *hi sinh* and was my own person in the universe. My next life circle was opening with the power of love—of the smiling Buddha—behind me.

What could possibly go wrong?

NINE

Circle of Vengeance

MOVING ACROSS TOWN involves a thousand details. Moving across an ocean involves a million. My friends told me I couldn't do everything at once, but that didn't stop me from trying.

My first challenge was economic. Dan was doing well but I didn't want to depend on him—or any man—for my security. I called my friend Annie, a bright and sensitive woman who worked in real estate, and asked for an appointment with her company's property manager. I had three houses to rent and I couldn't keep track of tenants and repairs and all of that from Honolulu.

Annie's associate, Thomas, was good-looking and happy-go-lucky. Frankly, I wondered if he was tough enough to look after my assets with his easygoing manner. I was American, yes; but still Oriental enough to picture landlords as scowling mandarins.

We made a grand tour of my "empire"—from Temecula through Escondido to San Diego. I told Thomas like a stern mother what I expected from each house.

"The Escondido house should rent for two thousand a month," I said. "The San Diego house now goes for twelve hundred but I think we could get more. The one in Temecula is nine hundred and there's not much you can do with that since I still have an agreement with the Hollylinh to house their staff for a fixed amount. The main thing is that I need every penny and then some to service all the mortgages, so make sure you replace any tenant who moves out as soon as possible. Do you think you can handle it?"

"Hey," Thomas chuckled, "you're talking to the King of Collections. That's how I make my living. No sweat."

"So how much will it cost to keep me from sweating?" I asked.

"For three houses? Six percent of gross receipts."

"And Annie will be around to help you?" I was not sure I wanted to leave everything up to Thomas.

"Of course!" Thomas winked. "Couldn't get along without her!"

Six weeks later, everything was either packed or put into storage and we were camping in the shell of the Escondido house. At first, the boys had been cool to the idea of leaving their friends, even for the prospect of bikinis on tropical beaches, but Dan was a clever salesman. Although his promised check for our moving expenses never came due to one reason or another, he sent a continuous stream of clippings and information—from food prices and weather forecasts to movie, sports, and entertainment listings so the boys would know they weren't going to fall off the edge of the earth. He even sent Jimmy an application to the University of Hawaii, but Jimmy was halfway through his program at UCSD and decided to finish there. I would miss having him near, but I was now accustomed to thinking of him as his own man. Sometimes we can only keep those things which we are willing to let go.

I also got a pleasant letter from Dan's wife, Tuyet, which surprised me. She confirmed Dan's story that their decision to split was mutual. She said she bore him no ill will and realized he had been in love with me for a long time. She said that, since we were both Vietnamese "sisters" we should cooperate to make the transition as easy as possible, considering Dan's "problems." I had no idea what she meant, except that she seemed to think he couldn't be trusted and hadn't provided for his family very well. It seemed like spurned woman's talk and I discounted it. It made me feel that it was more important than ever for me to be by Dan's side. By the time our things were packed, everyone was more than ready to go.

Thomas came by regularly to show prospective tenants the house. They were all impressed but balked at the high rent I was asking. I had almost decided to drop it to seventeen or eighteen hundred, when Thomas showed the house to the Parrys, a nice couple moving in from Oklahoma. The man, Cliff, was tall and powerfully built, like a cowboy or oil worker, and his wife, Nancy, was well-dressed and very quiet. They had four kids. Their inspection was so meticulous that they seemed less like renters than buyers, which was what they apparently had in mind.

"Our house in Tulsa just went on the market," Cliff Parry said politely. "Would you consider selling the property?"

"Not right now," I said, wondering why Thomas had not made all this clear at the beginning. "I would like to hold on to it a while longer."

"Very wise," Mr. Parry said with a wink. "California housing prices are going straight through the roof. You've made a very wise investment."

They said their household goods were on the way from Oklahoma and, although they had a few more places to see, they liked the house very much and would make their decision soon. As they went to their big, late-model American luxury car, I told Thomas to do all he could to snag this couple. They seemed not only qualified to pay a high rent but thought like homeowners and would be sure to take care of the property.

My instincts were well founded. Three hours later, Thomas called to say the Parrys had decided to take the house effective the first of the month. They also had one additional request: Would the boys and I be willing to move out a little early so their things could be moved in right away? Mr. Parry, who apparently liked doing things in a big oilman's way, offered to put us up in the hotel of our choice, all expenses paid, between now and our departure for Hawaii. As an added incentive, he threw in free tickets to a big sporting event that the boys had talked about, so my sons lobbied hard on his behalf. They didn't have to. I was tired of camping out at home, and the prospect of a week or so in a nice hotel with maid service and room service and a swimming pool—a vacation before our vacation—seemed too good to pass up. I accepted Mr. Parry's offer with gratitude.

On the flight to Honolulu, I recalled the other passages I had made between Hawaii and the mainland, under vastly different circumstances. For once I wasn't running away but moving toward something positive. My motive was no longer mere survival, but renewal and growth. I thought again about the horoscope I had commissioned when I returned from Washington with Dan's proposal. It said, *"Loc den, tai duyen, dung nghiep"*—which meant that in the Year of the Dog (this year) I would be promoted to a "higher salary," gain wealth, and begin to realize my dreams, including my dream of a loving marriage. A few clouds would darken my horizon, the astrologer said, but those would quickly dissipate and show me a new dawn. So far, at least, it could not have fit my reality better. I couldn't imagine anything so bad that I couldn't handle it easily with Dan and my children by my side.

"*Colonel* Daddy" met us at the airport with flowered leis and a big grin. After my hug and a handshake for the boys, Dan talked to them man to man—not like a parent, but a friendly coach. Dan said he realized both boys were giving up a lot to come and live with him, and promised their sacrifice would be rewarded—with love and opportunities they had never dreamed about. Even in such small matters, my shining knight was a marvelous leader to "his troops."

He helped carry our luggage to a dusty, rusty used car, which surprised me. Maybe I expected him to drive a government staff car —I always remembered him in a jeep! But for some reason, the beat-up old car struck me as a bad omen: like a dog barking at midnight or a bird turning away from its flock.

"I've got to return my son's car this afternoon," Dan said as soon as the smoky engine coughed to life. "I couldn't very well borrow Tuyet's Toyota, so I've reserved a rental car for you up the street. It'll only take a minute. I thought you guys deserved a treat!"

He pulled into the loading zone and told me to go into the office and "pick up the paperwork" while he stayed with the jalopy.

Inside, the clerk had no record of a rental for DeParma. Instead he had one reserved under my name. I signed for the vehicle and started to go, but the clerk called me back.

"Sorry, Mrs. Hayslip," he said. "I have to run an impression of your credit card. It's the rules."

Back on the curb, wondering if this sort of Dutch treat was what Dan had in mind for our marriage, I waited for the agent to bring the car around.

"Hey, great!" Dan said as the clean little car squealed to a stop. "Now you and the boys can follow me to your hotel."

"Hotel?" I asked. "I thought we were going to your house?"

Dan blushed. "That was the plan, but Tuyet hasn't moved out yet. But don't worry—the hotel's not far away. You'll be very comfortable."

My heart sank when I saw the kind of neighborhood Dan thought would make us comfortable. The motel was in Aiea near the army post with lots of porno theaters, sex shops, and sailors' bars. I was not only a little miffed at Dan for these unexpected "surprises," I was disappointed. I wanted to sleep with my man, to begin our new life together right away, and not shiver alone in some cheap hotel bed while he continued to live with his ex-wife.

"Go ahead and pick up your key," Dan pointed to the office and began unloading the trunk.

Inside, the sleazy desk clerk told me the ridiculously high rate I'd have to pay—cash or charge, no personal checks—with the first night in advance. As I signed the register, the butterflies in my stomach turned to crows with long claws. *This was not how things were supposed to be!* I wasn't so much worried about paying my own way (although I couldn't do that indefinitely) as I was about Dan's not mentioning any of this before—about Tuyet's uncooperativeness, the transportation problem, the necessity of a hotel, sleazy or not. Still, we were souls in transition. What are a few nights in a crummy hotel compared to the things we had been through already—and the promise the future held?

We spent the next few hours sightseeing but came back early because we were tired and Dan had to return his son's car. He left us with some convenience-store groceries to tide us over.

I could see Tommy and Alan were as surprised by all of this as I was, so we had a brief "family meeting" to assess what I had gotten them into. We agreed to give things more time, that the "pot at the end of the rainbow" was worth a few sacrifices along the way. We just had to keep the faith.

The next morning, Dan gave the boys some bus fare and lunch money and suggested they "explore the island on their own." He drove me off in my rental car in the direction of Fort Shafter, where he worked. As we drove, he said, "Ly, I had a long talk with Tuyet last night. It's going to be a while until she moves out, so I think it's best if you took an apartment. I've already found a nice one just outside the gate. It's not too expensive and I think you'll be happy there until we get things squared away."

The apartment was located, as he said, at the army's "back door"

—where people put out the trash. The place was a dump, and worth about half of the $875 the landlord was asking in Honolulu's inflated rental market. The local area reminded me of Danang: the dirty markets, vagrants, street-corner hookers and drug dealers. Just to get out of there, I wrote a check for the deposit on the spot, but silently promised myself not to move in until a lot of questions about Dan and this whole bizzare episode were answered.

We picked up the boys and on our way to dinner at the Officers' Club, drove by Dan's house. Tuyet was home, so he didn't feel right about inviting us in (what happened to Tuyet's "sisters sticking together"?). The place looked worse than the apartment: a ramshackle wood-frame house with peeling paint, rotting steps, and an unkept lawn overgrown with weeds.

"A colonel lives here?" Tommy asked after Dan ducked inside to tell Tuyet where we were going.

"I guess so. Housing is very expensive in Hawaii." I didn't know what to say. It would be hard enough to show the boys the dank apartment they had traded for their big Escondido house, let alone to tell them that, if they were very lucky, *here* was where they would live for the next few years.

"I guess colonels don't make much money," Alan added.

"Money doesn't matter," I lied, realizing now how much we all had come to relish our comfortable California lifestyle. "What matters is that we'll be together. *Tinh thuong quan cung nhu nha, nha tranh co nghia hon toa ngoi xay*—With love, a shed is as good as a house; a cottage with love is better than a mansion without it." Still, I realized I was no longer a love-drunk little country girl willing to put up with anything to be with her man. If middle age does one thing, it makes you appreciate a dry roof and clean bed.

After dinner, we dropped the boys at a movie and drove into the hills, to a romantic spot overlooking the city.

After some halfhearted small talk, I said, "You know, Dan, things don't look so good for you here. Maybe if you explained what's going on, I might be able to help."

He squeezed the steering wheel until his knuckles were white and said, "The problem is Tuyet. She's been sick and has arranged to get all my paychecks. Hell—I'm still paying my parents back for the loan they made me in 1976 when I got remarried! I'm up to my eyeballs in debt to the credit union. My two adopted boys have gone to work to help out a little, but I'm just about bankrupt. She's taken me to the cleaners and after the divorce is final, she'll only get more."

The more Dan talked, the sicker I felt—not because of his problems or the fact that he didn't have money; I could relate to that very well. What terrified me most was how much he sounded like Dennis.

"What can I do to help you?" I asked, rubbing the sudden fire in my tummy.

"I need you to support us until I can retire and accept that civilian job. If I stay in the military, Tuyet gets everything and I'll never get back on my feet. I'll never be able to give you and the boys the things you deserve and help you with the humanitarian work that means so much to you."

"You know, you never told me about that big, important job. Don't you think you should now? What is it? Who is your employer? What do they want you to do for so much money?"

Dan stared out the window, biting his lip. The less he wanted to tell me about it, the more I felt I had to know.

"Well, this is confidential—just between you and me, okay? The government has rules about the kinds of jobs you can take after you've had a career like mine, and this one is pretty sensitive. But trust me—it will allow you to do everything you want: write your book, help your village, everything."

"Dan—what is this job?"

"Brokering arms."

"I don't understand—?"

"You know, selling weapons."

"What? You're joking!"

"No. What do you think I've been doing for the last twenty-five years? What do you think a military adviser does? I go into countries the U.S. is helping and teach them how to use the American-made weapons our corporations sell them."

"I can't believe it! You've been doing that for twenty-five years?"

"More or less. But as a civilian, I'll make money on the weapons themselves instead of just a crummy GI paycheck. That's why the government is very careful about letting senior officers take jobs with major contractors right after they retire. They don't want the officers to use their inside information to help one company against another, or to use their friendships with people still in the service to make sweetheart deals."

"Forget about the sweethearts—" I was dumbfounded. "I want to know if you sell guns to governments so they can go blow up women and children!"

Dan shrugged. "Now Ly, don't get on your high horse. It isn't that simple. That's why I didn't want to tell you. I knew you wouldn't understand."

"I understand war as well as anybody, Dan! Remember who you're talking to!"

"Then you know that if we didn't sell arms to these people, somebody else would—maybe the Communists. How would that make any of us better off?"

Guns and Communists! Is that all anybody in America thinks about? A wet sob caught in my throat. "But Dan, how can you sell weapons knowing they will harm innocent people?"

He shrugged again—a soldier's fatalistic shrug, the way veterans respond when you ask about their chances of being killed. "It's my life, Ly. It's all I know how to do. At least I'll get paid more for doing it—almost two hundred thousand a year with my retirement pay. Doesn't that make you happy?"

"Make me happy? Haven't you listened to anything I've ever told you?"

"You mean all that spiritual stuff?" He made a face and stared out the window.

"Not just that—but about my family, about my life! We're strangers, Dan. We don't know anything about each other!" We were silent a moment, and then I said, "Besides, you lied to me in Washington."

"I knew you wouldn't come out here otherwise. It was just a white lie, a little fib to get you to do the right thing. I knew once you were here, we would be happy."

I was so furious now I couldn't see straight. "Take me home, Dan," was all I could say, although I knew that home could never be on this island.

The next morning, while the boys slept in, I had a cup of coffee in the tropical sun outside our room and tried to sort things out. My mind was crawling with a thousand thoughts—none of them good.

My biggest disappointment was that Dan had lied to me: not just about his personal and financial troubles, but his whole way of life; and not just in Washington, but from the first time we met. I knew he was a professional soldier—with all the good and bad that goes with it. I never had (and still didn't have) any moral problems with soldiers. There are good soldiers and bad soldiers, just as there are good and bad monks or schoolteachers or hookers or politicians. At best, men in uniform are strong and self-disciplined and committed to doing what they think is right. At worst, they can be soulless killers who mock true patriots by using their uniform to mask their crimes. I thought Dan earned his pay by teaching allied soldiers to fight: to stay alive and serve their country with honor. Now, he appears to have been one link in the unsavory chain that turns human misery into cash—for arms dealers, weapons makers, and ambitious politicians—the whole reason I quit my job at NSC. I didn't want to be part of that terrible cycle of death-dealing then, and still didn't.

But I had even more personal reasons for mistrusting and fearing Dan. Even if I could forgive him for his deceit and the way he spent his life, I'm not sure I could ever recover from hearing Dennis's voice come from his mouth. Somehow, his "Vietnamese wife" was always plotting to ruin his life. I knew divorces could be terrible and that spouses of any race could be made a little crazy because of them, but how long would we be married before my differences with Dan became "subversive plots" to destroy him? Of course, his rejection of any spiritualism in his life prevented him from seeing that his own bad karma was contributing to his problems. Even Dennis realized this toward the end, although he couldn't do much about it. More than the sorrow of a lover slipping away, I felt the pain a mother must feel when she sees her young man-child dying without ever really knowing life.

After Dan got off work, he came by the motel to pick me up. We took a long walk on the pretty beach beside the fort and I told him what was in my heart.

"Dan, I don't think it's such a good idea that we get married. I just could not live on blood money that came from selling death to others. But even if I could accept what you would be doing in your new job, how would it look to the people I will depend upon for my humanitarian work? How can I ask people to donate money and equipment and their own sweat and blood to heal the wounds of war while you are out making new ones?"

"It's the way the world works, Ly," he said. "I can't change it, and wouldn't if I could. But forgetting all that for the moment—think about everything we've been through. Doesn't that mean anything?"

"Of course. It means a lot. You are the only man I've ever loved. You are one of the best friends I'll ever have. But I see now we are too different inside to be true soulmates. There was a time when I might have overlooked all that—when I did overlook such things—but it always led to bad mistakes. I will not make such mistakes again."

"So what are you saying, that you moved halfway across the Pacific just to be friends? To be my neighbor? I don't understand."

"No. I moved to Hawaii on the strength of a promise and my own wishful thinking. Now that the promise and those thoughts have proved false, I will make other plans."

"I see. You're pissed because I didn't send the money for your move. You're mad because you have to pay for your own car and hotel. You don't have to play games. Be honest."

I sighed. "You don't understand at all. It's true, I don't have much cash—everything I have is tied up in something else. The money from one asset is used to pay for another. It's stupid; a terrible way to live. I've had to dip into my life savings to come here—but that's all right. Either things would have worked out, or I would have learned the truth. Either way, I've stopped myself from stepping back into the circle of bad soul debt—from making more mistakes. You should be grateful, too. If we don't marry, you will be spared all the heartbreak Ed and Dennis went through. If I've learned one thing, it's that there's no such thing as one happy person in a marriage. If one is miserable, both are miserable. That's the way life works. But we still have a lot to be happy about. A lifetime ago, you were my one true love. You helped save my family and send us back to America, and for that I can only be grateful. It is a debt I can never repay. How could I betray that debt by knowingly making you unhappy?"

We stopped and turned back toward the army post. "So what does this mean?" Dan asked. "That you'll be going back to the mainland?"

"Perhaps. Or maybe we'll try to make a new life here. The boys are registered for school and I have no place to go. I own three houses but they're all lived in by somebody else! Don't worry about us. We'll get along fine. Worry about putting your own life in order. If I can help you do that without marrying you, I'm certainly willing to try. Right now, though, I'm in complete control of my own life. That's something I can never give up."

Dan glanced at me wistfully, "You sure are *dien cai dau*—one crazy lady—aren't you?"

He said it like a compliment, but I wasn't sure. Being independent and captain of your soul was one thing. Being alone in the world was something else.

As the days went by, Dan and I felt more secure in our decision to call the wedding off. Maybe he felt guilty for the way he tricked me into coming to Hawaii, I didn't know, but he acted like a gentleman and didn't badger me. The similarity to my relationship with Dennis amazed me: the closer I got to both men, the worse our lives became, full of deceit and jealousy and betrayal. As soon as we chose to separate, even in principle, honesty and consideration became no problem. Amazing!

I gladly forfeited my deposit on the hovel Dan wanted us to rent and found a more appropriate place in a nicer neighborhood (Hawaii Kai) for not much more money. We had a seventh-floor apartment in a twin-tower high-rise with a view of the ocean on the left and jungly green mountains on our right—the first time in my life I ever lived anywhere with something to see out my window besides automobiles or neighbors! When my trusty old Toyota finally arrived from the mainland, I felt my life was nearly back on track.

While the boys went to school, I began planning my Vietnam relief project in earnest. I realized there was little I could do as an individual; only by organizing a not-for-profit foundation could I gain the resources and exert the kind of influence I would need to open doors, hearts, and checkbooks to the people left behind by the war.

My first impulse was to name the foundation after my father, Phung Trong, but I felt somehow I would need his permission. In life he was not the kind of man to toot his own horn, and the idea of putting his name on something another person had made just didn't seem to be something he'd want. When he failed to materialize in any of my Honolulu dreams, I dropped the idea. On the other hand, staring out my window at blue water to the east and the rugged green hills to the west, another idea struck me. Although my goal was to help people stricken by the war, wounded bodies and souls could be found on *both* sides of the ocean—Vietnam had no monopoly on people who needed help. What I *really* wanted to do was bind my old country to my new one—to sponsor a healing handshake across time and space. Thus, *East Meets West—Dong Tay Hoi Ngo,* the daughter of my soul—was born, at least in spirit.

After a month or so, the boys got "island fever." They became homesick for their friends and all the places they missed in Southern

California. I, too, felt a little cut off. Letters from my friends on the mainland never came often enough and my money was running low. I would either have to get a job in Hawaii, where I didn't know anyone, or go back to San Diego. Either way, I would have to sell one of my houses to get cash. Fortunately, I already knew one tenant who was ready to buy.

After quick phone calls to Cliff Parry and Thomas, I caught a flight to the mainland to put my Escondido house into escrow.

Cliff picked me up and drove me to the hotel where he had arranged for my complimentary weekend stay.

"I appreciate your doing this for me, Cliff," I said. "I'm running short on money and every little bit helps. Still, I think you're getting a good price on the house."

"Oh, don't worry about that," Cliff said with a big Okie smile. "I'm just sorry that things fell through with Colonel DeParma. Annie says you and he went back a long way."

"Yes, to Vietnam. We met just before the war ended. But it's all for the best. My goal is to help the peasants recover from the war. With Dan's business interests, it just wouldn't have worked out."

"You know, I was stationed in 'Nam," Cliff said.

That was the first I'd heard he was a veteran. Maybe that explained his unusual kindness toward me and my boys.

"Oh really?" I asked. "Where?"

"In the South—in the highlands. I was in Special Forces."

"Oh, a Green Beret! I came from Danang. That's where my foundation will begin its work—back in my home village of Ky La."

"How do you plan to start?"

"Well, first I hope to publish my book, which is the story of my life and what we peasants went through in the war. All the other books about Vietnam have been written by generals or soldiers or politicians or scholars—nobody has told Americans what the war was like for ordinary people, villagers and farmers. That will be my job. I'm sure that once they understand what we went through, their hearts will open to my people."

Cliff was quiet a moment, then said, "Well, put me down as your first contributor, Ly. I went through quite a bit there myself and I'd like to help. Maybe we can talk about it before you go."

Maybe we can talk about it? I won't let you forget! I had run into several veterans who wanted to go back to Vietnam or do something to help the people they had harmed—but most of them had only big hearts, not big pocketbooks. Cliff was one of the few vets I had met who had both the desire and means to put his good intentions to work.

The next day, we signed all the papers, including a special letter Cliff prepared for my signature giving him the right to handle questions or take care of any problems with the house during escrow.

"It's just a formality," Cliff said, "a convenience for us both. As my own tenant, so to speak, there's no reason to keep Thomas in the loop and with you three thousand miles away, I'd just as soon keep things rolling so that you can have your money and I can have my house as soon as possible. Is that okay with you?"

I said, "Sure, of course. Why not?"

After our paperwork was done, Cliff took me to lunch.

"What do the Vietnamese-Americans think about your going back to the homeland?" he asked.

"It depends on who you talk to. The very old and the very young seem to think it's a good idea. The old want to honor our customs and the young are curious about a land they've never seen or can't remember. Only the people who remember the war and the suffering —they're the ones who object the most. They're like kids who have lost their parents. If they can't have a mom and dad, they don't want other kids to have parents, either. Consequently, they'll let their own relatives suffer and die if it hastens the downfall of the Hanoi government. They don't see those deaths as needless the way I do. That's why I want to get my relief work started right away. If you have any suggestions about organizing a small foundation, I would love to hear them."

Cliff grinned. "You will, Ly, you will!"

I returned to Hawaii but no matter what I did, I just seemed to spin my wheels—principally with my book. I concluded that I would probably need an experienced writer, a native English-speaker, to express my story effectively to American readers, and so went shopping for a collaborator. Although I corresponded with and interviewed several people, my efforts seemed to go nowhere.

Dan and I spoke only occasionally during this period and the boys seemed to prefer moping, instead of surfing, as an after-school activity. I couldn't fault them: more than anyone, I knew what homesickness was like. Still, my household goods were here, not San Diego, and even if I wanted to move back, I could not stand the cost of relocating until we closed escrow on the Escondido house.

Fortunately, good-natured Thomas came to my rescue.

"Ly," he said on long distance one evening, "bad news! Your San Diego tenant gave notice and I'm having a hard time replacing him. It looks like you're going to have a vacant unit for a while. Sorry—there's just nothing more I can do."

"What!" I squealed with delight. "That's great!"

"Huh?"

"Don't worry about finding a tenant. I'll move in myself. That's just the break I've been waiting for!"

"Well, if losing money makes you happy—hey, I'll double my fee and kick out your other tenants!"

I called the boys into the room and told them the good news: *We're going home!* Despite the troubles we'd had, Tommy and Alan had fond memories of our San Diego house and most of their childhood buddies still lived in the neighborhood. As for me, five years had passed since I felt my neighbors' cold eyes on my back. I was a new person, a woman with some accomplishments of her own and a mission in life. I could hold my head high next to anyone.

I called Cliff Parry and told him of our plans. He was surprisingly enthusiastic.

"Now we'll have a chance to work together on your foundation," he said.

The boys and I arrived at Lindbergh Field late on a Tuesday afternoon. After claiming our luggage, I stepped out on the curb to hail a cab. Before I could, a uniformed man stepped up with a cardboard sign reading HAYSLIP FAMILY.

"Excuse me," the young chauffeur said, "are you Le Ly Hayslip?"

How many other Vietnamese women with teenage Amerasian boys could be deplaning? "Yes, but I think you want somebody else. I didn't reserve a car."

"That's all right." He smiled. "Mr. Parry did. Will you please follow me?"

He led us to a white stretch limousine and opened the rear double doors. From inside, he pulled out a dozen red roses and offered them to me with a flourish. "From Mr. Parry," he said, "wishing you a happy return!"

An instant later we were speeding east on the freeway.

"Excuse me." I tapped the glass behind the driver. "Where are you taking us?"

The inside window glided down. "Mr. Parry has reserved a suite for you at the Radisson Hotel in Mission Valley—as his guests, of course, until your house is available. He hopes that meets with your approval."

Of course it did, although it left me speechless. The boys cheered and gave each other high fives and got ready to live high on the hog. But I wasn't so sure. Why would this nice man do all this for us? He had a financial interest in keeping me happy, of course, at least until our escrow closed. But this was way too much. I decided to call him as soon as we arrived at the hotel.

As it turned out, that wasn't necessary. As soon as we entered our room—a magnificent suite overlooking one of San Diego's posh new bedroom communities—the telephone rang.

"Cliff, is that you?" I recognized his chuckle.

"I hope you're feeling warm and welcome!" he said with a laugh.

"Of course, but this is all too much, really!"

"Just relax and enjoy yourself. You've earned it. I'll be by in the morning. We'll talk."

He hung up—but I did not perceive it as rudeness. He was just a "take charge" kind of man. Although this appealed to my feminine instincts, especially after my bad experience with Dan, it raised other flags of warning. I had enough cash to cover our hotel expenses if I had to, and the boys were already fighting over which cable channel to watch. I could afford to wait at least one more day to see just how charming this prince really was.

Cliff picked me up in a big car and presented me with the keys—our rented transportation until my Toyota arrived from Hawaii. Lunching at a beachside restaurant, I asked him again, "Cliff, why are you doing this? Be honest now—what's going on?"

He broke off his glance and fingered his silverware like a little boy, "I said I wanted to help you. This is my way of doing it. Finish your lunch. There's something else I want you and the boys to see."

We drove to Mount Helix in the secluded suburb of La Mesa, the "Beverly Hills" of San Diego. We stopped in the driveway of a magnificent house—half hotel, half castle—just incredible!

"Let's take a look inside, what do you say?" Cliff led me and the boys to the huge front door and introduced me to the occupant, a friendly man named Al, and his girlfriend, who took us on a tour of the palatial estate. Its seventy thousand square feet encompassed five bedrooms (each with its own fireplace), a completely furnished gymnasium and sauna, and a third-floor loft that was laid out as an office, with telephones and computers and desks and filing cabinets. Surrounding the second story was a terrace with a breathtaking view in all directions—from the saddle hills of El Cajon to the port of San Diego to downtown skyscrapers. It could have contained every house I had lived in to that point in my life under its broad roof, with room to spare.

"How do you like it?" Cliff asked as I gripped the terrace handrail, dizzy with excitement.

"It's wonderful! Who lives here?" I asked.

"Why, you do!" Cliff beamed.

"I don't understand . . . !"

Cliff leaned against the railing. "I'll make a confession to you, Ly. Ever since I met you, something's happened to me inside. You're a very special person. You're very independent and smart, of course—I mean, look at where you came from and how far you've come. But you're also very compassionate. It's as much a part of your nature as the way you walk or talk or sing those old Vietnamese songs. The point is, I'm in a position to do something few people in this world ever get a chance of doing. I have a chance to help bring something *good* into this world and pay back a little something to someone who has suffered way too much in her life. What I'm saying, Ly, is that I want you and your boys to live here. Move in and write your book. Use the facilities for fund-raising parties or whatever you have to do to make your dream of helping others a reality. I'll bankroll the whole affair, you don't have to worry about a thing."

"But this is such a big house! It's like living at the Radisson as the only guest!"

"Forget about that. You see, if you expect to raise money from rich people, you've got be just like them. If you come on too poor—like Mother Teresa—they'll get suspicious. They'll think you're trying to snow them—or worse, that you don't know what you're doing. With a place like this, they'll feel at home. They'll think you're one of them. Believe me, Ly, I know what I'm talking about."

I believed that he did—but *still!*

"Anyway," Cliff continued, "after your book is written and your foundation is up and running and you fall in love with me, I'll move in here and you and I will get married. What could be better than that?"

"*What?* Cliff, what are you talking about? You're a married man!"

"No. No, I'm not. Nancy is not my wife. She's a widow, just like you. Her husband was a policeman who was killed in the line of duty. We met in Tulsa and I took her and her family under my wing because I felt sorry for her. She wanted to move to California and start a new life, so I made it happen for her."

"But you live with her as her husband!"

Cliff shrugged. "I admit it, I get lonely like anybody else."

"I know what you mean," I said. Still, I felt like I had been drugged. This couldn't be happening! "This is all too good to be true. Something about it just can't be right."

But Cliff was prepared for everything. He gave me another business card.

"Here's my CPA—a well-respected fellow. Call him whenever you like. He'll explain everything."

"I don't know what to say, Cliff—" I literally was speechless. On the one hand, I felt I should run from the house and not look back. On the other, *dan-ba nhu hat mua sa, hat roi gac tia, hat ra ngoi dong*— Women are like raindrops; some fall down on palaces, others on rice paddies. Why shouldn't I complete my stormy life's circle at the end of a big, beautiful rainbow?

"I hope you'll give me a few days to think all this over," I said, still breathless.

"Of course. We've got a lot to talk about, and now isn't the time to do it. Al and I have an appointment at the bank to sign the purchase agreement. Why don't you take the car back to the hotel and talk things over with your boys. Take as much time as you want."

The first thing I did at the hotel was call Thomas.

"This is very important," I said, still lightheaded, out of breath. "Please read to me the names on the lease of the Escondido house."

"Sure," Thomas said. After a minute, he returned. "Clifford Parry and Nancy Mills. Who did you think?"

"What does their financial statement say?"

After another short silence, Thomas said, "He's the original Mister Gotrocks. Parry has his own business in San Bernardino. He sent me lots of financial statements, tax returns—why? What's going on?"

"Nothing—and everything! Thank you, Thomas! I'll call you later!"

Early that evening, I dialed the number of the big house we had visited. When a male voice answered, I said, "Hello—is this Al?"

"Yes it is."

"My name is Le Ly—we met this afternoon?"

"Right—with Mr. Parry. How are you?"

"I'm fine. Listen, I want to ask you a couple of questions, okay? When did you first meet Mr. Parry?"

"Oh, about three months ago. He looked at the house and said he was moving in from Oklahoma. Nice fella, but he didn't seem too interested—until last week. Then he called back and asked if the house was still on the market. I said it was. You know, not everybody can afford a place like this. Anyway, he said he was ready to deal and to have my realtor draw up the papers."

"So what happened? Did you open escrow?"

"Oh yes. He put you down as the owner of record. The deal calls for a half million cash and an assumed loan of seven hundred thousand. He wanted all the furniture thrown in, too. He says it's an early wedding present. What a guy, eh?"

"Yes, some guy. Okay, Al, thanks for everything. See you soon."

I hung up, muttering to myself. I would have to slow things down; to proceed with due care. I was still on the rebound from Dan. I still hurt too much to be cured all at once. Still, as the Christians liked to say, God works in mysterious ways . . .

I moved into the La Mesa mansion in November 1986. It set into motion a chain of events that still amazes me to this day.

To begin with, once I became Cliff's dependent, I saw him less than ever. He traveled constantly and most of my contact regarding either the Escondido or La Mesa houses came through Nancy and Al. On weekends, when Tommy was home from school, he would remark on all the remodeling going on at the old house: a new patio and new porch and new landscaping (including a waterfall!) that replaced my tropical garden in the back.

Naturally, I had mixed feelings about this. Escrow hadn't closed yet, so technically the house was still mine—although I couldn't really complain since I was living like a queen on the buyer's generosity.

On the rare occasions that he was in town, Cliff would come by the mansion and take me and Alan and Tommy out to dinner and a show or to some sporting event for which Cliff always seemed to have front-row seats.

Shortly before Christmas, 1986, Cliff came to the mansion for a "heart to heart" talk.

"How's everything coming," he asked, "the book—the foundation?"

"How could they not be coming along fine!" I answered. I had finally found an agent and we were talking to several good writers about preparing a first-class proposal for major publishers. I'd been learning all about how to set up and manage a nonprofit foundation in California.

Cliff smiled—satisfied, indulgent, *big daddy*. "Good," he said, "that's great." Then his mood changed. "We need to talk about a couple of things, Ly—things that are very important to me. First, I want you to know that I'm going to be staying with Nancy a little longer than I planned. She's not getting established in her new life as fast as I hoped. But don't worry, we'll be together soon. If you and your soothsayer agree, I'd like to set our wedding date for March seventh. We'll throw the biggest Tet New Year's and engagement party this town has ever seen! You can invite all your friends. After that, we will begin our romance—the first day of the rest of our lives. How does that sound?"

"Don't worry about me, Cliff," I said, relieved that he would not be moving in soon, despite all the extra space. I could only envision a reprise of my life with Ed and Dennis and I was not anxious to take that risk. Fantasy and wishful thinking felt much better. "I'm getting along fine, although that house is so big—it's like living in my own hotel. What else is troubling you?"

He was silent a moment, then said, "I want to tell you about my experiences in Vietnam. I've wanted to tell you a long time now, but frankly, I didn't have the guts."

"What guts does it take to tell me?" I put my hand on his arm. "I went through the war too, just like you. Many other GIs have told me about their experiences, and most of them feel better after they do it. Don't make yourself wait any longer. You'd be surprised what I can take."

His eyes moistened as he began. "I enlisted in the army in 1965 when I was a kid of twenty-one. After boot camp and ranger school, I went to 'Nam and was assigned to Operation Phoenix. Do you know what that was?"

"I've been told it was an American program where U.S. advisers,

Republican agents, and village police assassinated local Viet Cong and VC sympathizers."

"Exactly. After the government agents gathered a list of names for a certain area, I would be called in to kill the leaders."

He paused a minute, as if debating whether or not to continue.

"Go on—please," I said and took his hand.

"So, as you can guess, I wound up killing a lot of people, Ly. A *lot* of people. Sometimes three or four a night, and occasionally as many as twenty. Mostly we used knives, because we didn't want to make noise. We'd slit their throats like chickens and leave them to die in the jungle. But that wasn't the worst of it. Sometimes we'd torture the target first—not to get information, but just because we hated those bastards so much. We'd cut off their ears or gouge out their eyes and take them back as evidence of the hit. If a guy really pissed us off, we'd cut off his dick and shove it in his mouth before we killed him. Our local agents always blamed these killings on the VC but I don't think many villagers believed it. We didn't care."

Cliff's voice quivered and he broke into tears. "I hated those motherfuckers—not just for being Commies and killing my buddies, but for making me do this to them! It was all their fault! It had to be their fault or I would've gone nuts! Maybe I went nuts anyway!"

His chest was heaving so hard now he couldn't talk. Tears streamed down his face and I held him in my arms—this big, confident, millionaire who wanted to take care of everyone and make the world perfect was now as helpless as a baby.

Cliff fished out his handkerchief and blew his nose. When he was more composed, he said, "Anyway, I got so good at my job, I was reassigned to the CIA. Their hits were more selective—big fish like Cho Lon, a rich Chinese guy who they thought was financing a local VC unit. Some of the people I hit, though, were eliminated just because they refused to go along with the program. The CIA was into a lot of bad shit in those days—drugs, gun-running, white slavery, you name it. Hell, one time another agent waxed the Vietnamese girl I was shacked up with. We were supposed to avoid close contact with any Vietnamese nationals outside channels, so they killed her— slashed her pretty little throat from ear to ear, can you believe it? I was really pissed—really angry. Of course, I took it out on my job. When I got a target, I didn't just take out the target; I included the poor bastard's wife and kids and housekeeper and gardener and anybody else unlucky enough to be around. I was in hell, Ly, pure hell. But I didn't know how to get out. All I knew was to keep on killing and the more I killed, the better I got at it and the more targets they gave me. Do you know what it's like being in a business like that? It's like being eaten inside out."

He wept for several minutes and I just held him. I couldn't think of anything to say or do. What could anyone say to salve this poor man's tortured soul? He was, in one person, the whole war—the whole experience: killer and victim.

"What's going to happen to me, Ly?" he sobbed. "I'm *so* afraid!"

I patted his back like a mother. "I don't know, Cliff. You are a Christian. You and Nancy go to church every Sunday. Maybe you can confess and find forgiveness with your God. As a Buddhist, I only know the laws of cause and effect: *Soi giay oan cuu, nghiep chuong nang me.* You have made very bad karma and your soul debt will come due, if not in this life, then another."

"Yes—you see!" He looked up and wiped his cheeks. "Now you know what all this has been about—the big house, the fancy car, helping Nancy and her family, helping you. It's the only way I know to put things right—big favors to right big wrongs."

I hugged him again and spoke like a different sort of mother. "Cliff, I understand, but I think you have it wrong. If you want to help me—help me finish my book and start a relief foundation—that's fine. But my mission doesn't need to be housed in a mansion. It doesn't need a big car to get around. Its house is the world—thatch roofs as well as tile. Its vehicles are the hearts and minds of people. Do you understand?"

"I'm trying to, Ly. I'm really trying." Cliff composed himself and washed his face. The phone rang and it was for Cliff, which was quite unusual at the La Mesa mansion. When he returned he said, "I have to go. Something unexpected has come up and it may be a while before I get back. I'm really glad we had this talk Ly. Thank you. We'll talk again."

I had learned by now not to ask questions when Cliff left.

On December 30, 1986, we had a Christmas and engagement party for about a hundred people. All my girlfriends came and we laughed and cried like the little kids we were before the war. I was Cinderella at the ball but had forgotten what happens after midnight.

A few days later, Cliff called. I answered the phone cheerily but he sounded terrible.

"I'm sorry, princess," he wheezed, "things got out of control."

"What are you talking about?" My breath caught in my throat. "Where are you?"

"I can't tell you. All I can say is that I'm in a hospital. I was beaten by a couple of guys."

"What? What happened? Did you get mugged? Does Nancy know?"

"God no! And she must never find out—about this, about Vietnam, about anything. She's not as strong as you are, Ly."

"What happened?"

"I can't tell you now. Maybe later. I just wanted you to know I was okay—to hear your voice again. I love you."

He hung up.

My mind raced with all the horrible possibilities I had carefully suppressed in the preceding weeks. *Was Cliff somehow still connected with the CIA? Even worse, was he involved with his ex-partners who went freelance after the war, smuggling guns and drugs and killing people for profit around the world?* That would certainly account for all the cash and his long, unexplained absences from home. It would also explain why people would beat him up and why he would have to lie low. No matter how hard I tried, I could not think of an innocent or even simple explanation for the behavior of this strange and complex man.

What was worse—for my sons and my own karma—by becoming Cliff's dependent, I had put myself and the future of my mission more and more in his power and my ability to fairly and clearly see my own situation was clouded by that dependence. I needed guidance and I needed it quick. I could not go to the police or the FBI—I had proof of nothing but my own bad judgment and wishful thinking. I decided that the best place to start would be my monk.

I phoned the temple and asked my *su* to visit. I knew he might have trouble swallowing my unbelievable story, and the huge, empty —and now evil-seeming—mansion would be eloquent testimony to this whole bizarre episode.

After a quick tour of each elegant and sterile room we adjourned to my loft, where my desk and typewriter and shrine were located— the room where I not only worked and read, but now often slept and took my meals. We prayed awhile and meditated, then I told him everything I knew about Cliff.

"Master," I concluded, "what will happen to his soul? I am very worried. His bad karma seems to be catching up with him. I feel I am only making things worse for him and for me."

"First, *phat tu,* you must make peace with your own troubled spirit. We have talked about this before, but perhaps only now do you see its truth. Hate and violence—rape and murder—are as much a part of the natural universe as birth and charity. Each is both a lesson in itself and an object for future lessons. A man who kills will suffer murder himself until he learns the lesson of nonviolence. Consequently, we should never hate thieves and killers, but offer them our compassion and a chance to learn about growth and giving."

As was so often the case, the monk's advice was undoubtedly true but short on solutions. I decided to call Annie, who had known Cliff from the beginning.

After hearing my story, she was almost as alarmed as I.

"He's definitely involved in something illegal," she said. "You should talk to my fiancé. He's a private detective and will know just what to do."

Unfortunately, Annie's fiancé, Jack, only poured gasoline on my smoldering fears. He checked the house with electronic equipment for "bugs" (it was clean) and even called over a bodyguard, a man as big as a tow truck with two automatic rifles!

This was too much.

"That's enough," I cried. "All of you—get out!"

Coincidentally, as soon as Jack and his goon left, Cliff called "just to check on us" but offered no information about where he was or what he was doing. I told him I couldn't live like this anymore and that I didn't want to see him again until he was ready to tell me what was going on. I then called Al and told him that I would probably be moving out. He sounded disappointed, but admitted that Cliff had some "unusual" ways of handling his business affairs. Still, Al wanted the sale to go through (the big La Mesa house was nearing the end of escrow) and reminded me of how well Cliff had treated me and my boys.

"I think you should give him a chance before you do anything rash," he said.

At two in the morning, the telephone rang. It was Cliff.

"Ly." His once strong, confident voice sounded chewed up and defeated. "I'm calling to say goodbye. This is the last time you'll ever hear from me. I hope you and the boys have a happy life. I hope all your dreams come true. Mine haven't. It's time to say goodbye."

The phone went dead. I had no idea where Cliff was calling from or if his fatalistic "goodbye call" meant he was about to be murdered or was going to leave the states in a hurry or what. But I did know someone who *might* know where he was or what was going on—a person who, at Cliff's request, had been left "out of the picture" too long. Still, I had to be careful.

I phoned an old friend in Escondido where Tommy was staying. Tommy was out, but I told his host I thought there might be problems at our old house—would he mind checking on Nancy and calling me back?

An hour later, he did.

"Ly," he said, "you were right. There's been a lot of trouble down there. I just talked to Pastor Sam, who's with the family. It seems Mr. Parry is in the hospital. He just tried to commit suicide."

I thanked him and hung up. Although the crisis seemed to be over, the mystery had only deepened. I hated to trouble Nancy, but I needed answers. I decided to see her the following afternoon and get to the bottom of things once and for all.

The next morning, though, a banging on the front door woke us up. It was Al.

"Where the hell is Cliff!" he demanded.

"He's in the hospital. Why?"

"It's nothing that concerns you, at least for the moment," he said brusquely. I had never seen Al so upset, let alone with Cliff. "Why is he in the hospital?"

"Apparently he tried to kill himself. Maybe you should tell me what's going on, Al. Please—come in and have some coffee. Calm down and let's see if we can work this out together."

Al's story was short but far from sweet. "Well, Ly, the deal for this house is dead. Everything's back in my name, including title to your old house in Escondido."

"What? Cliff and I haven't closed on that house! It still belongs to me! Even if something has happened with Cliff to make you change your mind about this deal, the Escondido house has nothing to do with it!"

"I'm afraid it does. Cliff's check bounced higher than a kite. I've got losses and claims—expenses to recover. I've put a lien against Cliff's assets. According to the county clerk, one of those assets is your house."

As soon as Al left, I called the escrow company.

"Yes," the officer said, "Mr. Parry was here with a notarized copy of your bank's deposit record for his down payment on the Escondido house—some twenty-five thousand dollars. We closed escrow on December nineteenth. Remember, you signed a form giving him permission to act on your behalf. Why—is anything wrong?"

Numb with disbelief, I called Pastor Sam, which was just as well, because he had been trying to contact me ever since Cliff's attempted suicide. In addition to being a clergyman, Sam was a Vietnam vet and marriage counselor who always struck me as a pretty straight shooter. We met at his home in Escondido.

"We have a lot to talk about, Ly," he said as he ushered me into his modest house. "About Cliff and what he's done to you and your family—and why."

"I know what he's done!" I said, not bothering to hide my anger. "He lied to everyone and stole my property!"

"Yes, and he regrets it deeply. More than you think. You know, this is his second attempted suicide. The first was a few weeks ago."

That explained his strange call from the hospital!

"The point is," Sam continued, "he's too ashamed of what he's done to explain things to you in person. He's asked me to do it for him in the hope that you'll forgive him."

"Go ahead, Sam, let me know the whole story."

It seems Cliff Parry was a professional swindler—a pathological liar and con man—with a long list of aliases. He had lawsuits filed against him by physicians, landscaping companies, three banks, a security company, and the owner of the big house in La Mesa—and that was just in California. He paid for his high-rolling lifestyle by covering the costs of one deal with the assets of the one before it. When it all finally caught up with him, he tried to take his own life. It was an old story, as old as war and money and corruption, and I couldn't believe I had walked right into it—this time as a victim. Sam answered all of my questions except one, which for me was perhaps the most important.

"Tell me, Sam, was Cliff ever in Vietnam?"

The clergyman shrugged. "Who knows? He's a very accomplished liar."

I felt myself uncoil inside. Cliff, or whatever his real name was, might have a lot to regret in his life, but slaughtering my people may not have been one of them. I could only hope and pray that his war stories, too, were a lie—but who could be sure?

I left Sam's house and went straight to my temple. I told my monk everything that had happened since our last meeting.

"So, *phat tu,*" he asked, "how do you feel?"

"I feel good that Cliff may not be a murderer. But I also feel stupid. I fell for a line of sugar-talk I would only have laughed at in Danang. Cliff saw all my weaknesses and knew just how to play them. Take a poor farm girl and give her a mansion—no questions asked. Take a crusader who wants to save the world and give her a sad war story with the promise to turn her dreams into reality. Take a mother who's worried about her fatherless sons and give them companionship and tickets to sporting events. I was a fool, master, ignoring every lesson I had learned in life. The only question I have now is why? Why did it happen to me and why did I go along with it?"

The monk did not chide me like a schoolmaster, but spoke softly the way a nurse comforts the sick. "Perhaps you had soul debt to repay in this area, my child. Perhaps you were a swindler in a past life. What's important now, though, is where all this has left you. Look into your heart. Has any man ever come into your life who did not have a lesson to teach: soldiers in your youth? Your husbands? Dan? Have any of these lessons been so bitter that you have not thanked these men later for helping to free you from *soi day oan nghiep*—your karmic soul debt?"

I left the temple and drove to the beach at Del Mar. The sun was setting and the beach was almost deserted. The sea wind was brisk, sending up horsetails of sand and salt spray along the horizon.

As the monk suggested, I thought about all the men in my life and the lesson they taught me. Yin and Yang, love and hate, woman and man—one needs the other to have meaning, to be complete. All my life to this point had been a search for that balance, that completeness.

As a child, I was taught to venerate my elders and subordinate myself to a husband. I would care for his family and he would care for me. That was not the life I found. After having been raped at fourteen, I could forget about ever having a man or a family of my own. Of dire necessity, I learned the ways of men myself—to survive and provide. But to be independent, I also learned, was not to forswear companionship. Even a lone wolf has a mate, and I never gave up hope of finding mine.

I also had bad karma to contend with. Even if I had not been a soldier or torturer or rapist or cheater in past lives, each man that I met with those marks had, in some way, prevented me from going on to something worse. The Republican and Viet Cong soldiers abused me, but they put me on a path away from war. Anh took advantage of me, but he put me on a path that led toward Ed and to America. Because I knew family love as a girl, I felt its loss in this alien land even more acutely and let that pain obscure the lessons I had learned. Dan rescued me from my mistake with Ed and taught me womanly love, but, had we stayed together, his own bad karma would have taken me a step backward toward war. Dennis, despite our trouble, kept me from Dan, and I can only thank Dennis for that. Is Cliff, who taught me a final lesson about trust and charity, any less worthy of gratitude?

Everyone searches for something to make his or her life complete. I thought I needed a man to fill the void created by the loss of my native land, my family, my innocence. What I discovered, though, was the nature of my own true higher self: that it is my karma to love mankind better than any one particular man. This revelation did not turn the men of my life into saints, but it made me realize they were not devils. Who am I to ignore my father's voice and his example? Who am I to betray my teachers?

I drove home and gathered the boys for a family meeting.

"The police say we weren't the only people Cliff took advantage of," I told them. "They want to know if I'm going to press charges. You are all young men now. What do you think I should do?"

Jimmy, the oldest at twenty, spoke first. "I don't think it's worth it. Cliff has no money left and even if you win a lawsuit, what will you have gained? We're pretty well off compared to his family. We still have two houses and a car and enough to eat. Remember how you felt when you got back from Vietnam?"

Jimmy's views fit mine perfectly, but I wanted to hear from my other boys, too.

"Tommy?"

His handsome face darkened, "I think we should slash his tires and break his windows. I hate the Parrys! I think we should really pay them back for what they did!"

I let Tommy speak his mind and did not interrupt. His Phung warrior blood is strong and passion is the province of youth. When he was finished, I turned to twelve-year-old Alan.

He looked up, sad-eyed, like a little old man and said, "I don't know, Mom. Don't we have enough troubles now? I don't think we should make any more."

Tears filled my eyes—tears of hope and love and gratitude. How many eons of needless karmic suffering had Dennis and Cliff saved little Alan? I began to suspect that the body of my youngest son harbored a very old soul.

"Then I think we have decided," I said, wiping my eyes. "If we go after Cliff, we will only be keeping past hurt alive. We would be wiser to bury our pain and start over. Each time we have done so in the past, we've been better off, isn't that right?"

The boys agreed, even Tommy.

Al evicted us from the big fortress at La Mesa just as he had evicted Nancy and her children from my old home in Escondido. I gave him title to the house just to escape its liens and debts, including the biggest of all: Cliff's soul debt, *soi day oan nghiep*. The Parrys moved in with Pastor Sam and lived off the charity of their neighbors. Cliff soon faced civil and criminal consequences for his acts. All his victims and creditors, except one, pressed him unmercifully for retribution, took what little he had, and put him in jail for a long time.

The one exception was me.

I sold my San Diego house and bought a smaller home in the hills of Escondido. It was not too far from my old neighborhood, but with a view that expanded my horizons. It was also close to an old Indian burial ground, and its great spiritual energy gave my tired soul new strength and inspiration.

Cinderella had turned back into a pumpkin. But for an old Danang farm girl, it really wasn't so bad.

TEN

Ghosts from the Past

THE EPISODES with Dan and Cliff convinced me that if I was truly going to make humanity the object of my love, my life's companion, I would have to become a better student of "cause and effect" —of seeing things as they actually are.

One of those things for which I gained a clearer perspective was the art, as well as the soul, of writing a book. In dictating the rough draft of my story to Jimmy, I relived every moment of pain and terror as the words left my lips. Although simply saying "I was terrified" or "I was sad" was enough to reawaken those feelings in me, it did not always do so for others. The feedback I had gotten from publishers only confirmed that living through a harrowing story is a different challenge from communicating it to readers.

I had been working with different writers to express my story in a way that was close to how I felt it—but without much luck. I finally found such a writer in Jay Wurts, a man about my age but with a very "old soul"—a person who, in my opinion at least, had seen enough karmic cycles to understand what my story was about, feel what I had felt, and live those feelings on paper.

While publishers perused our revised book proposal, I turned all my energy to the foundation. I learned a lot more about the way charitable institutions worked, raised money, coordinated effort, and found willing hearts and hands in faraway places. With my friends and alone, I went to lectures sponsored by all kinds of humanitarian organizations. Whenever possible, I volunteered to help with fund-raising events—luncheons, seminars, and dinners—to learn how efficient organizations worked.

Once, I went to hear an old man talk about how mothers should protest against nuclear arms. His speech put into words many things I had felt for twenty years: that mothers were the guardians of life on the planet, that their sons and daughters should not be used as pawns in the mortal struggles of ambitious men. I was further astonished to learn that this kindly old fellow who spoke with such intensity had been put into jail *five times* during the Vietnam War for saying much the same thing. Most of all, I learned from Dr. Benjamin Spock that you can't make a splash unless you jump in the pool—that all that evil needs to flourish is for good people to do nothing.

I was also intrigued by a group called Youth Ambassadors of America (YAA) that specialized in "citizen diplomacy"—improving relations between the United States and the Soviet Union through direct people-to-people contact. It was impossible to live in the United States and not know that the "evil empire" of the Soviets was viewed by many as the source of most trouble in the modern world. I still had no clear idea of what "communism" really was, except that it seemed opposed to the system allowing me to improve my life in the United States and that it was terrified of the free speech we enjoyed. If I were forced by circumstances to do my Vietnam relief work in cooperation with (or at least without the obstruction of) a Communist government, I felt I should know a little more about it. What better classroom could there be than one-on-one contact with the people who invented that system?

The three thousand dollars needed to participate in a teachers' delegation to the western Soviet Union tore a great hole in my five thousand dollars of life savings. However, the knowledge and contacts I would gain gave me courage to take such a risk (or at least justified the foolishness!).

YAA's route into this vast and ancient land was indirect—through Finland, a country that, like Thailand, made its fortune by being in between. Although I had been advised to dress warmly, the notions of cold to our Moscow hosts and a California tourist were as different as the systems that governed them. My coat, adequate for tepid San Diego winters, let the vicious wind from Central Asia bite me to the bone. As a result, most of what I saw of Russia was from behind the frosted windows of trains, buses, and hotels.

Like every other nation, the heart and soul of the Soviet Union seemed defined by its wars—especially World War II. While my countrymen and the French were resisting (or toiling under) the Japanese, the Soviets were sacrificing a whole generation to stop Hitler's war machine. Few countries could have endured the terrible losses and privation caused by the Great Patriotic War (as the Soviets called World War II)—which were not unlike the sacrifices and hardships demanded of the Vietnamese in the French and American conflicts. Like the trees in the great forests, the struggles the Russians survived in their youth seem to give them strength in their maturity. The laws of karma dictate that something good must be in store for both nations.

In Leningrad or Moscow, the picture was the same: clean streets, hardy workers, imposing but soulless buildings, long lines and empty shelves. At every stop we met families who offered us food and drink they couldn't spare. Their true gift, however, was their friendship. Our pretty Russian guide, who had just returned from a tour of America, summed it up best:

"American women are nice, but very spoiled. They are like darling little children who don't know what they have until they have to do without it. As for the men, they are free to say and do anything they wish, but they do little but stay at home and complain about their government. Believe me, freedom that is not used is no freedom at all. Why they make themselves prisoners of their own idleness is beyond me."

For me, the highlight of the trip was our visit to several Soviet schools and afterward, an audience with a pair of highly placed officials. To my surprise, the kids performed flawless skits of *Pinocchio* and *The Wizard of Oz*. The children, clad in neat navy blue uniforms and red scarves, were very curious about America. We had an opportunity to clear up many misconceptions about our country generated by TV in both the United States and the Soviet Union. We told them that the newsreels and movies depicting demonstrators, unemployment lines, drug busts, and mass murderers were noteworthy precisely because they were exceptions. We felt it was a tribute to the American people that they kept their troubles, rather than just their accomplishments, in front of their eyes so that their problems might be solved and not forgotten.

The teachers said the main trouble with Soviet TV was that real problems went unreported in order to show the people as "one big happy Soviet family." I realized now that the same thing went on in Vietnam, and not just because of the Communists. It is an old Oriental tradition to keep your troubles "in the family"—*tot khoe xau che*—show only what's good and hide the bad. It was the first time I really appreciated the significance of the painful newscasts I used to watch with the Munros at the height of the Vietnam War. Problems that were out of sight were quickly "out of mind," which helped no one but the mischief makers who profit from such problems, no matter what the country.

In our later meeting with the government officials, we asked questions and exchanged views of a more general nature: about economic reform, cultural exchange, war and peace. I asked our hosts: "I am a Vietnamese American who grew up in the war zone. Not long ago, I returned from a visit to my homeland and was shocked by how poor it was. During the war, America gave billions of dollars in weapons and assistance to the South and you gave the North billions of rubles in weapons and supplies. Now the U.S. and the Soviet Union are becoming friendlier. My question is: What happened to Vietnam? Neither country seems to remember the Vietnamese—to want to help them out—now that the war is over."

One official said apologetically, "We're doing the best we can—we still send aid and advisers—but as you can see, we have problems of our own. Your adoptive country, on the other hand, not only refuses to help, it actively stands in the way of nations who want to try. It prevents the World Bank from making loans to the Vietnamese and discourages allied nations from trading with their old enemy. Perhaps you can do something as an American citizen to get your government to reconsider its policy. We would like nothing better than to see our old friends in Vietnam and our new friends in America shake hands and forget their past difficulties, as they have done with the Germans and Japanese."

I realized that two officials did not make a government and a few school kids and "sanctioned host families" did not represent a nation. But we all came away with the same basic impression: that the cold war was something invented by generals and politicians, not peasants, workers, and businessmen. Communism and capitalism—neither was better or worse than the people who governed or tolerated each system. Left to themselves, the average person knows very well what it takes to make a better life. I never once heard a person on either side say that war and hate were the necessary ingredients.

Back in San Diego, I volunteered to be a YAA sponsor for an American visit by two Soviet children. It cost three hundred dollars, which I couldn't afford by myself, so it was an early test of my fund-raising abilities. I was pleased to discover that many people who could not be sponsors were happy to support others who would.

Ivan and Niklaus were young teenagers who did not have the showcase children's mastery of English, so I felt their encounter with America would be genuine and relatively free of prejudice. They went sightseeing and lived with me and Tommy and Alan (just like our foster family!) for two weeks. Unlike our Vietnamese wards, though, their blond hair and blue eyes and new American clothes let them blend easily with the native surfers at the warm San Diego beaches that, next to the well-stocked supermarkets, proved their favorite attraction. Jimmy gave them a farewell party at a friend's house in Del Mar and they took back to their capital two tangible signs of at least this one little thaw in the cold war: a pair of San Diego Padres baseball caps and a ball and bat for organizing the "great American pastime" in Moscow's frozen parks.

Just before New Years, 1987, my agent called to tell me our proposal had sold.

My book had sold!

I broke down crying. The silent echoes of all the suffering people —not just me and my family, but Vietnamese peasants everywhere— would finally be given a voice. Whether or not my story would be noticed by anyone important, whether it would change any lives or not, whether or not I would even be around to see it in print was immaterial. What mattered was that my American "brothers and sisters"—people like Mom Munro and Erma and Dennis's sister and the cashier at Safeway and anybody else who could read—would now have access to a hidden side of their own national experience. My paddy had become the printed page. I had sowed thoughts and feelings like rice and in return reaped words to nourish my readers' spirit.

I had accomplished my father's business. I knew he would be pleased.

I now felt secure about my future and the progress of my mission. My attorney, Milton Low, filed papers to incorporate my nonprofit organization under the name of East Meets West. I began immediately to plan a return to Vietnam. I had three goals.

First, I wanted to take stock of the medical needs of my home province, Quang Nam. I had discovered that people who were reluctant to donate money for anonymous "good works" were more than happy to sign a check for a specific project or piece of medical equipment.

Second, I needed to find out which officials gave permission for what activities. In my last visit, my brother Bon Nghe offered to help, but with the labyrinth of ministries, bureaucracies, and officials, even he didn't know where to start.

Finally, I wanted desperately to complete some unfinished business: to return to my home village of Ky La—to burn incense at my father's shrine and sleep in the house he had built with his own two hands. Although, like the first trip, I would be traveling unaccompanied, I knew I would not be alone. This time I felt not only my father's spirit, but the buoyant spiritual energy of a million souls who were counting on me to tell their story.

At the travel agency, I met a Vietnamese woman, a little older than I, who was making her first trip back into the country. She was scared to death, but, as I had been, was driven to persevere. When I told her who I was and where I had been last year, and that I was going back soon, she burst into tears and begged me to go with her.

At first I told her she was just being silly and tried reassuring her with comforting words. Then it occurred to me: paranoia feeds on just such words, such conflicting stories. The more I tried to convince her that her worries were false, the more suspicious she became. The same was true with the veterans I had talked to during the past few years. The same was true with early drafts of my book. Words are cheap. Actions mean everything.

I told her I would be willing to delay my trip for a day or two and accompany her into the country. I empathized greatly with this woman's terror and if such an easy sacrifice on my part would sooth a sister's spirit, it was cheap at twice the price. As things turned out, that little delay would profoundly change the course of my mission, if not my life.

With an extra day at my disposal, I tried to contact the Ohio chapter of the Vietnam Veterans of America, the VVA. According to a newspaper article, they would be visiting Vietnam at about the same time. I had learned from my other volunteer work that "cooperative" ventures among smaller humanitarian groups often made the difference between mere good intentions and results. I also believed that, with my book due out the next year, the time was right to make East Meets West known to like-minded Americans. Unfortunately, I failed to get through to the VVA organizers, and for good reason. They had already left for California on the first leg of their journey. Fate brought us together quite by accident on the big jet to Bangkok.

Don Mills, leader of the fifteen returning GIs, was not your typical Vietnam Vet activist. Bearded but well groomed, tall and soft-spoken, with a glance that was at once cryptic and pleading, he had the look of a determined dreamer. I introduced myself to him and he introduced me to his group.

For most, it was their first time "back across the pond." Like my Vietnamese companion, they were suitably worried—not for legal or political reasons, but of their own reactions to the past.

One of the three women touring with the group was Barbara Cohen, a trim, strong, ex-army psychiatrist with feathered gray-brown hair. Because of her gender, her profession, and her knowledge of war, we had an instant and good rapport. Being a successful female in institutions dominated by men, she had learned long ago to master her own feelings. She was also writing two books: a novel telling the war from the Vietnamese perspective, and a Vietnam guidebook for Americans she hoped would follow in her footsteps. We were kindred spirits.

One of Don's vets had been back many times: Bill Fero, a man of great heart, a big smile, powerful arms, and no legs. He had managed to put the hell of war and his own great suffering behind him years ago and I admired him greatly for that. Even more, he used his reservoir of strength to help vets or veterans' families on both sides who had been broken by the war. His formula was simple: "I tell them I forgive them, then ask them to forgive me. Sometimes we go through hell to get there but it's always worth it. Vietnam cost me a lot but it's given back a lot more."

Bill lost his legs to a Viet Cong mine "south of Danang" somewhere near my village. I remembered, as a child, making booby traps for American and Republican soldiers: shallow holes filled with sharpened bamboo stakes or nails that we hoped would defeat the enemy's thick boots. The traps using metal nails were often found by mine detectors and since I seldom handled explosives, I doubted that Bill's misfortune was directly due to me. Still, at that moment, I felt as though I had pulled the tripwire myself.

"So, how do the Vietnamese treat a GI who lost his legs to them?" I asked.

Bill was able to laugh. "My reception was a big surprise. I thought everybody would hate me because of what I represented. You have to remember, the last time I saw the country was through the door of a gunship over two bloody stumps. My legs were lying somewhere out there in the elephant grass. I hated every Vietnamese—North and South—because I thought I was going to die. After I knew I was going to live, and *how* I was going to live, I hated them even more. By the time I got out of the hospital, I hated everybody who had anything to do with the war, including most Americans. I guess I first went back to Vietnam hoping for a confrontation—hoping I could show how I whipped them, at least psychologically. Boy, was I wrong. They treated me like a king—like a favorite uncle." His face froze in a smile but tears started down his cheeks. He wiped them gruffly, with a farmer's hand. "I thought, One trip to kill the ghosts and that's it. Now I'm on my third visit. Who'd have thought it?"

Later, Bill confessed how this transformation took place.

"After my discharge, I went back to my family's farm in Wisconsin. You don't see too many farmers in wheelchairs, so you can imagine how tough it was at first. I was really bitter. Anyway, in 1975, after the fall of the South, the refugees started to arrive and I sponsored as many of them as I could. I wanted them to work on my farm—but not for the reasons you think. I wanted to get those little bastards under my thumb so I could pay them back for what they made me go through. Jesus—I was a real asshole! I made those motherfuckers work from dawn till dusk for starvation wages. I cussed them and threatened them and told them I'd send them back to the Commies if they didn't do everything right. And you know what? The tougher I was on them the more they tried to please me. Hell, to them I was a savior and could do no wrong. Maybe they thought they had to do penance for losing their country, I don't know. Anyway, I started to see that these people were victims just like me. The big difference was, they were trying to get on with their lives and make something of themselves while I was just refighting the war. That's when I got the idea of going back to Vietnam, to give myself the final test. By the time I got back to the States, I knew that the Vietnamese were my brothers and sisters. I'm not kidding. I love these people like my own family."

I had tears in my own eyes now and clutched Bill's hand. "So, it's your third trip. What do you plan to do now?"

"Whatever I can. Each visit I bring in some medicine and clothes and help out at a big orphanage in Saigon, but it's just a drop in the bucket. Until the U.S. government drops its trade and travel restrictions, we'll just be putting Band-Aids on a gator bite."

Passing through Vietnamese customs sobered me. Once word had gotten around in the Vietnamese community that I was going back again, I was besieged by Viet Kieu who wanted me to hand-carry letters to their relatives: letters bearing messages and photos and thoughts the senders were unwilling to entrust to censoring postal officials. Many of these people wanted to spike their letters with green cash or gold leaf for *li xi nam moi*—good luck for Tet—which means I would have to smuggle the letters sewn into my garments or in the lining of my suitcase. It was a common practice, but I refused.

I did not want to run afoul of the authorities and risk everything I was trying to start with my foundation. And some of the senders were more interested in profit than charity. It was usual for Viet Kieu couriers to charge a percentage rebate or service fee for every hundred dollars they smuggled into the country, or to convert their greenbacks to *dong* on the black market, which paid higher rates, then remit the proceeds to the beneficiary at the official exchange rate, thereby increasing the profit. Sometimes the courier just hijacked the shipment or replaced a valuable piece of jewelry with one of lesser value so that the relative could still report that "the cookies arrived safely" if that was their codeword for a diamond ring.

Anyway, the Vietnamese customs officials were very strict about this and were even stricter and more wary of me on my second trip, so I made no effort to hide my one thousand dollars in Tet money (some Viet Kieu came with as much as thirty thousand!) and the twenty-eight letters I carried. I invited the officials to inspect each of them for cash or contraband, which they did. You'd think that they would encourage Viet Kieu to send in as much of anything they wanted, including greenbacks, and just tax it, so that the citizens and the government would both get much needed foreign exchange, but that was not their style. In a society where absolute obedience was the measure of success, not material or physical or spiritual health, such policies made perfect sense.

"Why don't you tell us the truth, Miss Ly," the inspector said. "We don't want any trouble with our returning countrymen. You have many letters but little cash. That doesn't make sense."

"I told you, brother, I came for Tet, not to deal on the black market. Please, search again if you want to, but I have nothing more to declare."

They continued to riffle through my things and yet a third inspector came over. They just couldn't believe I was as poor (or stingy) as I appeared and things were quickly deteriorating into a war of wills.

"Why do you carry all these letters if you do not bring cash?" the third official asked.

"Next week is Tet. If my friends had mailed the letters, they would've arrived too late. It was the least I could do."

"Then you don't know what's in the letters? How do you know it's not subversive propaganda?"

"No, my friends would never do that."

"How do you know? I'm sorry, we'll have to confiscate the letters and check them thoroughly." The official gestured toward a glass-enclosed office. He said, *"Moi chi di hop*—Step over here so we can talk."

I couldn't believe this was happening! The other inspectors followed with my belongings.

Inside the little office, a fourth official, obviously a supervisor, wrote out a citation on brittle brown paper and handed it to me.

"Here you are, Miss Ly," he said. "I'm afraid I have to cite you for *lam trai luat chinh phu.*" Which could mean almost anything—literally, it was a "general misdemeanor against the government."

"You will have to appear in court, downtown in Ho Chi Minh City, on this date. Of course, if you simply tell us where you've hidden the money, I can tear up the ticket."

I stared at the citation in disbelief. "I wish I had something to show you, brother. But in truth, you've already seen everything. There is simply nothing more I can do."

"That's very well for you to say," the senior man said, "but what if we find more cash or contraband? What do you think will happen then?"

"I would pay for my crime, of course. But I won't have to pay because I haven't done anything wrong." I would have asked *Why don't you believe me?* but I knew already why he didn't. Mistrust—paranoia—was standard operating procedure. While we were talking, the other agents had already started work on my things: disassembling the little tape recorder I'd brought for Tinh and squeezing out all my toothpaste—a favorite hiding place for jewels.

"What's this?" one inspector asked, holding up a metal can.

"If you bring hot water," I said, getting angry now, as well as scared, "I'll make you some very nice coffee—*ngon lam,* delicious French roast, unless you think that's too subversive."

After three hours of tedious searching, which included breaking the heels of every shoe I'd packed, the senior officer finally said, "Okay, take her away."

I was led into a sparsely furnished room without windows of any kind—never a good sign. Inside was a nice, fatherly man in his late fifties. He offered me a seat. His pleasant voice was a refreshing change from his comrades' increasingly belligerent tone.

"I'm sorry for this unfortunate, episode, Miss Ly," he said. "It is not the sort of reunion we try to make with our *con em Viet Kieu*—daughters who live overseas. But you'll agree, the black market is a terrible thing. There was too much of it during the war and there's too much of it now. That's the only reason we're being so harsh. We all have better things to do. Now, if you just tell us the truth, show us or tell us where the money is hidden, I'll sign this pass and you can be on your way. No citation, no fines, no court hearing, nothing. It will be as if all this never happened."

I sank back in my chair. This was just like the interrogations at the district jail when I was a girl. I had been alternately beaten and cajoled, given pain and then relief, to make me cooperate. Then, as now, I felt righteously innocent. I also recalled how irrelevant that innocence was.

"Bac, con noi roi—Uncle, I've already told you, I have no more money."

The man looked very disappointed, got up, and walked out. Two women came in immediately and ordered me to disrobe. They didn't carry rubber hoses or electric prods, so I felt better and complied. Still, taking off your clothes before strangers is one of the most humiliating things you can do in a peasant culture, where our dignity and the clothes on our backs are often our only possessions. The two matrons, obviously big-city police girls, showed me no mercy, just hard stares until I complied with their orders. They checked my shirt, slacks, bra, and underpants, then had me spreadeagle against the wall and inspected me thoroughly where even doctors are quick to finish.

When they were through, one slid my wadded-up clothes across the table and ordered me to get dressed. The other went to the door.

"Khong co gi het anh a!—We found nothing, brother," she called.

A moment later I was back in the front office. The senior official was gone, but an underling pointed to my suitcases, which looked like a bomb had exploded in them, and told me I could repack. I gave them all dirty looks and shoved my things together as fast as I could. I had just finished repacking and stepped outside the office with my belated customs clearance when they announced the arrival of the second flight from Bangkok—the one containing the rest of the VVA party.

"What happened, Ly?" Don asked, pushing Bill's wheelchair past the customs table. I was the last person they expected to see at the airport. "Are you okay? Did anything happen? Did they want money from you?"

I gritted my teeth and felt tears pool in my eyes. I wanted to cuss out the small-minded bureaucrats, but that would not have encouraged these nervous-enough GIs. "Yes, something happened, but nothing important. I'm okay. It's no big deal. I've been through a lot worse."

That was true enough, but I still felt raped by the matrons and the whole paranoid system. After telling the truth unsuccessfully for three hours, I only wished my tormentors had been by Bill's wheelchair to hear me lie so effectively on their behalf. What angered me most, perhaps, was the fact that Viet Kieu wishing to smuggle in big amounts of cash could still do so by bribing the officials, so little fish like me got all the hassle. We had a saying during the war: Robbers are those who steal at night; those who steal in broad daylight are called officials!

These officials were young men and women about the age of my Jimmy and Tommy. Denied a decent family upbringing, the state was their parent and they liked to put on airs, particularly in front of seemingly wealthy Americans. It was all so unnecessary, stupid, and wrong.

As I left the terminal, I was pleasantly surprised to see familiar faces pressed against the picture window: Anh, Jimmy's father; Yen, his second wife who had been my cordial hostess during my first visit; and several of their children.

We greeted each other like the old friends we had become and Anh asked *what the hell* had happened to me at customs for the last three hours. I told an even more abbreviated and sanitized version of my story while we went to the bus—a big difference from the limousine Anh used to take to and from the airport during the American occupation!

After helping Yen with dinner and putting the kids to bed, I begged off and went to bed myself, although sleep was a long time coming. I was hurt and angry over the confiscated letters that had been entrusted to me. Now the twenty-eight local families would have to pay all kinds of "official fees" to hear their beloved relatives' voices—assuming the letters were even delivered. I could already hear some of my friends complaining behind my back, "What's with Ly? She refused to take money to our families, then dumps the letters as soon as we're out of sight! What kind of friendship is that?"

I was even more concerned about my "court summons." Even if the case was dismissed, such documents had a way of hanging around —a black mark they could use against me. If there was one thing Vietnam's oppressive bureaucracy did well, it was keep very thorough records. If I was to be given this kind of reception on every trip, I would never be able to get complex medical equipment, perishable medicine, crates of bandages, and a hundred other items through to the people who needed them. If my relief supplies were to be detained or confiscated and I was to be treated like a criminal, my good works would be stopped before they started.

When I finally fell asleep, I dreamed I was beside the Vinh Dien River as it coursed, swollen with rain from the winter monsoon, toward Danang harbor and the sea. I was about nine years old, as I often was in my dreams of home, and felt full up with anger. I picked up one stone after another from the riverbank and threw it with all my force into the raging water. Each stone was larger than the next and I had to creep farther down toward the deadly current in order to reach and throw it. By the time my feet and face were wet and the biggest rock of all was in my hand, I felt strong fingers grab my waist and pull me up the bank.

My father plunked me down in a stand of grass and took my little face firmly in his hands.

"Bay Ly—what do you think you're doing? *Dung gian nguoi dam bung minh*—don't stab yourself to punish someone else! When you pull the tiger's whiskers, don't you expect him to growl?"

"Yes, Father," I cried, and probably out loud from the couch in Anh's living room.

"Besides," he continued, "who knows better than you how young men and women behave when they're given uniforms to replace their rags. Go home now and get to work in the paddy."

The stone slipped from my hand and I hugged my father.

The VVA group assembled in the lobby of their hotel precisely at eight the next morning. My Viet Kieu companion was supposed to go with us, but she never showed up and I wasn't worried. She looked a lot less anxious after clearing customs and I knew what family reunions were like. If she "forgot" our morning rendezvous and side trip, I was the last person who would hold it against her.

Our first stop, as it is for all Saigon visitors, was the infamous "Orphanage No. 6," home to Vietnam's most physically and emotionally damaged children, after which we went on to Orphanage No. 1, Nha Tre Mam Non, a larger, sister institution on the outskirts of Saigon. Its scarce resources were barely sufficient for the care and feeding of the inmates, so the physical grounds were neglected and made it a depressing place to grow up—for those lucky enough to make it. As we entered, Bill pointed to one of the three fat milk cows grazing by the rusty iron gate.

"See that cow?" he said like a proud dad. "Our last tour group pooled its cash and bought it for the kids. Turned out it was in foal, so now the kids have a calf to care for. Give love and get milk in return. Pretty good deal, huh?"

Inside the compound pale blue paint peeled from chipped concrete walls below a heavily patched roof. The children who greeted us had well-trimmed bangs and scrubbed faces. They were wearing their best hand-me-down clothes topped with the obligatory red kerchief.

When they finished a cheery song of greeting, the director, a fifty-ish woman named Nhu and our translator (a thin fellow who looked too young to have been a fighter but old enough to have seen the war) welcomed us formally and showed us to the reception area for morning tea.

"This whole place was made possible by Americans," Nhu said in Vietnamese, followed by the young man's English translation. "The teachers, supplies, and food were all donated through the Catholic church. During the war, many wealthy Vietnamese sent their children to parochial school here because it had American teachers."

Don asked her what she had done to earn such a responsible position.

"I was a teacher here myself, as well as a Viet Cong agent. I would note whatever the rich children said about their parents' activities and pass it on through channels. You'd be surprised how much we learned about the government's war effort through these innocent eyes and ears, although a lot of it got distorted, as you would expect. After the war, my service was honored by Hanoi and I was given the directorship."

I remembered my own experiences as a schoolgirl during the war, not all of them so pleasant. Both sides tried to exploit the children and forced them to participate in "patriotic" war games and political rallies. By day we would play "government soldier" and pretend to kill the VC, parading around with placards honoring President Diem. By night we would sing revolutionary songs and have our deeds (minor sabotage or spying) noted on the VC's "blackboard of honor." Instead of indoctrinating us to one side or the other, which was the organizers' intent, such tactics only made us view the war as a game—a game, that is, until we saw our loved ones killed. At least the kids in this school, pitiful orphans though they were, did not wake up to thundering artillery or spend endless nights watching insects wriggle through the dirt wall of a family bunker.

After tea, we took a tour of the facility. It was like a run-down summer camp between sessions. The wooden tables and benches were scarred, and rickety bunkbeds and wooden cribs filled the dormitory rooms. But there were no games, sporting equipment, or echoes of happy memories trapped within the walls. Toward the back was the saddest sight of all: the "factory" where older kids (and most of the crippled orphans, some deformed by Agent Orange) made rice paper for sale to government and private buyers. Part of the facility was upstairs on a mezzanine, which was a problem for Bill in his wheelchair. Without a word from their director, a group of bigger kids gently lifted his wheelchair to the landing. The rest of us were speechless with emotion.

We ended our tour where we began, in the tea room by Don's gift cows and a new water pump purchased by other American benefactors. Here, under the glare of lights from a veteran's video camera, Don made the formal presentation of his group's gift—cases of medicine and vitamins and candy. I put a hundred dollars on top of one box and added a few words to Don's, but the gifts spoke more eloquently than either of us.

Miss Nhu made a gracious speech of acceptance, ending her remarks with a plea for better U.S.-Vietnamese relations. We were all a little stunned at the warm feelings vibrating through the room, as if the war—and all the tragedy around us—had never happened.

As she finished, a curious thing happened. Our translator, who previously had relayed the words in a calm and businesslike way, suddenly covered his face and broke down weeping. Don, standing closest, looked bewildered, then tears rolled down his cheeks too. He took the young Vietnamese into his arms and cradled him like a baby. The video lights snapped off. Everybody sniffed back tears, then applauded when the young man, composed and smiling now, pulled back, blotted his eyes with a handkerchief, and finished his translation.

On the morning of my "court summons," I took a *siclo* to customs headquarters, an old cement building on the Saigon river. The judge said he did not have enough "evidence" to decide the case, and ordered me to go home and prepare a *tuong trinh*—a written report that described the incident from my perspective. This was not the way I had planned to spend my limited time in Saigon, but I had no choice. Along with many other Western amenities, the new regime does not believe in lawyers.

I dashed off a four-page report that, while not mincing words, at least concealed my contempt for the whole process. I brought it back to the judge that same afternoon, hoping for a speedy dismissal. Instead, he scowled at the pages and told me to return for his verdict in the morning.

The next day, the judge came into his chamber with great ceremony and took out my file, which already looked alarmingly thick.

"Why did you carry all these letters into the country?" he asked, waving the bundle.

"As favors to friends. If they went through the post, they could not arrive before Tet."

He frowned and replied, "You claim you didn't read them. If you didn't read them, how do you know they're not *phan dong*—reactionary propaganda?"

"My friends would never do such things."

"Well, if they did, you would be fined heavily and thrown into prison. Did you ever think about that?"

"I have thought about it constantly. That's why I have chosen my friends so carefully."

The judge leafed through some of the letters which, as we both knew, had been thoroughly screened by others. He saw plainly that nothing subversive was involved. Still, I could see he had no intention of letting me go scot-free.

"Well, I see one violation, anyway."

My eyes popped open. "What's that?"

"These letters are international mail. By hand-carrying them into the country, you have evaded the lawful postage. I hereby fine you the equivalent value of the stamps these letters would have used. Case closed."

After Saigon's trial of the century, the group and I traveled to Danang where we temporarily parted company. I could not afford a hotel and Tinh had agreed to put me up, despite the gossip of her neighbors. She thought living in her ramshackle house would involve a sacrifice on my part, but nothing was further from the truth. What millionaire wouldn't prefer a family's warmth to a cold and empty mansion?

My niece greeted me at the door with a kid on each arm. It was a heartwarming sight, though I still had trouble picturing the skinny little peasant girl I grew up with as a mother of six.

Tinh said she told "Grandma Phung" I was coming home for the holiday, which was now a day away, so my mother had come up from the village. She was out visiting friends, so Tinh and I went to the market.

The old Danang market was jammed as usual with vendors and shoppers, although there were few goods to buy and even less money to be spent. The *spirit* of Tet was the thing. A couple of Tinh's neighbors greeted us coolly but Tinh told them my visit would bring good luck for Tet—although the aroma of *banh tac banh chung* (sticky

rice in banana leaves), *mi quang* (Central Coast noodles with pork
and shrimp), and *xao* (vegetable chow mein) wafting through the
street did more to put them in a holiday mood than my big smile. I
drank in the festive aroma of fragrant flowers and the sweet smoke of
burnt offerings from bubbling stovepipe chimneys. I also drank some
country fruit juice, which would turn out to be a big mistake.

My mother was home when we got back. She acted as though I
had never left from my visit the year before.

"Wipe your feet, Bay Ly," she groused, bent like a gnome over her
tied-straw broom, "I just swept by the door!"

"How are you, Mama Du?" I dropped my bundles and gave her a
big hug and kiss. Unlike our first reunion, she did not pull away. I
knew my sisters Hai and Ba (and Ba's family) would be over later,
but Tinh had said nothing about my brother. "Where's Bon Nghe?"

My mother avoided my glance. "He moved to the South last
month. I don't think he'll be coming this year." I suspected, given the
coldhearted bureaucracy, it was probably more difficult for my beloved brother to return a few hundred miles for Tet than it had been
for me to cross thousands of miles of ocean.

After dinner and a good visit with my sisters, I began to feel sick.
My stomach had been nervous all day and at bedtime the dull ache
exploded like Tet fireworks. I emptied myself from both ends all
night, and when it was time to catch the VVA bus to the city of Hue,
which I had never seen and was anxious to visit, I could only lie weak
and exhausted in my bed.

Unfortunately, many of the vets still harbored deep fears and anger
about Hue, the scene of the heaviest fighting during the North's
infamous 1968 Tet Offensive. This deceptively beautiful city on the
legendary Perfume River had been the site of a terrible month-long
battle. One of my foster children's best friends, in fact, had lost his
parents in this massacre, and my own father committed suicide not
long thereafter. The Tet Offensive was for him and many other
Vietnamese what Gettysburg had been for the Confederacy in the
American Civil War: the beginning of the end. The VC considered
Tet their worst defeat. For many Americans, however, it removed the
last traces of patriotic self-delusion that said their all-powerful country was somehow destined to win no matter what. It was a typical
paradox in a war famous for turning things upside down. I had
promised Don and Bill, rain or shine, I would be there to help
translate, cope, and counsel.

A few hours after the bus had left, I felt well enough to drag myself out of bed, pack my things, and kiss my mother goodbye. Sick stomach aside, I felt bad leaving in the middle of the holiday, and promised to return as soon as I could. I hired a car to take me to Hue —$120 I could not afford and which would have been better spent on my family—but it was either "hurry up and catch up" or break my word to people who were counting on me. I just couldn't let them down.

I arrived in Hue at midafternoon after a therapeutic drive through some of the most breathtaking scenery I had ever seen. Lush greenery was now reclaiming such picture-book areas as the Hai Van Pass, land once scarred by bombs, hilltop forts, and roadside trenches. When we pulled up to the Song Huong Hotel, though, that sinking feeling returned.

The Dien Binh, or victory parade of the Northern Army, had just finished. The VVA group looked shaken and nobody wanted to talk. Instead, they headed for their rooms to prepare for dinner. In the middle of a peaceful city in its holiday dress, they seemed battle-shocked and alien, more lost and out of place than ever.

The last time I had celebrated a peaceful Tet in Vietnam was twenty-six years before, about the time of my twelfth birthday. Our neighbors were helping us build a room for my brother, Sau Ban, and the bride with whom we all thought he was destined to grow old. My sisters, Lan and Hai, came up from Saigon to be with us, and only Ba, whose policeman husband, Chinh, was still "on the outs" with my family, was away. Now, I had given up my first family Tet in two decades to be with a roomful of sorrowful ex-GIs who, at this moment, would have preferred to be anywhere else.

Amid the flowers, flags, and strands of fireworks waiting to be lit, we convened in the hotel's banquet hall to soberly toast the Year of the Dragon. Musicians plucking *ty ba*—a pear-shaped Oriental guitar —strolled around us, so I decided to liven up the party with a song, which drew the attention of two other groups at the end of the hall, both Vietnamese, celebrating the new year. Since our party contained "honored guests" from abroad, the hotel manager broke out the best rice wine, imported beer, Chinese champagne, and even some old bottles of American whiskey, which the other Vietnamese also did not fail to notice. When I saw them eyeing us, I sidled over and asked if they'd care to join us. They did not have to be asked twice.

The first to come over was an elderly man in an old army tunic covered with rusty medals. He plunked down between me and Bill at the end of the table, facing Don so that I could translate between them. At first I thought the bold, eccentric fellow was a bum— perhaps a homeless NVA veteran crashing one of the Vietnamese parties for a little holiday cheer. We almost fell over when we learned he was Phung-Van, the VC leader who organized the Communist uprising in and around Hue during the Tet Offensive. He was a hero revered all over the new Vietnam; by their own reckoning, the "Viet Cong John Wayne."

At first, Don and Bill didn't know how to react. I could see their polite instincts battle silently with their soldier's pride. Not knowing what else to say, Don asked Mr. Van to explain his medals—something most veterans of any army are quite happy to do. Mr. Van was no exception. After a few moments, Don produced combat decorations of his own—as did other U.S. vets. One by one, everyone around the table, Vietnamese and American, started nodding and smiling and exchanging admiring glances and compliments.

Suddenly, Don took one of his medals and pinned it to Mr. Van's shirt. The old soldier's eyes moistened and he stood up, raising his glass. The chattering around the table stopped instantly. I translated Mr. Van's words as he spoke.

"Our dirty war killed and wounded many good people. We've all seen too many boys reach out for their friends and loved ones just before death closed their eyes. Let's leave these fallen comrades in their graves. As survivors, our business is the future. My Vietnam is poor but proud—proud enough to ask humbly for America's help. Let us all march together in the cause of peace."

Wet-eyed, the assembly drank to his toast, to the health of this remarkable old man. "May you see many more Tets," Don responded, raising his glass, and everyone drank to that, too.

At midnight, after an instant's hush, a million fireworks exploded and loudspeakers everywhere blared hymns of welcome to the new year's dragon. Crowds of young revelers surged down to the Perfume River to sing and dance in the moonlight. The bell from the Thien Mu Temple, Hue's most famous pagoda, rang in the night, beginning the monks' prayer vigil: for food, peace, health, and a blossoming of love among brothers and sisters in Vietnam and around the world.

The vets in the hotel slapped each others' backs and hugged and clanked beer bottles and sang the words of one country's songs to the tunes of the other's. There was nothing left to translate.

The next day, after a tour of the ornate gravesites of Vietnam's thirteen great kings, we departed for Danang. On the way, we asked the driver to stop at a military cemetery at An Hoa. The GIs piled out with their cameras, anxious to get a few shots of the "Vietnamese Arlington Cemetery." As Don got ready to shoot, he spotted an old man dressed in black moving slowly along the headstones about a dozen yards away.

"Ly, go see what that old fellow's doing, would you?" he asked. I guess Don hoped to get a photo of some ritual.

"*Thua Bac, bac tim ai a?*—Uncle, who are you looking for?" I asked politely.

The old man glanced up, bewildered, then looked past me to the group. His voice, when he answered, was thin as the wind around the headstones.

"He says he's looking for his son who fought against the Americans."

Don let his camera fall on its strap. "You mean, he's going to pray at his son's grave?"

"Not exactly. I mean he literally doesn't know where his son is buried—in this cemetery or somewhere else. He doesn't even know if his son is buried at all." I thought of my own brother, Sau Ban—a Viet Cong "MIA"—and felt my throat tighten. The Vietnamese had more than 300,000 missing in action.

"Come on," Don said. "Let's help."

With the frail old man in tow, we walked down row after row of the raised cement "caskets" that served as Vietnamese headstones. Most markers had names, but too many simply read MAT TICH—Missing in Action—or CHIEN SI VO DANH—An Unknown Hero. The old man stuck his thumb at the group and whispered to me, "Miss, are they Russians?"

"No, Uncle—Americans."

He stopped, turned down the last row of headstones, and walked out the gate.

I missed my family and wanted to share with them the last few hours of Tet. The driver dropped me at Tinh's house and before I got out, I asked the state-supplied guide, who was also our security supervisor, about the group's itinerary.

"Tomorrow we go to Marble Mountain—a very beautiful place. Have you seen it?"

"Of course," I said. "I'm from Ky La—I'm sorry, its new name after liberation is Xa Hoa Qui—a village just south of town. Perhaps you and the group would like to visit my village after you've seen the Buddhas and VC caves?"

I crossed my fingers for luck. On my last trip, I had gotten as close as a mile to the village of my birth, but could not convince either the officials or my family to take me farther. Perhaps this trip, already so different from the last, would be different once again.

The tour guide scratched his cheek. "Go to a peasant village, eh? I don't know. We'll have to see what the group wants to do, and, of course, I'll have to check with the local *du lich,* the tourist committee-man. I'll let you know in the morning."

"I understand. I must also ask my mother if she minds all these Americans poking around."

The guide looked past me to the hovel that was Tinh's house.

"So this is where your family lives, eh?" He shook his head. Like so many others, the guide didn't know what to make of me. He must have thought I was a spy—for the CIA or the *cong an,* the government's own secret police, using my relatives' humble living quarters as some kind of cover. Most Vietnamese thought that anyone with American relatives would live high on the hog. Perhaps my niece's poor dwelling convinced him that if I were a spy, I at least worked for Hanoi and was as poor as everyone else. In any event, my request put him in a quandary—between what he saw with his eyes and what he felt he should believe. I could only leave him and the committee-man to work things out and hope for the best.

Inside Tinh's house, dinner was almost finished. Everyone greeted me with hugs and kisses and I clapped my hands at Tinh's beautiful decorations. Every table in the house had been shoved together and covered with food and *hoa mai,* peach blossoms and incense that symbolized the holiday spirit. Tinh put me in the place of honor, next to my mother, and gave me a big plate of food, which I could hardly touch, given my weak stomach and the encounter at the cemetery.

When the table was cleared, the men went into the other room to put their feet up and the children got ready for bed. I asked my mother, "Mama Du, I want to go home to the village. I want *dot nhang cho cha*—to burn incense at my father's shrine. I would also like to bring some Americans with me so that they can see how we peasants live after the war."

I prepared myself for the worst. Last year, this request drew a horrified response, a cry for pity. This time, my mother only shrugged. "I don't see why not."

"Mama Du! I don't believe it! Last year you almost fainted when I asked you the same question! What's happened to change your mind?"

"I haven't changed. The government is changing. Things are different now, so my attitude is different too. We are told to encourage all Viet Kieu to come home. The officials want Americans to see how open we are. Being seen with Americans now is a real status symbol. You would make me a celebrity with the committeemen. How can I say no?"

I gave her a squeeze. *I couldn't believe my good luck!* "Of course," I added, "I have not yet received permission from the committee in Danang."

"And I will ask the committee in the village, but I don't see any problems. The Americans are rich. Visiting at Tet, they will bring everyone good luck."

I was so excited that the next day's tour with the VVA group passed in a blur. Marble Mountain is the thousand-foot-high pile of rock and jungle famous for its Marine Corps outpost on the summit and Buddhist shrines within. Ironically, it also harbored a massive Viet Cong hospital deep within its bowels. The noisy crowds of pilgrims and Amerasian children hoping for Western contacts put me immediately in mind of the last Tet I had spent at the place.

In 1962 the whole family had gathered not just for New Years, but to celebrate Sau Ban's wedding. I had just received my first "grown-up" *ao dai* brought all the way from Saigon by Lan and Hai. They hadn't remembered how puny I was, so it was too big, and while everyone laughed at how funny I looked, I imagined I was the most beautiful "woman" at the party.

With cymbals and lyres playing, we climbed the steep stairs to the *su tu* guardian lions bearing the words *Ong Thien* (Mr. Good) on the right and *Ong Ac* (Mr. Evil) on the left. These twin spirits follow us through life and write down our ethical choices. When we die, we appear before *Ong Troi* (Mr. Sky), the chief god, and Thien and Ac present their notes. If this had been Dennis's Western God, we would've been judged harshly and sent to hell. But in the East, Ong

Troi just points to the evidence and asks us to judge ourselves: "Are you satisfied with the life you have led?" Because spirits have clear vision and can no longer deceive themselves, one's self-judgment is invariably fair and tempered with mercy. After all, Mr. Sky—the cosmic god—wants understanding, growth, and harmony, not vengeance and retribution.

Just as my family did on that wonderful Tet twenty-six years before, the vets and I burned incense and asked these guardian spirits for permission to enter the enormous cave. With three vent holes on the vaulted ceiling illuminating our path like spotlights, we descended into the main cavern where religious relics, Buddhas, various shrines, and now, a VC museum, are maintained. Don was amazed that "the enemy" could run such an enormous operation underground without detection by the troops on the summit.

"It's not such a mystery," I said, and showed them a fork in the path. One led up toward the summit; the other down into the labyrinth of tunnels used by the Viet Cong. "Everybody knew about the big cavern and religious shrines and the 'path to heaven' at the top, but the monks said the second path led directly to hell. If you were leading a squad of soldiers, would you want to follow the second path?"

So both sides coexisted throughout the war: the marine base unknowingly protecting the mountain from air attack; the VC installation, in turn, protecting the marines from saboteurs—a model, perhaps, for cooperation between the two countries now that the war was over.

Barbara Cohen, the army psychiatrist, seemed overwhelmed for the first time on the trip.

"I was here many times," she recalled, smiling but sniffing back tears. "This was a very soothing place for GIs with combat fatigue. If these walls could only talk, the stories they'd tell! Speaking of old ghosts, Ly, I'm going going to visit our old hospital. Would you like to come?"

The guide had mentioned nothing yet about my request to take the group to Ky La—even if it was a "group" of one: me! It would be just like the bureaucrats to stall until it was too late, and so avoid having to make a decision at all.

"Actually," I said, "I was hoping to visit my village this afternoon and burn incense at my father's shrine. It's quite close—an easy walk from here. Perhaps you'd like to come with me, then we can catch the bus to your hospital."

Miracle of miracles—she agreed. I told the guide we were going to "knock around" the local area before returning to Danang. If the guide took that to mean Marble Mountain and China Beach—the main tourist trap—so much the better. It wasn't a lie, just not the whole truth. It was the way most things seemed to get done in this new Vietnam.

After the group departed, we stood by the highway and I scanned the countryside, excitement rising, wondering how best to proceed. While we stood there, local kids began to gather—amazed by this tall American ("or was she Russian?") and her short Vietnamese escort with frizzy Westernized hair. We started walking down the road and the children followed.

"These kids are darling, aren't they?" Barbara reached into her purse for gum or candy to give them but I stopped her quickly.

"I wouldn't do that," I said nervously. "Once they know the store is open, they'll go tell their friends. No joke—we'll be mobbed."

What I feared was already beginning to happen. The cute little kids drew their bigger sisters and even bigger brothers. Before long, swarthy, hard-eyed teenagers—out of work and maybe looking for trouble—crowded out the harmless children. I couldn't help but remember the war years when the bodies of women—not just prostitutes, but anybody unescorted—turned up daily in garbage cans and scrub brush—brutalized, raped, dismembered.

"Barbara," I said, walking so fast I was almost running, "I think we should get the hell out of here!"

I spotted a *xe lam* motorized *siclo* coming toward us on the highway and waved my arms frantically. Thank god the driver stopped. Maybe he recognized our plight or maybe he was just curious or anxious for a fare, but he smiled and motioned us aboard. Some of the more aggressive kids ran after us for a while but quit when it was clear we weren't going to stop. It was then that I realized the "stodgy bureaucrats" might be right in discouraging visits to the countryside. I would either have to trust the committeemen or come up with a better plan.

After motoring a few miles, Barbara directed the driver to a small clinic—a three-room hovel on a concrete slab—built by Americans during the war. Two midwives, the only "technicians" on duty, greeted us at the door. I told them Barbara was a visiting army doctor and I was a Viet Kieu hoping to build and equip a clinic for the peasants. Had I known what we were about to see, I would have added, ". . . and to tear down old ones like this!"

I don't know who was more shocked: me, as an American consumer used to the best health care in the world; or Barbara, a professional who understood the difference between what was just unsightly and what was truly dangerous.

In the birthing room, we saw a rusty delivery table covered with mottled sheets. Floors were swept but not mopped or disinfected. The stained walls weren't scrubbed but merely brushed periodically for cobwebs. The medicine cabinets were bare except for laundered rags. Umbilical cords were cut with a pair of rusty scissors.

In the recovery room, a young mother lay resting on a straw mat with her hours-old baby. Barbara took their picture with her Polaroid and gave it to them as a souvenir. The girl's eyes teared over this priceless gift and we both wished her well, hoping silently that she and her baby would stay healthy enough to keep out of this place. Still, the midwives talked with glowing pride about their facility—a showcase maintained by the government as a "reward" to the local heros who fought against the Americans at China Beach.

I still hadn't solved my problem of how to get to Ky La when Don asked if I would like to go with the group to Hanoi. How could I say no?

Not only was the city famous in both ancient and modern legend, but it had been home to my brother Bon Nghe and countless other youths from the South after the country was partitioned in 1954. Similarly, tens of thousands of people, mostly Catholics, migrated from Hanoi to the South at the same time because they believed they would not be allowed to practice their religion under the Northern regime. To accuse someone of "being a Communist" simply because he or she came from Hanoi only shows the accuser's ignorance of Vietnamese history.

Hanoi's association with communism is fairly recent. Vietnamese in every era have dreamed of visiting this most ancient and revered of cities just as Americans think of traveling to New York or Washington, D.C., to learn their cultural heritage. Of course, some of the modern legends about Hanoi aren't flattering. American Viet Kieu gossip that Hanoi is filled with treasure looted from the South and I was curious to see for myself. I also had the small supply of American medicine I had brought as a gift. Perhaps by leaving it at a hospital in Hanoi, under the noses of the health ministers themselves, I could curry a little favor with those upon whom the success of future missions would depend.

From older legends, I expected Hanoi to be decked with gardens and monuments and ancient temples and palaces as befits a national capital, especially one the Viet Cong cadremen always talked about in such glowing terms. Reality was something else.

Approaching Hanoi for landing, we saw a countryside pock-marked with craters from massive B-52 raids during the war. Block after block of what once had been shops and housing stood in ruins or as vacant lots cleared to recycle the rubble. It was as if half the damage done to Nazi Germany in World War II still greeted gawking European tourists as late as 1960. There may have been postwar "miracles" for other ravaged American foes, but not for the Vietnamese. Even undamaged buildings looked weathered and worn, weeping rust and mildew. The public parks were weedy and unkept. Even the weather was wet and cold—more like Korea than Vietnam—and the few vehicles we passed in the mostly unpaved streets were mired in mud or hordes of sullen pedestrians. Compared to the long-faced North, Saigon with its own great troubles was like a sunny Caribbean island.

All Hanoi visitors first call on the "home" of their host: the tomb of Ho Chi Minh. Like Lenin's tomb in the Soviet Union, "Uncle Ho's" mausoleum is half church, half monument—the closest thing the secular government has to a religious shrine. Long lines of people sometimes wait hours for a glimpse at the fabled leader, founder of this new, reunified Vietnam. Flower shops for blocks around turn a profit while other businesses go begging. The rest of the city may rot, but no expense is spared to honor and preserve the Communists' own special "Buddha."

I felt my excitement rise as the line inched closer. For my first twenty years of life, hardly a day went by without my hearing Ho Chi Minh's name either praised or reviled. Although the two sides could never agree if he was saint or sinner, everyone agreed that his ideals and personality ignited the war and kept it burning. Mothers like my own willingly sacrificed their sons to secure his vision of an independent Vietnam. It made little difference that his brand of "independence" brought a totalitarian system that could not feed and care for its own people. Whether visitors came to see a philosopher-king, soul of his nation, or an unspeakable monster, nobody walked away unmoved from that tiny, brown-suited body sleeping the sleep of ages behind reliquary glass. I could only think of how this one man's influence so radically shaped my life and changed the course of history for both my old and adopted countries. The guards at the tomb must have thought I was Uncle Ho's most loyal follower. How could they have known that my tears were for all those souls on both sides who would never stand in my place, or go back to "home villages" of their own?

Barbara and I were concerned about the monument's impact on some of the veterans, but our worries were unjustified. Indeed, some members put on their Vietnam Veteran jackets for the first time on the trip. If there was little in Hanoi to make a North Vietnamese gloat, there was less at the monument to make an American veteran ashamed.

As it turned out, the real test was ahead of us at Bao Tan Quan Doi, the national war museum, where a sustantial portion of the five billion dollars in U.S. weapons captured from the South or shot down over the North seems to have found a home.

The North Vietnamese Army's museum resembles a junkyard, but not out of disrespect. The country simply lacks the resources it needs to trumpet its victories in the style of the West or even the old Vietnamese kings. Wandering through the collection of stacked rifles, battered jet engines, and shredded aluminum (some with U.S. aircraft insignia still visible), I felt as if I were rummaging through somebody's attic, and maybe that's not so bad. There are worse places than a forgotten attic to store the tools of war.

The guide rattled off statistics: more than 58,000 American dead versus 1.9 million Vietnamese—almost 33 Vietnamese deaths for each American killed—surely one of history's costliest victories. While American politicians and distraught families aggravate old wounds over the relative handful of remaining American MIAs, Vietnam *still* can't account for almost a third of a million of its brothers and sisters, sons and daughters, North and South. And an equivalent number are permanently disabled from the war. When will the multitude be allowed to rest in peace?

I was especially worried about some of the vets who had histories of severe post-traumatic stress disorder (PTSD), particularly since they would be going home the next day. These veterans were unlike any others in our group, but very much like people I had seen in the village and in Danang after too many years of bombings and torture and fear. They did not trust easily and kept to themselves. When they spoke, their glance was usually on the ground and their voices on the edge of tears. Their topics of discussion never drifted far from the objects of their hate: the U.S. government, the people who had led them on and let them down, the unfairness of it all.

After our tour of Hanoi, they were worrisomely quiet.

I asked Don what he made of it.

"I don't know, Ly," he answered. "I guess I have to look past my own mixed feelings. Some have already told me the trip has helped them. Others won't say a word. I'll say this for the quiet ones— they've got more guts coming here than the rest of us put together. On my last trip, we had one guy who spotted somebody in an NVA hat and tunic and just flipped out. I mean, he was hysterical. He started running around and screaming for his rifle. It took five of us to hold him down. The Vietnamese on the street just stared at us. I can't remember what they said—"

"Dien cai dau?" I prompted. "Crazy in the head?"

"Yeah, that was it. I guess that's their way of dealing with PTSD. We don't seem to do much better. Ly, if you ever bring vets over here yourself, be very, very careful about who you let into your group. Everybody deserves a chance to get straightened out, but not everyone's ready for this. If you aren't sure you can handle them, send them to us at the VVA. At least we've been down this road before."

Don's advice was prophetic.

On a later trip with veterans, physicians, and teachers, I would learn that these troubled vets had more than their own flashbacks and nightmares to contend with. Sometimes they are pushed by desperate wives and relatives to take risks they're not ready to make. They talk themselves into believing that "Miss Ly" is some kind of magical healer (forgetting that it is *they* who must help themselves) and arrive in Vietnam with not only psychic pain and guilt but enormous pressure to be "healed" before their ten days are up. More likely, the poverty and misery they find only makes them more depressed. Although everyone on our trips must sign a release and pledge to follow certain rules, they quickly ignore their formal promise and fall back on old habits and beliefs. They become more paranoid than our hosts and whisper that everyone is spying on them. They complain that the food and accommodations aren't like the United States—of course they aren't! In short, they act like sick people—how could they do otherwise? In the end, they disappoint themselves and their loved ones once again and feel no better for the effort.

One thing I discovered was that many troubled vets, with a history of PTSD or not, already had problems, or were disposed to have problems, that their war experience only made worse. Some of these involved drugs or alcohol, or spouse or child abuse, but some simply had the same troubles with money and marriage that other people suffer. I truly believe their main problem was with their karma, not the service. Uncle Sam did them no favors by exposing them to events with which even healthy hearts, minds, and spirits have trouble coping.

To such people I can only say: Persevere in your quest for a better life. Do not expect to find miracles in me or your wife or children or in the poor people of Vietnam. The god that made you did so for a purpose. Don't reject the gift of life, no matter what has happened to you in the past.

The next morning, I thanked Don, Bill, Barbara and the rest for everything they had done—just as they thanked me—and waved them off on their bus to the airport.

For the last ten days, I had watched a small group of troubled souls come to terms with themselves. Somehow, the group had begun to transform memories of pain and terror into feelings of acceptance, forgiveness, and hope. When they think of Vietnam now, and for the rest of their lives, they will see a place with a human face: their own face—the face of god. If the monks were right, and nothing happens without a cause, then the result of my long hegira—from bombed-out village to the streets of Saigon and Danang to my life with Ed and Dennis and, finally, on my own—was to arrive at this watershed moment.

All my life I had been *caught in the middle*—between the South and the North, Americans and Vietnamese, greed and compassion, capitalism and communism, not quite peace and almost war. Now, instead of resisting that fate, I saw that *in between* was where I belonged. Only when you stop resisting the forces that shape your life (trying to "hold up the sky with a stick"—*be nan chong troi*, as my mother would say) and begin to use them in the service of your soul, do you find happiness—no matter which soil lies beneath your feet or which man walks beside you. Certainly, I could not speak for every

Vietnamese, but I was every Vietnamese's sister and, like it or not, all our umbilical cords lay buried in the land of the Viet. I could not speak for all Americans, but as a U.S. citizen of Asian descent I was as entitled to my spot in the U.S. melting pot as any Caucasian, Hispanic, or black woman, or any other race that made up the American soul. Peel away our colorful skins and we are all children of one planet. Our creed of choice—freedom and independence, responsibility and compassion—is the core of our humanity. We can no more reject it than we can reject the spark of life which fate or luck or god has given us. Many people may be better suited by education or talent to bring this message to East and West, but one handhold on that burden has fallen to me. I will not neglect my father's business.

My first stop after saying goodbye to the VVA group was the Central Commission of the Ban Viet Kieu, the bureaucracy overseeing relations with expatriate Vietnamese throughout the world. I intended to produce a copy of the proposal I presented to the UN Mission and announce that I wanted permission to conduct ongoing humanitarian work. I wanted to impress them with my sincerity and capabilities, but I also wanted some assurances that the nightmarish experience I'd had with customs wouldn't recur. To my amazement, *they* did all the "selling."

Two officials apologized for my harassment and gave me all sorts of information about whom I should see and the kinds of clearances I'd need. To top it all, they invited me to move into guest quarters in the building for the remainder of my stay in Hanoi. I could have asked for or expected no greater hospitality from family.

For the next few days, I talked to people in virtually every government ministry plus a number of Viet Kieu visiting from Europe. From these discussions, I learned many things, the first of which was that people are always suspicious of "humanitarians." Strangely enough, the capitalist West seemed the only place where charitable works were accepted at face value. In a country where the government was supposed to take care of every need, people seemed very reluctant to pick up the slack when it didn't.

After a week of interviews and note taking, I was getting lightheaded with details while my heart was growing heavier. I missed my boys in America and regretted the time I was not spending with my family. My god, I had been here over three weeks and I had not yet seen my only surviving brother, Bon Nghe!

I returned to Danang and went straight to Tinh's. Except for my niece and a couple of her kids, the place was deserted.

"Where is everyone?" I asked. "I thought brother Bon was going to come North for a visit after all?"

"Grandma Phung is with Hai in the village," Tinh said, "Uncle Bon was here, but went back to Saigon after a day."

"Such a short visit! Didn't anyone tell him I was here?"

Tinh didn't reply, but tried to keep a happy face. Something was going on.

"Be honest with me, Tinh. Why didn't Bon Nghe stay for a visit? For that matter, why did he move to Saigon? Last year, his family seemed very happy. He had a good, responsible job and he seemed anxious to help. What happened after I left?"

"Oh, you know how people are." Tinh pretended the dictatorship of village gossip didn't matter but I could tell she was trying to think of a nice way to give me bad news. "After you visited last year, the neighbors started talking. Some of them went to Bon's boss. Rumor had it that you brought a lot of money into the country from America and we were all rich—especially Uncle Bon. Despite the new official policy to encourage contact with American Viet Kieu, his boss and co-workers started spying on him, trying to see what he was doing with all that money. Maybe someone in the government thought he had sold himself as a spy for the Americans—who knows? Anyway, Bon's feelings were hurt and he got angry. He said he didn't deserve this treatment and applied for a transfer, which his department was only too happy to approve."

I couldn't believe it! Twenty years ago, *I* fled into exile to Saigon— the victim of malicious, dangerous, small-minded, paranoid gossip. Now, the same thing was happening to my brother! Didn't the war teach these people anything?

"How is his family?" I asked, knowing the toll such things can take on the people around the victim.

"His wife Nhi is okay. She's Northern tough, remember? His son Nam, though, is always sick. The Southern air is no good for his asthma. Of course, there's no medicine, so he has to be very careful." Tinh began peeling some sweet potatoes for dinner. Still seething, I picked up a knife and helped.

"Aunt Ba and Grandma Phung were hassled a little bit too, but for different reasons," Tinh continued. "The People's Committee invited them to a meeting and I thought they would both have heart attacks.

As it turned out, the meeting was for everyone who had relatives in the States. They were urged to write letters to invite their Viet Kieu family home for Tet. It was a major government program. You know, the authorities don't do much to support our old family ways, but when they want something, they sure turn to the network of grandparents, aunts, and uncles fast enough."

This was all beyond belief. With its right hand, the government was earnestly trying to cut a deal with me to bring in American medical aid to the rural peasants, always the last to be helped. They were even pressuring my family to get into the act. Now, with its left hand, it was terrorizing my brother for "being seen" with the same woman the government was trying to attract! The real tragedy was that, in this new Vietnam, it all made perfect sense.

I had to do something. The logical place to begin would be with my mother, the focal point of my family.

"Tell me, Tinh, has anyone contacted you from the local Ban Viet Kieu office about my request to visit Ky La?" I dropped a peeled potato into Tinh's bucket. With kids laughing in the background and the sweet odor of fresh vegetables and hot tea, it was, for an instant, as if I had never left home.

"Two men stopped by a couple of days ago and told Bien it was okay if you stayed with us instead of at a hotel. As far as Ky La goes, I— Oh, here's Bien now. He can tell you himself."

We heard the kids yelling "Papa! Papa!" as Bien parked his bicycle and walked back through his storefront barber shop toward the living quarters. He peeked into the kitchen and smiled when he saw me.

"Di Bay! You're back!" he said. "Everyone missed you. Your brother Bon sends his regards."

"That's not what I heard." I put down my potato and knife and rolled down my pants legs. "I've got to straighten everything out with the family before I go. I want to burn incense at my father's shrine. I know he will use his power to put compassion back into people's hearts if I can only get to Ky La. It is the one hole in my own soul that has yet to heal."

"Go to Ky La?" Bien scratched his chin. "I don't know. The committeemen said it was okay for you to stay here, but they didn't say anything about the village—except how much trouble they would be in if anything happened to you. I think they want to leave everything up to the Village Committee so it won't be their problem."

"There, you see? That means I *must* go to the village." I was ready now to say anything to get to my old house, but I didn't want to get anyone else in trouble. "You talked to the committeemen in Danang. Perhaps you can go with me."

Tinh nodded. "She's right, Bien. You can always say you're applying to the village council on behalf of the committee in Danang. The worst thing Bay Ly could do is try to go there alone. Then everyone would really be suspicious."

Bien wasn't quite convinced. "You know, Di Bay, if we get caught and they don't buy my story, you could be sent to prison. Your whole trip—everything you want to do for our country—could go up in smoke."

I swallowed hard. How much risk was too much? I felt like the Vietnamese woman I'd met at the San Diego travel agency on the eve of the trip. She was terrified of going, but more terrified of what would happen to her soul if she stayed away. *The path to Nirvana is always steep and winding,* my monk had said. I had a gap in my being that only the sights and sounds of my birthplace and the shrine of my father could fill.

"I don't care," I said in a voice so certain it surprised even me. "It's a risk I have to take."

"Okay," Bien said. "Mid-afternoon tomorrow, the village kids will be back in school and most of the adults will be in the fields. That's when we'll go. We'll leave tomorrow well after lunch. And after we've all said our prayers."

Bien gave me a final inspection before we left. I wore Tinh's black pajamas, rubber sandals, a conical sun hat, and no makeup. Except for my frizzy Americanized hair, I would look like any other Vietnamese lady shuffling along the highway headed south toward Marble Mountain.

"Good." He squared my hat. "You look terrible. Just like us."

We rode double on Bien's bike until a beat-up minibus filled with construction materials and workers stopped to give us a lift. Bien climbed on top to hold his bike and I slid in by the driver. I could tell the peasants had sized me up pretty quickly because the bus got very quiet. Since the war, holding your tongue in the presence of strangers was usually the best defense. What you didn't say couldn't get you in trouble. I was disappointed, though, that my disguise was so transparent. So was Bien.

When we got off at the narrow road at the top of a dike ("ambush trail" we used to call it) that led, after a mile or so, to my village, Bien said, "That was too close. You're not fooling anyone with that hair. We've got to be more careful."

If I'd had shears, I would have cut if off right there. We were so close to my village that I could smell the lunch pots boiling.

"Come on," Bien said like a sergeant on patrol. "And when we get to Ky La, don't dawdle. Burn your incense fast and we'll get out of there."

I climbed back on Bien's handlebars. Unfortunately, Bien's bike didn't share his sense of urgency. We bogged down immediately in the heavy, sandy soil, and wound up walking the rest of the way, which didn't bother me at all since it gave me more time to soak in the salty air, sights, and sounds of my youth. In fact, I could have told Bien from experience that his bike wouldn't hold two people away from the hard-packed road. I used to wait on this spot for my brother Sau Ban to come back from one of his construction jobs, and we'd walk and talk and get caught up on village gossip along the way. Now, if I weren't careful, I could become the hottest gossip these fields and kitchens had seen in a long time. The prospect didn't thrill me.

After a few minutes, we passed a stand of trees and some huts. A path to the left led through some scrubby brush into Khai Tay and Man Quang, where my father and mother were born. The path to the right led to Ky La and then to Phe Binh and the swamp where I was raped and almost killed. I was amazed at how everything was so close together. As a kid, I could range around the area all day and return thinking I had traversed half the country. A few steps farther, and we came across a graveyard I didn't remember at all.

"What's this?" I asked Bien.

"After the war, they dug up all the bodies that had been buried in a hurry and moved them here. Lots of people from the surrounding villages are buried here. A little further on, there's a military cemetery for the Viet Cong."

I thought of all the VC fighters and relatives and villagers my family had buried during the course of the war. They had been wrapped quickly in bamboo mats and shoved in shallow graves just to hide them from Republican and American troops. I wondered how many more went undiscovered and unlisted in the mass exhumation.

I wondered if my brother Sau Ban lay in some similar graveyard further south, just another Vietnamese "unknown soldier."

We arrived at Ky La when the afternoon shadows were long. Bien took a path around the perimeter that led to the old well by our house from which I had drawn water so many times as a girl. Clean water was a treasure and we never took it for granted. Now, the well looked dry, a home only to lizards, bugs, and the souls of soldiers. I remembered the bushes being large, but now they seemed scarcely tall enough to hide an adult, even one as short as me.

"Stay here and keep out of sight," Bien said as if planning an ambush. "I'll go ahead and if anybody's watching, I'll distract them so you can sneak into the house. If I see your sister Hai, I'll tell her where you are. You two can take things from there."

I hunkered down as Bien walked away. This was just the sort of thing I'd done countless times during the war, but after twenty years in America with supermarkets and freeways, playing guerrilla warrior again seemed silly, like a role in a schoolgirl's play. Unfortunately, the penalty for getting caught was real enough. The reward for a good performance would be survival.

While Bien was gone, I risked a peek at my house. The trees around it were a lot taller and more plentiful than I recalled. After I left for Saigon and Danang, the fighting around Ky La intensified. The village was half destroyed in one battle, and much of the rest was bulldozed to make a "killing zone" for a permanent American firebase. After that, between the shells and bombs and chemicals sprayed on the area, everything started to die. The green village, surrounded in part by the lush jungle I remembered as a girl, had been a loamy desert by the time I left. Now, by nature's plan or man's, I couldn't tell, Mother Earth was reclaiming what was hers. It was wondrous to see.

More unsettling was the difference between what I took to be my house and the house I remembered in dreams and visions. It was smaller, of course, moss-streaked and unpainted and ill repaired like everyplace else, and less imposing. Ours had been one of the first concrete houses built in Ky La and one of the best. Now, other huts built to government specifications dotted the main street, making my father's handiwork dwindle. Still, it bore the twin shrines he had built outside—one for our ancestors, who felt crowded inside, and one for any wandering spirit who needed shelter. The big concrete numerals 1962 overlooked the front door, a monumental birth date added by the proud builder. The house rested in the shadow of an ancient pepper, or *sau dau,* tree that had stood beside the plot long before our first house, which had been burned by the French, was built. Undoubtedly, my memories had altered the vision as much as time, history, or Mother Earth. But it was and always would be *home.*

I was home.

I fought back tears and tried to be quiet but wasn't doing much good at either. All I could think about was how much I missed my father and Sau Ban. The old house itself was a kind of mother, issuing loved ones who came and went—a loving mother, yet as indifferent as the trees to our mortality. *God—how long my life has been!* From 1949 until now—two wars and a journey to another world! I felt as weathered and ancient as the stones.

Bien had doubled back, walking his bike now, and spotted Hai coming toward him from the lake with shoulderpoles on both arms. She saw Bien, dropped the buckets, and waved hello. Bien walked over, spoke quickly, and Hai looked straight at the well. I felt terrible for putting her through the same hell as I did on my first trip in 1986 when I "surprised" her selling snails at the Danang market—but what else was I to do?

Bien went off with his bike, trying to look casual, and Hai scurried into the house with her buckets. She came out a moment later with a bag of seed and began scattering it at the ducks and chickens that followed her around the house like begging kids. She scanned the area once or twice and, satisfied that curious eyes were busy elsewhere, waved frantically at the well. I dashed through the brush and over the path and past the chickens into the house.

As I turned, Hai was already closing the door behind me. The interior was dark as a tomb.

"What do you think you're doing?" she demanded, which was not the welcome I expected, although the one I probably deserved. I wanted to look respectfully at my oldest sister, my surrogate mother (who, at sixty, now looked like our mother herself) or just drop my glance contritely while she chewed me out, but I couldn't. I could only look around the house and stare. *There* was the same bamboo bed and well-worn dirt floor I had slept on with my mother. *There* was the thatch roof—pierced with a thousand pinholes of light that admitted soft rain and geckos and red *ran* house snakes to eat the mice when the weather turned cold. *There* was my father's shrine, with its sepia image of Phung Trong taken during Sau Ban's wedding, dressed in his "Mandarin" best, a suit his daughters had bought for him in Saigon.

"Are you listening to me, Bay Ly?" Hai demanded. "Sit down!"

"Yes, Hai Ngai," I said and perched on my mother's bed. I was sobbing, the air knocked out of me by the fist of sudden emotion. I had no idea the sight of my old home would overwhelm me so much. After six generations of Phung families, I was the only one to leave the dragon's spine of Vietnam, set foot in the larger world, and return.

"Why did you come back? What are you trying to do?"

"I only want to burn incense—"

"I know what Bien said!" she snapped. "Just burn your incense and get out of here, fast! You always cause us trouble! I can't believe it! Did you know that a woman in the next village last year, shortly after you left, visited an American Viet Kieu relative in Danang? She came back filthy rich—paraded around in jewelry and fine clothes. You know where she is now?"

"No, I don't—"

"She and her whole family had to move away! Her neighbors wouldn't leave her alone so they lost their ancestral farm. Do you want that to happen to us? Go do what you came to do, then leave us alone!"

Hai lit the altar lamp, then went back outside to feed her ducks.

I approached the altar and caressed my father's portrait. His eyes gazed down at me impassively, immortal. I imagined his strong wife, my mother, and all of his children arrayed around him like playing cards—king and queen, princes and princesses of his little domain. I remembered 1962, the year the picture was taken, the last year my family was together. Sau Ban's little portrait rested by itself on a smaller altar. Because he died so young, he could not be displayed with the elder spirits.

I lit a box of *nhang*—special incense. I knelt and placed my palms together and bowed deeply. I was about to place the smoking wand in the *bat nhang,* the incense bowl, when Hai burst back into the house. She blew out the lamp and snatched the incense and snuffed it out and rolled it under our mother's bed. Without saying a word, she grabbed my arm and hustled me into our family's secret "hiding closet," which I remembered quite well from the war. It was pitch black inside, but my eyes became slowly accustomed to the dark. As they did, I noticed an old American *bi dong*—GI canteen—an ammunition box (empty, but useful as a sturdy storage container), and olive drab entrenching shovels and picks. Hidden in our secret place, they could have been army souvenirs, but more likely, they were Hai's and my mother's reserves for a rainy day: goods they could barter or sell for food and medicine.

I heard a little girl's voice outside, "Who ran into your house, Di Hai?"

Hai answered, "What are you talking about?"

"You know, the person who ran past you. Didn't you see her?"

"No, silly girl. I was feeding the livestock. Do you really think somebody sneaked into my house?"

"Yes, she was dressed in black but she wasn't from here."

"Come on then," Hai said. "Let's look for her." She made a big show of going noisily from room to room, which didn't take long in the small house. "There, you see? Nobody's here."

"But I'm sure I saw somebody."

"Well, maybe you're right," Hai said thoughtfully. "You're too young to remember, but they fought some terrible battles outside by the old well—"

"That's where the person came from!" the little girl squeaked.

"There, you see? What did I tell you! It's war ghosts. They're all over the place. I sweep them out but they just keep coming back. Come on, let's look for them again!"

"That's okay. I have to get home for dinner. Sorry I disturbed you. Goodbye, Di Hai—" Little footsteps trailed off.

The door to the hiding closet flashed opened and Hai yanked me out.

"That was too close," she said. "She might just come back with her friends to see the ghosts, so you'd better finish up and get going."

I worked as fast as piety permitted. I asked our ancestral spirits to forgive me for failing to burn ceremonial money or clothing as was proper. I asked special blessings for my father and Sau Ban, and any other wandering spirits who might need comfort. I had in mind especially the Ong Thay Dong's admonition in San Diego about the very ancient spirit that had been dogging me since birth—the one who would declare himself when my mission was complete—but I didn't have time to wait for the spirit sense to move me.

Bien stuck his head in the door, "Come on, Di Ly! What's holding things up?"

I finished my prayer and took a last look around the room, filling my memory like a treasure sack to be sorted through later. The sun was now well down behind the western mountains and the air had begun to chill as I followed Bien into the street. I didn't even look back to tell Hai goodbye. Bien was twenty yards ahead of me and widening the gap. I assumed he didn't want us to be seen together in the village, and would give me my seat on the handlebars once we reached the main highway.

"Ba-dien!" a little voice behind me yelled. *"Ba-dien bo ba vao tu!—* Mad lady, lock her away!" I walked faster and didn't look back. Some kids had spotted us and I continued my prayer—this time for myself. Shuffling footsteps and more children's voices. I passed the new graveyard but kept my eyes glued to Bien's back.

It was dark by the time we made the dike road and, although the children didn't follow us past the graveyard, I heard spirits rustling in the trees. I slipped a couple of times and got one foot wet in a flooded paddy but we made it to the highway okay.

Bien looked scared and angry as I climbed on. He said nothing but pedaled furiously into the wind and the oncoming headlights. I gripped the handlebars, legs dangling, and shut my eyes. When we finally got back to Tinh's, around nine o'clock that night, my mother was waiting for me.

"Where were you?" she demanded.

"Out." I pulled the cord of my sun hat from my chin, untied my kerchief, and shook out my hair. "I was with Bien, didn't Tinh tell you?"

"I know where you were," my mother growled. "You went to the village. Stupid girl! Now I'll have to go home and save Hai! Our neighbors will tear her apart!"

"No, Mama Du," I took her by the shoulders and held her close. "It's dark and windy outside. You can save her tomorrow."

"You're not taking this seriously, Bay Ly. Oh, why do you do this to your poor mother?" She wrung her hands and pulled at her hair.

"Listen to me," I said, sounding just like Hai. "You said yourself that the government wants Viet Kieu to come back. I just spent a week meeting with their officials in Hanoi. Everybody wants me to help the village. Now, if that isn't official permission to go to Ky La and visit my father's house, it's the next best thing. Be reasonable."

"Lenh vua thua le lang—Reason has nothing to do with it!" my mother snapped. "Oh, Bay Ly, have you forgotten everything? The government is one thing but the people are another. You spend all

your time with Americans now. Even on this visit—nobody knows where you're going or what you're doing. You don't even give me time to work things out with the committee. Bon Nghe came home for Tet only when he knew you wouldn't be here. He can't afford to be seen with an outsider. You're making things dangerous for him—for all of us."

"Mama Du, I'm not working for the government—Vietnamese or American. How can I prove that to you?"

"You can't. Only time will show if you're telling the truth. In the meantime, stay out of trouble. Let the officials work things out. How can anybody trust you when you go sneaking around by yourself?"

"I come from America, Mama Du. People there can come and go as they please."

"Yes, you're a spoiled American—that's true enough! But you forget what things were like in the war. Do you remember having to get permission from the Viet Cong and the Republicans and the Americans and the civil police and the local village commander if you wanted to go anywhere? Don't make us lose what little bit of freedom we have today!"

"The war is over!" I couldn't believe I was arguing with my mother, but I believed I was right. She just didn't understand. "I've told everybody I want to help the peasants in Quang Nam. I've told them in Saigon and Danang and Hanoi and New York and everyplace else. I don't know what else I can do!"

My mother grunted. *"Tram nghe khong bang mat thay!*—Doing something once is better than saying it a hundred times! Show the villagers with deeds, then you'll get the freedom you desire. Then we can all sleep well again at night!"

I sighed. "Okay, Mama Du. Whatever you say."

My mother shook her head. "Ignorant girl."

ELEVEN

Two Halves Make a Whole

AFTER A FINAL WEEK at Tinh's, I realized my mother had been right. Actions speak louder than words, even when those words come from the heart. It was time to demonstrate my good intentions.

Immediately upon my return to the States, Jimmy and I began writing follow-up letters to everyone I had met on the trip, and I developed a slide presentation about the war and its effects on the Vietnamese people. Some of it was pretty rough stuff, like my pictures of Tu Du hospital's "specimen room" whose shelves were lined with deformed fetuses with three heads and split-open stomachs and monstrous faces—all products of Agent Orange and other wartime chemicals. I also put myself on the mailing list of as many humanitarian organizations as I could find. On a quest into a land so dark, many people must carry torches.

One of the first to reply was Fredy Champagne, founder of Veterans-Vietnam Restoration Project. VVRP was a nonprofit organization in Garberville, California, that takes U.S. vets back to Vietnam in order to build medical facilities. We agreed to meet on his upcoming fund-raising trip to San Diego.

In person, Fredy was far from the polished executives I had run into in big foundations. Like many of the vets he recruited, Fredy was wrestling with middle age while coming to terms with his own Vietnam trauma. Instead of a "presidential" necktie and suit he wore jeans, old tennis shoes, and a T-shirt. His fuzzy mustache and ever-present baseball cap crowned a ready smile and lively eyes. He greeted me with *"Han hanh duoc gap co"*—a rusty "Nice to meet you."

I got a lot of good information from Fredy about organizing a grass-roots foundation while Fredy learned a lot from me about establishing contact and doing business with the Vietnamese bureaucracy. He subsequently went to the UN Mission in New York and received permission to build a small health clinic in the village of Vung Tau.

"Why Vung Tau?" I asked when Fredy called with the good news. I was a little disappointed that we could not collaborate to put the first facility near Danang, which had a bigger population and more pressing needs.

"Because my group passed through Vung Tau on our last visit and the village council asked us to build one. I didn't know of a better place and the Health Ministry honchos liked the idea because I already had local permission. Anyway, it's a start. The next one goes to Danang, I promise."

Despite my disappointment, it was good news for Vietnam and a good start for both of our organizations. Our collaboration quickly took the form of friendly competition to see who could raise more money and contribute most to our joint goal. Fredy's VVRP had the advantage of mailing lists and contributors and volunteer workers to draw on. I had none of these yet, and as East Meets West's organizational costs spiraled—for long-distance telephone calls, flyers, and travel—I had trouble paying my bills. Even worse, a lot of people perceived me as "the enemy"—not a U.S. vet, but somebody who was on the wrong side of the war. However, what I lacked in personal resources, I made up for in another way.

In May 1989, my book was published.

Virtually overnight, hundreds of thousands of Americans, not just book buyers, but people who heard, saw, or read my interviews or the book's reviews, learned about my life during the war and my return to find my family in 1986.

The first phase of my life's mission was accomplished. The steep climb toward the goal my father had set for me, and that I had accepted reluctantly, began to level off. The stumbling blocks around me—hearts stone cold with prejudice and wartime hate—miraculously began to bloom with empathy and compassion. We were on our way.

After *When Heaven and Earth Changed Places* arrived in bookstores, my own life turned upside down. Requests for interviews and lecture invitations multiplied. Major newspapers and magazines all over the country recommended it to their readers, calling it a unique look into the face of the enemy and the dark heart of war.

I felt terribly excited, but terribly unprepared. I wanted very much to reach these big new audiences, but felt my accent and old clothes and farm girl manners just weren't up to the task. What gave me the courage to persevere—to say yes to these opportunities instead of copping out—was to take my own advice. People were hailing my book for its message of forgiveness, and that meant forgiving myself for my own shortcomings. It also required me to acknowledge that my purpose for writing it had been fulfilled. Even if I died tomorrow, if no clinic were built, if things somehow just got worse, the book— my father's message of hope—would live on, a beacon to light the way for someone else.

And that's nearly the way it happened.

The *Los Angeles Times* ran a condensed excerpt and many of my family pictures in a cover story in their February 5, 1989 Sunday magazine. I was in New York when the piece came out. When I returned, my answering machine (that and my kitchen table were all there was to East Meets West—we wouldn't get a real office until a San Diego patron donated storefront space in 1990) was filled with messages, not all of them congratulatory.

"I'm going to kill you, damn Viet Cong bitch and Communist sympathizer!"—*beep*—"Sister Ly, this is Representative Tran at the UN Mission, please call us right away. We must discuss your article!" —*beep*—"Ly, this is your sister Lan. Have you seen the Vietnamese newspapers in Little Saigon? They're out for your blood! What did you do?"—*beep!*

Although many of the calls were favorable and supportive, my attention was naturally focused on the complaints and threats: *Why didn't I reach this person?* As it turned out, many people who disapproved of the piece hadn't even taken the time to read it.

"All I saw was the word 'Viet Cong' and I picked up the phone," one person who had complained wrote after reading the whole book. "It was my old hurt and prejudice that motivated me, not anything you or the reporter said. To tell you the truth, I didn't even read the article."

That attitude was confirmed by the magazine's editor, who said the article drew the largest *negative* response of any similar piece published in her years with the paper. One of the messages (all calls to the editors are recorded) contained a particularly credible threat that was referred to the FBI. Although I didn't speak with my old friend Agent Tracy, the case was passed to the local police, who located and interrogated the caller. The man making the threat, it turned out, was not Vietnamese—not Chong Cong, the right-wing militarists (which relieved me greatly)—but a U.S. vet who saw the magazine's cover while drinking with his buddies and decided to impress them. Like so many other callers, he did not bother to acquaint himself with "the other side" before he drew his conclusions. I told the man through the authorities I would not press charges as long as he read the whole book, even if he had to borrow it from the library. I never heard from him again, which I assume is good news.

I realized that truth and clarity alone were not enough to overcome some people's deep-seated hatred and fear. If books alone could improve the world, we would need none other than the Bible, the Koran, the *Tu-Khe Tinh Tam,* and the other great spiritual testaments. The road to nirvana is always steep and winding.

In the same month the book was published, Fredy Champagne and fourteen of his Garberville veterans completed the first structure built in Vietnam by American hands since the war: a fourteen-room, 2,500-square-foot clinic in the coastal village of Vung Tau. In a television interview following their accomplishment, Fredy said, "We are giving back to the people what we took away during the war—life. The first time we came, we came with guns and bombs. Now we come with hammers and shovels." In a small but tangible way, East and West had met and helped each other. It was a partnership that, having sprouted, could only produce more flowers.

Danang and my home village were next.

I gained approval from the minister of foreign affairs in Hanoi for East Meets West to operate in the country, and after that, I traveled to Danang with Fredy and met with officials in the Foreign Economic

Relations Department, International Red Cross, and Ministry of Health in Danang. During a break in these sessions, I went to visit Tinh and check on my family for the first time since my arrival. The news was not good.

"Your mother is very ill," Tinh said, looking suddenly much older than her thirty-five years. "She can't get out of bed. Hai is caring for her, but it doesn't look good."

I felt the floor drop out from under me. "What about Bon Nghe? Has he been told? Has he brought a good doctor? He must be able to do something!" This was what my relief work was all about. What horrible irony it would be if my Ky La clinic was not ready in time to save the one person I wanted most to help!

"He's come up to visit her, of course, but he won't stick around. He knows you're in the country and is still afraid to be seen with you at the village."

"That's absurd!" I cried. "Our mother's sick, maybe dying, and he's still afraid of the village committee? That's got to stop. This has all gone far enough!"

I left Tinh's house determined to resolve this endless cold war. The place to start was the high council in Danang.

This time I was armed for my committee meeting with a group of American veterans who were more than tourists. They were officially designated heroes for their charitable work at Vung Tau. The commissars had no choice but to approve my visit, and they did. My escorts to Ky La would be the first Caucasian-Americans to set foot in my village since the last marine withdrew in 1973.

Fredy, three vets, and I arrived at the old dike road shortly after sunrise and set out for the village. The horde of curious children met us again, but this time kept their distance, even though the My Bo Doi American "soldiers" carried cameras and tote bags full of gifts, not guns and grenades.

We entered the village like a circus parade. My house was one of the first buildings on the right, and I headed straight for it. I could see Hai—who had just propped open the doors for what looked to be a hot and dusty morning—regard us with puzzlement, then terror.

"It's okay," I said, smiling as I drew close. I didn't want to violate village protocol by being too familiar or too pushy with my older sister, particularly in front of Americans. "We have permission to be here from the high council in Danang. I'm here to see our mother."

I ducked into the doorway and encountered her lying in a scuffed wooden bed facing the wall.

"Mama Du," I said softly. Outside Hai, Fredy's men, and half the village stared in through the door and windows.

The old, gray-topped face turned toward my voice. Her thin purple lids opened over sunken eyes. A bulb-knuckled hand, tough as a work glove, trembled in the air.

"Bay Ly," her dry lips whispered, "little one. I didn't think I'd see you again."

I cried and embraced what little was left of her. I heard cameras click behind me and a fist curled in my stomach. I wanted to shout *Go away!*, but these were friends and the only reason I was allowed to come. I gritted my teeth and let it pass.

I reached into my bag and withdrew a copy of my book. Its cover was as tan as the sand at China Beach; the letters of the title as red as warrior's blood. A frosty blue picture of me decorated the jacket.

"When heaven and earth changed places, Mama Du." I showed her the book. "Remember when you said that on my first visit? When you were telling me what happened after the war? Look, these are your words, right here, over my picture! People will see them all over the world. What do you think about that?"

I couldn't tell if the curl on her betel-black lip was a smile, but she said, "It almost makes me wish I had learned to read, Bay Ly."

"It's the story of our family—the story of my life and what everybody we knew went through in the war. It's the story of my visit three years ago. You're in it too, Mama Du, all over the place!"

"Nobody cares about that," she said, as if it were true.

"They will, Mama Du. I promise."

She looked at the doorway, *"Ho la ai?*—Who the hell are all these people?"

"They are my friends, Mama Du. You said to bring *Ong Ba My*— Mr. and Mrs. American—to the village. Here they are."

"Okay, they can stay. But the kids have to go. They're too noisy."

Hai turned to shoo the children away but they returned as soon as the shooing stopped. Fredy and the rest of the men blinked back tears.

I turned to Hai. "Where is brother Bon?"

"Gone to get supplies." She edged away from Fredy's veterans, still afraid to get too close. "Some of the neighbors have been giving him and Mama Du a hard time. They think you've been bringing her lots of money and can't understand why she doesn't share it with them. Bon's angry because you brought all this trouble with you. Mostly though, he's frustrated because he can't do anything about it."

I looked back at my mother. "You're not going to die, are you, Mama Du?"

"I should be so lucky! No, I'm not going to die. I'm just a sick old lady. I've been through worse. Right now I just want to sleep."

"Okay. Rest well, Mama Du."

I kissed her on the forehead and went to the family altar to burn incense to my father and pray for her recovery.

Despite my preoccupation with my mother's illness, the work session in Danang was very productive. The Health Ministry had drawn up plans for a small clinic near Ky La, but kept postponing it for lack of funds. Fredy brought out the blueprints his group had used for the new facility at Vung Tau, and everyone agreed the new plan was better—especially if it was funded by Americans! It was a good time to bring up my brother's problem.

"Some of you know that I have not seen my brother during my last two visits." I cast my eyes along the row of officials on the other side of the table. "Most of you don't know why. I am an American citizen —a Viet Kieu—trying to use the resources of my new country to help my old one. When I'm not here, I will have to leave my affairs in the hands of somebody I can trust. I know I can trust my brother, but he is afraid to trust me. He's worried that if he gets too close to me, he will lose your confidence and respect. My mother's jealous neighbors only make matters worse. I respectfully wish to place this issue before the committee so that we can work out a solution."

To my mild surprise, the second lieutenant governor of the Quang Nam People's Committee, Nguyen Dinh An, spoke right up.

"We have already discussed this problem with your brother. We agreed that if he gets involved with your foundation—to receive materials on your behalf, for example, to ensure they do not fall into the hands of black marketeers—he must first give up his current duties so that there can be no conflict of interest. I am prepared to submit a written request that he be transferred to the Health Ministry or to the Red Cross or to whatever other department you and he desire. As far as the problem with your neighbors go, I suggest we hold an open forum in Ky La to finalize the plan so that everyone can witness things for themselves."

The following day the People's Committee of Quan Nam Province convened a "town hall" meeting among our group, representatives of the Red Cross, Ministry of Health, the Foreign Economic Committee, and virtually every ambulatory resident of Ky La. As the villagers crowded around our long table, I was surprised and pleased, and ultimately a little saddened, to see my brother Bon Nghe, dignified in a clean white shirt and dark pants, slip into the back of the crowd. Although his future was the focus of the meeting, he was still too afraid of "village justice" to take a place at the main table. After all, our group would go back to America and the high officials would go back to their city offices, but residents of Ky La would stay on—to police themselves and their kind as they had for a thousand years.

The president of the committee convened the meeting and read a declaration authorizing a clinic to be built with the aid of foreign labor and materials. Several officials made short speeches, then the president opened the floor to questions.

I was astonished to see that the first person standing to speak was my sister Hai.

"Sister Ly," she shouted in my direction, though her eyes cut around the crowd, "you have caused our family a lot of pain. You come to the village and talk about everything you are going to do. You act as if you are rich and can build a whole hospital like that"—she snapped her fingers—"no problem! I want you to know, Sister Ly, that people talk. People say that if you are rich enough to do this, you are rich enough to give your family money, although we have received nothing except a little cloth and candy and medicine. Still the rumors fly. That's how it has been since you first came back—nothing but trouble for everyone. Our poor mother has no peace anymore. I have no peace anymore. When I try to sell snails in the market, people ask me, 'Why don't you just use your American dollars to buy what you want?' When our mother eats her bowl of brown rice, people ask her, 'Why don't you just use your American money and eat beef and duck or go to a restaurant in town? It's always the same thing now—money, money, money! I wish you had never come back!'"

Hai sat down and covered her face and I felt the blood rush into mine. Of course, she had to make some show in front of the neighbors—at least a symbolic rejection of me and what I represented. Nobody could conceive that a "rich" American sister would not first line the pockets of her family before she undertook any charity for her village. I would have to make a similar, suitable reply.

I stood up and cleared my throat. "Okay, it's time everyone knew what is going on. I have been an ungrateful daughter and sister and I now admit it to you with great shame. When I first came back in 1986, I could have given my mother and brother and sisters great wealth but I did not. I was too afraid of going to jail. When I came back a second time, my fortunes had changed and I did not have much money at all—just enough to come home for Tet. During that time, I decided to devote my life in America to helping the people in my homeland. I can make the same promise to my relatives here, though, that I make to you all: the money I raise in the future will be spent in Vietnam for the good of our people—for things everyone can use, like this health clinic. All I ask from you is that you allow my brother Bon Nghe to work on your behalf—to receive the money and material I send in to the country for our work. Otherwise I will do nothing and things will go on for you as they have in the past. As for my sister Hai and my mother, I ask that you take pity on them for having such an ungrateful sister and daughter. Don't make their burden any more difficult to bear. That's all I have to say."

The meeting broke up and Hai went home in the company of some neighbors who seemed to be consoling her. But Bon Nghe slipped away. Fredy and his group left for Danang, where they would depart from Vietnam the next day. The crowd dispersed and I went quietly to our house.

My mother was feeling better and was able to sit up and go out to the latrine. Hai brought some vegetables home for dinner and we hugged, each understanding the other. At least everything was out in the open now, which made gossip a lot less profitable. After dinner people began hanging around the house to eavesdrop, although now they seemed more like curious neighbors than jealous spies.

"Bay Ly," my mother said after dinner, "everything is in your hands now—the future of the whole family. *Mot nguoi lam nen ca ho duoc cay; mot nguoi lam bay ca ho mang nho*—If one of us is successful, we all depend on her; if one disgraces us, we all share her shame. If you don't build your clinic, people will be convinced you've just used it as an excuse to ship money in for us and if they don't kill us outright, we'll be ostracized to death."

"Mama Du, I will build the clinic. You'll hold your head up high and laugh at all the people who caused you trouble. Bon Nghe will be a respected man and loved by the village just like Father was before the war."

I had to apply through State Department channels for permission to export aid to Vietnam, then to seek collateral waivers from the Treasury and Commerce Departments to avoid penalties under the Trading with the Enemy Act, which went all the way back to World War II. I also needed testimonial letters from a variety of senators and congressmen known to be both for and against normalized relations with Vietnam. You would think I was running for office!

To finance the campaign, I wrote pamphlets and traded volunteer labor for a couple of good mailing lists and made countless calls. When I got too tired from phone calling and letter writing, I prayed at my shrine for providence to keep my mother alive. I now wanted more than anything for her to see me fulfill my promise and restore our family's good name in the village.

I also sponsored, alone and with other groups, Oriental banquets (doing most of the cooking myself) and auctioned off some of the artwork I had brought from Vietnam a long time ago. But the funds produced from these events, plus dues from East Meets West's growing membership, weren't enough to complete the clinic, although we shipped a half ton of medical supplies and broke ground for the project. We needed a lucky break and hadn't a clue as to where it might come from.

A few months later, my financial outlook and the prospects for East Meets West improved when a paperback publisher and book clubs and foreign presses began to discover *When Heaven and Earth Changed Places*. People unfamiliar with publishing, like me, thought this would mean lots of money, but what it really meant was the *promise* of future earnings. Still, these sales were enough to make second-mortgage payments and keep Tommy and Alan fed and clothed and healthy until they finished school. It also allowed me to finally take my three sons on my next trip to Vietnam—to meet their Vietnamese relatives and, in Jimmy's case, to meet the father he had never known.

My boys envisioned a Vietnam not too different from the Mexican towns familiar to American tourists. They were therefore astonished by what poverty actually meant in the rest of the world.

Clearing customs with our cases of medicine was still tedious, but easier than it would have been even a few months before. And as icing on the cake, the boys were received like rock stars. Even Jimmy, who is one hundred percent Vietnamese, stuck out like a sore thumb —his average American college-student clothes flashier to his ethnic countrymen than an Elvis suit. The biggest difference, of course, was in my kids' height and healthy bodies. Although they were average by American standards, their well-fed physiques towered over their Vietnamese counterparts. When I had first arrived in America, I thought the huge refrigerators, jammed with food, were the reason Americans grew so big. Perhaps that ignorant little farm girl's naive observation wasn't so far from the truth.

Our first big event was at our hotel in Saigon, where Jimmy would meet his father for the very first time. An American news crew was traveling with us, and it was the first of several occasions when I would question the high emotional cost of publicity, however much my struggling foundation needed it. I did not want to put more stress on Jimmy and Anh than they would already feel, and the scurrying technicians and bright lights did nothing to calm our nerves. Even worse, Jimmy was closeted in his room so he would not stumble onto his father prematurely, spoiling the *genuine moment* the producer wanted to capture. I could not understand how something so contrived could be anything but awkward and uncomfortable. It just seemed like another way of betraying your soul—of "selling out"— but it is what I had agreed to do, so I kept my mouth shut and so did my son.

Just before Anh was scheduled to arrive, I went to see Jimmy in his room.

"How are you doing, Mr. Movie Star? Do you want to throw up?"

"No," my big son grinned. "I just don't know what I should do."

"The producer says just be yourself. Whatever you feel like doing will be fine."

"But what should I say? I don't even know how to say 'Hi, Dad' in Vietnamese!"

"Chao Ba," I said. "See how easy it is?"

"Chao Ba. Chao *Ba*. So, should I shake his hand or hug him or what?"

I laughed. "It's best if you bow. That's how Vietnamese do it. Just be polite and go with your feelings and you'll be fine. They want you to be natural, so it's impossible to make a mistake. Still, I'll ask them to turn off the cameras as soon as possible."

"That's the best idea yet," Jimmy said nervously.

A moment later, the producer came to the door and said, "He's here! Come on!"

Jimmy entered the room from one door and his father, Anh, entered the other. The camera was already whirring and a few flash bulbs popped. Jimmy stopped and crossed his arms and bowed stiffly like Charlie Chan.

"Chow Bah," he said gravely.

Anh paused, smiled in amusement—a genuine moment—and replied in Vietnamese. I was so taken with the image of my firstborn son towering over his middle-aged father—both of them bathed in white light like angels—that I forgot to translate.

Of course, Jimmy didn't know what Anh said and could only reply in English, "It's good to see you after all these years." I finally snapped out of it and called them to the table, where I served some tea.

I translated their small talk and began to feel that things were very anticlimactic. I had built these two halves of my life up so big that their coming together could never match my romantic and motherly fantasies. And there was no reason that it should. These were two men in front of me, strangers tied in blood, knowing each other only by stories, pictures, and reputation. Both had reasons for old grievances—Jimmy's birth had embarrassed Anh and caused him problems with his marriage; Anh's abandonment had caused his son a lot of hardship. Yet both survived worse things and now were here together. More than anything else, I felt Jimmy's life—his fate and future—being taken from my hands and placed into his own. No mother likes that feeling, yet we all pray for the day when a young man finally grows beyond his parents. In truth, it didn't make any difference if Anh had never seen Jimmy before or if Jimmy had lived with Anh every day of his life. Jimmy was now embarked on his own life circle. Universal law was working. I was one step closer to my ancestors and Jimmy was one step further on his own adventure. The sparkling aura that surrounded and bound us was an image the camera could never see.

"*Tiep tuc hoc, lam nhieu. Dung hoc huot can sa bich phien,*" Anh said. "Continue your studies, work hard. Stay away from drugs."

Jimmy laughed. "Now you sound just like Mom!" A native Vietnamese son would never be so familiar under such circumstances, but would be humbler and more subservient. It reminded me of just how Westernized my boys really were.

Anh knew Jimmy was about to graduate from college. *"Ba rat tiet la ba khong lo cho con duoc."*

I leaned toward Jimmy. "He says he regrets not taking care of you when you were little."

Jimmy shrugged, still smiling. "I understand. Tell him, if he had, I would never have gone to America. My life has been good—just fine. He has nothing to feel bad about."

I translated this for Anh and he leaned into me and spoke quickly, seriously.

When he finished, I said, "Okay, everybody, can we turn off the lights? Did you get enough pictures?"

Anh had said he was at a loss for words. He felt uncomfortable with all these strangers around. This was not a public event. Gratefully, the lights snapped off.

Anh rose and shook hands with the crew and our traveling companions. He shook Jimmy's hand, paused, then pulled him close, something he would never have done with the camera turning. Jimmy hugged him back and looked, despite his greater size, like a little boy in his father's arms.

The next morning we flew to Danang where we distributed our medical supplies among several local orphanages and the hospital. The facilities were full because of a recent typhoon that had struck Quang Nam, killing 78 people and leaving another 150,000 homeless. The materials didn't last long. The doctors took only enough time to accept our provisions ceremonially and pose for a picture or two, before ripping desperately into the supplies. Accommodating this need was genuinely satisfying, although I felt anxious to move along. I had received permission to take my boys and the crew into Ky La and the long fingers of home were already beckoning me.

Our little caravan turned off the highway at the familiar dike road and, with my warning to the driver unheeded, we immediately bogged down in the dirt. We crossed the last blistering mile on foot, carrying the video equipment like ants.

As we passed the new cemetery, the usual gang of village children ran out. *"Ong Ba My!"* they cried. "Mr. and Mrs. American are back!" By the time we reached my house, we had attracted an enormous crowd. With all our equipment, we must have looked like the marines returning to China Beach!

Because they knew we were coming and had, after my last visit, made peace with the gossip-mongers, my brother Bon Nghe and sister Ba Xuan were there to greet us, as well as Hai and my mother. I was doubly moved when my brother, the Communist, produced an offering of food and incense for our father's shrine—a practice strictly discouraged under the postwar regime. In a Communist state, even a small step backward can mean a giant leap forward for the common people.

"Thang Hung dau?" my mother called when she saw us approach, asking where Jimmy (Hung, in Vietnamese) was.

"Ba Ngoai!" Jimmy hugged his startled grandmother.

"Oi chu cha troi, oi lon qua!" she gasped.

"What did she say," Jimmy asked, eyes dancing.

"She says she can't believe your size," I translated. "She says you're a giant!"

My mother asked if Jimmy remembered her.

"Of course," Jimmy grinned. "You're the woman who used to scratch her back on the wooden posts in our house!"

I translated this for my mother and everyone laughed. In accordance with family protocol, my mother next turned to Tommy, saying *"Con thang Chau dau?*—And where is Chau?"

"Hi, Ba Ngoai!" Tommy, too, smothered this frail old lady.

She looked into his face a moment, perhaps wondering if her attempts to darken his skin and flatten his nose as an infant—her attempt to make Ed's boy look more Vietnamese—bore any fruit. Whatever she saw, it continued to make her happy.

"And this is Alan," I said in Vietnamese. "The grandson you haven't met. His father saved Nam Lan and her boys in 1975."

She squinted at Dennis's son, who, although still in elementary school, towered above her. She squeezed his meaty arms and gave me a wide, toothless grin, obviously pleased.

She asked the boys many grandmother's questions: "What do you study in school? Do you have many friends? Do you stay out of trouble and do your homework? Do you help your widowed mother get along?" To Jimmy, whom she regarded as a handsome young god just jumped down from a temple ornament, "Do you have a girl picked out yet? When are you going to give your mother grandsons?

Do you remember the things we used to do in Danang? Do you miss me at all?"

I burned incense and other offerings at our shrine and my mother thoroughly enjoyed her role as hostess and matriarch. She gathered everyone around and sang a song. Her voice had surprising strength and sweetness:

> *Who will come to Ky La*
> *With its sands like fluffy cotton?*
> *Steer clear of the flooding river,*
> *And her mud-washed roads.*
>
> *Why go to Bai Gian, or see*
> *The rich farms of Thi An?*
> *Kai Thay is surrounded by graves,*
> *Filled with casualties from Hai An.*
> *And in Hue Dong, the land is poor,*
> *Where people burrow for rice.*
> *All year they work in the fields,*
> *And forget what it's like to live.*
>
> *But in Ky La we sing proudly,*
> *"Don't work so hard to be unhappy,*
> *"When you can work a little harder*
> *"And get so much more!"*
>
> *Other villages have two seasons,*
> *In Ky La we have four—*
> *Like the corners of the earth.*
> *In Ky La we fight bravely;*
> *And bow our heads to no one*
> *Except Mr. Sky.*

She laughed and covered her mouth shyly while everyone applauded. I translated the words, changing only the last line, which as she sang it went, "After they destroyed our village, many Americans were killed by our leaders." Hardly an ancient song existed that had not, in the course of two decades of fighting, lost its original words to war.

Just before sundown, the TV crew asked if I would take them into the swamp and show them the spot where I was raped and terrorized by the Viet Cong. It was a short enough walk—I remembered seeing the lights of my house easily from the little island where it all happened. But the spiritual distance was enormous, and I was not sure I had the strength to tell the story on the very place it happened. Nonetheless, it was a rare chance to document for others what still burned so vividly in my mind, and (as I had been advising U.S. vets for years) there might be some healing quality in revisiting the site of old wounds.

Crossing the checkerboard rice paddies on the dikes with the setting sun warm on my face was like moving back in time. As we splashed through a shallow causeway onto the island, my legs felt younger and a song popped into my head—one I remembered hearing my mother and sister Hai sing during the war with the French. It's about a Viet Minh fighter returning home after being too long at the front. I sang it softly:

> *So long ago I left this place*
> *Of home-cooked meals,*
> Rau muon *soup and purple eggplant,*
> *And villagers toiling in the fields.*
> *Under hot noon sun or foggy morning,*
> *They carry buckets and plant new rice.*
> *I must return to this sacred spot:*
> *The motherland that gave me life.*
>
> *Back I've come now to my farm.*
> *I'll plant crops and take*
> *One meal in the morning and one at night,*
> *From the land, all that she gives.*
> *Vietnam gives rain*
> *To wash away death and make plants grow;*
> *And from the draught inside my heart*
> *Make rivers of happiness overflow.*

When the song ended, we were standing in a clearing just big enough for a couple of kids to kick around a ball. Near a line of brush a few yards away was a shallow indentation, barely perceptible, and its sister pile of dirt eroded by twenty years of wind and rain— yin and yang of what this nighmare playground and those years had been all about. I think the crew was a little disappointed at this pint-sized "killing field." It was not a graveyard or even a place of execution, but an area set aside by the Viet Cong to make its victims think it so. Still, at the time, it had been enough to do its job. I always felt very uncomfortable thinking about this place and now I realized why. It was not just the unfair trial and threatened execution or even my rape—as horrible as those things were—that tormented me. What I hated and feared most about this place was that, for at least a little while during my stay on earth, other humans had taken away my spirit—my will to love. I had talked and written a lot in the last few years about forgiveness. I had been able to forgive the two VC guards, Loi and Tau, for the terrible things they did to me, but that was easy compared to what the cosmic god was now calling on me to do. I now had to forgive myself for the biggest sin of all from those years: turning my back on life. I now knew why coming back to this place, and starting the clinic nearby, was so important. Others may call it charity, but I was really saving my soul.

In the vans going back to the hotel, I asked the boys what they thought about the place where their mom grew up.

"Is it always this hot?" Jimmy asked.

"This is a nice day," I laughed. "Wait for the summer monsoon!"

"We had enough trouble carrying all that video gear in shorts and T-shirts," Tommy added. "I can't imagine GIs patroling the paddies in fatigues and backpacks. Even if you got up the energy to move, you'd sink in the mud up to your knees. Unbelievable! I wonder why they never dressed for the occasion?"

"At least I got to ride on a water buffalo," Jimmy said.

"You mean that dinky little cow I saw you sitting on when we got back?" I teased.

"Well—it's a lot bigger when you get close up."

"It was just a small cow!"

"Let's just tell people I rode a water buffalo, okay? And leave it at that."

The next day, after seeing the television crew off, Tommy met some girls who invited him to a concert in Danang. When he returned, the other boys teased him to death.

"Hey, Tom," Jimmy said, "you want Mom to call the village matchmaker?"

"You're just jealous 'cause they're cuter than that cow you dated in Ky La."

Bathroom towels, wrapped into whips, snapped like gunfire and I thought they would wreck the hotel room.

"Okay, okay, that's enough!" I shouted. "Of course, Jimmy, Grandma Phung is right. You're a young man now. Pretty soon you'll be finished with college and ready to settle down. I can have Ba Ngoai start looking for a nice Vietnamese girl for you."

"Whoaa—hold it! Time out!" Jimmy made a T with his hands. "Vietnamese girls are too shy. Tom says you can't even hold their hands while you're dancing. All they want to do is practice their English and talk about school."

"Of course," I said proudly. "These are village girls! They want to impress you with their seriousness. You have to be patient. In America, finding love is like grabbing a Big Mac. Here, it's like planting rice. You can't sow and reap in the same evening, for goodness sake!"

"How about just spreading some fertilizer?" Tommy asked.

I belted him with a pillow myself and the other boys jumped on top of him.

"If you talk like that, you'll never find a girlfriend in Vietnam," I said. "These girls are too nice for you!"

I sounded just like my mother. Secretly, though, I could think of nothing better than for my sons to discover the love of their life among the poor girls of Vietnam—I knew what strong hearts and willing hands they could bring to a marriage, to complement and fulfill a good man's life. I also knew, of course, what any rural girl would be up against in America, even though my boys had my example—written down now, like a textbook!—to advise them. But I wouldn't hold my breath. There were some things, in the East and West, each generation insists on learning for itself.

We left Vietnam a slightly different family. In many respects, the trip had brought us closer together. The boys had seen their mother's origin and no longer had to imagine it from books, old photos, and stories. In other ways, though, the hairline gap of age and culture that had always existed between me and my sons now grew into the gulf that always and inevitably separates the generations, especially in the West. I could no longer pretend that my boys were somehow displaced Vietnamese—surrogate villagers provided by god to decorate my life with familiar things. More clearly than I, they saw Vietnam's wretchedness as part of the bigger wretchedness of all mankind. Their perspective was one of globe-straddling, well-educated Americans—businessmen, doctors, lawyers, artists, whatever they would become—not a country girl with a third-grade education trying to heal in a day the wounds of an entire people. Just as each trip instructed me further about my mission, so it caused me to realize that my American sons truly had life missions of their own. Without question, our lives and missions would intersect from time to time, but their karma was their own. Such is the discovery every mother makes and the lesson every child must learn. As for us, we could not have asked for better teachers.

Back in the United States, the movie rights to my book were optioned by Oliver Stone, an Oscar-winning filmmaker who was a Vietnam veteran himself. He saw in my story the third installment of his great Vietnam trilogy, which began with *Platoon* and continued with *Born on the Fourth of July*. We met to discuss the project and I found him to be a down-to-earth, creative person who tried unsuccessfully to hide his big heart and generous spirit. Like so many veterans I had worked with, he still held in a lot of anger about the war. But he also had the god-given soul of an artist, which allowed him to appreciate his feelings and transform them into compelling, and ultimately healing, images on film. I saw in Oliver a kindred spirit who could help my story touch a much bigger world audience that only movies can reach.

He was also a man who liked to make things happen.

Three days after he had asked to see plans for the Mother's Love Clinic and background information about East Meets West, he donated a check for the amount needed to finish our work. Just as miraculously, as if triggered by this first domino, we received our license from the State Department to build our clinic and our waivers to the 1942 Trading with the Enemy Act. Brick by brick, the wall that had isolated my old from my new country was coming down.

In September 1989, I was back in Vietnam. Several uncles had arrived at Danang and were going to Ky La for the clinic's grand opening two days hence. I hitched a ride with them and appeared at my mother's door shortly after sundown.

"I'm going to spend the night in my village," I announced to my mother and Hai. Once the clinic was opened, the village and its spirits would enter a new life cycle. These would be the last two nights I could recapture the world of my youth.

Hai checked all the windows for eavesdroppers and my mother

blew out the lights to discourage visitors. With my uncles, we sat together on the floor like kids telling ghost stories in the dark.

"This reminds me of 1975," Hai said with a laugh, "when the North took over Danang. Everyone ran to the American Army PX at China Beach because they were giving away the food. I grabbed a couple of empty sacks and went down myself. I was a little angry that the Republicans were charging an entry fee, but I paid and filled my bags. When I came out, a Southern soldier took my loot—yes, just grabbed it. They were using the peasants to do their dirty work! I started shouting and punching the soldier when shots rang out. Somebody yelled '*Giai phong, giai phong!*—Liberate the people!'— and quick as a wink, the Republicans had shed their uniforms and hidden their rifles. The man who had just stolen my bag tried to trade it back for some of my clothes—can you believe it? Anyway, the Northern soldiers surrounded the place. They arrested the Republicans and tied them to the heavy bags so they couldn't run away, then let the peasants go. I hated to lose that big bag of loot, but it was good to see those bullies get what they deserved!"

Everyone laughed but my mother. "Tonight reminds me of the night the village psychic told me about Sau Ban—"

I stopped laughing, too. This was news to me.

"Somebody told you what happened to my brother?" I asked.

My mother shifted her tiny body on the mat and looked up, as if she could see the stars through our thatched roof.

"Not long ago, Bon Nghe hired an *ong thay xac dong* down South to locate Sau Ban's remains. He interviewed a lot of villagers and believes he knows what happened. Sau Ban was serving with a cannon squad in the Dai Loc District just before the Tet Offensive in 1968—just before your father died. He was scouting from a hilltop fort and spotted a column of American tanks. He signaled his gun crew to fire but they missed the lead tank, and a moment later every cannon in the U.S. column had zeroed in on their position. His crew was wiped out in the first salvo, although Sau Ban, who was gravely wounded, was able to crawl away before the American troopers came. He lay in the sun all day until a VC medical team came along and took him to an underground hospital. They arrived about midnight, but it was too late. Your brother died and his body was buried at Dai Hong. Some of the older villagers have corroborated this story. That's where we'll go to find him—someday."

A mosquito buzzed in my ear and I swatted it away. My mother was right. The house—each building in every village—had a spirit separate and apart from the generations of people who inhabited it. That spark of life, granted by Mother Earth, is what animates the world and binds a people to a place. Into this ancient, vibrant web, I was about to introduce a new entity, a place of healing, like a wandering herbalist come to help the sick and give the dying a little comfort. The day after tomorrow, my old world would be gone forever. We could only hope the new one would be better.

After talking a little more about Sau Ban, I turned to my mother, "So, Mama Du, you're happy with your life?"

"What kind of question is that for an old lady? You have to be my age to realize that just being alive is a blessing—a miracle! From the smallest bug to the biggest whale, everything rejoices at being alive. When you stop to think about it, that's all that counts. Hai Ngai and the others talk about independence from invaders and I suppose that's okay. It gives people something to think about from the time they're born and have everything to learn and the time they die and have forgotten it all. To tell you the truth, I'm looking forward to passing over into the spirit world. We have a lot of new ghosts out here in the countryside."

"What do you mean, Mama Du?"

"I mean that a lot of people sacrificed in the war have come back as babies, and many of those are now young men and women. They're dissatisfied with what now passes for peace. They want to make things better and, one way or another, they're going to do it. How do you think your clinic got built? If the old ghosts didn't want it, it wouldn't be here. That's what this country is all about now, Bay Ly—life, not death. Your clinic is just one of its new green shoots."

At eight the next morning, all the honored guests had arrived: officials from the Health Ministry and Red Cross; physicians and nurses from town who would rotate shifts in the clinic; minor functionaries from a variety of provincial departments; and, of course, every villager who could walk and many who could not.

Bon Nghe's crew set up a podium and PA system and a few dozen folding chairs for the dignitaries. From the roof of the clinic, they unfurled two banners: one reading GRAND OPENING, with the Red Cross and East Meets West logos, like a new drugstore in a California shopping mall; the other WELCOME TO THE MOTHER'S LOVE HEALTH

CLINIC. A marble plaque by the front door bore this name and the names of many of our benefactors, including Oliver Stone's.

After a lot of speeches and handshakes the village children in the back were getting restless. I was the last to be asked to get up and say something. As I walked up, it seemed like a thousand years since I had been a little kid like them, but in reality it had been only forty-two years. *Forty-two*—the Ong Thay's magic number! I floated to the microphone, amazed and grateful.

My mother was too timid to sit up front, where I had saved her a seat. I spotted her in the back, where she stood proudly in a fluttering *ao dai*—the one I had seen her wear only twice before in my life: at Sau Ban's wedding and at my father's funeral. Next to her in his worn white shirt was my oldest brother, Bon Nghe, head of the Phung Trong family.

After thanking everyone, including fate or luck or god, for giving me a chance to heal myself with this project, I said, "To the people of Hoa Qui, or Ky La, as it was called when I lived here, I want to humbly apologize. Everybody wanted my sisters and me to marry nice village boys and raise traditional Vietnamese families. Well, I didn't do that. My karma took me elsewhere, to America. I can tell you now, though, from firsthand experience, that America is not your enemy and never was, even during the war. Back then, America picked me up when I was scared and bloody and cared for me and educated me and helped me to raise my three wonderful sons. It made me a citizen and has let me come back with these presents which she gives you freely and without reservations. What she wants more than anything, I think, is to forgive you and be forgiven by you in return. When she comes to you over the next few years with businessmen and tourists and assistance workers, please welcome her with open arms. We are all brothers and sisters. We must all repay our mother's love."

Big scissors then cut the red banner and fireworks exploded overhead. Little kids beat on drums and the evil spirits that had been lurking in the swamps grew thin and fled before the joyful noise.

EPILOGUE

A Song of Tu *and* Dao

OUR CLINIC'S FIRST PATIENT was a former soldier who had carried pieces of a fragmentation grenade in his hand for the last twenty years. Government doctors who had last examined him thought the operation was too minor to consume their valuable time, so the patient was advised to "grin and bear it." Until today, that's just what he did.

Today, he had come to ask the local doctors if there was anything they could do. They X-rayed the damage and saw three metal slivers embedded near the bone. With the patient lying comfortably on a sparkling white table, the doctors administered a local anesthetic, just arrived from America.

When the hand was numb and swabbed with disinfectant, they began to work, using the X-ray as their guide. A half hour later, they presented three jagged fragments to the soldier as a souvenir, his last from the war.

In the clinic's log book, the first patient's name was entered: "Louis Block, U.S. Viet Nam Veteran from Plummer, ID, USA; On tour-of-duty mission with East Meets West Foundation, Oct. 22, 1989; Da Nang, Quang Nam Province, Viet Nam."

Since the Mother's Love clinic opened, it has treated more than 16,500 patients and delivered 300 babies. East Meets West is currently constructing a twenty-acre rehabilitation center for the homeless and handicapped amid the white sands and tall pines of China Beach. Called Peace Village, it occupies a site where, exactly twenty-five years earlier, more than 3,500 marines landed to begin the American buildup. Phase one of the project—a full-service medical center that treats over seven hundred patients a day, and a school for a like number of poor children—has already been completed.

Also since the clinic has opened, a bloody and tragic—but blessedly short—American-led war was fought in Iraq, paying off and creating soul debt all its own. The Vietnamese government has ended its military occupation of Cambodia, opening the door to the first real peace in Indochina since before World War II. North Vietnam's staunch ally, the Soviet Union, has vanished, not even leaving its name. East Germany has met West Germany and that nation no longer stands divided. Except for China, North Korea, and Cuba, the Socialist Republic of Vietnam stands alone, pondering from a distance a world rediscovering freedom. Internally, it has begun a vast policy of *doi moi,* or economic renovation, designed to improve the standard of living for everyone in the country. The leopard has not changed its spots, but it has certainly changed its diet. Whether this will be enough to save the country is anyone's guess, but at least it is a start.

For America's longest war, the circle of vengeance appears to be breaking. The U.S. State Department has devised a four-phase plan for normalization of political and economic relations with Vietnam, beginning with the March 1992 lifting of its ban on organized travel to the country and a grant of $4 million for humanitarian assistance. Further steps depend on continued Vietnamese cooperation in search for American MIAs and progress toward free elections in Cambodia. *Hat tieu no be no cay; dong tien no be no hay cua guyen*—The pepper is small but hot; the banknote is small but powerful!

Still, not everyone agrees that the circle should be broken.

One Green Beret vet responded to my invitation to return to Vietnam with, "Hell, no, I'll never go! Not while the Communists are in charge!"

After I gave a lecture on a midwestern college campus, one Vietnamese in the audience asked, "Who is paying you to do this work?"

"Nobody is paying me," I answered. "Everything I do in Vietnam comes from donations or my own pocket. I have refinanced my house twice and borrowed against my car to raise money. I am ten thousand dollars in debt to my friends. I wish what you say was true, but it simply isn't. This job has cost me a lot of money."

Another asks, "In your story you say that the Southern government and the Americans did terrible things to you. What about all the people in the Communist re-education camps right now? What about the POWs and MIAs? Why don't you talk about them?"

I answered, "I would talk about them if I had any information, but I don't. I only know what others have told me, and that is that the government has exhausted all means of locating their remains. Whenever a reward is offered, people fabricate evidence to get rich. Whenever the government exacts penalties, people complain about brutality. The government wants to put the POW/MIA issue behind them, too, just as much as people in the United States. The problem is, some people in Vietnam, just like some people in America, refuse to admit the war is over. They have been terribly hurt and want to keep on hurting 'the enemy.'"

A Vietnamese woman stood up and said, "What about the refugees from the South—the boat people and all the hardships we've had to endure? We've suffered, too! Why don't you write about us?"

"I didn't write about the boat people because I did not come over on a boat. Personally, I think every side of the story should be told."

Another young woman stood up and shouted, "If the Buddha ignores my prayers and lets you live, please take this message back to your Communist masters in Vietnam: Tell them to go to hell! Tell them to let all the people out of the torture camps! When we go back, it will be with guns in our hands and we do not want to find our relatives dead!"

I answered, "Do you really think that forty years of war—with the Japanese, the French, the Americans, the Khmer, and with each other, isn't enough for us Vietnamese? Do you think that all we need is a few more years of fighting and everything will be fine? Do you think that is what we were put on earth to accomplish?"

After sessions like these, I am usually greeted by older Vietnamese and more mature students, who quietly say things like "It is terrible that some Vietnamese act like that in front of Americans. It makes me feel like a barbarian. I am ashamed to be Vietnamese."

"Don't be," I reply. "Be proud of yourself and our people. Would you scold your child for feeling ill? After all we've been through, our future is bound to be wonderful. *Ai oi hay o cho lanh kiep nay chang gap de danh kiep sau*—Live a good life: if in this existence you do not find happiness, then you surely will in the next.

Time and again, images of healing appear in my talks, in what I write, in my informal conversations, in my dreams. Of course, much of it has to do with my work, but I had not forgotten the words of the Ong Thay Vu Tai Loc and Paul, the medium who told me about the ancient guardian spirit, the medicine man, that has dogged my steps since birth—a higher entity, a soul older even than even my father's —whose identity would eventually be revealed.

In 1990, I went to Ky La to visit my mother, now eighty-four and more fragile than ever. I knew the number of times we would meet on future trips was numbered, although god only knew what that final number would be.

"Mama Du," I asked, "if you had one wish, what would it be?" I was hoping she'd give me a clue about something from the West that would make her remaining time easier.

"One wish? Oh, that's easy," she said. "You know, after all those years of war, we have relatives scattered in shallow graves all over Vietnam. Their souls are lost and lonely—I can hear them howling, sometimes, when the wind comes up from China Beach. If I had one last wish, it would be to gather up all the remains and bury them in the new cemetery near your father. That would make him happy, I think. And make me very happy, too."

"Find all the old bodies, eh?" I couldn't even conceive how that might be done.

"Oh, don't look so glum," my mother poked me. "All you need to do is hire an *ong thay xac dong.*"

"A spirit guide? Like the man who looked for Sau Ban? What can he do?"

"Why, contact the wandering ghosts. They'll lead him to their graves. All he'll have to do then is dig them up and bring them to Ky La."

"How many remains are we talking about?" I asked, still unconvinced.

"About fifty or sixty," she said as if it were nothing. "Of course, that's all I can remember. That only goes back six generations. Your father knew about many more."

My mother seemed very animated by this project and I wanted very much to complete it for her, but my time on this visit was short. Besides, only the head of the family could authorize such an undertaking, and now that was my brother Bon Nghe.

"Surely you're joking," he said when I asked.

"No, I'm not. And neither is our mother. I've heard stories and seen newspaper articles about some government officials using mediums to try and locate American MIAs. You did it before for Sau Ban. Can we do any less for our ancestors?"

Bon Nghe shook his head and grumbled, but I knew what his answer would be. We had already accomplished bigger miracles than this.

On my next trip to Vietnam in March 1991, the *ong thay xac dong* Bon Nghe hired greeted me.

"The remains of all your ancestors on your father's side are waiting for you at the graveyard, young lady," the nearly toothless old fellow said. "The spirit energy around Quang Nam is a lot lower now that they've found a proper place to rest, I'll tell you! I even sleep better myself."

I went to fetch my mother and Hai and we followed the *ong thay* to the cemetery by the old dike road where the reliquary jars, linen-wrapped bone fragments, transplanted caskets, and marble markers were all lined up like troops for inspection.

I had no way of telling if these bones—especially the ones without inscriptions—were true Phung ancestors or not; but my mother seemed happy. I lit a stack of incense and passed in review, praying to each spirit as it identified itself through its tablet or through the *ong thay's* voice.

At the end of the line was the oldest ancestor of all. The finely carved antique marble showed that the interred either died very rich or was highly revered by his contemporaries. I placed a smoking stick of incense by the headstone and a chill ran down my spine. The inscription read:

ONG TIEN HIEN THAY THUOC—Ancestral Herb Healer

I dropped the incense but quickly picked it up and replaced it. The tree leaves rustled—a spirit voice laughing. Tu *and* Dao, it said, *the spiritual way and the earthly way coming together as one. Was that so difficult a lesson to learn?*

The afternoon sun sank onto the western hills. Workmen placed the remains into a specially excavated plot and carefully arranged the new headstones. My mother and sister Hai stood close together in the sunset, chatting like schoolgirls—rejuvenated by the reunion of so many generations. Farther down, the group from America chatted pleasantly through their guide with a handful of villagers—East meeting West as naturally and easily as the roaring surf kisses the sand at China Beach.

In the distance, the shadow of the old pepper tree by our house inched closer to the Mother's Love clinic. Now—at last!—it made no difference if the soil beneath my feet was American or Vietnamese. Mother Earth was my home and all her children, my brothers and sisters.

I could feel the herb-man turn over and sleep soundly in his new bed. One dream was ending. Another had begun.

ACKNOWLEDGMENTS

THIS BOOK is about *debt*—the debt we owe to the cosmic god for creating us; the debt we owe to our mothers for bringing his creation onto this earth; the soul debt we accrue and pay off by the choices we make in life. We owe similar debts to the people who guide, shape, and help us. We may not always be able to repay these debts, but we can at least acknowledge the ways in which they have made our journey through life richer and less steep.

I wish first to thank all those who showed simple human kindness to me and my sons since we first dried our feet on America's "golden shore." Most of the time, we never knew your name and could not or did not thank you sufficiently. Let me do so now. If another incarnation finds you an immigrant—lost and lonely in a foreign land—you will know and appreciate fully what I am saying. May I be that grocery clerk or bureaucrat or teacher or friendly neighbor who helps you with a smile and encouragement when you need it most.

Specifically, I want to thank the Munro and Hayslip families: those still living and those who have joined their ancestors. From my husbands and their relatives, I learned how to be an American. I also want to thank most humbly my sister Lan, who followed me to these shores. Because of all of you, I have learned that flowers can bloom in any soil. When our life lessons caused me and my boys to feel grief, please know now that I understand why those things happened. The road to nirvana is always steep and winding and those who climb only on sunny days will never know the beauty of a rainbow.

My thanks go also to all the people who read *When Heaven and Earth Changed Places,* and helped it to find its own life as an independent creation—another son who has made its way in the world. If it were not for Doubleday's continuing faith in me and my life's story—especially that of our editor, Casey Fuetsch, and so many others—much goodness could not have entered the world. At the time of this writing, my "daughter," the East Meets West Foundation (a world-peace and relief organization) has built, or participated in building, two health clinics in rural Vietnam and is well on its way to completing a regional Peace Village at China Beach, the very spot where, a quarter century ago, American marines first landed to begin our two countries' long march together. How can a debt like that be repaid in one lifetime?

This literary child has given birth to children of its own, and their midwives deserve my thanks and gratitude as well. To Rachael Klayman, our paperback editor at Plume Books; Michael Viner and Nancy Kwan at Dove Audio; and to the editors and translators of the foreign language editions in ten other countries, I give my sincerest thanks for helping to spread my message of peace and forgiveness to those who, although they may have watched the Vietnam War only from a distance, have suffered wars of their own. To Oliver Stone, Lynwood Spinks, Kathryn Sommer, Mario Kassar, Christina Rodgers, Robert Kline, and others who have worked, and continue to work, so hard to tell my story on film, my deepest thanks. You are helping to extend its healing message to millions around the world who may only be reached through the special magic of images and sound.

My gratitude also goes to all the print and broadcast journalists, and to the many colleges, universities, high schools, and charitable organizations that helped raise my one small voice into the great chorus of human discourse—in the United States and around the world. Because of you, many people have had a chance to pause and hear the temple bell. From the thousands of letters I have received, I know that many have sung the song of enlightenment as well.

Bringing East and West together sometimes means moving mountains. I wish to thank Steven Pinter, Michael Marine, and Jeff Braunger at the U.S. Teasury Department and Marc Kron at the U.S. Commerce Department, as well as many, many people at the Department of State, for granting us the special licenses we need for our work in Vietnam to continue. For similar assistance and support, I thank Ambassadors Trinh Xuan Lang and Nguyen Can at the Vietnamese UN Mission, Ambassador Empassi in Bangkok, and Messrs Nguyen Co Thach and Dang Nghiem Bai and their staff in the Foreign Affairs Office in Hanoi. Also in Vietnam, I wish to thank the vice president of the People's Committee, Mr. Nguyen Dinh An and Mr. Ngo Van Tran and his staff in the Foreign Economic Relations office; Dr. Dinh The Ban, vice director, and Dr. Ly of the Department of Health; as well as the staff of the Red Cross, the local officials of the villages of Hoa Hai and Hoa Qui (Ky La), and all the people of Quang Nam Da Nang Province who have helped me, my family, and the Foundation to build the medical clinics the people of Central Vietnam so desperately need. Because of your ongoing work, the circle of vengeance that still grips some in both our countries has become a little smaller.

I thank particularly all the people who have traveled with East Meets West on our missions of relief and discovery. Thank you for putting up with the less than first-class hotels and simple food and not so elegant transportation and other annoyances you would not have endured if you had stayed comfortably at home in the United States. Thank you for rolling up your sleeves and pitching in and giving your sweat and love to a people and a place abandoned by America so many years ago. Although much remains to be done, those mountains are a little closer because of you.

I wish to extend my special thanks to my brother and sister Viet Kieu who took, and continue to take, great risks to revisit and nurse back to health the "land where our umbilicus is buried." In a very real way, this new book was written for you. As members of one great family, what happens to one of us happens to us all. *La se rung ve coi, nuoc se chay ve nguon. Lay thu lam ban, an oan xoa ngay. Nguoi con nuoc Viet Ta thuong nhan cung.*

Sometimes we owe the greatest debts to people who hear our words of gratitude least: those closest to home. To my oldest son, Jim, my new coauthor and as fine a young man as any mother could want, my thanks for reliving with me the not always pleasant memories of our tumultuous life in America. Along with your brothers, Tom and Alan, who figure so prominently in our story, the time and ideas you have lavished on your "poor old mom"—especially with other voices calling you all so loudly—has moved me more than you can know. Truly, we have planted and nourished our own sau dau tree in the rich soil of America. We cannot forget, either, the others who have toiled in our garden: Jay Wurts, for adding his literary voice to ours; and Sandy Dijkstra, Kathy Goodwin, and Mary Ann Grode for opening new doors and helping us harvest the fruit of our labor.

I also wish to thank most humbly the many Vietnamese and American people who have served on the East Meets West board of directors, honorary board, and board of advisers, as well as those who have served steadfastly in the ranks of unpaid volunteers. Your long hours of sacrifice have earned my love and the deepest gratitude of those you've helped; and, I hope, more than a little satisfaction for yourselves.

My deepest gratitude, too, goes to the many physicians from across the United States and from other countries who have collected the supplies, equipment, medicine, and money needed to stock and support our clinics in Vietnam. With so much of the world's wealth still lavished on the apparatus of war, your generosity in our crusade for peace is overwhelming.

Closer still to home—although four thousand miles away—I wish to thank my relatives in Vietnam: my mother, my brother Bon Nghe, my sisters Ba Xuan (and husband Chin) and Hai, along with my niece Tinh, and all their families, who have helped and put up with me during my many trips to our homeland over the last few years. With our good health and many reunions, we are luckier than most. Let us continue to repay that great debt with good works that honor our ancestors and all the *am binh* soldiers. As part of my "spiritual family," I must also thank my monks, the Venerable Thich Giac Ngoi, Thich Giac Nhien, Thich Tri Chon, Thich Man Giac, Thich Phap Chan, and Phuoc Thuan. As far as I feel I have come, I would not be half so close to my destination in this life if it had not been for you.

I would like to print the names of everyone who has helped East Meets West with a contribution or supported us with prayers and encouraging words, but that would require a book in itself. Suffice it for now to list below, on a special roll of honor, those who have helped in a thousand and one ways whenever they were asked. To any valued friend inadvertently left off the list, let me now acknowledge my debt and assure you that my heart continues to tend the shrine of our affection. To any friend I have yet to meet, but whose compassion has been drawn across the ocean by these words, I invite you to call or write:

East Meets West Foundation
725 Washington Street
Oakland, CA 94607
(510) 834-0301

In a world running headlong into the light from the shadows of its own dark past, we must not forget a people left behind. Many lessons remain to be taught and learned. Much work remains to be done.

PHUNG THI LE LY HAYSLIP
San Diego, California
March, 1992

Tony Abat
Dee Aker
American Legion Post 33
    (Kasson Legion)
Mr. and Mrs. Doan C. An
Bill Backner
Dean Barad
Thomas Bass
Patrice Basse
Lowell Blankfort
Louis Block
Vickie Block
Jeff Brown
Dr. Richard Buchta
Le and Lan Bui
David Bushnell
Fredy and Sherry Champagne
Steve Chang
James Chapman
Joan Chen
Geoffrey Clifford
Luc Do
Chanh Doan
David Donnan
Robert Donnan
Robert and Judy Dunn
George Elson
Mary Emeny

Michael Feldstein
First Unitarian Church
Dave Gallo
Loraine Gardner
Louis Gotlib
Dee Gove
Steve Graw
Kathy Greenwood
Ailill Halsema
Lambert Halsema
Doan Thi Nam Hau
H.M. & T. Cohn Foundation
A. Kitman Ho
Doan Thi Nam Hoa
Doan Thi Nam Hue
Marie Huhtala
Le Van Hung
Laurens J. Jansen
Chuck Jones
Russell Jones
Don and Carol Kenyon
Victor Kempster
Ron Kovic
Dr. Judy Ladinsky
Jeanne Lang
Andrew Le
Dr. William Lenon
Jean Lovejoy

Milton Low
Don Luce
Marvin May
Barry McMahon
Medic of Illinois
Nguyen Tang Mien
Jim Miller
Mr. and Mrs. Lu Van Moch
Hiep Nguyen
Tanya Nguyen
Northwest Airlines
Vu Thi Van Nuong
Bernard O'Gara
Pacific Unitarian Church
Richard Pardo
Herbert Paas
Peace Development Fund
Val Petersen
John Pritchard
June Pulcini
Binit Rama
Morria Ratcliff
Dr. R. C. Reznichek
Michael and Monica Rhodes
Jim Robinson
Timothy Rogers
Dr. John Romine
Roger Rumpf
Steve Russel and the Landmark
    Theater Corporation
San Diego Foundation
Nguyen Thi Sanh

Dolie Schien
Dr. Edward Sherwood
Michael Singer
Dr. Peter Singer
Bob Sioss
Mike Snelling
Kathy Sommer
Perry Steinberg
Oliver Stone
Rose Stone
Shirley Sun
Mai Phuoc Thien
Nguyen Thuan
Clayton Townsend
Tom Tran
University of California, San
    Diego Medical Center
U.S. Committee for Scientific
    Cooperation with Viet Nam
U.S./Viet Nam Friendship Aid
    Association
Nick Ut
Nam C. Van
Linda Vo
Jennifer Wall
VVAF/Washington, D.C.
James Watson
Putney Westerfield
The Wonderful Foundation
Janet Yang
John Sacret Young
Azita Zendel